PSYCHOLOGY LIBRARY EDITIONS:
COMPARATIVE PSYCHOLOGY

Volume 2

THE BEHAVIORAL SIGNIFICANCE OF COLOR

THE BEHAVIORAL SIGNIFICANCE OF COLOR

Edited by
EDWARD H. BURTT, JR.

Routledge
Taylor & Francis Group
LONDON AND NEW YORK

First published in 1979 by Garland Publishing Inc.

This edition first published in 2018
by Routledge
2 Park Square, Milton Park, Abingdon, Oxon OX14 4RN

and by Routledge
711 Third Avenue, New York, NY 10017

Routledge is an imprint of the Taylor & Francis Group, an informa business

British Library Cataloguing in Publication Data
A catalogue record for this book is available from the British Library

ISBN: 978-1-138-50329-8 (Set)
ISBN: 978-1-351-12878-0 (Set) (ebk)
ISBN: 978-1-138-57496-0 (Volume 2) (hbk)
ISBN: 978-1-351-27044-1 (Volume 2) (ebk)

Publisher's Note
The publisher has gone to great lengths to ensure the quality of this reprint but points out that some imperfections in the original copies may be apparent.

Disclaimer
The publisher has made every effort to trace copyright holders and would welcome correspondence from those they have been unable to trace.

The Behavioral Significance of Color

Edward H. Burtt, Jr.
Department of Zoology
Ohio Wesleyan University
Delaware, Ohio

Garland STPM Press
New York & London

15 14 13 12 11 10 9 8 7 6 5 4 3 2 1

Library of Congress Cataloging in Publication Data
Main entry under title:

The Behavioral significance of color.

(Garland series in ethology)
"Based on a symposium held as part of the Animal
Behavior Society's meeting in June 1977."
Includes bibliographies and index.
1. Color of animals. 2. Animals, Habits and
behavior of. I. Burtt, Edward H., 1948-
II. Animal Behavior Society. III. Series.
QL767.B413 591.5 77-14618

ISBN 0-8240-7016-X

Printed in the United States of America

Contents

Preface ix

Contributing Authors xi

Introduction xiii
Edward H. Burtt, Jr.

PART I: PHYSICAL PRINCIPLES

1. Physics of Light: An Introduction for Light-Minded Ethologists 3
B. Dennis Sustare

Emissivity, A Little-Explored Variable: Discussion 28
C. Richard Tracy

PART II: PHYSIOLOGICAL FUNCTIONS OF ANIMAL COLORATION

2. The Influence of Color on Behavioral Thermoregulation and Hydroregulation 35
David M. Hoppe

Further Thoughts on Anuran Thermoregulation: Discussion 63
C. Richard Tracy

Maximization of Reproduction: Discussion 69
William J. Hamilton III

Audience Questions: Discussion 70

3. Tips on Wings and Other Things 75
Edward H. Burtt, Jr.

The Evolutiono-Engineering Approach: Discussion . . 111
C. Richard Tracy

Where is the Evidence for Ultra-violet Damage: Discussion .114
William J. Hamilton III

Audience Questions: Discussion. 120

PART III: PHOTORECEPTION

4. Extraretinal Photoreception 127
Herbert Underwood

Extraretinal Photoreception: Words of Caution: Discussion 179
C. Richard Tracy

5. Mechanisms of Color Vision: An Ethologist's Primer 183
Samuel H. Gruber

6. Visual Discriminations Encountered in Food Foraging by a Neotropical Primate: Implications for the Evolution of Color Vision 237
D. Max Snodderly

Comments on Coevolution: Discussion 280
C. Richard Tracy

Are Selection Pressures Different? Discussion . . .282
William J. Hamilton III

Audience Questions: Discussion. 284

PART IV: COLORATION FOR COMMUNICATION

7. Environmental Light and Conspicuous Colors 289
Jack P. Hailman

Audience Questions: Discussion. 355

8. Optical Signals and Interspecific Communication . . 359
Jeffrey R. Baylis

9. The Use of Color in Intraspecific Communication . . 379
William J. Rowland

Visual Functions of Color: The Predictive Approach: Discussion 422
C. Richard Tracy

Audience Questions: Discussion. 424

10. Conclusion 427
Edward H. Burtt, Jr.

Index 433

Preface

This volume grew out of a symposium presented at the meeting of the Animal Behavior Society in June 1977. The chapters are based on the papers read before the society, but the authors have included new material not presented and frequently unknown at that time. Each chapter is followed by a discussion that includes comments from C. Richard Tracy or William J. Hamilton, III or both, questions from the symposium's audience, and answers prepared by the author of the chapter. I hope that such a format captures the enthusiasm and spontaneity so evident at the symposium.

Animal coloration has received too little study. If this book excites further thought and research into the world of colors and patterns of color, then it will have fulfilled its purpose.

Many are those who have contributed to this book. Edward O. Price, Program Chairman for the Animal Behavior Society, was an invaluable source of encouragement during the planning and organizing of the symposium. The authors have been exceptionally pleasant and cooperative and have made outstanding contributions. Although the questioners are infrequently identified, their queries and the ensuing discussion add immeasurably to the book. The symposium was organized while I was a member of the Department of Psychology at the University of Tennessee; I am grateful to the department for its support of the entire project, especially to Becky George and Lorraine Simmons, who typed many letters and relayed many telephone messages. The Department of Zoology at Ohio Wesleyan University provided facilities for the preparation of the manuscript; to the members of the department, especially A. John Gatz -- whose advice was freely given -- and to Ohio Wesleyan University, I offer heartfelt thanks. Gladys Hummel, who typed the entire, edited manuscript, has earned my eternal thanks as have Brian Fortini and Donna Wierbowicz who helped with the proofreading. And for George Narita, our long-suffering but ever helpful publisher, I offer the hope that the book is worthy of his expectations.

Now I leave the reading to you and return to the family too often neglected during the past months of writing and editing.

Edward H. Burtt, Jr.
5 March 1978

Contributing Authors

Jeffrey R. Baylis
Department of Zoology
University of Wisconsin
Madison, Wisconsin

Edward H. Burtt, Jr.
Department of Zoology
Ohio Wesleyan University
Delaware, Ohio

Samuel H. Gruber
Division of Biology &
Living Resources
University of Miami
Miami, Florida

Jack P. Hailman
Department of Zoology
University of Wisconsin
Madison, Wisconsin

W. J. Hamilton III
Division of Environmental
Studies
University of California
Davis, California

David M. Hoppe
Department of Zoology &
Entomology
University of Minnesota
Morris, Minnesota

William J. Rowland
Department of Biology
Indiana University
Bloomington, Indiana

D. Max Snodderly
Eye Research Institute of
Retina Foundation
Boston, Massachusetts

B. Dennis Sustare
Department of Biology
Clarkson College
Potsdam, New York

C. Richard Tracy
Department of Zoology &
Entomology
Colorado State University
Fort Collins, Colorado

Herbert Underwood
Department of Zoology
North Carolina State University
Raleigh, North Carolina

Introduction

Coloration and the pattern of coloration of animals play a central role in behavior -- even among species in which vision is not the dominant sense. For example, an animal's color or pattern is often related to its display movements (Lorenz 1941, Tinbergen 1952, Blest 1957, Cullen 1957, Hailman 1977a, 1977b); cryptic coloration often goes hand in hand with cryptic behavior (Ruiter 1952, 1956, Cott 1957, Hailman 1977b); and coloration that absorbs solar energy may show a close relation with thermoregulatory behavior (Ohmart and Lasiewski 1970, Burtt 1973, Storer 1974). Despite these pervasive correlations between behavior and coloration, we understand few of the principles that predict the specific pattern or color that best serves a particular function in conjunction with behavior. This volume brings together diverse experts and disparate facts as a step toward understanding the behavioral significance of animal coloration. Hypotheses that account for the coloration of animals fall into three major categories: (1) physiological functions of pigmentation; (2) coloration that affects the animal's visibility to other animals, including conspecifics; and (3) coloration that affects the animal's own vision. Predicative hypotheses in all three categories are outlined and data relevant to these hypotheses are presented in the chapters, discussions, questions, and answers that follow.

REFERENCES

Blest, A. D. 1957. The function of eyespot patterns in the Lepidoptera. *Behavior* 11: 209-256.

Burtt, E. H., Jr. 1973. Warbler leg coloration and migratory behavior. *Amer. Zoologist* 13: 1263.

Cott, H. B. 1957. *Adaptive Coloration in Animals*. Methuen, London.

Cullen, E. 1957. Adaptations in the kittiwake to cliff-nesting. *Ibis* 99: 275-302.

Hailman, J. P. 1977a. Communication by reflected light. In *How Animals Communicate*. T. A. Sebeok (ed). Ind. Univ. Press, Bloomington.

Hailman, J. P. 1977b. *Optical Signals: Animal Communication and Light*. Ind. Univ. Press, Bloomington and London.

Lorenz, K. Z. 1941. Vergleichende Bewegungsstudien on Anatinen. *J. f. Ornithol.* 89: 194-294.

Ohmart, R. D., and R. C. Lasiewski. 1970. Roadrunners: energy conservation by hypothermia and absorption of sunlight. *Science* 172: 67-69.

Ruiter, L. de. 1952. Some experiments on the camouflage of stick caterpillars. *Behavior* 4: 222-232.

Ruiter, L. de. 1956. Countershading in caterpillars. An analysis of its adaptive significance. *Arch. Neerl. Zool.* 11: 285-342.

Storer, R. W. 1974. Sunbathing in grebes. *Abstr. 16th Int. Ornithol. Congr.*

Tinbergen, N. 1952. "Derived" activities: their causation, biological significance, origin, and emancipation during evolution. *Rev. Biol.* 27: 1-32.

Part 1

Physical Principles

Chapter 1

Physics of Light: An Introduction for Light-Minded Ethologists

B. Dennis Sustare

Introduction
Electromagnetic Radiation
    Waves or Particles?
    Mathematical Description
What is Color?
Geometrical Optics
    Reflection
    Refraction
    Focal Points
    Diffraction
Sources of Electromagnetic Radiation
    Properties of Black Bodies
    Emissivity
The Measurement of Radiation
    Inverse-Square Law
    Radiometry
    Photometry
Sunlight
    Solar Spectra
    Sunlight's Earthly Fates
    Polarization
    Interference
    Water and Light
Zoochromes and Phytochromes
Bioluminescence
Recommended Reading

INTRODUCTION

Energy is absorbed, reflected, and radiated by all plants and animals and most animals use some of the information carried by radiant energy to modify their subsequent behavior. Regardless of the behavior examined, the unceasing flow of radiant energy affects the behavioral system. Hence ethologists must renew or make their acquaintance with the physical properties of radiation. For the sake of those whose memories are rusty, I briefly survey some features of the physics of electromagnetic radiation.

ELECTROMAGNETIC RADIATION

Waves or Particles?

Electromagnetic radiation can be thought of as little packages of energy, each package being a discrete unit. The amount of energy in a package characterizes the type of radiation. Along the bottom scale in Figure 1, energy is plotted in attojoules. As a reminder, a joule is the energy required to apply a force of one newton over a distance of one meter, a sizable amount of energy. Because the metric prefix *atto-* corresponds to a factor of 10^{-18}, an attojoule is a very tiny unit of energy. You can see in Figure 1 that there is little energy in the packages of a radio wave; infrared, visible light (what we can see), and ultraviolet show increasing amounts of energy/package respectively. If the figure continued to the left, more highly energetic radiation would be displayed, for example, X rays.

Energy/package is only one way to characterize electromagnetic radiation. Under some experimental conditions, electromagnetic radiation acts like a stream of particles; under other conditions radiation acts like waves. The more energetic each package of radiation, the more it acts like a particle. High-energy radiation can be more accurately located in time and space and tends to penetrate substances better than low-energy radiation. Low-energy radiation is very wavelike; it bends around objects easily, and is hard to locate in time and space. However, regardless of the energy content, any radiation may demonstrate wave properties, such as the ability to interfere with other radiation in the same way that water waves or sound waves interfere,

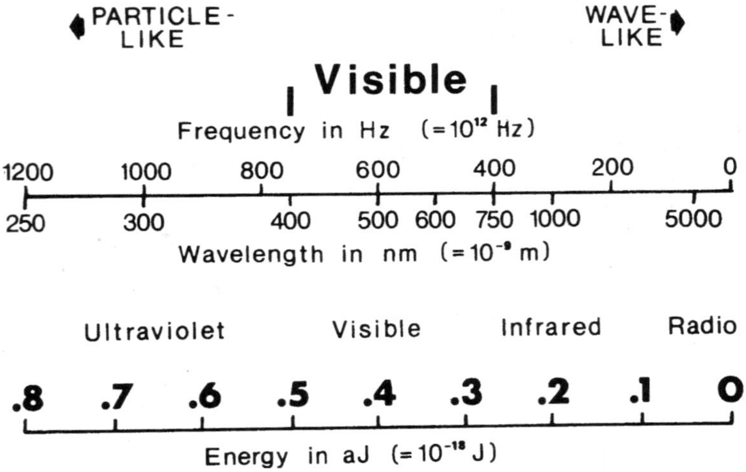

Fig. 1. Lower scale: Energy of photons, measured in attojoules. Spectral equivalences are shown above the scale (only shown to 0.8 aJ). Upper scales: Correspondence between frequency and wavelength of photons that have the amount of energy shown on the bottom scale. Only that portion of the spectrum up to 1200 THz is shown.

adding in some places, canceling in other places. Radiation tends to seem more wavelike when it is being transmitted through space, and more particle-like when it interacts with materials.

High-energy radiation acts as though its waves were very close together, with a high repetition rate, or frequency, and a very short distance between adjacent wave crests. On the upper scales of Figure 1 are the frequencies and wavelengths corresponding to the energies plotted on the lower scale. Frequency is measured in hertz, one hertz being one wave crest/second; a terahertz is 10^{12} hertz. Wavelength, the distance between adjacent wave crests, is measured in nanometers in Figure 1, one nanometer equaling 10^{-9} meter. Interestingly, visible light displays a good mix of wave and particle properties, given the scale and sensitivity of our usual measuring devices.

Note that the perceived color of a beam of light is a function of the beam's energy. Radiation at the low-energy end of the visible light segment appears red. As we progress toward higher energies, the light appears to pass through the colors of the rainbow: red, orange, yellow, green, blue, and violet, the last being at the high-energy end of the visible range.

Mathematical Description

There is a direct relation between the frequency of the radiation and the energy in one radiation package, called a quantum or photon. Note that frequency and energy are plotted arithmetically in Figure 1; they differ only by a constant factor:

$$U = h\nu \qquad (1.1)$$

where U represents the energy of a single quantum and ν is the frequency of that quantum. If energy is measured in joules, and frequency in hertz, the proportionality constant is h, Planck's constant (6.6256×10^{-34} J•s).

There is also a regular relationship between the wavelength and the frequency of radiation. The speed of an object is the distance it travels per unit time. If you multiply the wavelength, a distance, by the frequency, the reciprocal of time, the result is the speed of light (or any other electromagnetic radiation):

$$c = \lambda\nu \qquad (1.2)$$

where λ is the symbol for wavelength and c for speed of light. One useful fact about electromagnetic radiation is that *all quanta travel at the same speed in a total vacuum* (approximated by outer space), no matter what their energy content; speed is independent of the wavelength or frequency of the radiation. This speed is very close to 3×10^8 m•s^{-1}. You may find the wavelength (λ) by dividing the speed (c) by the frequency (ν); similarly, divide the speed (c) by the wavelength (λ) to find frequency (ν); but be careful that your units are consistent.

WHAT IS COLOR?

What happens when light strikes something? (The following discussion deals with the behavior of a beam of many quanta or packages, not with the behavior of a single quantum.) In general, three things may happen to the light.

It may bounce off the surface (reflection), it may be absorbed and transfer its energy to the absorbing material, or it may pass entirely through the substance (transmission). Often all three processes occur, with some quanta meeting each fate according to the relationship:

$$I = R + A + T \tag{1.3}$$

where I is the number of incident quanta, R the number of reflected quanta, A the number of absorbed quanta, and T the number of transmitted quanta.

The perceived color of an object depends on the frequencies of visible light remaining *after* absorption. If the object reflects frequencies that we would call green, then we call the object green. Similarly, if we look at an object by transmitted light, we would call it green if it transmits green light, i.e., light in the frequency range of about 540-600 THz (about 0.36-0.4 aJ or 500-555 nm).

The color of an object is determined by the light that is *not* absorbed by the object. If you shine a green light on an object that absorbs green light, it appears black. The process of absorption is complicated, and is not discussed in detail; but, briefly, absorption of light by the molecules of the substance causes those molecules to become excited, i.e., to have more energy. The molecules may give up this energy by reradiating it (but at a lower frequency, and hence with less energy, than the radiation absorbed--a phenomenon called fluorescence), or by bumping into a nearby molecule and giving up some of the energy to the bumped molecule, or by flying off from the surface or otherwise converting the energy into work performed.

GEOMETRICAL OPTICS

A quantum (package of radiation) is in motion during its entire existence and tends to maintain its direction, all other things being equal, in a manner similar to the inertia of objects in motion. Those "other things" add many complications that are of little or no importance to ethologists, so I will not discuss such other things as strong gravitational fields, or what "maintain its direction" really means. The movement of radiation in straight lines allows some useful approximations, called geometrical optics, to be developed.

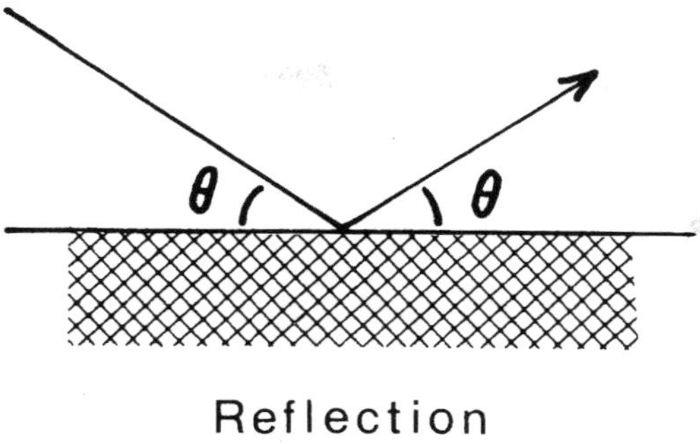

Fig. 2. Reflection: The angle of incidence equals the angle of reflection; here, it is measured relative to the surface plane rather than to the perpendicular with the surface.

Reflection

If light strikes a mirror and bounces off again, the angle between the reflected beam and the mirror is the same as that between the impinging beam and the mirror (Fig. 2). These angles are customarily measured with respect to the perpendicular to the mirror surface rather than as in the figure, but you will recall from your high school geometry that this makes no difference in the equality of angles entering and leaving.

Refraction

When light passes from one medium into another, it changes direction, bending closer to the perpendicular when it enters a denser medium (Fig. 3). This process is called refraction. The relation between the angles is not as simple as with reflection.

$$\sin \theta = n \sin \phi \tag{1.4}$$

Equation (1.4) states that the sine of one angle is a constant (n) times the sine of the other angle. What is this constant of proportionality? You may have noticed the earlier qualification, that the speed of light is constant *in a vacuum*. The qualification is necessary because radiation moves more slowly when passing through a medium. The

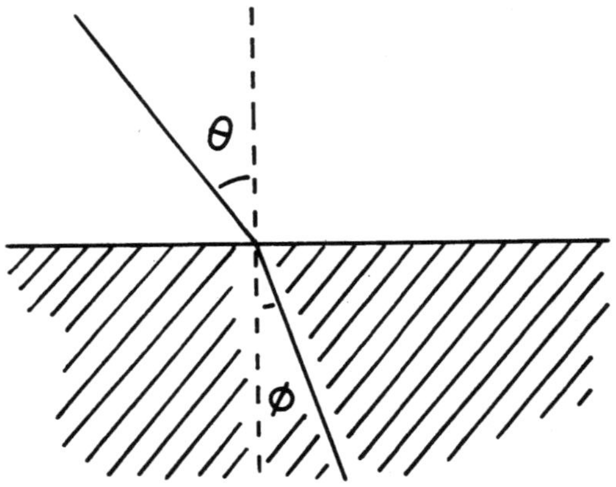

Fig. 3. Refraction: the light bends as its speed undergoes a transition between two media differing in refractive index.

amount of slowing depends on the medium: slower in water than in air; slightly slower in air than in a vacuum. The frequency of the radiation does not change as it enters the new medium, so that with a new speed the distance between wave crests (wavelength) must change. Wave crests for the waves on both sides of the interface between two media must have the same spacing along the interface, so that there must be a bending for rays that strike the interface at an angle other than the perpendicular.

Now, for the proportionality constant *n*: it is the ratio of the apparent speeds of the radiation on the two sides of the interface,

$$\frac{\text{speed after interface}}{\text{speed before interface}}$$

and is called the index of refraction. Equation (1.4) is sometimes called Snell's Law. I stated that the amount of bending depends on the density of the medium. More precisely, the index of refraction depends on the number of charges (i.e., electrons) per unit volume in the material. The index is also a function of the frequency of the radiation, being somewhat higher (more bending) for blue light than for red light. This is why a prism separates the frequencies of light in a beam of white light, bending the blue components more than the red. What appears white to us is of course a combination of frequencies, not light of a single frequency.

One interesting effect of refraction is a change in the apparent depth of an object located in a different medium (Fig. 4). In Figure 4, consider a source of radiation located at point *O'*. When the rays reach the surface of the glass and enter the air, they bend outward, according to Snell's Law. If one is in the air region and looks toward the source, the rays appear to be coming from a point source located at *O*. Therefore the source is actually deeper in the glass (or water) than it appears to be.

Bringing many electromagnetic rays together at the same point is called focusing (Fig. 5). The bending of

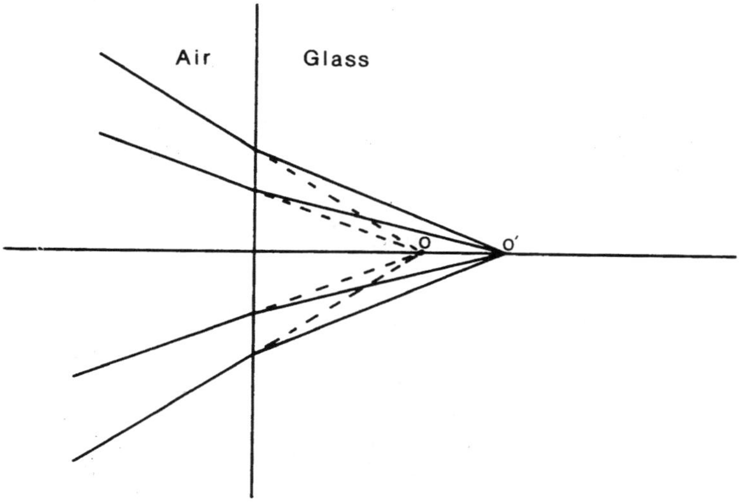

Fig. 4. Change in apparent depth due to refraction. Due to the refractive bending of light, a light source in the glass at point O will appear to be at point O' to an observer in the air.

Focal Points

Bringing many electromagnetic rays together at the same point is called focusing (Fig. 5). The bending of radiation by glass or other materials allows the construction of focusing devices such as a lens. In the upper part

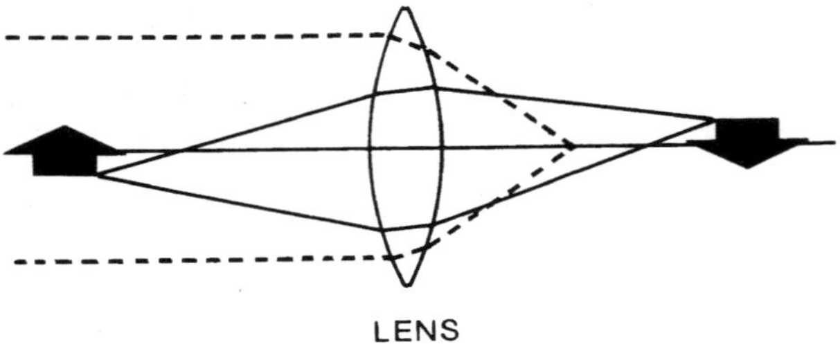

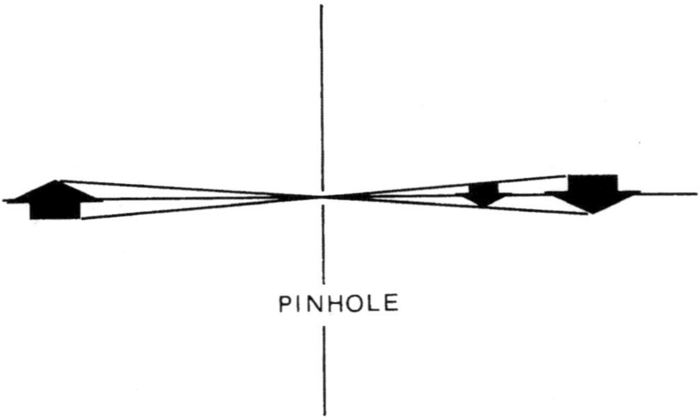

Fig. 5. Top: Focusing by means of a lens. The dotted lines show the focusing of parallel rays (from an infinitely distant source) at the focal point of the lens. The solid lines show that rays may follow different paths to reach the same point in the image. Bottom: Focusing by means of a pinhole. Note that the image is in focus at all distances on the other side of the pinhole, but that there is only one path for light originating at any one point at the source.

of Figure 5, the dotted lines show parallel rays from an infinitely distant source reaching the lens and bending to focus at a point. The distance from the lens to this point of focus (ignoring the size of the lens itself) is the focal length of the lens. Placing a source at the focal point produces a collimated beam of radiation, i.e., a beam in which all the rays are parallel. If an object, such as the arrow in Figure 5, is located farther away than the focal point (but not at infinity), visible light from each point on the object passes through the lens and comes to a focus at one point on the other side of the lens, beyond the focal point. If the lens is properly shaped, light along many paths will come to the same focus, forming an image of the object. The proper shape can be difficult. Figure 5 represents a lens with a spherical surface on either side, which gives a fairly good approximation to a perfectly focusing lens. Nevertheless, rays passing near the center of the lens will not focus at the same point as rays passing near the edge, causing what is called spherical aberration. If you recall that different frequencies are bent by different amounts, you might anticipate that another source of focusing error is due to the failure to focus all frequencies at the same point, called chromatic aberration when referring to visible light.

Having a properly designed lens to form an image is one way to resolve the ambiguity caused by radiation traveling outward in all directions from each point of an object. This principle is used to form an image on film in a lens-type camera. The lower figure shows another way in which an unambiguous image may be formed on film in a camera: using a pinhole instead of a lens. Note that there is only one route for visible light (or any other type of radiation) leaving a point on the object. Unlike the lens, which is in focus at only one distance for an object at a fixed distance from the lens, the pinhole forms an image that is in focus at all distances. Conversely, objects at all distances from the pinhole are in focus at any given plane on the other side of the pinhole. Thus a pinhole camera has an infinite depth of field; the more a conventional camera is stopped down by closing up the hole in the shutter through which the light passes, the greater its depth of field. One problem with the pinhole, of course, is that it lets very little light pass. The lens is able to collect light that was going in different directions and bring it together at a point; the pinhole selects only one ray of light from each direction.

Diffraction

Another phenomenon that appears with the pinhole is diffraction (not to be confused with refraction). Diffraction is another source of bending, and occurs when radiation passes through a small opening or past a sharp edge. Diffraction is tied to the interference of waves, and is linked to the uncertainty principle. In any case, all that need be remembered is that diffraction tends to fuzz up images and reduce resolution. Diffraction is a drawback to trying to form an image through a very small pupil of an eye.

SOURCES OF ELECTROMAGNETIC RADIATION

Passing from optics to the properties of radiation sources, let us consider what happens when a source radiates. One easy way to get an object to radiate is to heat it. You need not heat the object much; all objects above absolute zero constantly radiate. What's more, every macroscopic object radiates at all frequencies; you are, in theory, radiating visible light, radio waves, and X rays as you read this chapter, simply because your temperature is greater than -273°C (0°K). Why aren't we all dazzled by the glare? Of course, it is because the probability of radiating is not the same at all frequencies.

Properties of Black Bodies

An object that absorbs all radiation that falls on it, no matter what the frequency, would be an ideal black body. No radiation is reflected, so that the object must appear black. However, blackbody is a misnomer, since any blackbody above absolute zero (as it must be as soon as it absorbs energy) is radiating energy. Nonetheless, this theoretical model is convenient for discussing radiation, since the complications of differential absorption and emission may be ignored.

So what kind of radiation does a heated blackbody give off? Figure 6 shows the radiation given off by a series of blackbodies, at temperatures ranging from 200°C to 6000°K; the latter is the temperature of a blackbody whose radiation approximates that of the sun. The radiation spectrum is plotted as wavelength, with short wavelengths (high frequencies) to the left. The line marked VIS indicates the visible spectrum. Notice that increasing the

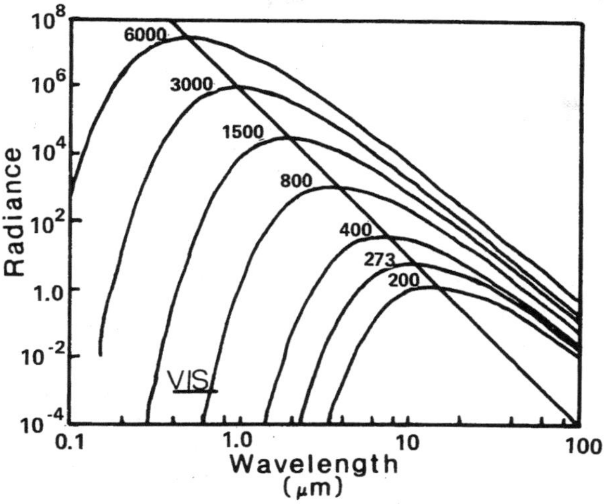

Fig. 6. Radiation from blackbodies. Each curve represents the radiance from a blackbody at a given temperature (in Kelvins). Wavelength is plotted on a log scale, in micrometers, with the shortest wavelengths (highest frequencies) to the left. The line labeled VIS indicates the visible spectrum. Radiance is measured in $W{\cdot}m^{-2}{\cdot}sr^{-1}{\cdot}\mu m^{-1}$. The diagonal line intersects the curves at their maxima (after Barnes 1968).

temperature increases the energy radiated at *all* wavelengths, though the maxima of the curves shift to the left with higher temperatures. This result should not be surprising; heating up the black body results in photons of higher energy (thus, higher frequency) being radiated. Note how the energy from the 6000°K source is at a maximum in the visible range. Notice also that radiation from the earth at a temperature of 273°K, the freezing point of water, is concentrated in wavelengths longer than the visible, in the infrared region, with a peak between 10 and 20 m. The shift in maxima with temperature is known as Wien's Displacement Law.

Emissivity

The radiant emittance from a hot surface is a function of the temperature of the surface, even in the case of real objects that deviate from the behavior of ideal blackbodies. In fact, the radiant emittance varies as the fourth power of the absolute temperature; doubling the temperature increases the radiant emittance by a factor of 2^4, or 16. If you consider two objects that are near one another, they are of course radiating to each other. The net flow of energy depends on their relative temperatures:

$$Q_R = \sigma\varepsilon_1\varepsilon_2(T_1^4 - T_2^4)A \qquad (1.5)$$

where Q_R is the net radiative transfer (in watts) and T is the absolute temperature, measured in degrees Kelvin. The term A is the view factor, the area through which the radiation passes between the two sources. The emissivity, ε, tells how well the source approximates a blackbody; a perfect black body would have an emissivity of 1.0 at all frequencies. The Stefan-Boltzmann constant, σ (5.6697×10^{-8} $W{\cdot}m^{-2}{\cdot}{}^\circ K^{-4}$) is a proportionality derived from a combination of K (Boltzmann's constant), the speed of light in a vacuum, and Planck's constant. Equation (1.5) is at the heart of any model dealing with the exchange of thermal radiation between objects.

The emissivity of biological tissue is approximately 1.0 in the middle infrared portion of the spectrum, due largely to strong absorption by water in these frequencies. The high emissivity is independent of pigmentation in the visible region. Plants and animals act very nearly as black bodies in the middle infrared. They absorb and emit these radiations very effectively. These are the frequencies of maximal radiation for objects at normal living temperatures. Therefore, coloration has essentially no effect on the gain and loss of infrared radiation by organisms. Emissivity in the visible portion of the spectrum varies with coloration. Hence, organisms with dark skins, feathers, or fur absorb more visible radiation than those with light surfaces; recall that the peak of solar output is in the visible range.

THE MEASUREMENT OF RADIATION

Inverse-Square Law

Energy from a point source is radiated in all directions. In a vacuum, with nothing to intercept the rays, they spread out as they travel away from the source. The amount of energy passing a cross section of a radiating cone in a unit of time is the same for any section of the same cone. This means that the intensity of radiation per unit area in the cross section decreases as the area increases. Doubling the distance from the point source causes a fourfold increase in the area of the cross section of the cone. Hence, the intensity per unit area decreases with the square of the distance from the source: the Inverse-Square Law of radiation from a point source.

Radiometry

The measurement of radiation can be very confusing, since there are many ways to take a measurement. Many persons have fallen prey to this confusion, and are not aided by the similarity of some of the terms used in the measurement of radiation, known as radiometry. Consider radiation emitted from a source, passing through an intervening medium, and striking a target. Measurements may be relative to the source of the target; total energy or energy per unit time may be recorded; radiation may be measured in all directions or only in certain directions.

A rather cumbersome diagram (Fig. 7) outlines some of these concepts. Electromagnetic energy represents the total output of the source, over an infinite range of frequencies. Any real sampling device can detect only a portion of that range, of course, though radiant energy refers to an attempt

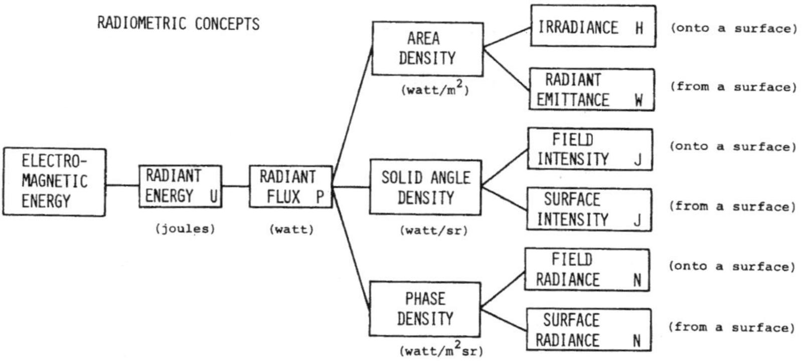

Fig. 7. Logical relationships of radiometric concepts; further explanation in the text (after Preisendorfer 1976).

to measure the energy at all frequencies without respect to the sensitivity of our eyes to perceive the radiation. Radiant energy is measured in joules, and is an indication of the total ability to perform work. The key concept in this diagram is that of radiant flux, defined as the rate of flow of radiant energy across a theoretical surface. This is a measure of power, or energy per unit time, and thus is in units of watts (joules/second). Since flux is measured across the spectrum, there is the problem of breaking up a continuous distribution into small bands of equal frequencies, unless you have a source that radiates at only a single frequency. This is a problem of integrating measurements across the distribution; it is not discussed further. The next step is to consider the geometry of the measurement. If a parallel flow of quanta through an area is considered, the area density of radiant flux is measured (in watts/m^2), sometimes called the flux density. If a measure is made of the solid angle density of radiant flux from a point, this is recorded in units of watts/steradian (the steradian being a measure of the solid angle). The solid angle density of radiant flux is sometimes given the shorthand name of (radiant) intensity. A combination of the two modes of measurement considers the little cones of radiation from each point in an area, called the phase density, measured in watts/$m^2 \cdot sr$.

Unfortunately, there is one remaining complication in this diagram. A distinction is made between the flow of radiant energy *onto* a surface and *from* a surface. When this is done, each of the three densities may have either of the two interpretations. The names and customary symbols for these measures are shown in the right-hand column of boxes. Each pair of boxes is measured in the same units as given for the generating density; i.e., irradiance and radiant emittance are both examples of area density measures of the radiant flux.

Photometry

Now that there is no confusion as to how one measures radiation, it is time for another monkey wrench (Fig. 8). Because most scientists are human beings, and vision is an important part of our sensory world, a complete alternative scheme of measurement has been devised for visible light, based upon the sensitivity of the human eye. In order to measure visible light in units that correspond to our perception of the brightness of light, the photometric system was developed. Photometric units are based on the selective

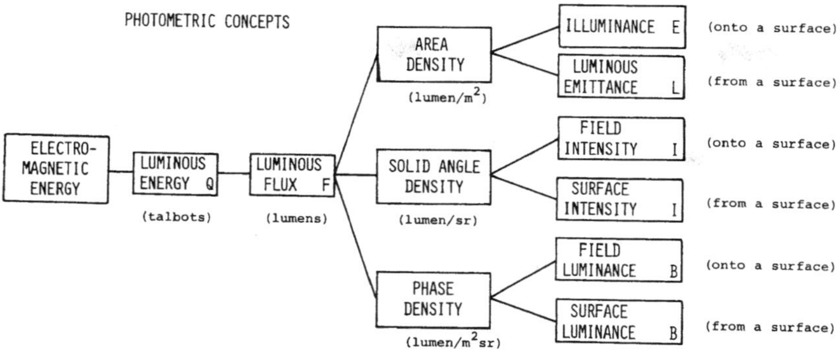

Fig. 8. Logical relationships of photometric concepts (after Preisendorfer 1976).

sensitivity of the light-adapted (as opposed to dark-adapted) human eye to the various frequencies of visible light. Figure 8 is the photometric counterpart of the radiometric diagram (Fig. 7).

The key concept is luminous flux, measured in lumens. Notice the modification of certain terms: illuminance replaces irradiance, luminous emittance instead of radiant emittance, and so forth. Properly speaking, all of these measures should be made with the light-adapted human eye. Use of other types of light sensors will introduce inaccuracies in proportion to their departure from the sensitivity curve of the human eye. An additional unit, the candela, is equal to one lumen/steradian, a measure of luminous intensity.

Figure 9 compares radiant and luminous flux. The ordinate measures absolute luminosity, expressing the ratio of luminous flux to radiant flux. Hence, the ratio is a conversion factor with the units of lumens/watt, and is plotted on a log scale in Figure 9. The right-hand curve (labeled *Photopic*) shows the luminosity for the light-adapted human eye, and is the basis for the relation between the photometric and radiometric measures. Notice that since the eye is not equally sensitive to all frequencies of light, a conversion between the two measurement systems must take into account the frequency of visible light (the curves here are plotted on a wavelength scale). The general procedure is to break up the spectral curve of a radiant source into numerous

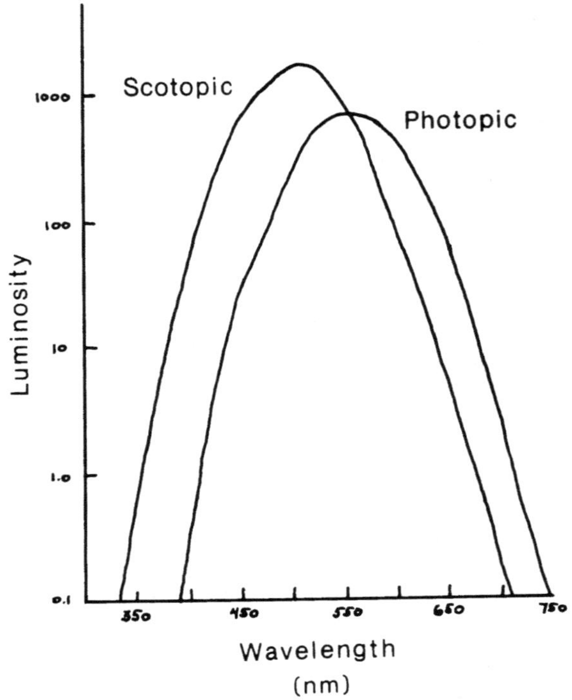

Fig. 9. Absolute luminosity curves as functions of wavelength (response of the human eye to radiation of a given wavelength). Absolute luminosity is measured in lumens/watt. Photometric units are based on the photopic response of the light-adapted human eye (after Barnes 1968).

small intervals and apply the appropriate conversion factor at each of these intervals.

The left-hand curve shows the luminosity for the dark-adapted human eye under low light conditions; this scotopic response is dominated by the rod photoreceptors in our eyes. Note that the peak luminosity for the scotopic curve is located at a shorter wavelength (i.e., shifted toward the blue) than is the peak for the photopic curve. The photopic peak luminosity is at a wavelength of about 556 nm, whereas the scotopic peak is at about 511 nm. The peak luminosity for scotopic vision is greater than that for photopic vision because the standard light source used to define the lumen (the standard candela) radiates less energy in the blue-green, where scotopic vision peaks, than in the yellow-green, where photopic vision peaks. The difference in peak luminosity is not due to differences in sensitivity of the two types of vision, although the scotopic system is more sensitive than the photopic system.

SUNLIGHT

Solar Spectra

The primary radiant source for all organisms is the sun. Figure 10 shows the spectral distribution of sunlight reaching the surface of the earth. The dotted line is a curve of black body radiation at a temperature of 5900°K, and is a very good approximation to the solar irradiance curve outside the earth's atmosphere. The solid line shows the irradiance of the sun as measured at sea level, after the atmosphere has absorbed certain portions of the spectrum.

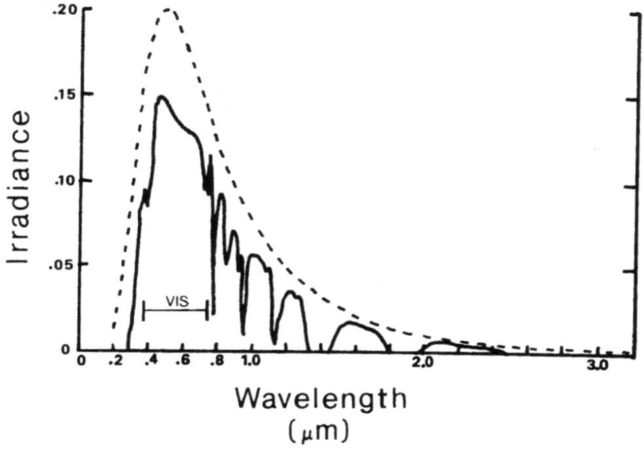

Fig. 10. Spectral distribution of sunlight reaching the surface of the earth. Spectral irradiance measured in $W{\cdot}m^{-2}{\cdot}A^{-1}$. The dotted line represents the theoretical curve for a black body at 5900 K. Position of the visible spectrum is indicated (VIS) (after Barnes 1968).

There are three molecules responsible for most of this absorption. Ozone absorbs strongly in the ultraviolet and part of the visible range. Absorption through the infrared is due mainly to water vapor and carbon dioxide. Notice the concentration of solar irradiance in the visible spectrum.

Sunlight's Earthly Fates

In addition to absorption, particles in the atmosphere also scatter sunlight. Scattering is a complex phenomenon that depends on the refractive index and size of a particle, the frequency of light striking the particle, and the angle at which the particle is viewed. You may even have scattering from a nonabsorbing material when that material is in bulk form. The atmosphere scatters blue frequencies more strongly than red frequencies, which is why the sky appears blue. On a clear day at sea level about one-fifth of the total illuminance (remember, illuminance refers to the light-adapted human eye) of the earth's surface is from the sky rather than directly from the sun. When you look at the setting sun it appears red because the blue light has been scattered during the long passage through the atmosphere at a narrow angle above the horizon. Some animal colors are produced physically through scattering by small particles in feathers or other integumentary structures. Scattering produces the blue color of kingfishers (*Alciedinidae*) and blue tits (*Parus caeruleus*) (Auber 1957) as well as the blue in certain insect wings and in the cuticles of some other invertebrates (Gardiner 1972). Colors produced by scattering from integumentary particles do not change their characteristic frequency (and wavelength) with slight changes in the viewing angle.

When the sun shines on water, the amount of visible light penetrating the water depends on the angle of incidence. A flat air-water interface reflects about 2% of the visible light that strikes perpendicular to the interface, with the percentage reflected increasing as the angle from the perpendicular increases. If the interface is ruffled by wind or waves, slightly more light is transmitted at every angle.

Polarization

Some other interesting phenomena may occur at the air-water interface, including polarization and interference.

Electromagnetic radiation is transmitted as transverse waves; i.e., the displacement vector of the wave is normal to the axis of propagation (like water waves, but unlike sound waves, which are longitudinal waves). If the displacement vector of the wave is always in the same plane, the wave is plane-polarized. Normally, radiation from a source such as a heated object has unpolarized waves, oriented in random directions normal to the axis of propagation. When a beam strikes a nonmetallic surface, the tendency for the radiation to be reflected or to penetrate the surface depends on the polarization of the radiation, resulting in a partial polarization of the reflected beam, and dependent on the angle of incidence of the beam. Waves whose displacement vector is parallel to the surface tend to be reflected; waves whose displacement vector is oriented otherwise tend to be absorbed. Certain materials (such as Polaroid sheet) are dichroic, that is, they selectively absorb visible light that is not in a "preferred" plane of polarization relative to the orientation of the dichroic material. These substances can be used to produce polarized, visible light. Numerous arthropods can see polarized light, and can use the directional information provided by the polarization produced by scattering and reflection of light in their environment.

Interference

When two radiation waves are superimposed slightly out of phase, they tend to cancel each other through the process of interference. Interference may also produce an adding effect, causing a local increase in light intensity when two light waves are in phase with one another. A thin film may cause interference by the action of light reflected from the first surface interfering with light reflected from the second surface. The thickness of the film must be comparable to the wavelength of the light for this to occur. Such interference produces the iridescence seen at the surface of soap bubbles. Interference between a transmitted ray and a doubly reflected ray at a thin film may produce similar results. One characteristic of thin film interference is that the frequency of interference depends on the angle of incidence of light (and thus the path length traveled through the film). This is why an oil film on a water surface changes color as you change your angle of view. Interference at the surface of the integument (or at the surface of pigment granules within the integument) is another source of animal colors, such as the iridescent or metallic colors of pigeons (Columbiformes), hummingbirds (Trochilidae), peacocks (*Pavo eristatus*), mallard ducks (*Anas platyrhynchos*) (Fox and Vevers 1960), and many insects (Gardiner 1972). Most of the blues and greens (the latter in combination with pigments) of bird feathers are produced by structural colors involving scattering or interference, rather than selective absorption by pigments.

Water and Light

Once the radiation passes the surface of the water, refraction has caused the rays to bend so that an underwater observer is effectively looking out of a manhole, with an angular radius of about 48°. Beyond this angle there is total internal reflection from the surface, according to Snell's Law. As the radiation descends through the water column, the infrared is absorbed very rapidly. Infrared comprises about half the total irradiance at sea level on a clear sunny day; this is essentially all absorbed by the first meter of water, falling off in an exponential fashion. Other frequencies of light show this exponential decay as well, though the decay rate is frequency-dependent. For natural waters the irradiance transmittance is usually maximal in the 460–500 nm range; i.e., blue light tends to penetrate the deepest in the water column. Transmittance falls off very rapidly at wavelengths above 580 nm, so that red light is filtered out very quickly.

ZOOCHROMES AND PHYTOCHROMES

Probably the key source of coloration for most plants and animals is pigmentation, the presence of materials that absorb in the visible range. Figure 11 shows absorption curves for two of the earth's key pigments, chlorophyll a and b. Each pigment shows two major peaks, one in the spectral region we call blue and one in the red. Failure to absorb in the green provides chlorophyll with its green appearance. The chlorophylls are related to several other classes of pigments that contain four pyrrole units, including porphyrins, heme pigments, cytochromes, and bile pigments (Wolken 1975). The location of major peaks for some other plant pigments is shown in Figure 11: β-carotene is a common carotenoid pigment found in many species (the carotenoids include the carotenes and the xanthophylls); phycoerythrin and phycocyanin are two algal pigments. There are numerous other pigments in the biological world,

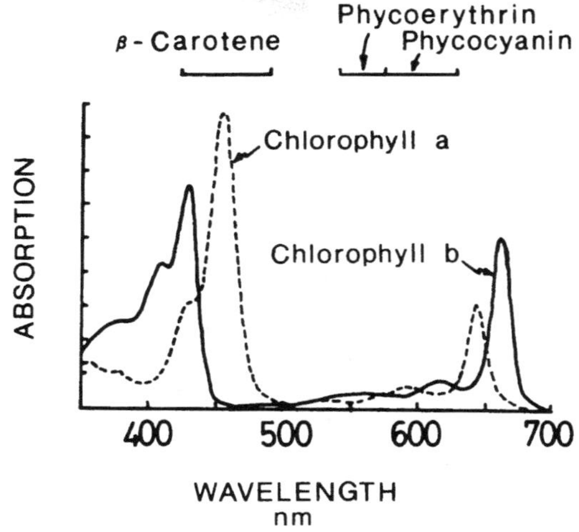

Fig. 11. Absorption spectra of chlorophylls a and b in ether. Absorption is plotted as specific absorption coefficient in the test apparatus used. At the top of the diagram are shown regions of the main peaks of three other plant pigments. The chlorophylls and β-carotene are found in land plants and most algae; phycoerythrin occurs in red algae; phycocyanin is found in both red and blue-green algae (after Seliger and McElroy 1965).

including several related to nitrogen metabolism, such as the indigoids, ommochromes, pterins, and melanins. Melanins are widespread, and account for black, brown, tan, and, less commonly, other colors. Melanin often occurs in specialized cells (melanocytes) that may allow for color changes by the animal. Note in Figure 11 the placement of absorption peaks along the spectrum. Marine algae that inhabit deep water tend to absorb at higher frequencies than marine algae that reside closer to the water's surface. Such a distribution correlates with the selective filtering of visible light by sea water.

BIOLUMINESCENCE

In the great depths of the ocean, all sunlight has been filtered out by the water column. Nevertheless, there is not total darkness, since a number of animals produce their own light, either by direct chemical means (bioluminescence) or by symbiotic use of bioluminescent bacteria. Terrestrial organisms may be bioluminescent as well, with many examples among land and marine organisms in diverse phyla (Gardiner 1972, Wolken 1975).

RECOMMENDED READING

To conclude, I would like to recommend two works for those who wish to investigate physics a little more deeply. *The Feynmann Lectures on Physics*, Vol. 1 (Feynmann et al. 1963) is a physics textbook that presents physical phenomena in a manner that relates to our everyday experience and is highly stimulating and entertaining, yet rigorous and thorough. Be prepared to go slowly. I also recommend *The World of Elementary Particles* (Ford 1963) for a gentle introduction to the fascination of physics at the most fundamental level, that of the most basic particles, forces, and interactions of the universe. The book is highly readable and requires no mathematics; it will give you a much better appreciation for what is *really* going on during light production and absorption, on the scale where the wave and particle nature of light are equally important.

REFERENCES

Auber, L. 1957. The distribution of structural colors and unusual pigments in the class Aves. *Ibis* 99:463-476.

Barnes, F. A. (ed.). 1968. *Electro-Optics Handbook: A Compendium of Useful Information and Technical Data.* RCA/Commercial Engineering, Harrison, N.J.

Feynmann, R. P.; Leighton, R. B.; and Sands, M. 1963. *The Feynmann Lectures on Physics*, Vol. 1: *Mainly Mechanics, Radiation, and Heat.* Reading, Mass.: Addison-Wesley.

Ford, K. W. 1963. *The World of Elementary Particles.* New York: Blaisdell.

Fox, H. M., and Vevers, G. 1960. *The Nature of Animal Colours.* London: Sidgewick and Jackson.

Gardiner, M. S. 1972. *The Biology of Invertebrates.* New York: McGraw-Hill.

Preisendorfer, R. W. 1976. *Hydrologic Optics*, Vol. 1: *Introduction*. U.S. Department of Commerce, National Oceanic and Atmospheric Administration, Environmental Research Labs. Government Printing Office, Washington, D.C.

Seliger, H. H., and McElroy, W. D. 1965. *Light: Physical and Biological Action*. New York: Academic Press.

Wolken, J. J. 1975. *Photoprocesses, Photoreceptors and Evolution*. New York: Academic Press.

Emissivity, a Little-Explored Variable:
Discussion

C. Richard Tracy

I appreciate very much Dennis' excellent review. Biologists are rarely equipped to talk about the physical, scientific aspects of the biological phenomena that they study. I think Dennis' paper helps to illustrate that biologists must know a considerable amount of physics, if they are to avoid a like amount of naiveté in their conclusions about biological processes.

I want to clarify a point central to Dennis' chapter. The wavelike energy which we see and call visible light is phenomenologically part of a continuum that includes X rays and radio waves. Of equal importance is the fact that electromagnetic radiation of varying wavelengths is emitted from different sources and sensed biologically by diverse senses. For example, nearly all of the sun's radiation that penetrates the earth's atmosphere to reach the biota of our planet is in the wave band between 290 and 2600 nm (Gates 1962). We can call this "solar radiation." On the other hand, all objects on the earth, and the earth's atmosphere, emit radiation in the band between *ca*. 4000 and 50,000 nm. We can call this "thermal radiation." In other words, there is a practical separation in these two forms of energy (each of which is extremely important to all animals). Thus, Dennis' broad treatment is excellent physics, but potentially misleading biology.

Dennis has told us that the average emissivity and absorptivity of thermal radiation by animals is always nearly 1.0. In other words, all animals act essentially as black bodies in the long-wave infrared spectrum. This is the case primarily because most animal surfaces contain water, which is a good absorber and emitter of thermal radiation. O. P. Pearson (1977) has discovered a possible exception to this dogma that animals act as black bodies in the thermal wavelengths. He has estimated that the South American iguanid lizard *Liolaemus multiformis* has a thermal emissivity of *ca*. 0.69! Pearson speculates that this is an adaptation by which this lizard can maintain an elevated body temperature due to reduced thermal radiant heat loss.

We already know that many animals have adaptations related to their exchange of heat involving differences in, or abilities to change, color or the absorptance of visible solar radiation (Norris 1967). We also know that essentially no animals have adaptations exploiting differences in thermal radiant emissivity. Thus, it might be useful to explore the circumstances under which an organism would "achieve" a greater advantage (in terms of an ability to maintain an elevated body temperature) from adaptations consisting of lowered (or an ability to physiologically lower) thermal emissivity as opposed to an increased (or ability to physiologically increase) solar absorptivity. I have preliminarily explored this question by manipulating an energy-balance model of a hypothetical animal. I assume the hypothetical animal is an ectotherm whose metabolic heat production and latent heat loss rates exactly balance (very often the case in lizards: Porter et al. 1973). It has a negligible conductive heat transfer, receives direct solar radiation on 25% of its total surface area, and receives scattered skylight (one-sixth as intense as direct solar radiation) on 50% of its total surface. The simplistic energy-balance model of this hypothetical animal (see Porter and Gates 1969, Tracy 1972) in thermal equilibrium is:

$$\text{Direct solar and skylight input} = \text{convective output} + \text{net thermal radiative output} \quad (1.6)$$

$$\alpha(0.25S + 0.50S/6) = h_c(T - T_a) + \bar{\varepsilon}\sigma(T^4 - T_e{}^4) \quad (1.7)$$

where

$\bar{\alpha}$ = average absorptivity to solar radiation (fraction)

S = direct solar radiant flux density ($W \cdot m^{-2}$)

h_c = convective heat transfer coefficient ($W \cdot m^{-2} \cdot K^{-1}$)

ε = thermal emissivity (fraction)

σ = Stefan-Boltzmann constant ($W \cdot m^{-2} \cdot K^{-4}$)

T = surface temperature of the animal (K)

T_a = ambient air temperature (K)

T_e = effective (average) temperature of the thermal radiant environment (K)

The partial derivative of thermal emissivity with respect to solar absorptivity

$$\frac{\partial \bar{\varepsilon}}{\partial \bar{\alpha}} = \frac{0.25S + 0.50S/6}{\sigma(T^4 - T_e^{\,4})} \tag{1.8}$$

will tell us the magnitude of difference in the thermal emissivity of the hypothetical animal that would exactly match a unit difference in solar absorptivity in terms of an effect on the equilibrium body temperature of the animal. Figure 12 shows the magnitude of this partial derivative as a function of the direct solar radiant flux density, S, and the average temperature difference between the animal and its thermal environment, $T - T_e$ (assuming that T_e is 283°K). This analysis shows that when the sunlight is intense (e.g., when $S > 0.7$ kw$\cdot$m^{-2}), a 1% change in $\bar{\alpha}$ is usually equivalent to a several-percent change in $\bar{\varepsilon}$. On the other hand, when there is little sunlight (e.g., when $T - T_e = 20$°K), a 1% change in ε is equivalent to a several-percent change in $\bar{\alpha}$. However, this latter set of circumstances is usually unlikely or even impossible. That is to say, an ectothermic animal is not likely to achieve a very elevated body temperature without a large amount of absorbed radiant energy. Therefore, it would appear that under most natural circumstances a small change in solar absorptivity would be equivalent to a larger change in thermal emissivity, and thus natural selection should usually favor morphological adaptations related to α more strongly than similar adaptations related to $\bar{\varepsilon}$. It seems, therefore, that animals such as *Liolaemus* represent a very interesting exception

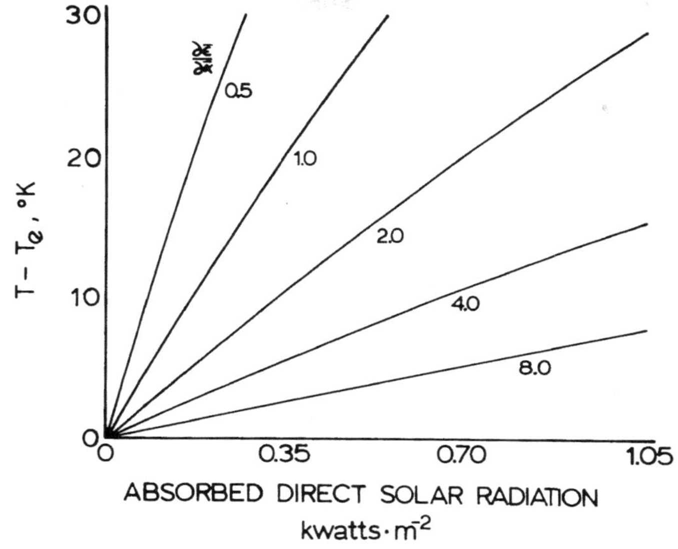

Fig. 12. The values of the partial derivative $\partial\bar{\varepsilon}/\partial\bar{\alpha}$ (see equation (1.8)): the steady-state energy-balance equation for a hypothetical ectothermic animal as a function of the direct solar radiation absorbed by the animal and the temperature difference between the animal and its environment. The combinations of environmental variables which give $\partial\bar{\varepsilon}/\partial\bar{\alpha} > 1$ represent situations in which differences in solar absorptivity, $\bar{\alpha}$, are more influential on the steady-state body temperature of the hypothetical animal than identical differences in the thermal emissivity, $\bar{\varepsilon}$. Combinations of environmental variables resulting in $\partial\bar{\varepsilon}/\partial\bar{\alpha} < 1$ are situations in which differences in $\bar{\varepsilon}$ are more influential on the energy balance than like differences in $\bar{\alpha}$.

to a logical rule, and must be exposed normally to unusual thermal environments.

ACKNOWLEDGMENTS

I would especially like to thank O. P. Pearson, who shared his ideas and a manuscript that was the focus of my discussion.

REFERENCES

Gates, D. M. 1962. *Energy Exchange in the Biosphere*. New York: Harper.

Norris, K. S. 1967. Color adaptation in desert reptiles and its thermal relationship. In *Lizard Ecology: A Symposium*, W. H. Milstead (ed.). Columbia, Mo.: Univ. of Mo. Press.

Pearson, O. P. 1977. The effect of substrate and skin color on thermoregulation of a lizard. *Comp. Biochem. and Physiol.* 58:353-358.

Porter, W. P., and Gates, D. M. 1969. Thermodynamic equilibria of animals with environment. *Ecol. Monogr.* 39:245-270.

Porter, W. P.; Mitchell, J. W.; Beckman, W. A.; and DeWitt, C. B. 1973. Behavioral implications of mechanistic ecology. *Oecologia* 13:1-54.

Tracy, C. R. 1972. Newton's Law: Its applicability for expressing heat losses from homeotherms. *BioScience* 22: 656-660 (erratum, 23:296).

Part 2

Physiological Functions of Animal Coloration

Chapter 2

The Influence of Color on Behavioral Thermoregulation and Hydroregulation

David M. Hoppe

Introduction
Thermoregulatory and Hydroregulatory Behavior
    Reptiles
    Amphibians
The Effect of Color on Absorption and Reflection
Study Systems for Examining the Role of Color
    Metachrosis in Lizards
    Metachrosis in Frogs
    Amphibian Color Polymorphism
    Desiccation Experiments with Chorus Frogs
    Reflectance Spectra of Chorus Frogs
    Distributional Aspects of Color Polymorphism
Adaptive Compromise

INTRODUCTION

Animal coloration represents many evolutionary adaptations. The first consideration by those seeking to identify coloration's adaptive value has often been the visual appearance to other animals of pigmented skin, scales, feathers, or hair. Investigators have considered and extensively studied such phenomena as cryptic coloration, aposematic coloration, parasematic coloration, and other aspects of inter- and intraspecific communication (refer to Chapters 8 and 9) as possible forces affecting the evolution of animal color. But color has nonvisual effects, through physical and biochemical changes that result from absorption and reflection of direct solar radiation and indirect or secondary radiations. Pigmentation of the skin and its derivatives influences the quality and quantity of radiation absorbed, and may filter out harmful radiation (see Chapter 3), or affect body temperature or the rate of evaporative water loss. Where radiation, temperature, or moisture is a critical factor limiting animal populations, color could have considerable adaptive significance through these nonvisual phenomena.

In this chapter, I review some of the evidence indicating that amphibians and reptiles behave so as to regulate body temperature or water content, or at least confine fluctuations within narrower limits than environmental conditions would otherwise dictate. I discuss the effect of color on some physical responses of organisms to solar radiation, and the behavioral responses that are affected as a consequence. I limit the discussion to responses of amphibians and reptiles, although some conclusions from my experiments with these ectotherms may apply to endothermal vertebrates as well. I consider the differential absorption of solar radiation by differently colored skin or scales, and I conclude by speculating on the adaptive significance of color in amphibians and reptiles from the standpoint of behavioral thermoregulation or hydroregulation, referring to studies of color change and color polymorphism in these vertebrate groups.

THERMOREGULATORY AND HYDROREGULATORY BEHAVIOR

Reptiles

Thermoregulatory behavior is well documented for many species of reptiles, and one can sort through literally hundreds of papers in reviewing this phenomenon. Perhaps the most widespread thermoregulatory behavior is basking; organisms gain heat by prolonged exposure to solar radiation (heliothermic basking) or to warm substrates (thigmothermic basking). Heliothermic basking is of more interest here, since color affects the absorption of solar radiation. Basking enables some species to attain body temperatures well above ambient air temperatures, a phenomenon most pronounced in high-altitude populations such as an Andean smooth-throated iguanid lizard (*Liolaemus multiformis*) (Pearson 1954, Pearson and Bradford 1976) that attained body temperatures as high as 30°C above that of the ambient air. Vitt (1974) reported that many species of high-latitude lizards and snakes achieve body temperatures higher than that of the ambient air or substrate by basking. Norris (1967) demonstrated similar thermal phenomena with three species of high-altitude American lizards of the genus *Sceloporus*.

The efficiency of basking can be increased by changes in the animal's posture or orientation with respect to incident radiation. For example, Brattstrom (1971) described several basking postures used by the bearded dragon (*Amphibolurus barbatus*), showed that these lizards orient themselves to maximize or minimize exposure to the sun or a heat lamp under experimental conditions, and demonstrated that such behavior is influenced by body temperature. Similarly, Cogger (1974) described orientation and posturing behavior involved in the basking of the mallee dragon (*Amphibolurus fordi*) and DeWitt (1967) showed that the desert iguana (*Dipsosaurus dorsalis*) adjusts its position with respect to incident radiation under laboratory conditions, thereby achieving quite precise regulation of its body temperature.

Further modification of basking behavior was shown by Case (1976), whose studies indicate that endogenous triggers to basking have become integrated with seasonal behavior of the chuckawalla (*Sauromalus obesus*). He showed that spring-collected animals readily basked, whereas fall-collected animals were hesitant to bask under the same conditions of temperature and light. This result suggests that endogenous controls allow for basking when increasing body temperature and metabolic rate is advantageous, but inhibit such behavior when the animal should be entering a winter torpidity.

Whereas basking and its modifications help to increase the body temperature, other action patterns are necessary to keep this temperature from reaching lethally high values under some circumstances. Mosauer (1936) reported that reptiles die from thermal stress due to insolation, not from ultraviolet radiation or desiccation. He also stated that a diurnal desert lizard cannot tolerate any more heat than a nocturnal snake, and therefore must adjust behaviorally to keep its body temperature down. Cole (1943) has confirmed Mosauer's finding that desert reptiles die from thermal stress when overexposed to sunlight. Some disagreement exists in the literature regarding thermal tolerance; however, as Cowles and Bogert (1944) state: "Contrary to previous reports, nocturnal reptiles not only tolerate but prefer temperatures lower than diurnal reptiles." Regardless of any comparison of diurnal and nocturnal forms in this respect, diurnal lizards (particularly desert species) can become lethally overheated in sunlight, and must behave so as to avoid this occurrence.

One tactic that minimizes heat gain from the surroundings is to reduce the surface in contact with warm substrates. For example, the lizard *Phrynocephalus mystaceus* adjusts its posture at midday so that its legs hold its body well off the substrate (Kashkarov and Kurbatov 1930). The shovel-snouted lizard (*Aporosaura anchietae*) arches its body, which limits the substrate contact to a small portion of its ventrum (Brain 1962). Brattstrom (1971) and Cogger (1974) also describe postures which serve to minimize substrate contact.

Avoidance behavior is another adaptation to unfavorable thermal environments. Shade-seeking, shelter-seeking, or burrowing, as in the reports of Cowles and Bogert (1944), Norris (1953), Brattstrom (1971), Cogger (1974), and Aleksiuk (1976), are behavioral patterns aimed at temperature regulation by retreating from unfavorable environmental conditions. By splitting their time between sunlight and shade, being in burrows or on the surface, and other such behavior, reptiles have been able to achieve rather precise control over their body temperatures. Thermoregulation can be assisted by heat-dissipating behavior, such as respiratory movements or panting (Cowles and Bogert 1944, Brattstrom 1971, Cogger 1974), or licking the lips to allow for evaporative cooling (Brain 1962). Further refinement of thermoregulatory behavior is seen in species such as the taipan (*Oxyuranus scutellatus*), which appears to behave so as to achieve an even more precise regulation of head temperature than body temperature (Johnson 1975). Johnson described specific reptilian action patterns (e.g., gaping, elevating the head above the substrate, tucking the head under or inside a body coil, or burying the head in the substrate) that may precisely regulate the temperature of the head. Specific regulation of head temperature may be an important factor when considering differences between coloration of the head and body of some species.

The significance of behavioral thermoregulation is further elaborated by studies of natural populations. Hamilton (1973) has reported that a large vegetarian lizard (*Angolosaurus skoogi*) spends most of its above-surface time on dunes, behaving so as to first increase body temperature, then stabilize it near 39°C, with only brief visits to feeding sites. These data suggest that the significance of thermoregulation may be in allowing for more efficient metabolic food processing rather than increasing activity capabilities of the whole organism for food-seeking and subsequent higher food intake.

Cost/benefit ratios may be important factors to consider in studying the evolution of thermoregulatory behavior. For example, Huey (1974) reported that a Puerto Rican anolid lizard appears to behaviorally thermoregulate in open habitat, but tolerates decreased and more variable temperatures in forest habitat where fewer and more widely separated basking sites are present. Another tropical forest species, *Anolis marmoratus*, is also more eurythermal than most lizards, showing little thermoregulation (Huey and Webster 1975). Thus, the energy expenditure or increased exposure to predation in seeking the less abundant basking sites may make behavioral thermoregulation disadaptive.

Amphibians

Some amphibians are thought to use behavioral thermoregulation. That thermal preferences are present in this group of vertebrates can be seen even in the larval stages. Brattstrom (1963) has reported that tadpole aggregations are sometimes thermotaxic, and that larval salamanders may select specific, favorable water temperatures within ponds. Licht and Brown (1967) found that both larval and adult red-bellied newts (*Taricha rivularis*) exhibit distinct thermal preferences. One report of thermoregulatory behavior among frogs is that of Lillywhite (1970), who studied the behavior of bullfrogs (*Rana catesbeiana*). He found that certain action patterns were correlated with air temperature, with stronger correlations seen for juveniles than adults. Such behavior included shuttling in and out of shade, shuttling between water and terrestrial surfaces, basking in exposed areas, and changing between prostrate and sitting postures. Valdivieso and Tamsitt (1974) have also reported basking behavior in semi-arborial neotropical tree frogs (*Hyla labialis*) which resulted in body temperatures higher than ambient air temperatures. Western toads (*Bufo boreus*) exhibit basking as a means of increasing body temperature (Lillywhite, Licht, and Chelgren 1973). Such behavior is more pronounced among juveniles than adults, and may serve to maximize growth rate. Some Peruvian toads were also shown to increase body temperatures somewhat by basking, but not nearly as well as lizards of the same region (Pearson and Bradford 1976).

The water-permeable skin of amphibians results in a problem not faced by the scaled reptiles, that of rapid desiccation. Thus there exists for amphibians a close relationship between thermal changes and body water balance. The resulting evaporative cooling may reduce or even eliminate the possibilities for amphibian thermoregulation. These relationships are pointed out in observations that "thermoregulating" toads gained heat inefficiently because they returned to shaded regions of lower temperature often, perhaps to rehydrate, but could be active during unfavorably hot, dry hours of the day, presumably due to evaporative cooling (Pearson and Bradford 1976). Similarly, an African toad (*Bufo mauritanicus*) may have adapted to hot, dry climates by losing water more rapidly and thus maintaining a lower body temperature through evaporative cooling (Cloudsley-Thompson 1969). The relationship of heat and water budgets is emphasized by the observation that heliothermic anurans are forms that remain close to permanent water (Brattstrom 1963). Tracy (1976) showed that there may be little thermoregulatory ability among leopard frogs. His computer simulations imply that under most natural conditions, these frogs would have a core temperature very close to the ambient air temperature, due to evaporative cooling, so thermoregulatory behavior, if present, would be very inefficient. My own work with chorus frogs, to be discussed later, confirms this observation.

Since amphibians lose water freely, many of their action patterns may be aimed at conserving body water, which I consider to be hydroregulation. Bentley (1966) described hydroregulatory behavior of amphibians occupying arid Australian regions, including burrowing when conditions are dry and emerging in response to rain, and becoming cryptozoic by seeking refuge under litter and in soil cracks. Such amphibians may seek shade or moist soil, or may position themselves so as to contact more moist substrate or to contact it with the more permeable skin of the groin region. Leopard frogs subjected to desiccation experiments (Gillis and Hoppe 1975) initially sat erect and attempted to escape, and later in the trials assumed a tucked posture that reduced their surface area and put more ventral skin in contact with the substrate. Salamanders may seek refuge under leaf litter, and coil to reduce surface area. The bullfrogs in Lillywhite's (1970) trials, in splitting time between water and terrestrial surfaces, may have been regulating body water content.

THE EFFECT OF COLOR ON ABSORPTION AND REFLECTION

Different pigments or densities of pigment are known to absorb solar radiation at different rates and in different qualities or quantities. In this way, the color of an animal can affect its temperature and possibly its water dynamics, thus influencing behavioral thermoregulation or hydroregulation.

Cole (1943) noted that a dark-colored animal is subject to more rapid heating than a lighter animal if exposed to the same intense radiation, and dark lizards overheated more rapidly than lizards of lighter color. He and other early investigators erroneously concluded, however, that the dark-colored animal also lost heat more rapidly than the light-colored animal by reradiating it, when sheltered from incident radiation. Norris (1967) detailed the reasons why a dark lizard is not necessarily a better emitter of radiation than a light one. This is a crucial point, since any advantage a dark animal holds in absorbing radiant energy would be lessened if it also emitted that energy more rapidly in shade or early evening hours, which would be the case if Cole's (1943) assumption were true. The thermal relationships of reptiles with respect to color have been well discussed by Norris (1967), and I refer the reader to that publication rather than reviewing the material here.

Bartlett and Gates (1967) reported that the total energy gain of a lizard would be altered by about 4% with a 10% change in the lizard's absorptivity. While 4% may seem a small amount, they concluded, "It would be worthwhile to examine the spectral variations of both individuals and ecotypes in these terms." I report the spectral properties of different color phenotypes of chorus frogs in a later section of this chapter.

That reptiles have adapted evolutionarily to meet thermal problems by altering the spectral properties of their surfaces is indicated by some observations of Hutchison and Larimer (1960). They pointed out that heat gain of some lizards via absorption of solar radiation is correlated to habitat, desert species absorbing least and tropical forest species the most. Lower heat gain was seen with increasing aridity and temperature. They also found that the light ventral surfaces of desert species reflect more of the radiation being emitted and reflected by the substrate, which may be another color-related thermal adaptation.

STUDY SYSTEMS FOR EXAMINING THE ROLE OF COLOR

Two types of color variation among reptiles and amphibians provide systems for studying the influence of color on the behavioral regulation of temperature or water content. One is the capacity for color change by individuals, a phenomenon which has been called metachrosis by some authors. This can be a distinct change between two visible hues, such as from brown to green, or a change in the saturation of a color, such as from light brown to a darker brown. The other is color polymorphism, where individuals of different genetically determined colors coexist in the same population.

Metachrosis in Lizards

Pronounced color changes have been studied in species of both reptiles and amphibians, most of which are affected by environmental conditions in a predictable fashion. Some of these changes have been shown to affect the thermal biology and consequently the behavior of the organisms involved.

The pioneering studies of Atsatt (1939) on sixteen species of desert lizards revealed that both geckos and iguanid lizards become lighter colored in response to high temperatures and darker when temperatures are decreased, which is adaptive for a temperature-regulating organism. Cogger (1974) reported that the melanophores of the mallee dragon (*Amphibolurus fordi*) expand to yield a darker color soon after emergence in the morning, increasing the efficiency of its basking. Norris (1967) also described cases in which lizards, after emerging and increasing their body temperatures by basking, become paler, some of them becoming "superlight," thereby greatly reducing their absorption of solar energy. These daily cycles of metachrosis appear to be adaptive strategies of thermoregulation among diurnal lizards, animals becoming darker in color when it is advantageous to absorb more light, and lighter when body temperature must be stabilized or decreased by reflecting more light. One might get into a "cause-vs.-effect" argument at this point. That is, the animal turns darker as an "effect" of lower temperatures (and perhaps changing intensities of illumination), so we should be careful of speaking teleologically in saying that the animal turns darker to "cause" greater absorption of radiant energy. Regardless of the viewpoint taken, such metachrosis seems to represent an evolutionary adaptation to modify the thermal changes occurring as a result of insolation.

Ontogenetic color change could represent another level of thermoregulatory adaptation. Fitch (1955) described a color pattern metamorphosis in the Great Plains skink (*Eumeces obsoletus*). In this species the hatchling is usually jet black dorsally, changing to a golden brown after the first hibernation period, and eventually to a dull, speckled adult pattern varying from "grayish brown or yellowish brown to olive, with irregular black markings." The darker pigmentation of juveniles, combined with their higher ratio of surface area to volume, allows them more capacity for gaining heat through thermoregulatory behavior, and results in an increased rate of growth.

Metachrosis in Frogs

Considerable research has been carried out which examines the phenomenon of color change in amphibians, the earlier work being summarized by Parker (1948). From this summary, Edgren (1954) generalized that "frogs respond to cool dark environments by release of melanophorotropic hormone and darkening of integument, whereas light and warmth result in melanophore contraction and light colors. . . ." Anyone who collects or maintains frogs for research purposes has probably observed the darkening of the skin that occurs when the organisms are refrigerated. Both leopard frogs and chorus frogs exhibited this type of metachrosis in my own research activities. In some species, most notably the tree frogs, environmental factors cause color changes between distinctly different hues. Edgren (1954), for example, noted that gray tree frogs (*Hyla versicolor*) remain brown under constant light conditions but turn green in constant dark, and that cold temperatures induce darkening of color. In fact, frogs with parts of their bodies exposed to different environmental conditions may show color differences between these body regions. For example, Porter (1972) described green frogs (*Rana clamitans*) which were bright green on portions of their bodies that were in direct sunlight, and a bronze or olive-green color where they were in the shade or under water.

These amphibian color changes could play a thermoregulatory role in addition to contributing to the cryptic coloration of the animals involved. Experimental data quantifying the thermal effects of amphibian color change are not presently available, however.

Amphibian Color Polymorphism

Some populations of a variety of amphibian species exhibit color polymorphism. By examining such phenomena as seasonal changes in the frequencies of various color morphs, environmental correlates with color morph frequencies, or other physiological traits that may accompany color phenotypes, the adaptive significance of color might be further elucidated.

One well-studied example of color polymorphism is the situation existing in Rocky Mountain populations of the boreal chorus frog (*Pseudacris triseriata*) (Matthews 1971, Hoppe 1975, Tordoff, Pettus, and Matthews 1976, Tordoff and Pettus 1977). Eight color phenotypes may occur in these populations; the dorsum can be brown, red, green, or red-and-green, and the accompanying spots or stripes can be brown or green. Chorus frogs do not change from one color to another, although they become darker or lighter in response to environmental factors as do other amphibians and reptiles previously discussed. The relative advantages or disadvantages of different colors appear related to sunlight or visual phenomena, since these frogs feed diurnally during most of July and August, whereas nearby prairie populations are largely nocturnal and contain only the brown dorsal color phenotype (Spencer 1964, Hess 1969).

Two types of experimental evidence, plus some observations regarding the dynamics of these mountain populations, contribute to my speculation regarding the nonvisual significance of color in chorus frogs. One experimental finding is that a green frog loses water more rapidly than a brown frog when exposed to direct sunlight. The other experimental finding is that green chorus frogs absorb and reflect radiant energy differently from brown frogs, in a manner that might account for their different desiccation rates.

Desiccation Experiments with Chorus Frogs

Two sets of desiccation experiments, designated dark and sunlight trials, were carried out in order to examine the role of color in the thermal and water dynamics of these frogs. The dark trials were performed under laboratory conditions similar to the method of Claussen (1969). The sunlight trials involved recording similar data, but the frogs were exposed to direct solar radiation during the experiments.

Dark desiccation trials were carried out by placing frogs in wire screen cages in a 0.05 m^3 oven at room temperature (21-23°C). Air was first pumped through a liter jar filled with Drierite ($CaSO_4$), then through the oven chamber from bottom to top at a rate of 2500 cm^3/min. An enamel pan containing another 800 cm^3 of Drierite was placed in the bottom of the oven, resulting in 10-12% relative humidity in the desiccation chamber. Frogs were acclimated for 24 hours at 18°C in petri dishes that contained filter paper saturated with distilled water to the point where a layer of standing water just covered the paper. Each frog was weighed before the trial, at half-hour intervals during the trial, and at the frog's critical activity point (CAP). Critical activity points were determined by using the combined criteria of Ray (1958) and Farrell and MacMahon (1969). These criteria are (1) loss of righting ability, (2) cessation of buccal movements, (3) dried appearance of the skin, and (4) ultimate survival of the frog upon immediate rehydration.

Temperature and desiccation responses to sunlight were determined by modifying the above procedure somewhat. Adults were acclimated as described above, then fastened to a sheet of white styrofoam by means of strings tied around the knees. They were placed in direct sunlight on a flat surface. Weight, dorsal surface temperature, and cloacal temperature were recorded initially, after 30 minutes, and at CAP. Dorsal surface and cloacal temperatures were measured electronically with flat surface and 20-gauge blunt needle thermistor probes, respectively. Air temperature, relative humidity, and wind velocity (which was negligible on the days selected) were also recorded. All trials were carried out between 1230 and 1400 Mountain Daylight Time (MDT) to standardize the angle of exposure to the sunlight.

Desiccation data were pooled from different days during which the weather conditions were similar enough that overall desiccation means were not significantly different. Least-squares regression coefficients of desiccation rate on initial weight were calculated with phenotype as a covariant. Analyses of covariance were then performed to examine the role of color phenotype in determining desiccation rate.

Changes in dorsal surface and cloacal temperatures of the frogs during the sunlight trials are shown in Table 1.

Table 1

Temperature Changes of Adult Frogs in Sunlight Trials, in °C

	Green		Brown		
Area Measured	*N*	$\bar{X} \pm$ S.E.	*N*	$\bar{X} \pm$ S.E.	*t*
Δ Dorsal					
30 minutes	14	−2.0 ± 1.3	20	−0.9 ± 1.0	0.696
CAP	13	+6.2 ± 0.8	18	+6.4 ± 0.6	0.159
Δ Cloacal					
30 minutes	14	−1.1 ± 0.6	20	−0.7 ± 0.6	0.471
CAP	13	+1.3 ± 1.2	18	+1.9 ± 0.5	0.472

Whereas the relatively large error factor in these data discourages rigorous analysis or interpretation, the data indicate that temperature response is probably not a major limiting factor for these frogs. The average environmental conditions to which they were exposed were temperatures of 26-29°C, relative humidities of 23-42%, and a dry substrate at a temperature of 29-33°C. But both surface and cloacal temperatures (initially 20-24°C) dropped by 1-2° during half an hour under these circumstances. Only when the animals reached CAP (which took 30-45 minutes under these circumstances) did these temperatures rise appreciably, and even at CAP the animals were usually cooler than the air and the substrate. In these trials, evaporative cooling was effective enough that frogs maintained temperatures below ambient, and would die of desiccation before encountering seriously high body temperatures. In fact, frogs which were not placed in water for rehydration immediately after reaching CAP did not recover. The final cloacal temperatures of these frogs ranged from 25-29°C. Since the critical thermal maximum (CTM) temperature of chorus frogs from these same populations, acclimated under similar circumstances, is reported as 37-38°C (Miller and Packard 1974), death must have resulted from desiccation in the sunlight trials discussed above, not from high body temperature.

Water losses of the frogs during these sunlight trials are summarized in Table 2, expressed as percentages of initial weight lost. Tolerance to desiccation, as indicated by percentage of body weight lost at CAP, did not differ between green and brown frogs, in either adults or juveniles. However, green adults lost water more rapidly than browns, losing 29.3% of their body weight in 30 minutes compared with 26.5% in browns ($p < 0.05$). Similar differences were not detected in juvenile frogs. I suggest that the high surface area/volume ratio of juveniles allows for such a high relative rate of loss that any differences due to other factors are less likely to be expressed. Also, the pigmentation of juveniles may not be completely developed, a suggestion supported by the observation that colors become more distinct during the first few weeks of growth of these frogs.

Table 3 contains similar data from adults and juveniles subjected to the dark, laboratory-chamber desiccation trials. Again, neither adults nor juveniles show different CAP values between the phenotypes. In these dark trials, differences in rates of water loss were not seen between green and brown frogs, juveniles or adults.

Table 2

Weight Loss Due to Desiccation of Frogs in Sunlight Trials, as Percentages of Initial Weight

Category	Green N	Green $\overline{X} \pm$ S.E.	Brown N	Brown $\overline{X} \pm$ S.E.	t
Adults					
30 minutes	21	29.3 ± 0.8	21	26.5 ± 0.8	2.462*
CAP	13	36.1 ± 0.6	18	35.4 ± 0.6	0.768
Juveniles					
20 minutes	12	21.9 ± 0.4	12	21.1 ± 0.4	1.536
CAP	12	38.3 ± 0.9	12	38.9 ± 0.9	0.479

* $p < 0.05$.

Table 3

Weight Loss Due to Desiccation of Frogs in Dark Trials, as Percentages of Initial Weight

Category	Green N	Green $\overline{X} \pm$ S.E.	Brown N	Brown $\overline{X} \pm$ S.E.	t
Adults					
1 hour	12	11.6 ± 0.6	12	11.5 ± 0.4	0.153
CAP	12	42.6 ± 0.5	12	42.1 ± 0.4	0.774
Juveniles					
1 hour	19	23.3 ± 1.2	24	24.9 ± 0.8	1.211
CAP	15	40.5 ± 0.9	23	38.6 ± 0.8	1.583

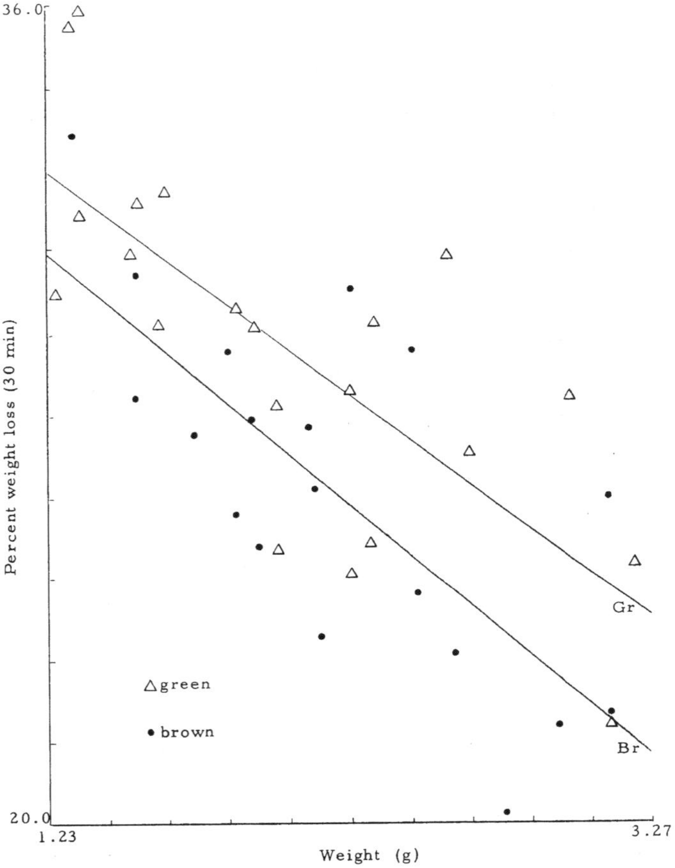

Fig. 13. Regression of adult weight loss on initial frog weight, sunlight trials.

Anurans can lose water at different rates due to their body size, as a consequence of surface area/volume relationships. Therefore, the desiccation data reported here have been plotted as functions of the frogs' weights (Figs. 13-16), in the format of Farrell and MacMahon (1969). The resulting linear relationships are similar to those of other hylids, as reported in the Farrell and MacMahon paper. *F*-statistics from analyses of covariance on each of these pairs of regression lines are listed in Table 4. (The roman numerals subscript to *F* in the two

Table 4

Analysis of Covariance[a] of Weight Loss Due to Desiccation of Frogs (Fig. 13-16)

Trial	F_I[b]	F_{II}[c]
Sunlight		
Adults	0.212	7.834**
Juveniles	0.060	3.956
Dark		
Adults	0.087	0.089
Juveniles	1.725	0.169

[a]Testing regressions of rate of weight loss of initial frog weight, with color phenotype as a covariant.

[b]Testing the hypothesis that the two slopes are equal.

[c]Testing the hypothesis that the two Y-intercepts are equal, given that the slopes are equal.

**$p < 0.01$.

right-hand columns refer to hypothesis I and hypothesis II, respectively.) The only significant difference indicated by these tests is between green and brown adults in the sunlight trials ($F = 7.834$, $p < 0.01$). The interpretation, as shown in Figure 13, is that a green frog of a given weight loses water more rapidly in sunlight than a brown frog of the same weight.

These desiccation findings suggest a terrestrial disadvantage of green frogs compared with brown frogs. Since these montane frogs feed diurnally, exposure to sunlight results in relatively more water loss in green adults, which

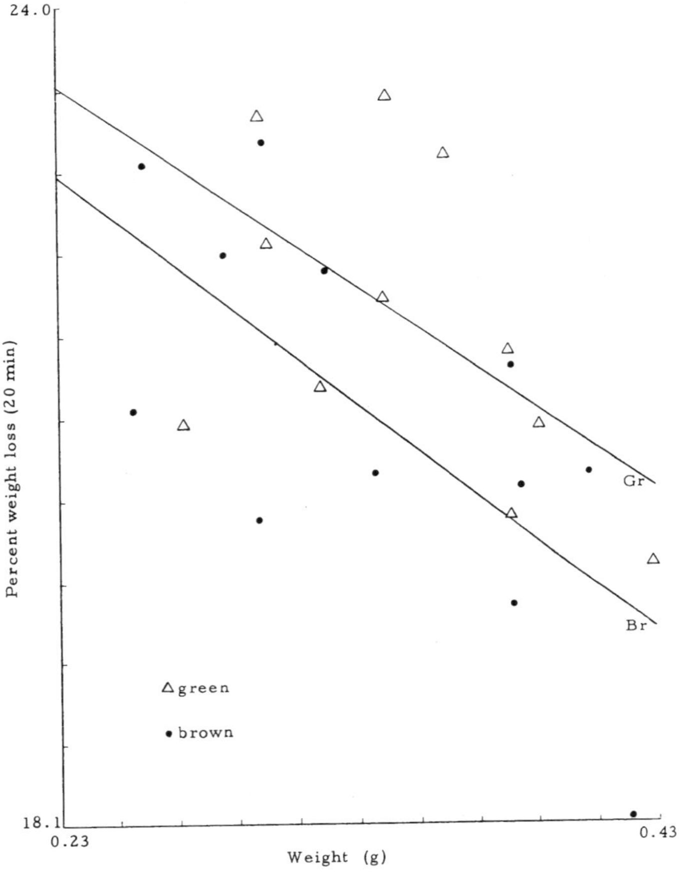

Fig. 14. Regression of juvenile weight loss on initial frog weight, sunlight trials.

may limit the distance traveled or time spent in feeding, or both. It may be argued that the frogs limit their activity to moist meadows, hence overcoming evaporative loss through continual water uptake. Two considerations tend to counter this argument. One is that the water balance model of Tracy (1976) suggests that under the desiccating circumstances of montane air temperatures, insolation, and wind, chorus frogs could not replenish their body water, even on water-saturated substrates. Secondly, as reported by Spencer (1964), these frogs migrate considerable distances across relatively dry terrain. Unless such

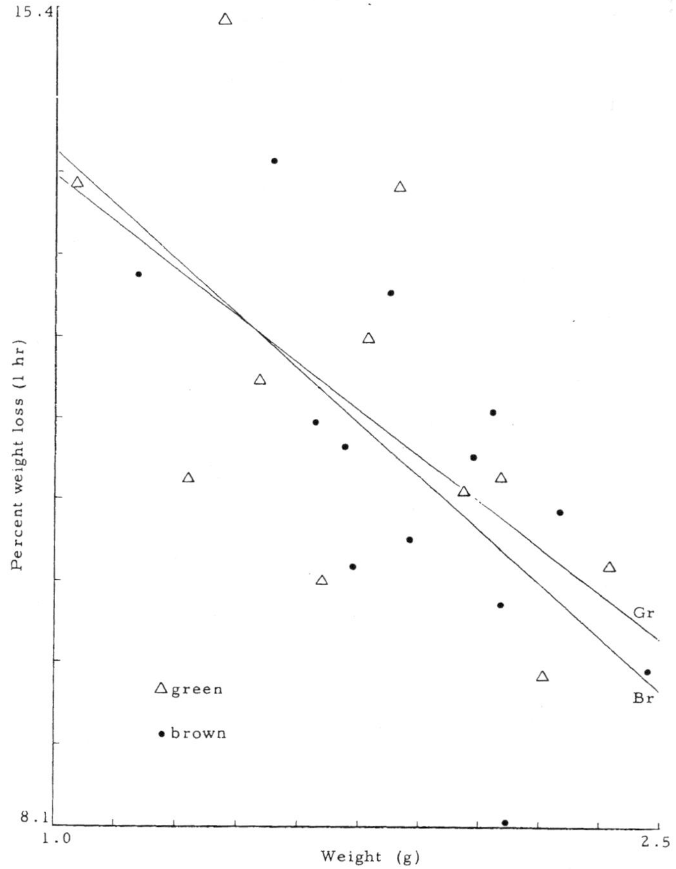

Fig. 15. Regression of adult weight on initial frog weight, dark trials.

migrations were completed during periods of rainfall or darkness, brown frogs would have a slight advantage in losing water more slowly while exposed to sunlight.

Reflectance Spectra of Chorus Frogs

Preliminary spectrophotometric data relate to the different desiccation rates of brown and green chorus frogs. Spectral reflectances of the dorsal surfaces of

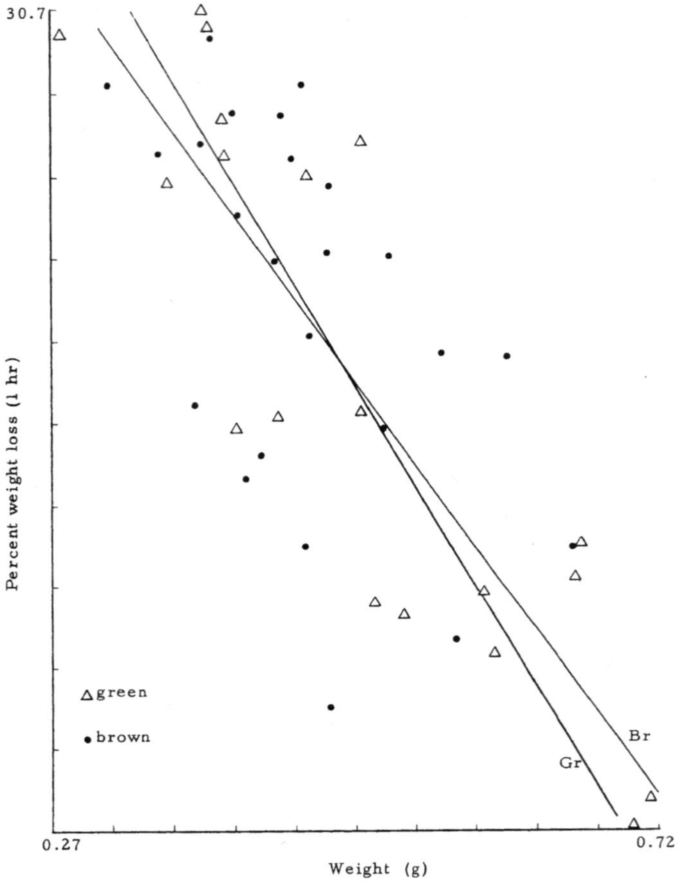

Fig. 16. Regression of juvenile weight loss on initial frog weight, dark trials.

these color morphs were determined with a Beckman DK-2A spectroreflectometer for the wavelength interval of 350 to 2500 nm. The response curves of two brown and two green frogs are shown in Figure 17. As illustrated, the percentages of light reflected by the frogs' dorsal surfaces were generally lower for green frogs than for brown frogs, particularly in the spectral interval of 500 to 1000 nm. In other words, green frogs absorb more of the incident radiation than do brown frogs, green acting as a "darker" color in this respect. It must be pointed out that these

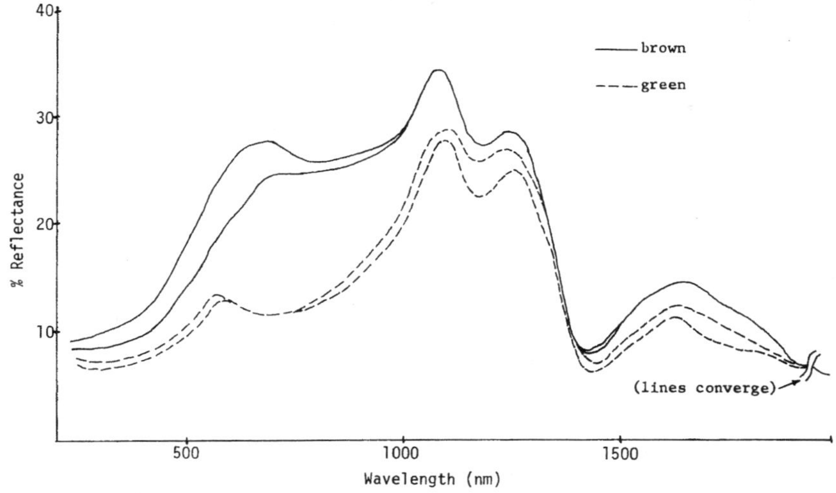

Fig. 17. Reflectance spectra of brown and green chorus frogs.

animals' surfaces are nearly perfect absorbers and emitters of long-wave or thermal radiation, regardless of color (see Chapter 1). However, the wavelength interval over which these color morphs differ in their absorptive properties contains significant energy which is converted to heat on absorption, and could therefore affect the thermal and water budgets of the animals.

Distributional Aspects of Color Polymorphism

Some distributional data regarding amphibian color polymorphism relate to the role of color in the thermal or water dynamics of the species involved. Data from at least two montane populations of chorus frogs indicate that the green phenotype may be favored in the aquatic phase of the life cycle, but at a disadvantage terrestrially (Tordoff 1971, Hoppe unpublished data). The frequencies of green frogs in these populations appear to decrease throughout the summer, during the period of time when the frogs are feeding diurnally. Similar phenomena were reported in two other species of hylid frogs studied. In populations of Pacific tree frogs (*Hyla regilla*), green individuals are favored in the spring, whereas non-greens are favored by late summer (Jameson and Pequegnat 1971). Similarly, in cricket frog populations (*Acris crepitans* and *A. gryllus*), green frogs appear to be favored in spring and early summer, but grays are favored by fall (Pyburn 1961, Nevo 1973). In Pacific tree frog populations again, the frequency of green frogs in West Coast populations is inversely proportional to aridity, relatively fewer green frogs being found in populations located in more arid regions (Resnick and Jameson 1963). All these distributional observations suggest that the increased solar absorptivity of small diurnal or semidiurnal frogs with a green dorsum may be placing them at an adaptive disadvantage in desiccating circumstances. Conversely, as long as they have adequate substrate moisture or standing water to replace evaporated water, these green frogs could possibly gain a thermal boost through more efficient basking.

For at least two reasons, I hesitate to apply my speculations to green versus brown frogs generally. One is that surface/volume relationships may mask any color effect. Sunlight desiccation trials similar to my experiments with chorus frogs were run with leopard frogs, and no differences in desiccation rate were seen between brown and green frogs (Gillis and Hoppe 1975). With the lower surface/volume ratio of the larger leopard frogs, the differences in absorptivity of the dorsal surfaces of the color morphs may not alter the thermal or water balance significantly. The other reason is that a green frog is not necessarily a "green" frog. All frogs that the human eye perceives as green do not necessarily have the same combination of pigments or the same spectral properties. Schwalm, Starrett, and McDiarmid (1977), for example, reported that some frogs that appear green reflect near-infrared light, whereas others do not, so the "green" color of these frogs may differ in its effect on their thermoregulatory or hydroregulatory abilities.

ADAPTIVE COMPROMISE

In oversimplifying some ectothermal color relationships, I have of necessity ignored a considerable volume of literature dealing with other effects of color, both from a visual and a nonvisual standpoint. The evolution of animal color in relation to thermal or water dynamics is interrelated with selection for cryptic coloration, aposematic coloration, parasematic coloration, protection from harmful radiation, and other selection pressures dealt with in other chapters. The relative importance of these factors varies with the species or the particular environmental circumstances.

The most obvious role of color and color change in several of the examples I have described is color-matching between the animal and its surroundings. For example, a number of species of desert lizards change color to match their surroundings. But among these, representatives of at least two genera tend to overshoot the ideal color-match by becoming lighter than their surroundings at very high temperatures (Norris 1953, Norris and Lowe 1964). Cowles and Bogert (1944) have pointed out the evolutionary compromise between cryptic color change and thermoregulation, noting that color change in diurnal desert lizards can extend their survival time when thermal conditions are marginal. Norris and Lowe (1964) have extended the consideration of adaptive compromise to discussing seven different phenomena which influence the degree of background color-matching in amphibians and reptiles. They have summarized that "background color-matching of color-labile reptiles in nature is most effective when the animal is within its activity temperature range, whereas the same animal is, to some extent, maladapted to concealing coloration during the warming period. Even during the warming period some radiation absorbing efficiency may be sacrificed to the maintenance of a degree of concealing coloration."

The ideas of adaptive compromise and sacrifice lead to another important consideration when studying animal behavior. The interacting effects of color on the various problems faced by an animal may necessitate more behavioral adaptation. For example, if the animal must sacrifice cryptic color advantage to gain more heat, then behavioral predator avoidance becomes important. If selection for cryptic coloration results in unfavorable spectral properties with regard to thermal or water dynamics, the species may have simultaneously been selected for more efficient thermoregulatory or hydroregulatory behavior.

ACKNOWLEDGMENTS

I am grateful to David Pettus for his advice and encouragement related to the chorus frog experimentation reported here, and for the use of his laboratory facilities.

Thanks also go to C. Richard Tracy for determining reflectance spectra for me, and to Barbara Hoppe for her many hours of assistance in the field and laboratory. The chorus frog desiccation data are part of a Ph.D. dissertation submitted to Colorado State University.

REFERENCES

Aleksiuk, M. 1976. Metabolic and behavioral adjustments to temperature change in the red-sided garter snake (*Thamnophis sirtalis parietalis*): an integrated approach. *J. Thermal Biol.* 1:153-156.

Atsatt, S. R. 1939. Color changes as controlled by temperature and light in the lizards of the desert regions of southern California. *Publ. Univ. Calif. Los Angeles Biol. Sci.* 1:237-276.

Bartlett, P. N., and Gates, D. M. 1967. The energy budget of a lizard on a tree trunk. *Ecology* 48:315-322.

Bentley, P. J. 1966. Adaptations of amphibia to arid environments. *Science* 152:619-623.

Brain, C. K. 1962. Observations on the temperature tolerance of lizards in the Central Namib Desert, South West Africa. *Cimbebasia* 4:1-5.

Brattstrom, B. H. 1963. A preliminary review of the thermal requirements of amphibians. *Ecology* 44:238-255.

Brattstrom, B. H. 1971. Social and thermoregulatory behavior of the bearded dragon, *Amphibolurus barbaratus*. *Copeia* 1971:484-497.

Case, T. J. 1976. Seasonal aspects of thermoregulatory behavior in the chuckawalla, *Sauromalus obesus* (Reptilia, Lacertila, Iguanidae). *J. Herpetol.* 10:85-95.

Claussen, D. L. 1969. Studies on water loss and rehydration in anurans. *Physiol. Zool.* 42:1-14.

Cloudsley-Thompson, J. L. 1969. Water relations of the African toad, *Bufo mauritanicus*. *Br. J. Herpetol.* 5:425-426.

Cogger, H. G. 1974. Thermal relations of the mallee dragon, *Amphibolurus fordi* (lacertilia: Agamidae). *Aust. J. Zool.* 22:319-339.

Cole, L. C. 1943. Experiments on toleration of high temperature in lizards with reference to adaptive coloration. *Ecology* 24:94-108.

Cowles, R. B., and Bogert, C. M. 1944. A preliminary study of the thermal requirements of desert reptiles. *Bull. Amer. Mus. Nat. Hist.* 83:265-296.

DeWitt, C. B. 1967. Precision of thermoregulation and its relation to environmental factors in the desert iguana, *Dipsosaurus dorsalis*. *Physiol. Zool.* 40:49-66.

Edgren, R. A. 1954. Factors controlling color change in the tree frog, *Hyla versicolor* Wied. *Proc. Soc. Exp. Biol. Med.* 87:20-23.

Farrell, M. P., and MacMahon, J. A. 1969. An eco-physiological study of water economy in eight species of tree frogs (Hylidae). *Herpetologica* 25:279-294.

Fitch, H. S. 1955. Habits and adaptations of the Great Plains skink (*Eumeces obsoletus*). *Ecol. Monogr.* 25:59-83.

Gillis, J. E., and Hoppe, D. M. 1975. Variation and possible adaptive significance of shape in *Rana pipiens* and *R. blairi*. *Bull. N. Mex. Acad. Sci.* 15:51.

Hamilton, W. J., III. 1973. *Life's Color Code*. New York: McGraw-Hill.

Hess, J. B. 1969. Changes in frequency of the green-spot phenotype in piedmont populations of the chorus frog. Ph.D. dissertation, zoology, Colo. State Univ.

Hoppe, D. M. 1975. Selection pressures affecting color polymorphism in montane populations of the boreal chorus frog, *Pseudacris triseriata*. Ph.D. dissertation, zoology and entomology, Colo. State Univ.

Huey, R. B. 1974. Behavioral thermoregulation in lizards: importance of associated costs. *Science* 184:1001-1003.

Huey, R. B., and Webster, T. P. 1975. Thermal biology of a solitary lizard: *Anolis marmoratus* of Guadeloupe, Lesser Antilles. *Ecology* 56:445-452.

Hutchison, V. H., and Larimer, J. L. 1960. Reflectivity of the integuments of some lizards from different habitats. *Ecology* 41:199-209.

Jameson, D. L., and Pequegnat, S. 1971. Estimation of relative viability and fecundity of color polymorphisms in anurans. *Evolution* 25:180-194.

Johnson, C. R. 1975. Head-body thermal control, thermal preferenda, and voluntary maxima in the taipan, *Oxyuranus scutellatus* (Serpentes: Elapidae). *Zool. J. Linn. Soc.* 56:1-12.

Kashkarov, D., and Kurbatov, V. 1930. Preliminary ecological survey of the vertebrate fauna of the Central Kara-Kum Desert in West Turkestan. *Ecology* 11:35-60.

Licht, P., and Brown, A. G. 1967. Behavioral thermoregulation and its role in the ecology of the red-bellied newt, *Taricha rivularis*. *Ecology* 48:598-611.

Lillywhite, H. B. 1970. Behavioral temperature regulation in the bullfrog, *Rana catesbeiana*. *Copeia* 1970:158-168.

Lillywhite, H. B.; Licht, P; and Chelgren, P. 1973. The role of behavioral thermoregulation in the growth energetics of the toad, *Bufo boreas*. *Ecology* 54:375-383.

Matthews, T. C. 1971. Genetic changes in a population of boreal chorus frogs (*Pseudacris triseriata*) polymorphic for color. *Amer. Midland Naturalist* 85:208-221.

Miller, K., and Packard, G. C. 1974. Critical thermal maximum: ecotypic variation between montane and piedmont chorus frogs (*Pseudacris triseriata*, Hylidae). *Experientia* 30:355-356.

Mosauer, W. 1936. The toleration of solar heat in desert reptiles. *Ecology* 17:55-56.

Nevo, E. 1973. Adaptive color polymorphism in cricket frogs. *Evolution* 27:363-367.

Norris, K. S. 1953. The ecology of the desert iguana, *Dipsosaurus dorsalis*. *Ecology* 34:265-287.

Norris, K. S. 1967. Color adaptation in desert reptiles and its thermal relationships. In *Lizard Ecology: A Symposium*, W. H. Milstead (ed.). Columbia, Mo.: Univ. Mo. Press.

Norris, K. S., and Lowe, C. H. 1964. An analysis of background color matching in amphibians and reptiles. *Ecology* 45:565-580.

Parker, G. H. 1948. *Animal Color Changes and Their Neurohumors*. Cambridge: Cambridge Univ. Press.

Pearson, O. P. 1954. Habits of the lizard *Liolaemus multiformis multiformis* at high altitudes in southern Peru. *Copeia* 2:111-116.

Pearson, O. P., and Bradford, D. F. 1976. Thermoregulations of lizards and toads at high altitudes in Peru. *Copeia* 1976:155-170.

Porter, K. R. 1972. *Herpetology*. Philadelphia: Saunders.

Pyburn, W. F. 1961. The inheritance and distribution of vertebral stripe color in the cricket frog. In *Vertebrate Speciation*, W. F. Blair (ed.). Austin: Univ. Texas Press.

Ray, C. 1958. Vital limits and rates of desiccation in salamanders. *Ecology* 39:75-83.

Resnick, L. E., and Jameson, D. L. 1963. Color polymorphism in Pacific tree frogs. *Science* 142:1081-1083.

Schwalm, P. A.; Starrett, P. H.; and McDiarmid, R. W. 1977. Infrared reflectance in leaf-sitting neotropical frogs. *Science* 196:1225-1226.

Spencer, A. W. 1964. The relationship of dispersal and migration to gene flow in the boreal chorus frog. Ph.D. dissertation, zoology, Colo. State Univ.

Tordoff, W. 1971. Environmental factors affecting gene frequencies in montane populations of the chorus frog, *Pseudacris triseriata*. Ph.D. dissertation, zoology, Colo. State Univ.

Tordoff, W., and Pettus, D. 1977. Temporal stability of phenotypic frequencies in *Pseudacris triseriata* (Amphibia, Anura, Hylidae). *J. Herpetol.* 11:161-168.

Tordoff, W.; Pettus, D.; and Matthews, T. C. 1976. Microgeographic variation in gene frequencies in *Pseudacris triseriata* (Hylidae). *J. Herpetol.* 10:37-42.

Tracy, C. R. 1976. A model of the dynamic exchanges of water and energy between a terrestrial amphibian and its environment. *Ecol. Monogr.* 46:293-326.

Valdivieso, D., and Tamsitt, J. R. 1974. Thermal relations of the neotropical frog *Hyla labialis* (Anura: Hylidae). *Roy. Ont. Mus. Life Sci. Contrib.* 26:1-10.

Vitt, L. J. 1974. Body temperatures of high latitude reptiles. *Copeia* 1974:255-256.

Further Thoughts on Anuran Thermoregulation: Discussion

C. Richard Tracy

Dave Hoppe's discussion of the role of color in regulatory processes (i.e., thermoregulation and/or hydroregulation) is cryptically complex. As Dave has suggested, it is extremely important to view any one regulatory process in terms of competition with other processes.

Consider the concept of thermoregulation in amphibians. Figure 18 illustrates a simulation of the body temperatures of a frog, *Rana pipiens* (using the model of Tracy 1976), and a lizard, *Sceloporus undulatus* (using the model of Porter et al. 1973), as a function of time during an idealized day at 40° N latitude at an altitude of 250 m where the maximum air temperature during the day is 26°C (see Porter et al. 1973 and Tracy 1975 for examples of this sort of simulation). The frog and lizard are each simulated as having two solar absorptivities, 0.65 and 0.85. Notice that the body temperatures of the lizard are remarkably influenced by a 20% difference in solar absorptivity, whereas the body temperatures of the frog differ by less than one degree Celsius. The reason for these differences in response to the 20% increase in absorbed radiation lies in the fact that increased radiation absorbed by the lizard is available to become stored energy, which changes the animal's body temperature (Porter et al. 1973), whereas increased radiation absorbed by the frog is used in vaporizing water from the frog's mucus-covered skin (Fig. 19), and thus, the frog's body temperature is very little influenced

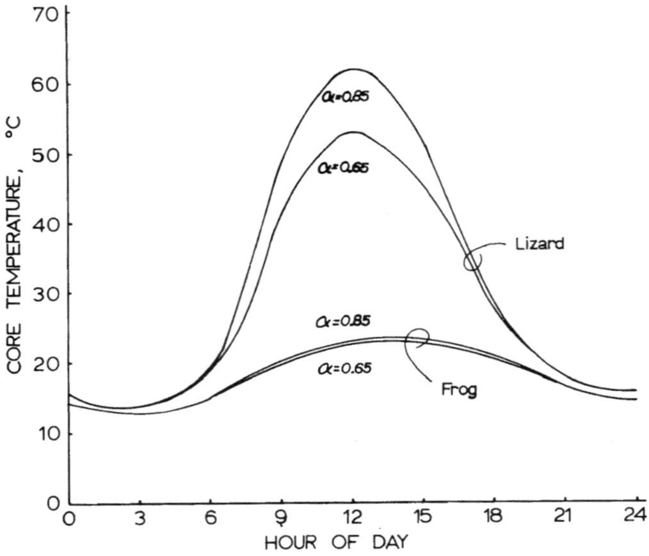

Fig. 18. Model simulation of body temperatures of a lizard, *Sceloporus undulatus*, and frog, *Rana pipiens*, as a function of time of day for an idealized clear and warm day. The animals were each modeled as having solar absorptivities of 0.85 and 0.65. The frog model is described in Tracy (1976), and the lizard model is described in Porter et al. (1973).

by increased radiant input (Tracy 1976). It is also important to notice that the 20% increase in solar absorptivity elicited an increase in evaporation rate of more than 1.2 $g \cdot hr^{-1}$, which is enough to dissipate energy at a rate of more than 0.81 watt.

The difference between lizards and frogs supports the hypothesis that selection for an ability to precisely control body temperature is strong in lizards and weak in frogs (Tracy 1975, 1976). The hypothesis predicts that lizards should generally regulate body temperature precisely and function best within a narrow range of temperatures. On the other hand, frogs should not regulate body temperature precisely and should function best over a wide range of body temperatures. These predictions have been tested by prodding *S. undulatus* and *R. pipiens* until they

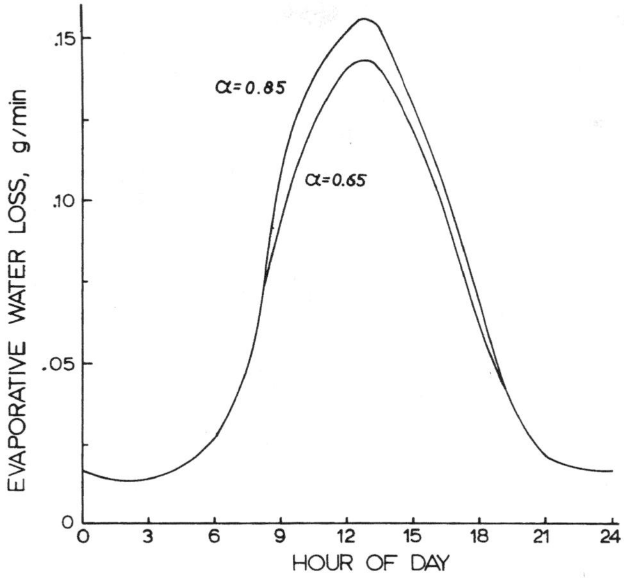

Fig. 19. Model simulations of the evaporative losses for the frog in Fig. 18.

"escaped" by running (lizard) or hopping (frog) away. *S. undulatus* was able to sprint fastest (Fig. 20) over a very narrow range of body temperatures, whereas *R. pipiens* was able to hop farthest (Fig. 21) over an extremely broad range of body temperatures. These data suggest that, in lizards, natural selection has produced physiological mechanisms for efficient bodily operation over a narrow range of body temperatures within which the lizard presumably maintains itself by behavioral and physiological thermoregulation. The frog, on the other hand, seems equipped to function equally well over a broad range of body temperatures which could be maintained by avoiding extreme environments. The conclusion is supported by the fact that body temperatures of frogs in the field (where the data were taken over a period of several days) span a wide range of temperatures (Brattstrom 1963). Hence the concept of thermoregulation in frogs may be one that needs reevaluation in light of the other regulatory processes that may operate simultaneously in this animal group (Tracy 1975, 1976).

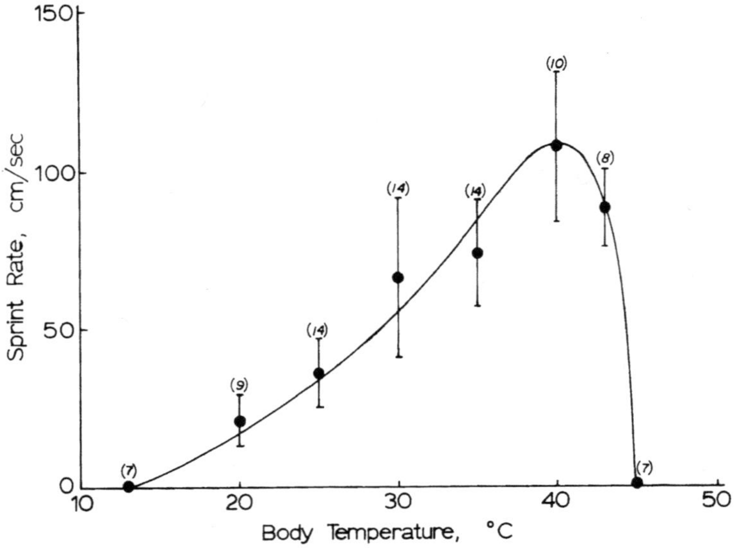

Fig. 20. The rate at which *Sceloporus undulatus* sprinted as a function of body temperature. Seven lizards were chased no more than two times each across a gridded "runway" one meter long. The sprints were recorded on super-eight motion picture film, and later transduced into a sprint speed by noting the number of picture frames that were necessary to photograph the lizard transversing the runway. The camera speed was calibrated to a digital stopwatch readable to the nearest 0.01 s.

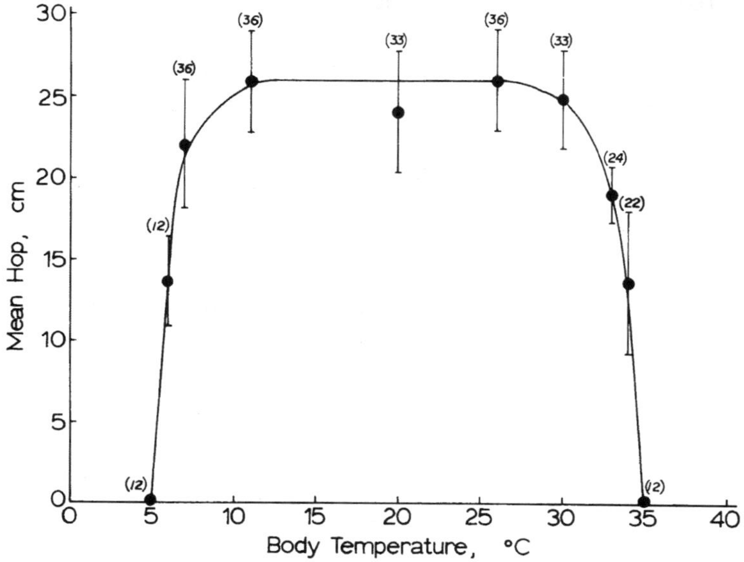

Fig. 21. The mean distance hopped by *Rana pipiens* as a function of body temperature. Each frog was induced (by tapping the hind foot) to jump three hops at each body temperature.

ACKNOWLEDGMENTS

I would like to thank Keith Cristian, Steve Waldschmidt, and Bobbi Tracy, who helped collect the empirical data presented in my figures.

REFERENCES

Brattstrom, B. H. 1963. A preliminary review of the thermal requirements of amphibians. *Ecology* 44:238-255.

Porter, W. P.; Mitchell, J. W.; Beckman, W. A.; and DeWitt, C. B. 1973. Behavioral implications of mechanistic ecology. *Oecologia* 13:1-54.

Tracy, C. R. 1975. Water and energy relations of terrestrial amphibians: insights from mechanistic models. In *Perspectives in Biophysical Ecology*, D. M. Gates and R. Schmerl (eds.). New York: Springer-Verlag, pp. 325-346.

Tracy, C. R. 1976. A model of the dynamic exchanges of water and energy between a terrestrial amphibian and its environment. *Ecol. Monogr.* 46:293-336.

Maximization of Reproduction:
Discussion

William J. Hamilton III

My view differs from Dick's (above) because my basic perception is that of an ecologist and field biologist. I see a thread of continuity that runs throughout lizards, across insects that I have studied, and across certain amphibians. The behavior of some insects is understandable only in terms of thermoregulation. I refer to species that maintain the body's core temperature between 38°C and 42°C, for example, many diurnal Namib Desert tenebrionid beetles (Hamilton 1971, 1973).

This may not apply to the montane chorus frogs discussed by David Hoppe, but we must address a basic question: Why did the frog come out of the water in the first place? Why is the frog sitting on the edge basking when it could be in the water? I think maximization of throughput and reproductive capacity through behavioral thermoregulation offers a viable explanation.

REFERENCES

Hamilton, W. J., III. 1973. *Life's Color Code*. New York: McGraw-Hill.

Hamilton, W. J., III. 1971. Competition and thermoregulation behavior of the Namib Desert tenebrionid beetle genus *Cardiosis*. *Ecology* 52:810-822.

Audience Questions:
Discussion

Question: What are the origins of polymorphism in chorus frogs?

Hoppe: There is little evidence that allows speculation as to the origins of polymorphism in chorus frogs. The literature, personal communications, and my own observations indicate that color-polymorphic populations of chorus frogs are not unique to the Colorado Rockies, but have been reported from Wyoming, North Dakota, Minnesota, Wisconsin, and Michigan, to cite a few populations. The widespread distribution suggests that whatever environmental factors have exerted selection on color phenotypes in the montane populations that I have discussed may have also played a role in the phylogenetic history of other populations. However, I think that speculation on the origins of color polymorphism must await an understanding of the maintenance of balanced polymorphism under present environmental conditions.

Question: Are color differences in chorus frogs correlated with sex or age?

Hoppe: Color differences among chorus frogs are not correlated with sex. The published genetic model (Matthews and Pettus 1966) indicates that dorsal coloration is controlled by three pairs of alleles at three autosomal loci; hence sex-linked inheritance is ruled out. In addition, the frequencies of differently colored phenotypes among males and females suggest no influence of sex on the expression of color genotypes.

Age-related differences in the frequencies of differently colored phenotypes may be found as a consequence of the seasonal selection to which I have alluded in Chapter 2. For example, in several populations a higher frequency of greens was found among juveniles than among adults. I have suggested (Chapter 2) that this may be a consequence of terrestrial selection against greens under some circumstances, since they desiccate more rapidly in sunlight than do brown frogs. There is no ontogenetic color change. The individual's coloration develops during the first few days after metamorphosis and remains unchanged throughout adulthood.

Question: Do similarly colored frogs pair more frequently than differently colored frogs?

Hoppe: No. There appears to be no assortative mating based on color phenotypes. This has been verified by analyses of the color combinations of breeding pairs of frogs captured in amplexus (Matthews 1971). Furthermore, these frogs breed nocturnally, so color perception is unlikely.

Question: What is the activity cycle of these frogs? Are they nocturnal or diurnal?

Hoppe: These montane frogs breed nocturnally during late May and most of June, then migrate to feeding meadows, where they are active diurnally during July and August. As I mentioned in Chapter 2, the nearby piedmont populations (in which green- and red-color phenotypes are not found) feed and breed primarily at night. This is one reason for my suggestion that the selection factors that maintain color polymorphism in the montane population relate to daylight conditions.

Question: Considering that animals absorb and emit long-wave thermal radiation at pretty much the same high rates (with emissivities and absorptivities of essentially unity), do you think that the reflectance differences you have shown between color phenotypes, which are pronounced only in the visual and near-infrared spectrum, significantly affect the thermodynamics of these frogs?

Hoppe: At the moment I cannot explain why the differently colored phenotypes desiccate at different rates in sunlight but at the same rates in the dark, except as a result of differential absorption of solar radiation. Light with wavelengths between 500 and 1000 nm represents energy that is converted to heat on absorption (Chapter 1) and that heat appears to increase the rate of evaporation from the frog's skin.

Consider also that chorus frogs in their natural surroundings are not exposed primarily to direct sunlight, but more importantly to light reflected and transmitted by the vegetation around them. In such light, visual wavelengths represent a much higher proportion of the energy than in direct sunlight, since much of the thermal radiation is absorbed by the surrounding vegetation.

Question: The fact that the absorption curves for green and brown chorus frogs diverge in the visible range and converge in the near and middle infrared region of the solar spectrum suggests to me that the adaptive significance lies in the color perception of predators, not in thermal adaptations. Otherwise one might expect that the infrared and unseen part of the spectrum would remain divergent. These animals have the potential to adapt to differences in the infrared, but have failed to do so.

Hoppe: The hypothesis of differential predation based on color-matching of frog and substrate has been tested by Tordoff (1971). He considered robins and gray jays to be the major predators, and tested their behavior when frogs were made available on substrates of different colors. The jays hunted by perching and scanning the substrate, and did prey more heavily on phenotypes that contrasted with the background color. The robins, however, hopped around on the substrate flushing the frogs, finding frogs when they moved rather than by their contrasting color.

The problem with selective predation as an explanation of color polymorphism is the lack of correlation between phenotypic frequencies and habitat heterogeneity. For example, if one population had twice as many green frogs as another population, the first population should have correspondingly more green background in its habitat, but such correlations have not been found. In fact, of the breeding populations studied by Tordoff, the pond with the highest frequency of greens (about 20%) is separated by only 490 meters from the one with the lowest frequency of greens (less than 1%), and the two populations share much of the same feeding habitat.

As to your statement that these frogs "have the potential to adapt to differences in the infrared," I assume this is based on reports that a few species of tropical tree frogs show differential reflectance in the infrared region of the spectrum. Richmond (1960) has pointed out that major climatic changes have occurred within the last 6000 years on the east slope of the Colorado Rockies. The montane populations of chorus frogs that I have studied have probably existed as semi-isolated entities under conditions approximating the present climate only 4500-6000 years. Conversely, the tropical tree frogs mentioned above may have had hundreds of thousands of years of relatively uniform conditions in which to evolve. Given this time factor, I consider it remarkable that the reflectance curves of different montane, color phenotypes differ as much as they do into the near-infrared spectrum, and see no "failure" to adapt in such a direction.

I do not deny that crypticity may be part of the adaptive significance of color polymorphism in chorus frogs. However, I think that no single selection pressure (e.g., color perception by predators, desiccating environmental conditions, or solar radiation for absorptive heat gain) can be paired with habitat heterogeneity to maintain this color polymorphism. Instead there are numerous selection pressures that change in intensity and relative importance both seasonally and sporadically, with the vagaries of montane weather and climate. I have emphasized the factors related to the absorption of solar radiation and deemphasized an array of other considerations in an attempt to stick to the topic of thermoregulatory and hydroregulatory behavior.

Question: Schwalm et al. (1977) demonstrate that the green color of some green frogs differs in the infrared region from the green coloration of the habitat. Thus colors that appear the same may not have the same reflectance spectra. Have you a comment?

Hoppe: I have alluded to those data in the previous answer and have discussed them in Chapter 2. The paper you have cited makes several points that arise in this symposium also. For one thing, we are throwing the term "color" around rather loosely. Are we speaking of a particular wavelength of light, a human perception, a biochemical pigment, or the printed appearance of exposed film of some type? Dr. Gruber (Chapter 5) will discuss the perception of color in more detail and Dr. Sustare (Chapter 1) has discussed the relationship between visible and other wavelengths of electromagnetic radiation. Schwalm's paper emphasizes that we cannot and must not generalize about "green vs. brown," or even "green frog vs. brown frog," based on our own perception of color. One should test the absorptive and reflective properties of the skin of some perceived "color" before speculating too freely on the adaptive significance of that color.

REFERENCES

Matthews, T. C. 1971. Genetic changes in a population of boreal chorus frogs (*Pseudacris triseriata*) polymorphic for color. *Amer. Midland Naturalist* 85:208-221.

Matthews, T. C., and Pettus, D. 1966. Color inheritance in *Pseudacris triseriata*. *Herpetologica* 22:269-275.

Richmond, G. M. 1960. Glaciation of the east slope of Rocky Mountain National Park, Colorado. *Geol. Soc. Amer. Bull.* 71:1371-1382.

Schwalm, P. A.; Starrett, P. H.; and McDiarmid, R. W. 1977. Infrared reflectance in leaf-sitting neotropical frogs. *Science* 196:1225-1226.

Tordoff, W. 1971. Environmental factors affecting gene frequencies in montane populations of the chorus frog, *Pseudacris triseriata*. Ph.D. dissertation, zoology, Colo. State Univ.

Chapter 3

Tips on Wings and Other Things

Edward H. Burtt, Jr.

Introduction
The Coloration of Warblers
  The Topography of a Warbler
  The Munsell Color System
  Measurement of Reflection and Transmission Spectra
Abrasion Resistance
  Statement of the Hypothesis
  Past Evidence of Differential Wear
  Tactics for Evaluation
  Experiments on the Abrasion of Warbler Feathers
    Methods
    Results
    Discussion
The Topography of Abrasion-Resistant Coloration
  Abrasion by Airborne Particles
  Abrasion by Airborne Particles in Flying Birds
  The Dorsum
  The Tail
  The Remiges
The Observed Distribution of Abrasion-Resistant Colors on Warblers
Conclusions Regarding Abrasion Resistance
Protection from Ultraviolet Radiation
  Statement of the Hypothesis
  The Molecular Basis for Damage from Ultraviolet Radiation
  The Potential for Ultraviolet Damage to Animals
  Protection from Ultraviolet Radiation
  Tactics for Evaluation

Reflection and Transmission of Ultraviolet Radiation
- Methods
- Results
- Discussion

Topography of Ultraviolet-Resistant Coloration
- Predicted Patterns of Coloration and Behavior
- Observed Patterns of Coloration and Behavior
    - Coloration
    - Behavior
    - Methods
    - Results

External Coloration as a Defense Against Ultraviolet Radiation: Evaluation of the Hypothesis

INTRODUCTION

Look at a monarch butterfly or a scarlet tanager and at once you are struck by their brilliant colors and bold patterns. Perhaps you have wondered why these and many other animals are brilliantly and boldly colored? Perhaps you have wondered what information is broadcast by these colors and patterns of color, or when and under what conditions the optical signal is broadcast, or for whom the signal is intended; but have you ever wondered about the noncommunicative functions of pigments, functions that are independent of the pigment's absorption, reflection, or transmission of visible light? In this chapter I evaluate the hypotheses that differently pigmented feathers resist abrasion differently, that the abrasion-resistance of differently colored feathers accounts for the general pattern of color of wood-warblers (Parulidae), and that external coloration protects underlying tissue from the potential damage of ultraviolet radiation. The hypothesized functions of color predict the behavior of differently colored wood-warblers. The predictions are tested by comparative study of the behavior and coloration of wood-warblers.

THE COLORATION OF WARBLERS

The Topography of a Warbler

I divided the warbler's body into twenty-two regions (Fig. 22). The eyebrow-stripe, eye ring, eyeline, and whisker are referred to collectively as the *face*. The nape, collars, and throat comprise the *neck*. The *dorsum* includes the back, rump, and upper tail coverts and the *venter* includes the breast, belly, and under tail coverts.

The Munsell Color System

I determined the coloration of male and female wood-warblers in nuptial plumage by using the Munsell color system in direct sunlight. The Munsell system is a spherical array of colored paper samples. The three dimensions are hue, value, and chroma. Ten hues are arranged in spectral order around the equator of the sphere. Value as measured along a central axis grades from black at one pole

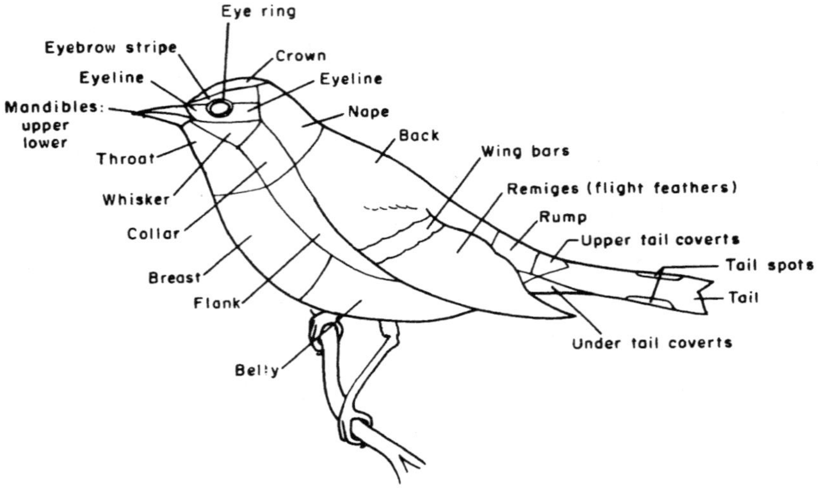

Fig. 22. Topography of warbler. (From Burtt, in press.)

to white at the other pole. The proportion of white, called the chroma, is measured along the radii of the equatorial plane from a maximum at the central achromatic axis to a minimum at the perimeter. Chroma approximates saturation. Every color can be specified by a numerical designation representing hue, value, and chroma. I used the Munsell color system to determine the coloration of the 22 body regions of 115 species of Parulidae.

The Munsell system recognizes ten hues: red, orange, yellow, yellow-green, green, blue-green, blue, purple-blue, purple, and red-purple. I followed the Munsell system except that I divided red into chestnut, red, and brown. If the color's chroma was less than two, then the color was close to the neutral (white to black) axis; and I called it white if its value was nine or above, black if its value was two or below, and gray if its value was between two and nine. I determined the hue of each of the nineteen feathered regions of the warbler. The chroma of the upper and lower mandibles and the legs was usually two or less. I categorized these three unfeathered regions by color value exclusively.

Measurement of Reflection and Transmission Spectra

The Beckman DK-2A spectroreflectometer determines reflectance or transmittance of a sample by comparing the reflection from a sample surface to the reflection from a reference surface. Reflectance is measured by comparing the reflectance spectrum of a white ($BaSO_4$) surface with the reflectance from a sample, such as a feather. To measure transmittance both the sample and the reference beams are reflected from $BaSO_4$ blanks. The specimen is mounted in the path of the sample beam and reflection from the blanks is measured and compared. For a more detailed explanation, see Burtt (in press).

ABRASION RESISTANCE

Statement of the Hypothesis

Knowledge of the structure of pigments and the effect of pigments on the structure of feathers makes it possible to predict the relative extent of damage to differently colored feathers. Melanin is a granular pigment whose granules are deposited in dense layers between layers of keratin. Furthermore, the deposition of melanin in the barbs and barbules induces increased keratin formation (Voitkevich 1966). Carotenes and xanthophylls are diffuse pigments and in moderate concentrations, such as found in warbler feathers, carotenes and xanthophylls have little effect on the structure of barbs and barbules (Brush and Siefried 1968). White in warblers is due to the reflection and scattering of all wavelengths from closely packed, unpigmented fibers in barbs and barbules. Only in feathers that contain melanin is there reason to expect increased resistance to abrasion. Therefore, if abrasion resistance is different in differently colored feathers, *Prediction 1*: melanin-impregnated feathers will be the most abrasion resistant.

Past Evidence of Differential Wear

Dwight (1900) appears to have been the first to associate differential wear with differently colored barbs, although much earlier Bachman (1839) concluded that birds change color without molting, simply by wearing away the differently colored edges of the feathers. For example, the black bib of the male house sparrow (*Passer domesticus*) is revealed in the spring when the buff edges of its throat feathers wear away. Averill (1923) observed that the white barbs of the recently shed primaries of gulls were worn away whereas the black barbs, although worn, remained intact. The observation was replicated by Test (1940) in the flight feathers of common flickers (*Colaptes auratus*) and by Bowers (1959) in the wrentit (*Chamnea fasciata*). Heinroth and Heinroth (1958) picture the molted primary of a peregrine falcon (*Falco peregrinus*) showing the worn appearance of the white barbs as contrasted to the unworn appearance of the black barbs. These examples show that black feathers resist abrasion better than white feathers. Because melanin is the black pigment, the implication is that feathers containing melanin are more resistant to abrasion than feathers that lack melanin. However, the examples fail to mention colors other than black and white, and they fail to assess the quantitative difference between black and white.

Tactics for Evaluation

The hypothesis that differently colored feathers resist abrasion differently was tested by subjecting feathers of different colors to a measured amount of abrasion. The effect of such abrasion was quantified and the results compared for feathers of different colors.

How are the feathers of living birds abraded? I discuss abrasion that results from airborne particles colliding with the feathers during flight. From this discussion emerge predictions of the location of the most intense abrasion and the areas most in need of abrasion-resistant coloration.

Experiments on the Abrasion of Warbler Feathers

Methods

The outermost left tail feather was plucked from warblers captured in mist-nets at Itasca, Minnesota, during the summers of 1973 and 1974 and from warblers killed at television transmitting towers in Madison, Wisconsin, on 26-28 September 1973. This feather was chosen because it was readily identifiable, easily removed, frequently contained a contrastingly-colored patch, and occurred in six different colors.

Prior to abrasion, all feathers were examined to ensure that there were no broken barbs or missing barbules. Only feathers in perfect condition were used. The feathers were individually tagged and traced so that the area of each feather or colored patch could be measured.

The feathers were abraded in the laboratory of K. Westphal with the help of B. Morgan, to both of whom I am greatly indebted for the use of their time and equipment. Each feather was exposed for one minute to a stream of powdered silicon from an air pressure gun. The feathers were held vertically with the ventral surface flat against a metal plate and the dorsal surface about 10 cm from the nozzle of the air gun. During the one-minute exposure, 0.4 g of powdered glass hit the feather.

Following abrasion I counted the number of broken and unbroken barbs. The percentage of broken barbs (P) for each feather was calculated from the ratio of the number of broken barbs (b), to the total number of barbs (B):

$$P = 100b/B \tag{3.1}$$

The mean percentage of broken barbs for each color was compared using an analysis of variance, and the individual means were compared using the Scheffé test (Roscoe 1975).

Following abrasion, each feather was again traced. I used a polar planimeter to find the area from the tracings of each feather before and after abrasion. The change in area was found by subtracting the area after abrasion from the area before abrasion. Size varied among the differently colored feathers. Therefore I calculated the percentage of area destroyed by abrasion (L), according to the equation:

$$L = 100(A-a)/A \tag{3.2}$$

where a is the area of the feather after abrasion and A is the area of the feather before abrasion. The mean percentage of area destroyed by abrasion was calculated for each color and an overall comparison made with the analysis of variance. Individual means were compared using the Scheffé test.

Results

A quantitative measure of the effect of natural abrasion cannot be made from Dwight's (1900) photographs of naturally abraded feathers, but the qualitative effects of natural and artificial abrasion are similar. In both cases the barbules have been stripped from large sections of the barbs and numerous barbs have been broken. Therefore artificial abrasion seems to be a reasonable substitute for a natural process that takes place throughout an entire year.

The mean percentages of broken barbs in differently colored feathers are shown in Figure 23. The percentages differ significantly from random based on an analysis of variance with 5 and 95 degrees of freedom ($F = 9.32$, $p < 0.001$). The results of comparing the mean percentages of

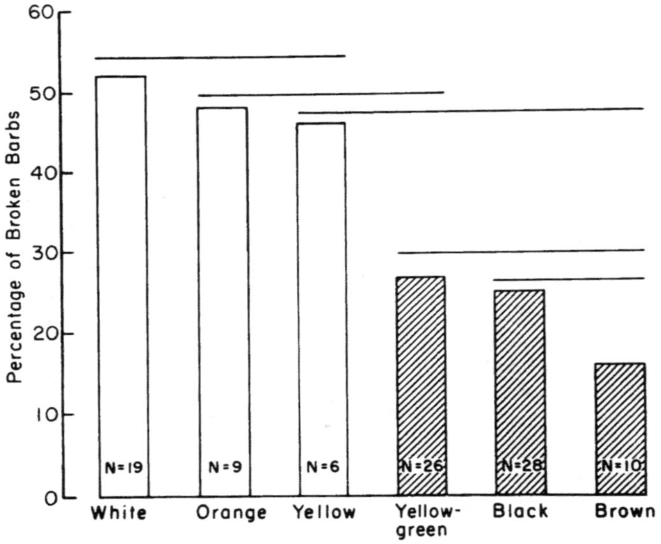

Fig. 23. The mean percentage of broken barbs in feathers of different colors exposed to equal amounts of abrasion. The number of feathers abraded (N) is indicated in the appropriate bar. The horizontal lines group feather colors in which the mean percentage of broken barbs is not significantly different. (From Burtt, in press.)

broken barbs for feathers of different colors are shown by horizontal lines (Fig. 23) that connect mean percentages that are not significantly different.

Black, brown, and yellow-green feathers, the only feathers that contain melanin, have a significantly lower percentage of broken barbs than white, which contains no pigment. Black and brown feathers also have a significantly lower percentage of broken barbs than orange feathers, which contain a carotenoid pigment but lack melanin. The percentage of broken barbs is not significantly different among black, brown, and yellow-green feathers, all of which contain melanin, nor is there a significant difference among yellow, orange, and white feathers, none of which contains melanin.

The mean percentage of area of differently colored feathers destroyed by abrasion is shown in Figure 24. The overall difference is significant (F = 37.65; df = 5, 92;

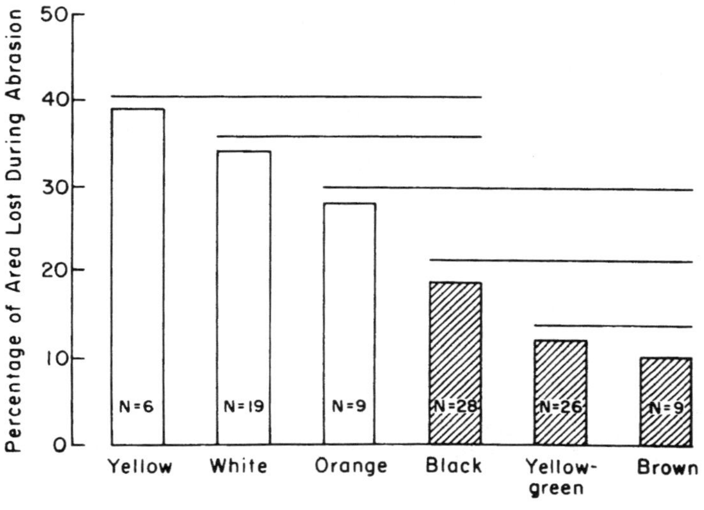

Fig. 24. The percentage of area lost by differently colored feathers exposed to equal amounts of abrasion. The number of abraded feathers (N) is indicated in the appropriate bar. The horizontal lines group feather colors in which the mean percentage of area lost is not significantly different. (From Burtt, in press.)

$p < 0.001$). The horizontal lines in Figure 24 connect means that are not significantly different. Brown and yellow-green feathers lost a significantly smaller percentage of area than yellow or white feathers. The percentage of area lost by brown, black, and yellow-green feathers is not significantly different, nor is there a significant difference in the percentage of area lost by orange, yellow, and white feathers.

Discussion

The hypothesis that differently colored feathers exposed to a constant amount of abrasion show different amounts of damage is strongly supported by the data. Feathers whose color is wholly or partially the result of melanin impregnation are more abrasion-resistant than those feathers lacking melanin (*Prediction 1*). The addition of moderate amounts of carotenoid pigment, such as found in yellow-green feathers, does not affect abrasion-resistance. The data suggest no difference in the abilities of carotenoid-pigmented and white feathers to withstand abrasion.

THE TOPOGRAPHY OF ABRASION-RESISTANT COLORATION

There are at least two sources of abrasion: that caused by the collision of barbs and barbules with airborne particles and that caused by feathers rubbing against one another or against a substrate. Only abrasion caused by airborne particles is discussed (Burtt [in press] discusses other types of abrasion).

Abrasion by Airborne Particles

Damage (D) from windborne particles depends on the kinetic energy ($K.E.$) of the particles at the time of collision (Probstein and Fasso 1970, Waldman and Reinecke 1971, Maki 1974, Schmel and Sutler 1974, Smith 1976):

$$D = f(K.E.) \tag{3.3}$$

Collisions of barbs and barbules with airborne particles are almost certainly nonelastic. The energy transferred from the particle to the barb or barbule struck is probably dissipated as heat or by the destruction of the keratin molecule.

If the extent of damage that results from the collision depends on the kinetic energy of the particle, then the damage will be greatest where the kinetic energy of the particles is greatest. Kinetic energy is energy due to motion. It is defined:

$$K.E. = \tfrac{1}{2}mv^2 \qquad (3.4)$$

where m is the mass of the particle and v its velocity in any direction. If we assume all particles to be some average size that is characteristic of the air of some habitat --for example, the air of boreal forests, which might contain conifer pollen as its primary particulate--then the kinetic energy of the particles depends only on the velocity of the particles at the point of collision with the barbs and barbules.

Abrasion by Airborne Particles in Flying Birds

The mass of an average particle traveling toward a collision with a barb or barbule is small compared with the mass of the feather. Therefore, take the feather about to be hit as the reference point: all changes in velocity of either the feather or the particle appear as changes in the velocity of the particle only. An airborne particle appears to approach along the bird's line of flight at a velocity equal and opposite to the bird's velocity, assuming still air.

If the velocity of the bird were the only factor that determined the velocity of the particles at the point of collision, then the head, neck, breast, shoulders, and leading edge of the wings would receive the most abrasion. However, the airfoil shape of the wings and possibly of the body as well means that air moving across the dorsum has a higher velocity than air moving across the venter, turbulence around the wings and tail means that these are areas of rapid air movement, and the wings move and therefore contribute their own kinetic energy to the collision. Because the velocity of the air moving past a flying bird varies according to a predictable pattern, the kinetic energy of airborne particles colliding with the barbs and barbules varies predictably, as does the potential damage caused by abrasion. The following predictions are based on the airflow pattern around a flying bird.

The Dorsum

If the bodily shape of a bird in flight deviates from teardrop shape, then air flow is not equal over all body surfaces. Figure 43 in Storer (1948, p. 30) shows a flight profile of an anhinga (*Anhinga anhinga*) that suggests an airfoil. When the body profile approximates an airfoil, the velocity of airborne particles moving across the dorsum is faster than the velocity of those moving across the venter and their kinetic energy on impact is greater. The wing must be an airfoil in birds that fly. Hence airborne particles moving across the dorsal surface of the wing have a higher kinetic energy than particles moving across the ventral surface. The wing anterior to the wing bars is included in the dorsum. *Prediction 2*: The dorsum is more likely to be melanin-impregnated than the venter.

The Tail

The tail is used to supplement the control movements of the wings, especially in the rapid aerial maneuvers of warblers. During such maneuvers the tail is spread to form an auxiliary surface behind and below the wings. Such a surface draws air over the main surface of the wings and so keeps the flow attached to the wings at high angles of attack, thereby increasing the maximum lift coefficient of the wing and lowering the stalling speed (Pennycuick 1972, 1975). Such use of the tail subjects the entire tail to rapidly moving air similar to the rapid flow of air across the dorsum, but also subjects the lateral and trailing edges to turbulence. The velocity of particles in areas of turbulence is greater than that of particles in the air moving across the dorsum or the dorsal surface of the tail because the air in the turbulence is moving relative to the nonturbulent flow of air. Where the velocity is greater, the kinetic energy of the particles is greater and the damage from abrasion is greater. The tail is subjected to abrasion from two sources: rapidly moving air and turbulence. *Prediction 3*: The tail and particularly the lateral and trailing edges of the tail are more likely to be melanin-impregnated than the dorsum.

When the tail is expanded, the more medial feathers overlie the adjacent, more lateral feathers with the lateral barbs of each feather above the medial barbs of the adjacent feather. Therefore, rapidly moving particles in the air from the dorsum and the wings abrade the medial tail feathers more than the lateral feathers, and the lateral barbs of each feather more than the medial barbs. When the tail is furled in rapid flight, the medial feathers are uppermost with the most lateral feathers on the bottom. During such flight, only the medial feathers of the tail and the lateral edges of the underlying feathers are exposed to abrasion from airborne particles moving around the tail. *Prediction 4*: The medial feathers and lateral edges of all tail feathers are more likely to contain melanin than other parts of the tail.

The Remiges

The remiges are subject to abrasion from the rapid flow of air that is characteristic of an airfoil. Such abrasion is similar to that occurring on the dorsum and tail. The remiges are also subject to abrasion from turbulence, as is the tail, but the remiges are subject to turbulence both at their trailing edges and at the wing tip. Unlike the other two regions, the remiges, particularly the distal remiges or primaries, are moving. From our reference point on the feather such movement appears as changes in the velocity of the particle. Since the wing moves at an angle with respect to the line of flight, the apparent change in the velocity of the particle is equal and opposite to a vector of the velocity of the remiges that is parallel to the line of flight. So the velocity of a particle approaching the remiges has increased velocity due to movement over an airfoil, increased velocity due to turbulence, and increased velocity due to flapping of the remiges. *Prediction 5*: The remiges are more likely to be melanin-impregnated than either the dorsum or the tail.

THE OBSERVED DISTRIBUTION OF ABRASION-RESISTANT COLORS ON WARBLERS

The occurrence on the dorsum of male and female warblers of colors whose abrasion resistance has been measured is shown in Figure 25. As predicted (*Prediction 2*), the most abrasion-resistant colors (brown, yellow-green, and black) predominate on the dorsum whereas white and yellow predominate on the venter (Fig. 26), but rarely occur on the dorsum.

The tail shows a much greater tendency toward abrasion-resistant coloration than the dorsum (*Prediction 3*).

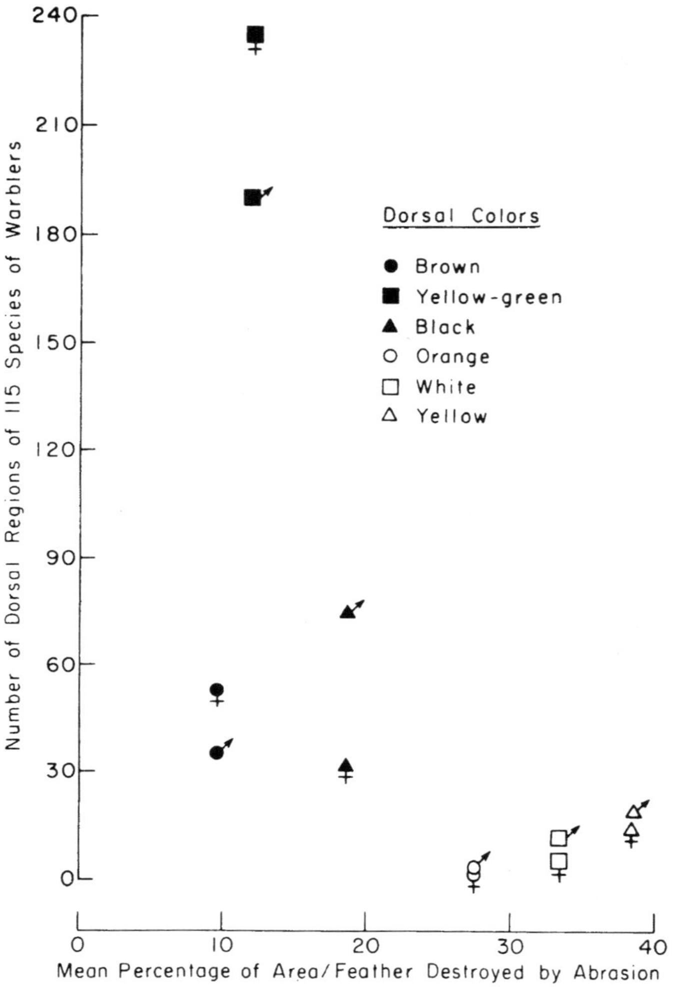

Fig. 25. The back, rump, and upper tail coverts comprise the dorsum. The number of dorsal regions of the indicated color is plotted as a function of the mean percentage of area/feather destroyed by abrasion. There are 336 dorsal regions in the males of 112 species, of which 1 region is red, 6 are chestnut, 97 are gray, and 27 are blue (all of which are untested colors). The remaining 205 regions have the colors shown. The females of 106 species have 318 dorsal regions of which 1 is red, 6 are chestnut, 81 are gray, and 10 are blue. The color of the remaining 220 regions is shown. (From Burtt, in press.)

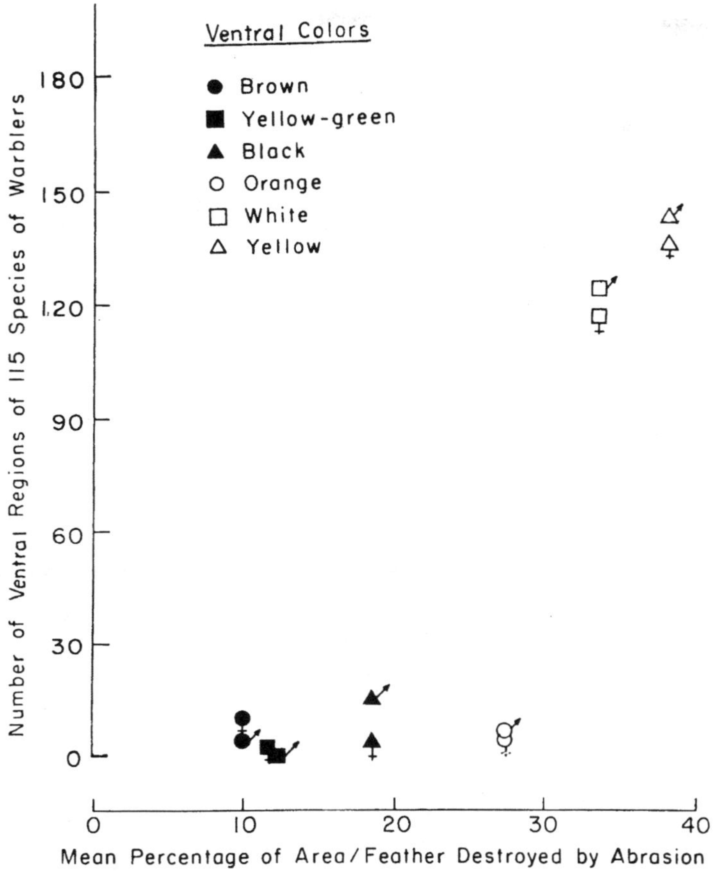

Fig. 26. The breast, belly, and under tail coverts comprise the venter. The number of ventral regions of the indicated color is plotted as a function of the mean percentage of area/feather destroyed by abrasion. There are 336 ventral regions in the males of 112 species, of which 15 regions are red, 11 are chestnut, 18 are gray, and none are blue (all of which are untested colors). The remaining 292 regions have the colors shown. The females of 106 species have 318 ventral regions of which 11 are red, 9 are chestnut, 19 are gray, and none are blue. The color of the remaining 279 regions is shown.

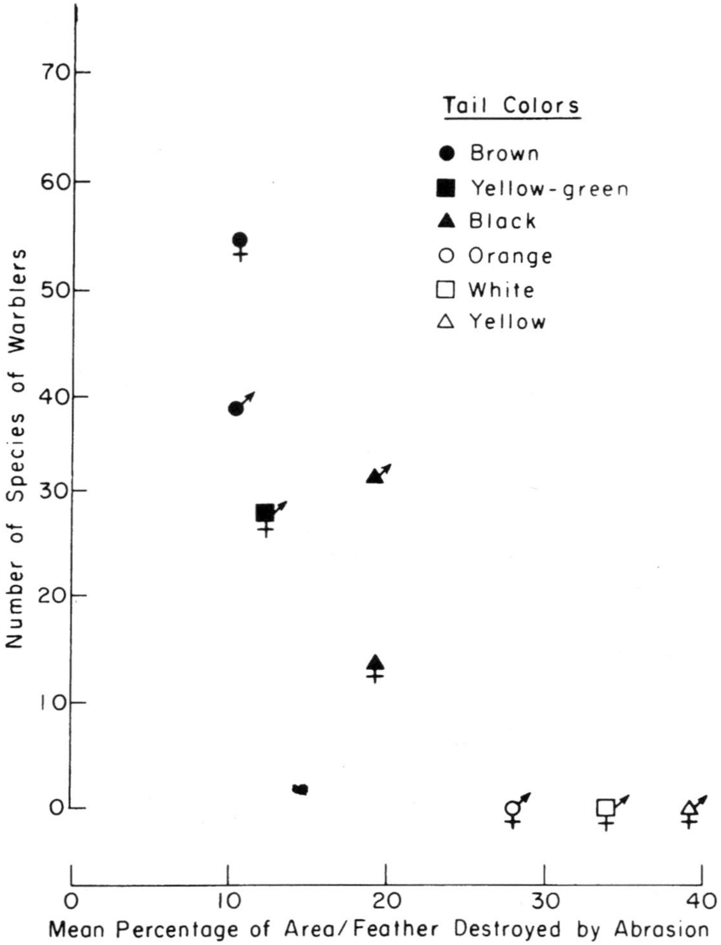

Fig. 27. The number of species of warblers whose males or females have tails of the indicated color plotted as a function of the mean percentage of area/feather destroyed by abrasion. The males of 11 species have gray tails, an untested color. The males of the remaining 101 species have yellow-green, brown, or black as shown. Females of 9 species have gray tails, whereas the tails of females of the remaining 97 species are the colors shown. (From Burtt, in press.)

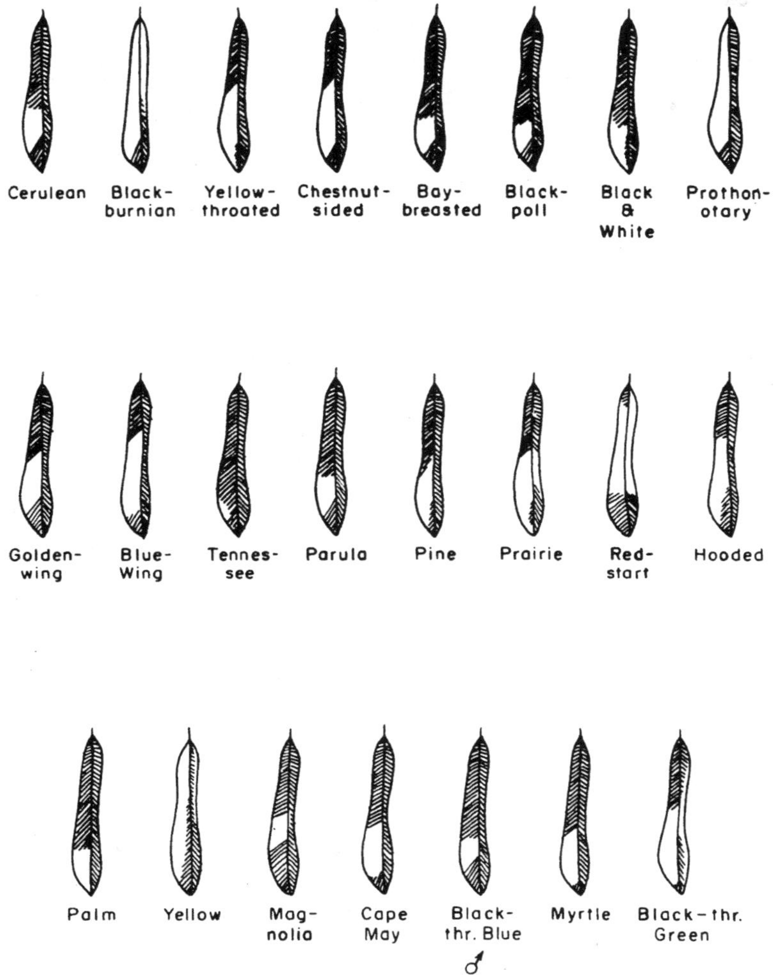

Fig. 28. Right outermost tail feathers of eastern North American warblers (adapted from Blake 1966).

There are no species whose predominant tail color is orange, white, or yellow (Fig. 27). Furthermore, brown, the most abrasion-resistant color, is more common in tails than on the dorsum.

The tails of many warblers have tail spots that are differently colored from the surrounding tail. However, as predicted (*Prediction 4*), the medial tail feathers are always melanin-impregnated as are the distal barbs of featl ers that possess light patches (*Prediction 3*). The right outermost tail feathers of eastern North American warblers

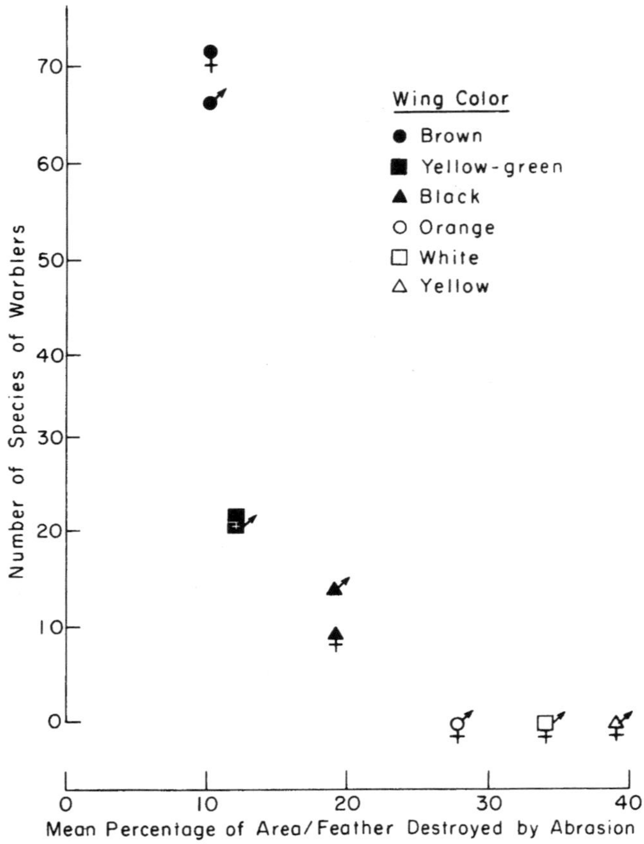

Fig. 29. The number of species of warblers whose males or females have wings of the indicated color plotted as a function of the mean percentage of area/feather destroyed by abrasion. Males of 9 species and females of 4 species have gray wings, an untested color. The males of the remaining 103 species and females of 102 species have yellow-green, brown, or black as shown. (From Burtt, in press.)

shown in Figure 28 illustrate this point, and in eighteen of the twenty-three species pictured the light-colored barbs are restricted to the medial side as predicted (*Predictions 3 and 4*).

The remiges (*Prediction 5*) show the greatest tendency toward abrasion-resistant coloration (Fig. 29). No species have white, yellow, or orange remiges, and the occurrence of abrasion-resistant colors is strongly skewed toward brown, the most abrasion-resistant color. In many species the wing bars are white, yellow, or orange, but the wing bars are located on the primary and secondary coverts where airflow, although rapid, is not turbulent and where movement caused by flapping is minimized. In other words, the location of the wing bars, which probably function in communication, is dictated by the need to protect the light, contrasting colors from abrasion.

CONCLUSIONS REGARDING ABRASION RESISTANCE

Results show unequivocally that melanin-impregnated feathers are more resistant to abrasion than feathers without melanin. Melanin-containing feathers cover all areas of the body that suffer excessive abrasion, as predicted from consideration of the pattern of airflow around a bird. These results are therefore consistent with the hypothesis that a strong selection pressure acting on coloration of wood warblers arises from the need to protect feathers from abrasion. However, dorsal coloration is subject to other selection pressures, concealment for example. Furthermore, the prediction that dorsal feathers must be more abrasion-resistant than ventral feathers rests on the supposition that the body is an airfoil. The airfoil shape of the body of a flying bird is suggested by a photograph in Storer (1948), but there are no quantitative data on the air flow pattern around the body of a flying bird (Tucker, personal communication).

PROTECTION FROM ULTRAVIOLET RADIATION

Statement of the Hypothesis

Exposure to solar ultraviolet radiation (290-400 nm) is potentially lethal to animals (Witkin 1966, Resnick 1970, Blum 1975, Caldwell and Nachtwey 1975). There are two strategies for coping with the effect of ultraviolet light: (1) shielding and (2) tolerance. Animals shield themselves from lethal intensities of ultraviolet light by absorption of the radiation into feathers, fur, or skin or by seeking protected habitats, for example, the shade of a forest. Animals tolerate damage from ultraviolet radiation through molecular repair mechanisms or through replacement of damaged parts, cells, or whole organisms within a population. Calkins and Nachtwey (1975) found that present flux rates of solar ultraviolet radiation are lethal to many classes of organisms, even when natural resistance and molecular repair processes are accounted for. Therefore, protection from intense ultraviolet irradiance is essential. These facts suggest the hypothesis that external coloration evolved to shield the animal from excessive ultraviolet radiation.

The Molecular Basis for Damage from Ultraviolet Radiation

Absorption of an ultraviolet quantum by a molecule raises an electron from a lower to a higher energy state (Chapter 1). The high-energy electron is unstable and immediately reverts to a lower, more stable state. When the electron reverts to the more stable state the previously absorbed energy is released. The released energy is transmitted to other molecules through electron transfer or emitted as light or heat. Alternatively, absorbed quanta provide sufficient energy to rupture chemical bonds. Such photochemical damage by ultraviolet radiation from the sun has been shown to inactivate biological functions of both DNA (Bollum and Setlow 1963, McLaren and Shugar 1964, Smith 1971) and RNA (Rupert 1964, Kleczkowski 1971, Murphy 1973). In simple cells (e.g., *Escherichia coli* and *Saccharmoyces cerevisiae*) damage from solar ultraviolet radiation leads to mutation or death (Kubitschek 1967, Harm 1969, Resnick 1969, 1970). In mammalian skin there is evidence that damage to DNA from solar radiation causes severe sunburn, freckling, and skin cancer (Blum 1975).

The Potential for Ultraviolet Damage to Animals

If there were no defense against ultraviolet radiation, its intensity within the abdominal cavity of lizards would be sufficient to cause injury. Porter (1967) calculated that if the side-blotched lizard (*Uta stansburiana*) lacked its black peritoneum, about 10.2×10^3 ergs·cm^{-2}·d^{-1} of energy in wavelengths shorter than 313 nm would penetrate the abdominal cavity. Doses of about 30×10^3 ergs·cm^{-2} are sufficient to induce mutations in the intestinal bacterium *Escherichia coli* (Hanawalt 1966, Witkin 1966). Because the effect of radiation damage is cumulative, the potential intensity of ultraviolet light penetrating the abdominal cavity of *Uta stansburiana* would be sufficient to cause damage were it not for the black peritoneum.

Protection from Ultraviolet Radiation

Animals shield themselves from ultraviolet radiation by pigmentation that protects ultraviolet sensitive tissue or by seeking microhabitats protected from ultraviolet light. Reptiles employ melanin to absorb ultraviolet radiation. The pigmented exuviae and skin of lizards absorb 90 to 95% of the incident ultraviolet energy (Porter 1967, 1975; Porter and Norris 1969). Melanin in the muscles of the body wall and around the blood vessels, nerve fibers, and gonads absorbs the remaining 5-10% of the incident ultraviolet energy (Porter 1967, 1975). Many reptiles and fish with little or no external pigmentation have a black peritoneum that shields internal organs (Watkins-Pitchford 1909, Klauber 1939, Cole 1943, Collette 1961, Porter 1967, 1975).

Body surfaces exposed to ultraviolet radiation are more absorbent than unexposed surfaces. For example, about 3% of the solar radiation incident on the dorsum penetrates to the peritoneum in Gilbert's skink (*Eumeces gilberti*); just over 6% penetrates the venter (Porter 1967).

Animals in habitats with high intensities of ultraviolet radiation are less transparent to ultraviolet light than animals in habitats with low intensities of ultraviolet light. Collette (1961) found a positive correlation between the degree of peritoneal pigmentation in six species of *Anolis* and the amount of time each species spent in sunlight. The heavily pigmented tissues of the diurnal desert iguana (*Dipsosauris dorsalis*) are opaque to solar ultraviolet radiation whereas the relatively unpigmented tissues of the nocturnal banded gecko (*Coleonux variegatus*) transmit up to 6% of the incident ultraviolet radiation (Porter 1975).

In the house finch (*Carpodacus mexicanus*) and the mourning dove (*Zenaidura macroura*) no ultraviolet light penetrates to the abdominal cavity through the rump unless the feathers are removed (Porter 1967). With the feathers removed, ultraviolet light with wavelengths as short as 295 nm penetrates the body wall of the house finch (Porter 1975). The intensity of ultraviolet light penetrating the finch's unfeathered body wall is greater by an order of magnitude than the potentially lethal intensity of ultraviolet light that penetrates the body wall of *Uta stansburiana* (see above, Porter 1975). These data suggest that the feathers and possibly their pigmentation are an important defense against the harmful effects of ultraviolet radiation.

Tactics for Evaluation

First I measured transmission spectra of differently colored feathers and legs of warblers. The transmission spectrum of the bill was not measured because the bill's small size and conical shape made accurate measurement impossible. Which colored feathers and scales transmit the least ultraviolet radiation? The transmission spectra answer that question.

The irradiance of ultraviolet light on the dorsum, venter, and sides of the body is estimated from data in the literature. If external coloration evolved to protect the animal from excessive ultraviolet radiation, then those colored feathers that transmit the least ultraviolet light will be on the surfaces exposed to the most intense radiation. The predicted distribution of color on the bodies of warblers is compared with the observed distribution in males of 112 species of warblers. If external coloration has evolved to shield the animal from excessive ultraviolet radiation, then species whose feathers or scales transmit the most ultraviolet radiation will seek habitats with low levels of ultraviolet light. The percentage of time spent in sunlight is compared with the ultraviolet transmittance of the feathers and scales of differently pigmented warblers.

REFLECTION AND TRANSMISSION OF ULTRAVIOLET RADIATION

Methods

I measured the percentage of transmitted ultraviolet (290-400 nm) radiation for ninety-eight feathers of six different colors and for legs of two Munsell color values from seven species. Mean transmittance for the feathers of each color was calculated and an analysis of variance (Roscoe 1975) was used to compare means. The sample size of differently colored legs was too small for statistical comparison.

Results

Differently colored feathers transmit significantly different amounts of ultraviolet (Fig. 30: $F = 125.51$; df = 5, 92; $p < 0.001$). Transmission is correlated with coloration of the feathers (Fig. 30). White, unpigmented feathers transmit the most ultraviolet radiation: more

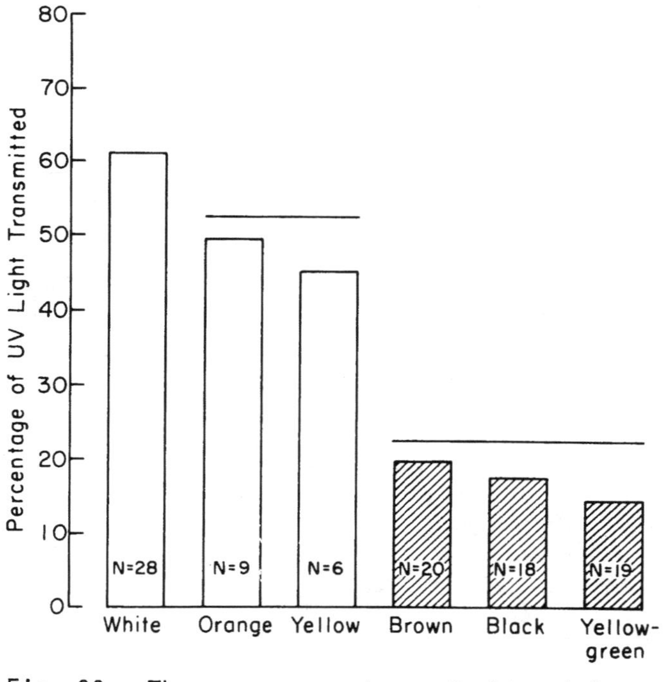

Fig. 30. The mean percentage of ultraviolet light (290-400 nm) transmitted by feathers of six different colors. The number of feathers measured (N) is indicated in the appropriate bar. The horizontal lines group feather colors in which the mean percentage of ultraviolet light transmitted is not significantly different. (From Burtt, in press.)

than 60% of the incident radiation. Orange and yellow feathers, both of which contain carotenoids, transmit significantly less ultraviolet radiation than white feathers and significantly more than feathers that contain melanin. Brown, black, and yellow-green feathers, all of which contain melanin, transmit the least ultraviolet radiation: less than 20% of the incident radiation.

Legs with a Munsell color value of two (dark) transmit no ultraviolet energy, whereas legs with a Munsell color value of six (light) transmit 0.6% of the incident ultraviolet radiation. Measurements of transmission through the legs may be underestimated because the light passed through the entire leg not just a layer of scales. However, light legs have a larger diameter than dark legs. Therefore, the ultraviolet beam passes through more tissue in the light legs. With the extraneous tissue removed the difference in transmission between dark and light legs may increase.

Discussion

The percentage of incident ultraviolet light transmitted to the skin through layers of differently colored feathers is unknown, but is undoubtedly less than the percentage shown in Figure 30. The feathers of birds overlap one another. Hence ultraviolet light must penetrate several feathers before reaching the skin. The intensity of the radiation is reduced by each feather the light passes through. Warblers with white, yellow, or orange feathers could reduce ultraviolet irradiance on the skin by increasing the number of feathers covering the skin. However, there is no evidence that such a strategy has been adopted (Wetmore 1936). Thus the best protection offered by colored feathers is provided by feathers that contain melanin. However, feathers that contain carotenoids transmit less ultraviolet radiation than unpigmented feathers and therefore offer some protection from exposure to excessive ultraviolet radiation. Ultraviolet flux increases with altitude. Likewise, the concentration of carotenoids in feathers of *Ramphocelus* tanagers increases with altitude (Brush 1970), although Brush does not attribute the correlation to ultraviolet-shielding. Melanin-impregnated scales offer complete protection from ultraviolet light, whereas unpigmented scales transmit small amounts of radiation.

TOPOGRAPHY OF ULTRAVIOLET-RESISTANT COLORATION

Predicted Patterns of Coloration and Behavior

Short-wave radiation is scattered by the earth's atmosphere. Therefore, the sky acts as a hemispherical source of ultraviolet radiation. As the angle between the sun and the zenith (zenith angle) decreases, atmospheric absorption and back-scattering of ultraviolet radiation decrease. Ultraviolet irradiance is most intense and most harmful when the sun is at its zenith (Shettle et al. 1975). With the sun at its zenith, about 50% of the ultraviolet radiation incident at sea level is direct radiation from the sun; the other 50% is diffuse radiation from the sky (Shettle and Green 1974, Allen et al. 1975). The sun approximates a point source. Therefore, when ultraviolet irradiance is most intense about half the radiation comes from a point source and half from a hemispherical source. Under these conditions a bird that is upright exposes the upper mandible, crown, nape, and dorsum to the most intense ultraviolet radiation. Less intense radiation falls on the face, collars, flank, wing patches, and remiges. If coloration of the warbler's external surface has evolved to shield the warbler from excessive ultraviolet radiation, then *Prediction 1*: The upper mandible, crown, nape, and dorsum will be darker than the face collars, flank, wing bars, and remiges, which will be darker than the lower mandible, throat venter, and legs. If tolerance of ultraviolet radiation (e.g., molecular repair mechanisms) and internal coloration are similar in all warblers, then *Prediction 2*: Species whose upper mandible, crown, nape, or dorsum is lightly colored will spend less time in direct sunlight than species whose upper mandible, crown, nape, or dorsum are dark.

Observed Patterns of Coloration and Behavior

Coloration

The upper mandible is significantly darker than the lower mandible (*Prediction 1*; Figs. 31 and 32). The percentage of regions that contain dark, melanin-impregnated feathers is highest in male warblers on the dorsal surface, less on the lateral surface, and least on the ventral surface (*Prediction 1*; Fig. 33). The pattern in females is almost identical. The legs are the darkest of the ventrally located structures. Almost 50% have Munsell color value two (dark).

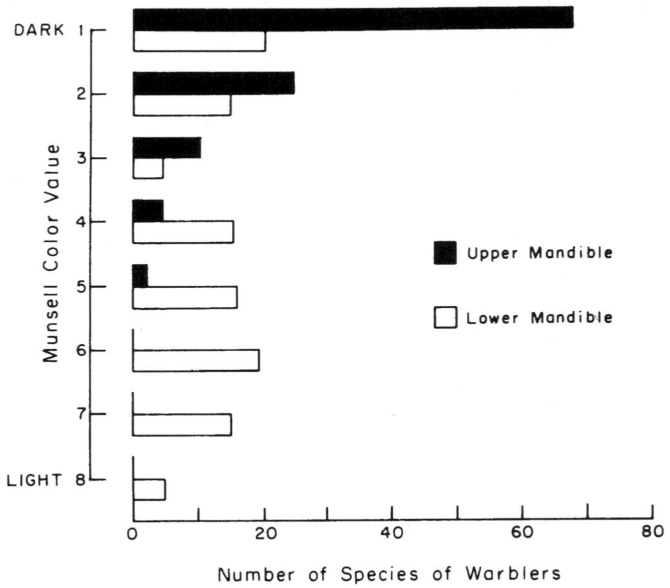

Fig. 31. The Munsell color values of the upper and lower mandibles of males of 115 species of wood warblers (Parulidae). (From Burtt, in press.)

Behavior

Variation exists in the coloration of the upper mandible, crown, and rump on the dorsal surface, and the legs are unusually dark for ventrally located structures. Therefore, the percentage of time spent in sunlight is compared in species whose upper mandible, crown, rump, and leg color differ.

Methods

I measured the time spent in sunlight for warblers breeding at Itasca, Minnesota, in 1974 and Chapel Hill, North Carolina, in 1975, and for warblers migrating through Madison, Wisconsin, in 1974 and 1975. I identified three light zones: sunlight, when the body was entirely illuminated; shade, when the body was entirely in shadow; and dappled, when the body was simultaneously in shadow and sunlight. I identified a warbler, waited ten seconds, and

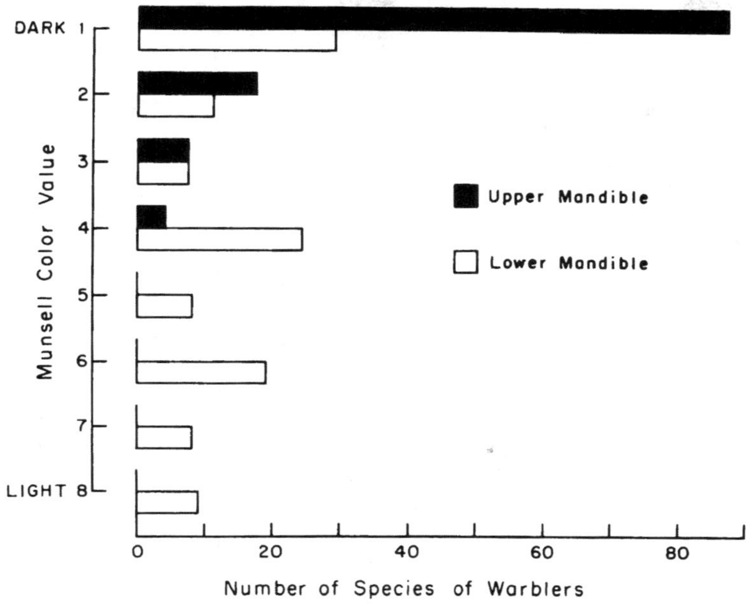

Fig. 32. The Munsell color values of the upper and lower mandibles of females of 106 species of wood warblers (Parulidae). (From Burtt, in press.)

then began recording on a tape recorder each change of light zones. I followed an individual for as long as possible or ten minutes, whichever came first. The time each species spent in sunlight is expressed as a percentage of the total time I observed the species under sunlit conditions. Percentages are used because the total time each species was observed varies greatly.

Dark legs (Munsell color value two) transmit no ultraviolet radiation whereas light legs (Munsell color value six) transmit some ultraviolet radiation (see above). Therefore, as Munsell color value increases (the color becomes lighter), more ultraviolet light is transmitted. Kendall's tau (Roscoe 1975) was used to evaluate the correlation between the Munsell color value of the upper mandible and the percentage of time spent in sunlight. The Pearson product-moment correlation coefficient (Roscoe 1975) was calculated to evaluate the correlation between the percentage of time spent in sunlight and the percentage

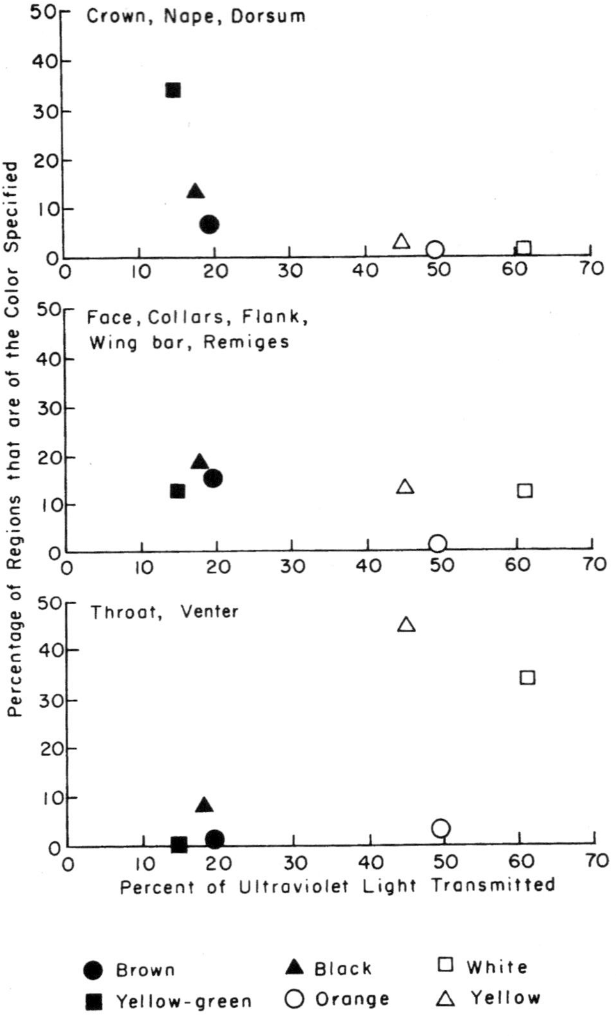

Fig. 33. Comparison of the percentage of differently colored regions on the dorsal, lateral, and ventral surfaces of male warblers. The percentages do not add up to 100: some of the colors that occur on warblers were not measured because suitable feathers could not be obtained. (From Burtt, in press.)

of ultraviolet light transmitted by differently colored feathers of the crown and rump.

The light falling on the legs was recorded separately from that on the body. I identified the species of warbler, waited ten seconds, and just before starting the taped record, I noted the light zone of the body and of the legs independently of the body. From these data I calculated the probability of exposing the legs to sunlight. A chi-square test was used to compare the probability of exposing the legs to sunlight in dark-legged (Munsell color value two) and light-legged (Munsell color values four, six, or eight) warblers.

Results

There is a significant negative correlation between the Munsell color value of the upper mandible and the percentage of time spent in sunlight (Fig. 34). Species whose upper mandible is dark (Munsell color values one or two) occasionally spent time in sunlight whereas species whose

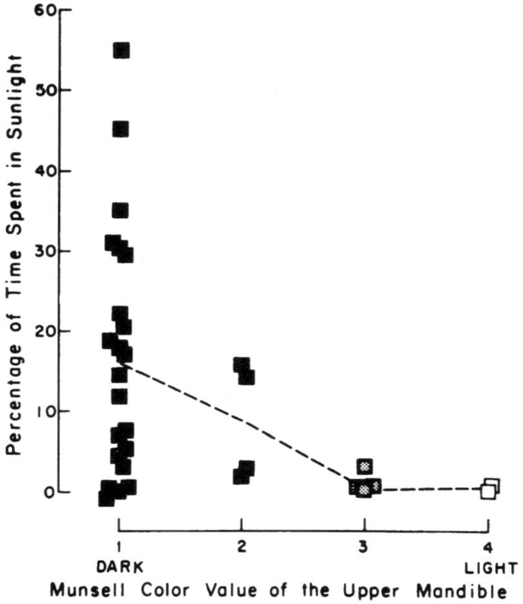

Fig. 34. Species of warblers plotted by the percentage of time spent in sunlight and the Munsell color value of the upper mandible. The dotted line connects median values. (From Burtt, in press.)

upper mandible is lighter (Munsell color values three or four) spent little time in sunlight. Among species I observed, only the bay-breasted warbler (*Dendroica Costanea*) is sexually dimorphic in the coloration of its upper mandible. The upper mandible of the male is darker (Munsell color value one) than the upper mandible of the female (Munsell color value two), and the male spent 7% of his time in sunlight as compared with 3% for the female. There is no correlation between the coloration of the crown and the percentage of time spent in sunlight by species with differently colored crowns ($r = 0.12$, $r^2 = 0.01$) nor is there a correlation between coloration of the rump and the percentage of time spent in sunlight by species with differently colored rumps ($r = 0.12$, $r^2 = 0.01$). The probability of exposing dark legs (Munsell color value two) to sunlight is not significantly different ($\chi^2 = 3.00$; df = 1; $0.10 > p > 0.05$) from the probability of exposing light legs (Munsell color value four, six, eight) to sunlight (Table 5).

Table 5

Number of Observations in which Dark- and Light-Legged Warblers Held Their Legs in Sunlight or Shade When the Body was in Sunlight, Dappled Light, or Shade (Species Combined)

Color of Legs	Sun	Shade
Dark (Munsell color value 2)	44	469
Light (Munsell color value 4, 6, 8)	25	169

H.: Exposure to sunlight independent of color value of legs.

$\chi^2 = 3.00$; df = 1; $\underline{p} = 0.10$. $0.10 > \underline{p} > 0.05$.

EXTERNAL COLORATION AS A DEFENSE AGAINST ULTRAVIOLET RADIATION: EVALUATION OF THE HYPOTHESIS

Transmission of ultraviolet light is correlated with pigmentation of the feathers. Melanin-impregnated feathers transmit significantly less ultraviolet radiation than feathers that contain carotenoids. Feathers that contain carotenoid pigments transmit significantly less ultraviolet radiation than unpigmented feathers.

The pattern of coloration of wood warblers is consistent with the hypothesis that external coloration evolved to shield the animal from excessive ultraviolet radiation. Feathers that contain melanin occur most commonly on the dorsal and lateral surfaces of warblers where ultraviolet radiation is most intense (*Prediction 1*). Only coloration of the crown and rump depart significantly from the predicted pattern.

The behavior of species with differently colored plumage is not consistent with the hypothesis that coloration of the plumage evolved to shield the animal from ultraviolet radiation. Species whose crown and rump feathers transmit large amounts of ultraviolet light spend just as much time in direct sunlight as congeners whose crown or rump feathers transmit little ultraviolet light (*contra-Prediction 2*). Therefore, the risk of damage incurred by exposure to ultraviolet radiation is outweighed by the advantages of bright, ultraviolet-transparent colors which serve communicative or other functions.

The density of melanin granules in keratin determines how dark the structure appears (Bowers 1959). Therefore, the varied shades of the mandibles and legs are due to different concentrations of melanin. Where the melanin concentration is low, in the light legs of the ovenbird (Munsell color value six), for example, ultraviolet radiation penetrates the keratin and reaches living tissue.

The upper mandible is darker than the lower mandible as predicted (*Prediction 1*) and species with lightly colored upper mandibles (Munsell color values three and four) avoid sunlight as predicted (*Prediction 2*). Therefore, both the coloration of the mandibles and the behavior of species with differently colored mandibles are consistent with the hypothesis that external coloration is an adaptation to protect tissue from ultraviolet radiation. However, see Burtt (in press) for other interpretations of mandibular coloration.

The legs of warblers are frequently as dark or darker than the dorsum (*contra Prediction 1*). Species with lightly colored legs show no tendency to shield the legs from ultraviolet radiation (*contra Prediction 2*). Therefore coloration of the legs of warblers is not explained by the hypothesis that external coloration has evolved to shield the animal from excessive ultraviolet radiation.

ACKNOWLEDGMENTS

I examined specimens of warblers through the courtesy of Melvin R. Traylor and the Field Museum in Chicago, Robert W. Storer and the University of Michigan, Frank B. Gill and the Philadelphia Academy of Sciences, and Raymond A. Paynter and the Museum of Comparative Zoology at Harvard. I thank Jack P. Hailman, Timothy C. Moermond, and Warren P. Porter for their criticism of my ideas and manuscript. My field work was supported by a Josephine Herz Fellowship from the University of Minnesota in 1973 and by the Frank M. Chapman Fund of the American Museum of Natural History in 1974. This chapter is based on a doctoral dissertation submitted to the Department of Zoology, University of Wisconsin, Madison, Wisconsin.

REFERENCES

Allen, L. H., Jr.; Gausman, H. W.; and Allen, W. A. 1975. Penetration of solar ultraviolet radiation into terrestrial plant communities. In *CIAP Monograph 5: Part 1--Ultraviolet Radiation Effects*, D. S. Nachtwey, M. M. Caldwell, and R. H. Biggs (eds.). Springfield, Va.: National Technical Information Service, pp. 2-78--2-108.

Averill, C. K. 1923. Black wing tips. *Condor* 25:57-59.

Bachman, J. 1839. Observations on the changes of colour in birds and quadrupeds. *Trans. Amer. Philos. Soc.* (Phila.) new series 6:197-239.

Blake, C. H. 1966. Warbler tail spots. *EBBA News* 29:54-55.

Blum, H. F. 1975. Ultraviolet radiation from the sun and skin cancer in human populations. In *CIAP Monograph 5:*

Part 1--Ultraviolet Radiation Effects, D. S. Nachtwey, M. M. Caldwell, and R. H. Biggs (eds.). Springfield, Va.: National Technical Information Service, pp. 7-87--7-103.

Bollum, F. J., and Setlow, R. B. 1963. The action spectra for ultraviolet-light inactivation of systems containing 5-bromouracil-substituted deoxyribonucleic acid. *Biochem. Biophys. Acta* 68:446-454.

Bowers, D. E. 1959. A study of variation in feather pigments of the wrentit. *Condor* 61:38-45.

Brush, A. H. 1970. Pigments in hybrid, variant and melanic tanagers (birds). *Comp. Biochem. Physiol.* 36:785-793.

Brush, A. H., and Siefried, H. 1968. Pigmentation and feather structure in genetic variants of the Gouldian Finch, *Poephila gouldiae. Auk* 85:416-430.

Burtt, E. H., Jr. The coloration of wood warblers (Parulidae). *Nuttall Ornithol. Monogr.*: in press.

Caldwell, M. M., and Nachtwey, D. S. 1975. Introduction and overview. In *CIAP Monograph 5: Part 1--Ultraviolet Radiation Effects*, D. S. Nachtwey, M. M. Caldwell, and R. H. Biggs (eds.). Springfield, Va.: National Technical Information Service, pp. 1-3--1-29.

Calkins, J., and Nachtwey, D. S. 1975. UV effects on bacteria, algae, protozoa, and aquatic invertebrates. In *CIAP Monograph 5: Part 1--Ultraviolet Radiation Effects*, D. S. Nachtwey, M. M. Caldwell, and R. H. Biggs (eds.). Springfield, Va.: National Technical Information Service, pp. 5-3--5-9.

Cole, L. C. 1943. Experiments on toleration of high temperature in lizards with reference to adaptive coloration. *Ecology* 24:94-108.

Collette, B. 1961. Correlations between ecology and morphology in anoline lizards from Havana, Cuba, and southern Florida. *Bull. Mus. Compar. Zool.* 125:137-162.

Dwight, J., Jr. 1900. Sequence and plumage of moults of the Passerine birds of New York. *Ann. N.Y. Acad. Sci.* 13:73-360.

Hanawalt, P. C. 1966. The u.v. sensitivity of bacteria; its relation to the DNA replication cycle. *Photochem. Photobiol.* 5:1-12.

Harm, W. 1969. Biological determination of the germicidal activity of sunlight. *Radiat. Res.* 40:63.

Heinroth, O., and Heinroth, K. 1958. *The Birds*. Ann Arbor: Univ. Mich. Press.

Klauber, L. M. 1939. Studies of reptile life in the arid southwest. *Bull. Zool. Soc. San Diego* 14:1-100.

Kleczkowski, A. 1971. Photobiology of plant viruses. In *Photophysiology*, Vol. 6, A. C. Giese (ed.). New York: Academic Press, pp. 179-208.

Kubitschek, H. E. 1967. Mutagenesis by near-visible light. *Science* 155:1545-1546.

McLaren, A. D., and Shugar, D. 1964. *Photochemistry of Proteins and Nucleic Acids*, Vol. 22. New York: Macmillan.

Maki, T. 1974. Prevention of wind frictional scratch on citrus fruit and the suppression of transpiration from eggplant by a surface coating agent. *J. Agric. Meteorol.* 30:39-44.

Murphy, T. M. 1973. Inactivation of TMV-RNA by ultraviolet radiation in the sunlight. *Int. J. Radiat. Biol.* 23: 519-526.

Pennycuick, C. J. 1972. *Animal Flight*. London: William Clowes.

Pennycuick, C. J. 1975. Mechanics of flight. *Avian Biol.* 5:1-75.

Porter, W. P. 1967. Solar radiation through the living body wall of vertebrates with emphasis on desert reptiles. *Ecol. Monogr.* 37:273-296.

Porter, W. P. 1975. Ultraviolet transmission properties of vertebrate tissues. In *CIAP Monograph 5: Part 1--Ultraviolet Radiation Effects*, D. S. Nachtwey, M. M. Caldwell, and R. H. Biggs (eds.). Springfield, Va.: National Technical Information Service, pp. 6-3--6-15.

Porter, W. P., and Norris, K. S. 1969. Lizard reflectivity change and its effect on light transmission through body wall. *Science* 163:482-484.

Probstein, R. F., and Fasso, F. 1970. Dusty hypersonic flows. *AIAA Journal* 8:772-779.

Resnick, M. A. 1969. A photoreactivationless mutant of *Saccharomyces cerevisiae*. *Photochem. Photobiol.* 9:307-312.

Resnick, M. A. 1970. Sunlight-induced killing in *Saccharomyces cerevisiae*. *Nature* 226:377-378.

Roscoe, J. T. 1975. *Fundamental Research Statistics for the Behavioral Sciences*. New York: Holt, Rinehart.

Rupert, C. S. 1964. Photoreactivation of ultraviolet damage. In *Photophysiology*, Vol. 2, A. C. Giese (ed.). New York: Academic Press, pp. 283-327.

Schmel, G. A., and Sutter, S. L. 1974. Particle deposition rates on a water surface as a function of particle diameter and air velocity. *J. Recherches Atmospheriques* 8:911-920.

Shettle, E. P., and Green, A. E. S. 1974. Multiple scattering calculation of the middle ultraviolet reaching the ground. *Appl. Opt.* 13:1567-1581.

Shettle, E. P.; Nack, M. L.; and Green, A. E. S. 1975. Multiple scattering and the influence of clouds, haze, and smog on the middle UV reaching the ground. In *CIAP Monograph 5: Part 1--Ultraviolet Radiation Effects*, D. S. Nachtwey, M. M. Caldwell, and R. H. Biggs (eds.). Springfield, Va.: National Technical Information Service, pp. 2-38--2-49.

Smith, K. C. 1971. The roles of genetic recombination and DNA polymerase in the repair of damaged DNA. In *Photophysiology*, Vol. 6, A. C. Giese (ed.). New York: Academic Press, pp. 209-278.

Smith, D. H. 1976. Debris shielding in regions of high edge velocity. *AIAA Journal* 14:94-96.

Storer, J. H. 1948. *The Flight of Birds Analyzed Through Slow-Motion Photography*. Bloomfield Hills, Mich: Cranbrook Press.

Test, F. H. 1940. Effects of natural abrasion and oxidation on the coloration of flickers. *Condor* 42:76-80.

Voitkevich, A. A. 1966. *The Feathers and Plumage of Birds.* New York: October House.

Waldman, G. D., and Reinecke, W. G. 1971. Particle trajectories, heating, and break-up in hypersonic shock layers. *AIAA Journal* 9:1040-1048.

Watkins-Pitchford, W. 1909. *The Etiology of Cancer.* London: William Clowes.

Wetmore, A. 1936. The number of contour feathers in Passeriform and related birds. *Auk* 53:159-169.

Witkin, E. M. 1966. Radiation-induced mutations and their repair. *Science* 152:1345-1353.

The Evolutiono-Engineering Approach: Discussion

C. Richard Tracy

Jed Burtt's approach to understanding the color patterning of warblers is what I called the "evolutiono-engineering approach." In this approach, you begin with basic physical and chemical principles and attempt to answer the question, "How can I best design this animal?" If the animals studied have the same design as that reasoned from the principles employed, you assume that the principles and processes originally *assumed* to be important in the evolution of particular adaptations are indeed important and that you have deduced some knowledge of the process and/or importance of particular adaptations. This approach differs from the more inductive process of surveying the adaptations of a large sample of animals, and then inferring knowledge about the process and/or importance of the adaptation studied.

I have two comments on the use of the evolutiono-engineering approach. First, this deductive analysis necessarily carries assumptions which should be tested individually. For example, Jed implicitly assumed that a one-minute blast of powdered glass on feathers was significantly related to the normal wear that feathers would get in nature. This assumption must be tested in some way, for if the normal wear on feathers is not great enough to cause reduced fitness in birds having feathers without the "appropriate" amounts of melanin, then the supporting predictions from the "wear hypothesis" must be reevaluated in terms of multicolinear support for alternative hypotheses. For example, Jed's *Prediction 2* (above) states that from the hypothesis of protection from wear, the dorsum of warblers is more likely to be melanized than the venter. If the prediction is supported by evidence, we also should ask how many alternative hypotheses does it likewise support. We know from the material given by Jed that a melanized dorsum also supports the hypothesis of protection from ultraviolet radiation. Thus, predictions in the evolutiono-engineering approach must be based on reasonable and/or well tested assumptions, and confirmed predictions must be evaluated in terms of alternative hypotheses or the entire approach could mislead us rather badly.

One way to strengthen the evolutiono-engineering approach is to form hypotheses in terms of optimality principles (Rosen 1967). Such principles do not generate hypotheses concerning evolutionary adaptations purely from the benefit derived from the adaptation, but rather from some benefit-cost relationship. That is to say, for every adaptation, one must evaluate and analyze the cost of that adaptation concomitant with the benefit derived from it. Indeed, if one were to make predictions entirely on the basis of benefit, and work strictly from the principle that melanin provides a benefit in terms of protection from abrasive wear, one would have to predict that warblers should be encased in feathers containing melanin. Since none of the warblers studied were completely armored with melanin, the prediction seems inadequate without also considering the *costs* of encasing the animal in melanin. The evolutiono-engineering approach using optimality principles of benefits and costs has yielded amazing insights into the selective advantages of complex biological adaptations (Parkhurst and Loucks 1972), and its use in ethological analyses promises very inventive breakthroughs.

The hypothesis that coloration can be involved in adaptations for protection from ultraviolet (Porter 1967) is very interesting and somewhat controversial (see Hamilton 1973). The initial assumption from which Jed has made predictions is that incident ultraviolet radiation exists in doses which are damaging to warblers. Thus, all of the predictions stemming from the ultraviolet hypothesis seemingly would have to be confirmed or else the initial assumption would not be true. In other words, any "damage," however slight, decreases fitness, so no adaptation implies no (or at least weak) potential for ultraviolet damage. Thus, it seems that each of Jed's predictions approximates a good null hypothesis, and rejection of any one should allow rejection of the overall hypothesis (that color patterning is a response to pressures from ultraviolet damage).

REFERENCES

Hamilton, W. J., III. 1973. *Life's Color Code*. New York: McGraw-Hill.

Parkhurst, D. F., and Loucks, O. L. 1972. Optimal leaf size in relation to environment. *J. Ecol.* 60:505-537.

Porter, W. P. 1967. Solar radiation through the living body walls of vertebrates with emphasis on desert reptiles. *Ecol. Monogr.* 37:273-296.

Rosen, R. 1967. *Optimality Principles in Biology*. New York: Plenum Press.

Where is the Evidence for Ultraviolet Damage?: Discussion

William J. Hamilton III

Jed has shown that a darkly colored dorsum may shield an animal from harmful ultraviolet radiation or increase the abrasion resistance of darkly colored feathers, fur, or scales; such hypotheses have received scant attention in the past. In addition, two classic hypotheses, absorption of solar radiation (Porter et al. 1973) and countershading (Ruiter 1956, Cott 1957), remain to be integrated into an overall hypothesis that can predict the coloration and pattern of color on the dorsum. The questions I pose, but cannot answer, are: How can we separate these four hypotheses? What is the relative importance of each selection pressure? Are the four hypotheses an inseparable, adaptive mix?

I suggest that, in the case of protection from ultraviolet radiation, despite all the effort to establish a quantitative argument, Jed and others who have concentrated on *comparative* studies provide the only evidence to date that melanic coloration shields the animal from ultraviolet radiation. Jed mentioned that the mutation rate of *E. coli* increases when it is exposed to the radiation levels that would reach the lizard's gut (where *E. coli* reside) if the lizard's black peritoneum were removed. However, *E. coli* is an internal organism that lives in a sheltered environment. Isn't it possible that, if *E. coli* lived in another environment, it would have a different tolerance to ultraviolet radiation?

What is the critical experiment, what are the critical data that will give us a *quantitative* measure of the relevance of the ultraviolet protection hypothesis? I fail to see such evidence. I see supportive evidence in Porter's (1967) comparison of the pigmentation of the peritoneum in lizards, in Collette's (1961) comparison of anole species, and in Jed's data from warblers. These studies provide supportive, circumstantial evidence that ultraviolet radiation is an evolutionary problem to free-ranging animals in natural environments. Can anyone show where quantitative data fit into the argument?

Burtt: Bill raises two important points: (1) the evolution of ultraviolet tolerance and (2) the lack of quantitative evidence that ultraviolet radiation is a potential hazard to lizards and warblers. Calkins and Nachtwey (1975) found that present flux rates are lethal to many classes of organisms even after tolerance mechanisms are accounted for. Hence these organisms must shield themselves. *E. coli* has a low tolerance for ultraviolet radiation and lives in an environment that shields it from the potentially damaging radiation. When *E. coli*'s shield, the lizard's black peritoneum, is removed, the bacterium's mutation rate rises. Hence the melanin-impregnated peritoneum is an effective shield beneath which *E. coli* is protected and without which *E. coli* is irreparably damaged.

As to quantitative evidence, there is none to show that ultraviolet radiation is a real hazard to warblers or lizards. Humans who are exposed to excessive ultraviolet radiation develop severe sunburn, freckling, and skin cancer (Blum 1975). I expect that the same conditions could develop in other vertebrates whose skin is exposed to excessive ultraviolet radiation, but a single lethal dose is unnecessary. Radiation damage is cumulative. Constant, low-intensity irradiation can cause damage just as surely as a single intense dose.

Hamilton: The human evidence is irrelevant because the human animal has been introduced recently into a habitat in which it did not evolve. An animal driving a tractor all day with its neck exposed is living outside its natural haunts. I would like to see evidence from the nonhuman world.

Question: Would you rephrase your question regarding quantitative data?

Hamilton: Are animals, living under natural conditions, ever exposed to excessive ultraviolet radiation? Is melanin an adaptation for shielding animals from excessive doses of ultraviolet radiation?

Question: Are you suggesting a more manipulative approach to the question of ultraviolet protection?

Hamilton: Yes.

Question: Relative to critical tests, what criteria would you use to assess radiation damage?

Hamilton: The animal dies after exposure to ultraviolet radiation, is denied profitable access to space or resources because of ultraviolet radiation, or reproduces or grows less rapidly when it is not exposed to ambient levels of ultraviolet radiation.

Question: Isn't the fact implicit in your question, that in order to define a critical test, you must know what you are being protected against? No one has referred to data that tell you what sort of damage occurs or where it occurs.

Burtt: On a macroscopic level the effects of excessive exposure to ultraviolet radiation are severe sunburn, freckling, and skin cancer (Blum 1975). These symptoms could serve as criteria, although their occurrence in nonhuman vertebrates is poorly documented.

Microscopically, absorption of ultraviolet occurs when the frequency of the incident radiation coincides with the resonant frequency of electrons in the outer shell of an atom or molecule. Absorption raises the electrons in the outer shell to a higher energy level. If the electrons are part of a covalent bond, that bond may rupture.

If DNA absorbs an ultraviolet photon into a thymine molecule, the hydrogen bond between adenine and thymine ruptures and two adjacent thymines on the same backbone unite to form a dimer linkage (Beukers and Berends 1960) that is more stable than the former hydrogen linkage. The result is a DNA molecule that fails to replicate properly (Setlow, Swenson and Carrier 1964, Hanawalt and Hayes 1967).

Question: Is there evidence that ultraviolet radiation affects metabolism?

Hamilton: Yes, but that is not my question. My question is: Where is the evidence that intensities of ultraviolet radiation sufficient to cause metabolic or genetic damage are relevant to animals living in their natural habitats? to animals living in a natural environment?

Question: Have the necessary experiments not been done in the natural environment?

Hamilton: How would you design such an experiment? Is the fact demonstrable only on a comparative basis?

Question: Is an albinistic animal a natural experiment?

Hamilton: No, an albinistic animal is a poorly controlled experiment. In many species albinos certainly have radiation problems. Such freaks also lack the repertoire of color adaptations to their particular color environment. The ultraviolet problems such individuals encounter are probably a consequence of a shift to an ultraviolet environment not encountered by the organism in its recent evolutionary history. Hence such problems cannot be evidence for or against the supposed evolutionary basis of pigments.

Tracy: Bill makes the important point that we have a problem with multicolinear effects. How can you separate one hypothesis from all other hypotheses, when all hypotheses make similar predictions? One test cannot single out one hypothesis; the results of that test can only support the possibility of several hypotheses. Bill's point is excellent and can be leveled at Jed's work. From the data presented we cannot conclude that the ultraviolet hypothesis dictates selection. At the same time Jed's thrust was not to conclude that potentially harmful ultraviolet radiation dictates coloration, his thrust was to say that there are many predictive hypotheses worthy of careful study. That is the real defense of Jed's work.

[*Hamilton*: Subsequent reflection following this conference has suggested to me one line of quantitative evidence which would demonstrate that ambient levels of ultraviolet radiation may impose limits upon the fitness of animals living in undisturbed natural environments. If *decrements* in ambient levels of ultraviolet radiation decrease mortality, increase reproductive or growth rate, or otherwise enhance fitness, the conclusion that ambient levels of radiation are hazardous and limiting would seem to be justified. It is experimentally much easier to increase radiation above ambient levels and to observe the result. Since such experiments are taking place under conditions not experienced in nature there is no selection pressure for adaptation to such conditions. It is thus not surprising that the general result is a demonstration of deleterious consequences. For marine algae, Lorenzen (1975) concludes that natural levels of ultraviolet radiation suppress photosynthesis in naturally occurring marine phytoplankton populations. To the extent that this is true, the case for ultraviolet as a barrier to further adaptation is apparently demonstrated. However, in interpreting such experiments it is critical to apply ultraviolet dosages available in the space and time occupied by the population under investigation.]

REFERENCES

Beukers, R., and Berends, W. 1960. Isolation and identification of the irradiation products of thymine. *Biochem. Biophys. Acta* 41:550-551.

Blum, H. F. 1975. Ultraviolet radiation from the sun and skin cancer in human populations. In *CIAP Monograph 5: Part 1--Ultraviolet Radiation Effects*, D. S. Nachtwey, M. M. Caldwell, and R. H. Biggs (eds.). Springfield, Va.: National Technical Information Service, pp. 7-87--7-103.

Calkins, J., and Nachtwey, D. S. 1975. UV effects on bacteria, algae, protozoa, and aquatic invertebrates. In *CIAP Monograph 5: Part 1--Ultraviolet Radiation Effects*, D. S. Nachtwey, M. M. Caldwell, and R. H. Biggs (eds.). Springfield, Va.: National Technical Information Service, pp. 5-3--5-9.

Collette, B. 1961. Correlations between ecology and morphology in anoline lizards from Havana, Cuba, and southern Florida. *Bull. Mus. Compar. Zool.* 125:137-162.

Cott, H. B. 1957. *Adaptive Coloration in Animals*. London: Methuen.

Hanawalt, P. D., and Haynes, R. H. 1967. The repair of DNA. *Sci. Amer.* 216:36-43.

Lorenzen, C. 1975. Phytoplankton responses to UV radiation and ecological implications of elevated UV irradiance. In *CIAP Monograph 5: Part 1--Ultraviolet Radiation Effects*, D. S. Nachtwey, M. M. Caldwell, and R. H. Biggs (eds.). Springfield, Va.: National Technical Information Service, pp. 5-83--5-91.

Porter, W. P. 1967. Solar radiation through the living body wall of vertebrates with emphasis on desert reptiles. *Ecol. Monogr.* 37:273-296.

Porter, W. P.; Mitchell, J. W.; Beckman, W. A.; and DeWitt, C. B. 1973. Behavioral implications of mechanistic ecology; thermal and behavioral modeling of desert ectotherms and their microenvironment. *Ecologia* 13:1-54.

Ruiter, L. de. 1956. Countershading in caterpillars. An analysis of its adaptive significance. *Arch. Neerl. Zool.* 11:285-342.

Setlow, R. B.; Swenson, P. A.; and Carrier, W. L. 1964. Thymine dimers and inhibition of DNA synthesis (in bacteria) by ultraviolet irradiation of cells. *Science* 142:1464-1466.

Audience Questions:
Discussion

Question: Unpigmented species of rodents frequently live in competition with melanistic species of rodents on white sands and adjacent black lava beds (Benson 1933, Hooper 1941). Could such a parametric situation be exploited to tease apart the hypotheses of abrasion resistance, ultraviolet protection, thermoregulation, and conspicuousness?

Hamilton: Let me speak to that, because I spent three months last year (1976) in the Namib Desert working with two species of tenebrionid beetle, *Onymacius*. One has a white dorsum, the other a black dorsum. They inhabit approximately the same environment, but have different activity rhythms.

The separation of hypotheses is enormously difficult. You must follow individuals in order to know their radiation dosage. You must know the longevity of individuals who have received different cumulative doses (see Jed's discussion, above) and you must know what constitutes radiation damage (see Jed's discussion, above). What we find is that inside the abdomen ultraviolet radiation is about equally intense in black and white animals, because the externally white beetle has a dark, melanized layer beneath its carapace. Predation pressures upon the two species are different and the white species loses water at almost twice the rate of the black one (Hamilton 1973), so the question arises: Is water a limiting factor in the desert environment? Hence, before you get an answer the whole web of adaptations comes into play. The approach you suggest is a valid one, but not an easy one.

Question: Have you thought about how the different texture, number arrangement, or pigment concentration of different plumages (e.g., natal down, juvenile plumage, first winter plumage, first nuptial plumage, and so forth) affects ultraviolet protection or abrasion resistance?

Burtt: I have thought about the variables you mention, but in an attempt to use the comparative method rigorously, I studied only adult wood warblers (Parulidae), a group of physiologically and morphologically similar birds. Hence I eliminated the variables you mention.

Morse: Many warblers are dark dorsally and light ventrally, but many of the light feathers are light distally and gray to black proximately. I hope you realize that.

Burtt: Yes, you raise an important point also illustrated by Bill's study of black and white *Onymacius* beetles (above, Hamilton 1973). The ultraviolet shield need not be on the animal's outermost surface. The feathers of birds and the cuticle of beetles are nonliving structures that are not seriously damaged by ultraviolet radiation. Living cells that are easily damaged by ultraviolet radiation (e.g., nerve cells, gametes) must be shielded. The melanin shield may enclose only easily damaged cells in the nervous and reproductive systems (e.g., *Dipsosaurus dorsalis*, Porter 1967), may lie just beneath the nonliving cuticle, feathers, fur, skin, or scales (e.g., the white *Onymacuis* beetle), or the shield may comprise external coloration of the body. The location of the ultraviolet shield is less important than the fact that the shield exists in all animals that are exposed to ultraviolet light. When the melanin shield is internal, external coloration is free to conform to other selection pressures. Indeed, the hypothesis of ultraviolet protection may be a poor explanation of external coloration because there is no necessity to absorb ultraviolet radiation at the outermost surface of the body.

Question: If melanin strengthens the cuticle, could one predict that raptors would have darker claws than birds that do not "abuse" their claws?

Hamilton: I do not know about that, but the most perfectly camouflaged crickets, green and beautifully matching their substrate, have black, melanic tips on the jaws and tarsal tips. A structural function whose benefits exceed the cost of more perfect camouflage is strongly implied.

Burtt: Are the claws of raptors subject to more abrasion than the claws of a sparrow or warbler that scratches on the ground for its food?

Question: Your prediction of abrasion resistance was based on evidence that airborne particles abrade aircraft. Have you any evidence that airborne particles abrade bird feathers? Could the wear be the result of repeated bending?

Burtt: I have only circumstantial evidence that airborne particles are the source of abrasion to bird feathers. The worn feathers pictured by Dwight (1900), the worn feathers of warblers that I have captured in mist nets, and the feathers I abraded with airborne particles all show a similar pattern of broken and pitted barbs. The pitted barbs and the irregularity of the breaks in the vane of the feather (e.g., one barb broken near its joint with the shaft of the feather whereas the adjacent barbs are unbroken) suggest collision with some small, hard object such as an airborne particle. Because the vane of the feather bends as a unit, breaks due to bending should extend uniformly across many barbs. Breaks from contact with twigs, branches, or the ground should involve many barbs and not infrequently the shaft. I commonly find such breaks, but they cannot account for the pitted barbs or the isolated, broken barbs. I recognize that the evidence is circumstantial, and I am working on wind tunnel measurements that may provide direct evidence for the particulate nature of feather abrasion.

REFERENCES

Benson, S. B. 1933. Concealing coloration among some desert rodents of the southwestern United States. *Univ. Calif. Publ. Zool.* 40:1-70.

Dwight, J., Jr. 1900. Sequence and plumage of moults of the passerine birds of New York. *Ann. N.Y. Acad. Sci.* 13:73-360.

Hamilton, W. J., III. 1973. *Life's Color Code*. New York: McGraw-Hill.

Hooper, E. T. 1941. Mammals of the lava fields and adjoining areas in Valencia County, New Mexico. *Misc. Publ. Mus. Zool., Univ. Mich.* 51:1-47.

Porter, W. P. 1967. Solar radiation through the living body walls of vertebrates with emphasis on desert reptiles. *Ecol. Monogr.* 37:273-296.

Part 3

Photoreception

Chapter 4

Extraretinal Photoreception

Herbert Underwood

Introduction
Insects and Extraretinal Photoreception
  The Role of ERRs in Entrainment of Insect Clocks
  The Role of ERRs in Insect Photoperiodism
Vertebrates and Extraretinal Photoreception
  Pineal System: Photosensitivity
  Entrainment of the Biological Clock
  Photoperiodic Photoreception
  Pineal Biochemical Rhythms
  Physiological Color Change
  Phototaxis and Photokinesis
  Orientation
  Photoreception in Adult Mammals
Conclusion

INTRODUCTION

For over a century we have known that vertebrates can respond to light by using photoreceptors other than the lateral eyes. Much of the earlier work concerned the phototaxic and photokinetic behavior of blinded animals and many early researchers assumed that light was perceived by photoreceptors in the skin--a so-called "dermal light sensitivity" (Steven 1963). Interest in extraretinal photoreception revived following the demonstration that important physiological and behavioral responses such as photoperiodism, changes in external coloration, or entrainment of the biological clock can be influenced by light after removal of the eyes. Recent studies show that extraretinal photoreception is a consistent and important aspect of the sensory repertoire of all vertebrates, with the possible exception of adult mammals. However, extraretinal photoreception is not confined to vertebrates. Many invertebrates (e.g., insects, molluscs, crustaceans) also employ extraretinal photoreceptors. This chapter discusses the role of extraretinal photoreceptors among the invertebrates only in insects since they have received more intensive study than other invertebrate groups. The reader is referred to Lickey et al. (1976) and Page and Larimer (1976) for recent reviews on extraretinal photoreception in other invertebrate groups.

The daily light-dark cycles associated with the earth's rotation and the annual changes in the length of the photoperiod are used by many organisms to time important physiological and behavioral events. By using alternating light-dark cycles to synchronize daily (circadian) rhythms animals can gain a degree of temporal coordination that would be impossible by utilizing more labile stimuli such as temperature or humidity. All eukaryotic organisms examined to date exhibit entrainment (synchronization) of circadian rhythms to 24-hour light-dark cycles. In addition, the annual change in day length offers a noise-free cue that relatively long-lived organisms can use to time annual cycles in such physiological and behavioral processes as diapause, fattening, migration, and reproduction. The adaptive significance of such photoperiodic responses is obvious--animals can anticipate and prepare for adverse conditions (e.g., diapause, migration) and they can confine reproduction to the time of year that is most conducive to the survival of the organism and its offspring. Most of the research into the role of extraretinal photoreceptors (ERRs) in insects as well as vertebrates concerns entrainment of the biological clock and photoperiodic photoreception.

INSECTS AND EXTRARETINAL PHOTORECEPTION

The Role of ERRs in Entrainment of Insect Clocks

In only two insects, cockroaches (Blattidae) and crickets (Gryllidae), is there evidence that ERRs (extraretinal photoreceptors) are not involved in entrainment of circadian rhythms. In both insects the compound eyes are the only routes by which daily light cycles can entrain the clock (Roberts 1965; Nishiitsutsuji-Uwo and Pittendrigh 1968a, 1968b; Loher 1972; Sokolove 1975; Sokolove and Loher 1975). Transection of the optic nerve, for example, produces a free-running (that is, the animal expresses its endogenous circadian rhythm) locomotor rhythm regardless of lighting conditions. The optic lobes of the brain appear to be the sites of the driving oscillators (or biological clocks) responsible for maintaining rhythmicity, since sectioning the neural pathways between the optic lobes and the rest of the brain or removing the optic lobes causes arrhythmicity in locomotor (cockroaches and crickets) or stridulatory (crickets) activity.

In all other insects examined, entrainment persists after removal of the compound eyes (Truman 1976). In the "long-horn" grasshopper (*Ephippiger sp.*), Dumortier (1972) showed that entrainment of the circadian rhythm of stridulatory activity persisted after removal of compound eyes or ocelli. However, localized illumination of the head area indicated that the compound eyes and/or ocelli also had an input into the grasshopper's biological clock.

In most insects the compound eyes are apparently not involved in the perception of entraining light cycles. Several investigators have used the daily rhythm of eclosion in order to reveal the nature and location of photoreceptors that have inputs into the biological clock of insects. Many insects exhibit a daily rhythm of eclosion; in a population of insects, individuals emerge from their pupal cases only during a restricted period of the day.

In *Drosophila*, for example, individual flies under natural conditions emerge near dawn, the coldest and wettest part of the day. Emerging flies lose water far more rapidly than mature adults and the wings may fail to expand properly if the humidity is too low. Although an individual emerges only once, the event is timed by the insect's biological clock.

The existence of ERRs in *Drosophila* was established by Engelmann and Honegger (1966) who found that the circadian eclosion rhythm of *Drosophila melanogaster* mutants, which lacked compound eyes and ocelli, entrained normally to an LD 12:12 cycle. Zimmerman and Ives (1971) determined the spectral sensitivities for both the compound eyes and the circadian eclosion rhythm of *Drosophila pseudoobscura* (Fig. 35). In this experiment, the spectral sensitivity of the compound eye photoreceptors was determined by an electrode placed on the corneas of immobilized flies. Action spectra for the eclosion rhythm were determined by exposing populations (white-eyed and wild-type) of

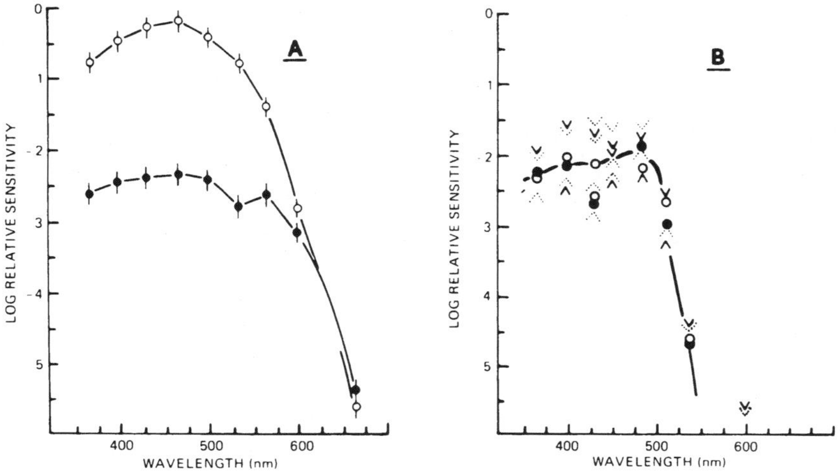

Fig. 35. Spectral sensitivity of the compound eyes of the adult (A) and the circadian rhythm (B) in white-eyed (open circles, dotted arrows) and wild-type (closed circles, solid arrows) *D. pseudoobscura* (Zimmerman and Ives 1971. Reproduced with the permission of the National Academy of Sciences).

Drosophila, which had been released from LD 12:12 into constant darkness (DD), to 15-minute light signals 5 hours after the light-to-dark transition. The populations were exposed to either monochromatic light, white fluorescent light (1100 lux), or no light (free-run controls). Action spectra were obtained by determining the relative number of quanta at wavelengths between 354 nm and 800 nm which generated a phase shift in the eclosion rhythm equal to about 50% of the saturating phase shift generated by the white light signal.

A comparison of the action spectra for phase shifting of the eclosion rhythm and the electrical response of the photoreceptor cells of the eye indicates that the two responses are mediated by different photopigments (Fig. 35). The eclosion rhythm is insensitive to light of wavelengths greater than 570 nm, but the eye is sensitive to light up to 666 nm.

The spectral sensitivities of the circadian rhythms of the few insects examined to date are similar to those described for *D. pseudoobscura*. The circadian rhythms of hatching, oviposition, and eclosion in the moth *Pectinophora gossypiella* are sensitive to blue but not to red light (Pittendrigh et al. 1970). A more complete action spectrum for the initiation of the larval-hatching rhythm of *P. gossypiella* is very similar to the *Drosophila* spectrum; the most effective wavelengths were between 390 nm and 480 nm and wavelengths above 520 nm were ineffective (Bruce and Minis 1969).

Another technique for determining the nature of insect photopigments takes advantage of the fact that in all known visual pigments the chromophore of the photopigment is the carotenoid derivative retinaldehyde. Carotenoids are synthesized by plants and can only be obtained by insects from their diet. Zimmerman and Goldsmith (1971) raised *Drosophila melanogaster* on diets without β-carotene and subsequently assayed both the photosensitivity of the circadian eclosion rhythm of the pupae to 15-minute monochromatic light signals and the photosensitivity of the compound eyes (Fig. 36). The photosensitivity of the visual receptors in carotenoid-depleted flies was about three log units lower than that of the carotenoid-supplemented flies. Most significantly, there was no difference between the deprived and supplemented flies with respect to the photosensitivity of their circadian rhythms. These results indicate that a carotenoid-deprived chromophore is not

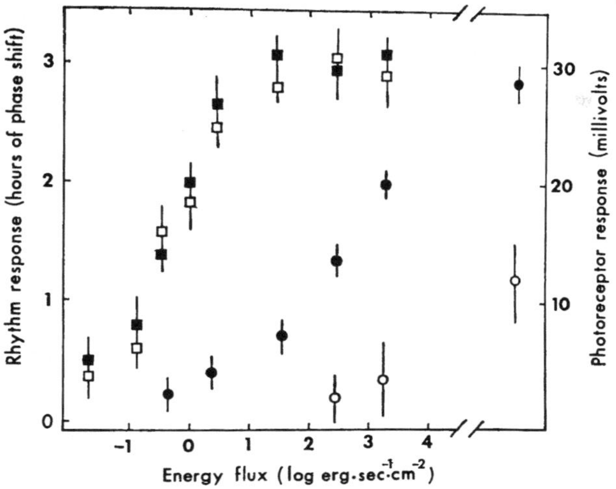

Fig. 36. Response-energy curves for phase shifts of the circadian rhythm (squares) and for the retinal action potential (circles) of *D. melanogaster* grown on aseptic diets with β-carotene (closed symbols) and without β-carotene (open symbols). The energy scale gives the light flux used in both experiments, but the exposures were 900 times longer for resetting the rhythm. The responses of the visual receptors shown to the right of the break in the abscissa were obtained with a bright white light (Zimmerman and Goldsmith 1971. *Science* 171:1167-1168. Copyright 1971 by The American Association for the Advancement of Science).

involved in mediating circadian rhythms. However, Zimmerman and Goldsmith (1971) point out that an alternative but less likely explanation of the results involves transmission of some carotenoids through the egg and preferential utilization of these carotenoids by the circadian system.

Drosophila ERRs are probably located in the brain. Opaquing (painting) the anterior ends of the pupae prevented phase shifting by dim monochromatic light whereas painting the posterior half did not (Zimmerman and Ives 1971).

The compound eyes have no role in the entrainment of the silkmoth flight activity rhythms (Truman 1974). A dim (one lux) light cycle was capable of entraining the flight activity rhythm of normal *Hyalophora cecropia* and *Samia cynthia*. However, silkmoths which had their heads, except the compound eyes, covered by black wax showed free-running activity rhythms even though the eyes were exposed to the light cycle. These results also indicate that the ERRs are located in the brain.

The relatively large size of silkmoths allowed various surgical manipulations which indicated that the brain was the site of both the circadian oscillators controlling circadian rhythms and the site of the ERRs (Truman and Riddiford 1970, Truman 1972). For example, if the brains of silkmoths are removed early in adult development, the eclosion rhythm of the brainless animals is abolished--they emerge at random times with respect to the light-dark cycles. Implantation of the brain into the abdomen of brainless animals restores rhythmicity, and the site of photosensitivity shifts to the abdomen. Implanting various parts of the brain into brainless hosts showed that the optic lobes are not required for entrainment of the silkmoth eclosion rhythm and the clock and photoreceptors are probably located in the cerebral region of the brain (Truman 1972). The location of the clock in these insects, therefore, is different from its location in cockroaches and crickets, where intact optic lobes are necessary for the persistence of rhythmicity.

The Role of ERRs in Insect Photoperiodism

Many insects have evolved time-measuring mechanisms whereby they can discriminate between day lengths and so initiate seasonally appropriate events such as induction or termination of diapause. The reduced metabolic rate which occurs during diapause enables insects to overwinter or to withstand a dry season. Another adaptive photoperiodic response which is common in insects is the control of seasonal morphs. For example, the long days of summer induce the production of viviparous parthenogenetic (virginoparae) aphids which can reproduce rapidly in the presence of abundant food supplies, whereas short days induce the production of egg-laying (oviparae) offspring (Saunders 1976).

Insects appear to measure photoperiod in two different ways. Measurement in some species appears to use an endogenous daily (circadian) rhythm of responsiveness to light (Pittendrigh and Minis 1964, Pittendrigh 1972). The second kind of time-measuring system envisages an "hourglass" or interval timer (Saunders 1976). This hypothesis assumes the accumulation of a reaction product during the dark (or light) which is inactivated during the other phase of the light-dark cycle. The duration of dark (or light) is "measured" by the quantity of substance that has accumulated; if enough substance accumulates, a photoperiodic response begins. This process begins anew with each cycle of the lighting regimen and lacks endogenous periodicity.

The existence of two different measuring systems for photoperiodic time, one involving a circadian clock, increases the likelihood that different photoreceptors are involved in the different measurement systems. The experiments of Pittendrigh et al. (1970) and Pittendrigh and Minis (1971) on *P. gossypiella* support this view. As discussed previously, Pittendrigh et al. (1970) demonstrated that several circadian rhythms in *P. gossypiella* are red-insensitive. However, the photoperiodic control of diapause in this insect is fully red-sensitive, suggesting the existence of separate photosystems for entrainment and photoperiodism. The results suggest that photoperiodic time measurement in *P. gossypiella* is accomplished by an hourglass mechanism. However, an equally plausible explanation is that the photoperiodic clock is a separate circadian oscillator coupled to light by a red-absorbing pigment.

Among insects, photoperiodic responses appear to be solely mediated by ERRs located in the brain. Williams and Adkisson (1964) showed that the site of photoperiodic photosensitivity in the oak silkmoth (*Antheraea pernyi*) could be transferred from the head to the abdomen by transferring the brain to the abdomen. The photoperiodic response of *A. pernyi* pupae persists after removal of the optic lobes (Williams 1969). Similarly, Claret (1966a, 1966b) transferred photoperiodic photosensitivity along with the brain in the cabbage butterfly (*Pieris brassicae*). These studies suggest that the ERRs for photoperiodic photoreception and entrainment of the biological clock are both located in the cerebral lobe of the brain, but whether these receptors are identical or not remains unresolved.

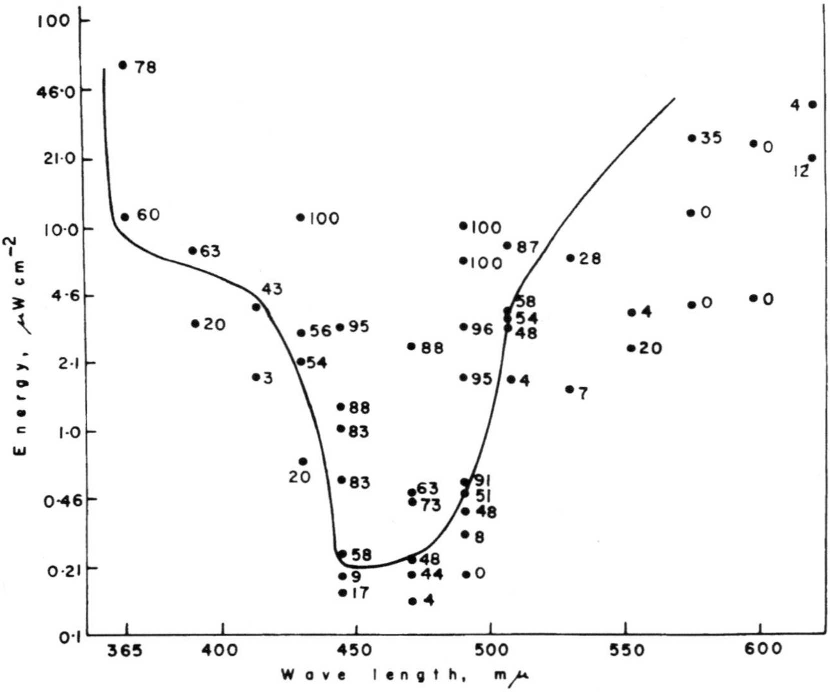
100
46·0
21·0
10·0
4·6
2·1
1·0
0·46
0·21
0·1
Energy, μW cm⁻²
365
400
450
500
550
600
Wave length, mμ

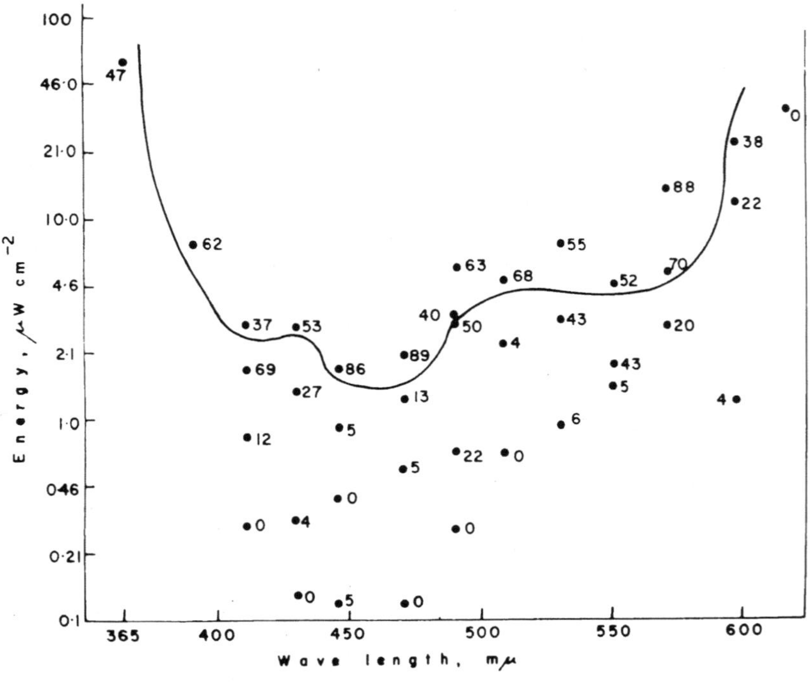
100
46·0
21·0
10·0
4·6
2·1
1·0
0·46
0·21
0·1
Energy, μW cm⁻²
365
400
450
500
550
600
Wave length, mμ

A technically different approach was utilized by Lees (1960, 1964) to localize the photoperiodic photoreceptors in the aphid *Megoura viciae*. Lees maintained parent aphids on a short day length (LD 14:10) but gave two hours of additional illumination to discrete areas of the aphid by means of fine light guides. If the additional illumination was positioned over the brain, the aphids reacted to the long day length (LD 16:8) and produced virginoparous daughters, whereas illumination of other areas of the body, including the compound eyes, was less effective and the aphids reacted to the short day by producing oviparous daughters.

Workers have investigated the photoperiodic spectral sensitivities of insects in an attempt to determine the nature of the photopigments. In general, most species are maximally sensitive to light in the blue-green region of the spectrum and largely insensitive to red, but exceptions are known (e.g., *P. gossypiella*). Saunders (1976) lists eleven red-insensitive species and five red-sensitive species. Assuming that these reflect the sensitivities of photopigments located in the brain, the screening effects of tissue overlying the brain may be a factor in modifying the intensities and spectral qualities of light. This screening will, of course, be of greater magnitude in larger insects.

One of the most complete action spectra studies for photoperiodism in insects was conducted by Lees (1971) with *Megoura* (Fig. 37). Parent aphids were exposed to a one-hour pulse of monochromatic light beginning 1½ hours into the dark portion of an LD 13.5:10.5 light cycle or to a ½-hour pulse placed 7½ hours after the inception of the dark period. These positions corresponded to an early or late night break, both of which induced the production of the long-day (virginoparous) offspring. The early night

Fig. 37. Action spectrum for the maternal control of virginoparaproduction in the aphid *Megoura viciae*. In (A) near-monochromatic light was applied in the early night, 1.5 h after the beginning of a 10.5-h dark phase. The curve is drawn for incident energies at which approximately 50% of the parent aphids become virginopara-producers. (B) Action spectrum showing the effect of 0.5 h of near-monochromatic light applied in the late night, 7.5 h after the beginning of darkness (Lees 1971. Reproduced with the permission of The National Academy of Sciences).

interruption showed a maximum sensitivity in the blue (450 nm-470 nm) with a threshold at that wavelength of approximately 0.2 $W \cdot cm^{-2}$. The maximum sensitivity of the late night interruption was also in the blue but sensitivity extended to 600 nm. The differences in action spectra indicated that different events, possibly involving different photopigments, occurred during these two times of night.

Other studies on spectral sensitivity indicate that the intensity threshold for photoperiodic responses may be quite low. The approximate intensity thresholds for photoperiodic responses of a total of eleven different species are listed in Saunders (1976) and Truman (1976). Most of these insects show thresholds between 0.1 and 10 lux.

Truman (1976) suggested that more advanced groups of insects show an increased reliance on extraretinal photoreception. In primitive insects such as cockroaches or crickets, circadian rhythms are exclusively entrained via retinal pathways, whereas in insects which undergo a complete metamorphosis, such as flies and moths, photoreception may be mediated entirely by extraretinal receptors located in the brain. Truman (1976) speculates that brain receptors may be of value during metamorphosis because they are unaffected by the extensive reorganization occurring in external structures (such as eyes).

VERTEBRATES AND EXTRARETINAL PHOTORECEPTION

Extraretinal photoreception is widespread among the vertebrates. Extraretinal photoreceptors participate in the responses of vertebrates to light in at least six general areas: (1) entrainment of the biological clock; (2) photoperiodic photoreception; (3) control of certain biochemical rhythms in the pineal; (4) control of physiological color changes; (5) phototactic and photokinetic responses; and (6) orientation. However, among vertebrates the only extraretinal photoreceptive system which has been definitely localized is the pineal system of fish, amphibians, and reptiles. The pineal system has attracted a host of investigators because of the grossly "eye-like" morphology of some components of the system and because of the ease with which the members of this system can be removed and probed cytologically, biochemically, or electrophysiologically. A comprehensive review of the pineal system is beyond the scope of the present discussion, but a number of excellent reviews can be consulted for additional information (Ariëns-Kappers 1965, Wurtman et al. 1968, Wolstenholme and Knight 1971, Quay 1974, Relkin 1976).

Pineal System: Photosensitivity

In many fish, frogs, and lizards the pineal system is composed of two elements, both of which are derived embryologically as evaginations of the roof of the diencephalon. In these cases one component, the pineal organ proper, remains attached to the roof of the diencephalon. The other component, the parapineal organ, seems to originate either as an outpouching from the pineal organ (as in frogs) or as a separate diverticulum from the diencephalon (as in some lizards) (Kelly 1962). The parapineal component is most often located just beneath the skin of the head and in many lizards is highly differentiated into an eyelike organ (the parietal eye) complete with cornea, lens, and retina. A less specialized version is common in anuran amphibians and is termed the frontal organ. Although some lower vertebrates lack the superficial component (e.g., urodele amphibians, snakes), practically all vertebrates retain a pineal organ.

Electron microscopy has revealed that both components of the pineal system in lower vertebrates possess a number of cells that resemble the photoreceptive cones of the lateral eyes (Wurtman et al. 1968, Wolstenholme and Knight 1971). However, many of these cells are more degenerate in appearance than the cones of the eyes and have been termed "rudimentary photoreceptors." Electrical responses to illumination have been recorded from the pineal organ of fish, the pineal organ and frontal organ of anuran amphibians, and from the pineal organ and parietal eye of lizards (Dodt and Heerd 1962, Dodt 1963, Dodt and Jacobson 1963, Dodt and Scherer 1968, Hamasaki and Dodt 1969, Hamasaki 1969, Hamasaki and Streck 1971). In general, the pineal organs give achromatic responses whereas the parietal eye and frontal organs show chromatic responses. The achromatic response typically involves inhibition of ongoing (spike) activity by all wavelengths of light. The chromatic response usually shows inhibition of electrical activity by shorter wavelengths and excitation by longer wavelengths of visible light. Some representative examples of the spectral sensitivity peaks of the (achromatic) pineal organs are: fish (*Salmo irideus*, 505 nm; *Scyliorhinus caniculus*, 500 nm; *Pterophyllum scalare*, 525 nm); amphibians (*Rana temporaria*, 560 nm); and lizards (*Iguana iguana, Lacerta sicula* and *Acanthodactylus erythrurus*, 570 nm) (Dodt 1963, Hamasaki and Streck 1971, Morita and Bergmann 1971, Dodt and Jacobson 1963, Hamasaki 1969). Examples of the peak chromatic responses from amphibian frontal organs and lizard parietal eyes are: amphibian frontal organs (*R. temporaria* and *R. esculenta*, 355 nm and 515 nm), and lizard parietal eyes (*I. iguana* and *L. sicula*, 460 nm and 520 nm) (Dodt and Heerd 1962, Dodt and Scherer 1968, Hamasaki 1969).

The achromatic responses of fish and amphibian pineal organs are typically very sensitive to light and threshold sensitivities of dark adapted (exposed) pineals range from 10^{-2} to 10^{-6} lux. The lizard's pineal is less sensitive and shows a threshold for exposed pineals of 4 lux (Hamasaki and Dodt 1969). In intact animals the skin and skull overlying the pineal reduce the amount of light reaching the pineal by factors of 100 to 1000.

In some cases both graded (slow) potentials and action potentials (spike activity) are observed. The graded potentials are most noticeable in frontal organs of frogs and lizard parietal eyes. In the lizard parietal eye, for example, there is a graded potential similar to the electroretinogram (ERG) of the lateral eyes (Dodt and Scherer 1968, Hamasaki 1969). With light stimuli in the blue range this ERG shows an "on" response that consists of a relatively rapidly rising positive wave. Stimuli of longer wavelengths elicit a rapidly falling negative wave. The positive component is associated with inhibition of spike activity whereas the negative component is associated with excitation of spike activity.

The photoreceptor cells in pineal and parapineal organs synapse with a single kind of neuron which sends its axons to the brain. A recent study by Engbretson and Lent (1976) shows the possibility of mutual interaction between the lizard's pineal and parietal eye. In the lizard *Crotaphytus collaris*, afferent fibers leaving the parietal eye pass over and possibly innervate the pineal on their way to the rest of the brain. Efferent fibers originating in the pineal organ can modify the parietal eye's response to light. The efferent nerves are not photosensitive but they are chemosensitive; norepinephrine and serotonin when applied to the pineal organ will initiate activity in these nerves.

The dual pineal system present in many lower vertebrates is absent in birds and mammals. The pineal organs of adult birds and mammals are apparently not directly photosensitive (Wurtman et al. 1968, Wolstenholme and Knight 1971, Quay 1974). The main cell type of bird and mammalian pineals is the pinealocyte, which is believed to belong to the same cell line as the photoreceptor cells of the lower vertebrates. The pinealocyte is an active secretory cell and is involved in the synthesis of polypeptides and biogenic amines such as serotonin and melatonin (Fig. 38). In this regard, the photoreceptive cells in the lower vertebrates, in spite of their obvious photoreceptive ability, are also active sites of chemical synthesis of such products as the biogenic amines. The only known innervation

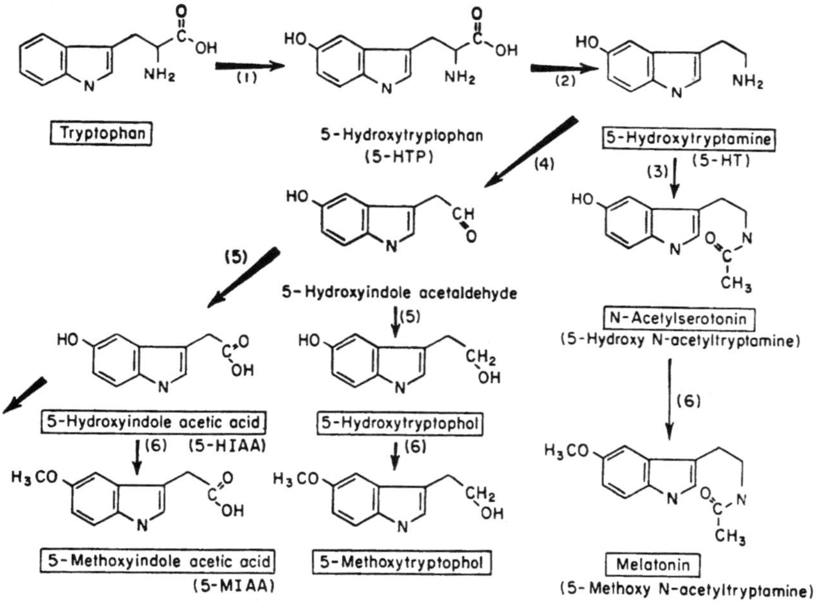

Fig. 38. Biosynthesis of biogenic amines from tryptophan in the pineal gland. Heavier arrows indicate the major pathways; compounds in rectangles are measurable within pineal tissue. Enzymatic steps: (1) tryptophan hydroxylase, (2) aromatic L-amino acid decarboxylase, (3) N-acetyltransferase, (4) monoamine oxidase, (5) aldehyde dehydrogenase, (6) hydroxyindole-O-methyltransferase. (Quay 1974. *Pineal Chemistry*. Courtesy of Charles C Thomas, Publisher, Springfield, Ill.).

of avian and mammalian pineals is sympathetic innervation from the superior cervical ganglia.

Entrainment of the Biological Clock

Entrainment of the circadian locomotor activity rhythms of fish, amphibians, reptiles, and birds to 24-hour light-dark cycles persists after removal of the lateral eyes (Eriksson 1972, Adler 1976, Underwood and Menaker 1976, Menaker and Underwood 1976, van Veen et al. 1976). Figure 39, for example, shows the locomotor activity rhythm of an iguanid lizard, *Sceloporus olivaceus*; neither blinding nor removal of the parietal eye or pineal organ prevented entrainment to an LD 12:12 (30 lux: 0) fluorescent light cycle. With the exception of anuran amphibians (Adler 1971), removal of the pineal system does not prevent entrainment in any vertebrate. Extraretinal photoreception occurs in fish, reptiles, and birds whether or not the pineal system is present, and localization experiments (reptiles and birds) have shown that the brain is the site of this photoreception. However, to date there are no data which eliminate the possibility that the pineal system may act as an alternate route of photoreception. The extraretinal photoreceptors are very sensitive to light; entrainment in blinded animals can be accomplished by light intensities as low as 0.05-0.1 lux (Underwood and Menaker 1976, Menaker and Underwood 1976).

In every case examined to date, the lateral eyes have been shown to have an input into the clock. For example, removal of the lateral eyes of lizards previously entrained to very dim light cycles can cause them to free-run (Underwood 1973). In birds entrainment can be accomplished or abolished by manipulating the amount of light reaching the brain or the eyes (Menaker 1968, Menaker and Underwood 1976).

Although the pineal organ is not necessarily a photoreceptor involved in entrainment in birds and lizards, it is an important component of circadian organization (Gaston and Menaker 1968, Zimmerman and Menaker 1975, Underwood 1977). Pinealectomy in the house sparrow (*Passer domesticus*) abolishes circadian rhythmicity; pinealectomized house sparrows are arrhythmic in continuous darkness (DD). The avian pineal appears to be hormonally, rather than neurally, coupled to other components of the circadian system since interruption of the nervous input and output of the house

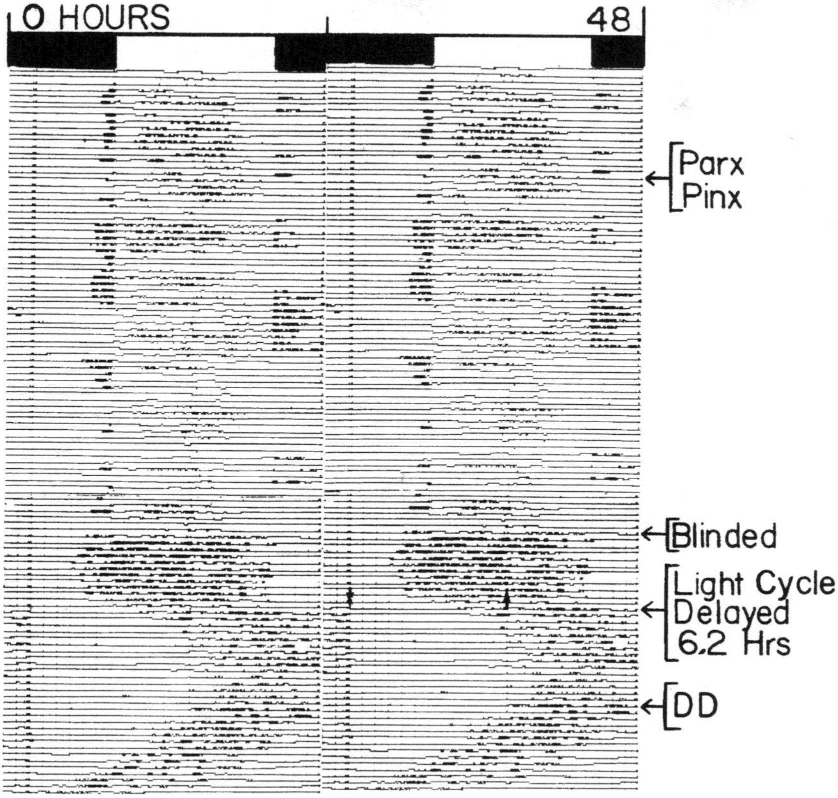

Fig. 39. Entrainment of *S. olivaceus* after removal of the parietal eye (*Parx*), pineal organ (*Pinx*), and lateral eyes (*Blinded*). The initial LD 12:12 fluorescent lighting regimen is diagrammed at the top of the record. To aid in interpretation the record is presented in duplicate, the right side displaced one day above the left. Each line, therefore, represents 2 days' recording (48 hours). Deflections of the line represent activity. *Light Cycle Delayed 6.2 Hrs* means the light cycle was shifted so that its onset (upward pointing arrow) now occurs 6.2 hours after the onset of the initial cycle.

sparrow's pineal organ does not abolish rhythmicity. Furthermore, birds rendered arrhythmic by pinealectomy in DD can be made immediately rhythmic by transplantation of a pineal organ into the anterior chamber of the eye. These studies indicate that the avian pineal is the site of a "master" oscillator that drives the overt rhythm of locomotor activity. Implanting melatonin into normal birds causes changes in free-running periods or arrhythmicity (Turek et al. 1976), suggesting that this is the hormone produced by the pineal which couples it to other elements of the circadian system.

Pinealectomy of lizards free-running under continuous illumination (LL) causes either a "splitting" of the activity rhythm into two circadian components, or arrhythmicity (Underwood 1977). Since lizard pineals are also capable of manufacturing melatonin, it may well be that melatonin released by the lizard pineal acts to couple circadian oscillators. In lizards, melatonin is manufactured and stored in the photoreceptive cells of the pineal organ, raising the possibility that light can directly control the release of melatonin from lizard pineals. However, autonomic nerves are seen in lizard pineals which may be similar to the autonomic nerves seen in bird and mammal pineals. In the bird and mammal, the pineal innervation is the end of a pathway which carries photic information to the pineal organ from the lateral eyes. In lizards, light, therefore, may at least potentially influence pineal secretory activity directly or via the retina.

Photoperiodic Photoreception

The role of ERRs in vertebrate photoperiodism was first demonstrated by Benoit (1935) in ducks. Benoit showed that ducks with either intact or sectioned optic nerves would respond to a long "stimulatory" day length by initiating testicular growth. Benoit localized the site of this extraretinal photoreception to the head, and subsequent experiments using light guides to discrete areas of the brain showed that illumination of the rhinencephalon, pituitary, or hypothalamus would elicit testicular growth (Benoit 1938, Benoit et al. 1950a, 1950b). Several kinds of experiments led Benoit to believe that both retinal and extraretinal photoreceptors were involved (Benoit 1938, Benoit et al. 1953, Benoit and Assenmacher 1954). Visible light in the orange-red region (617-740 nm) was most effective in stimulating testis growth in intact (unoperated) ducks (Benoit and Ott 1944, Benoit et al. 1950a). Presumably in these experiments, which used relatively high intensities of light, the orange-red light was stimulating both the extraretinal and the putative retinal receptors. Benoit attempted to define the action spectrum of the retinal receptors by exposing intact ducks to low intensities of monochromatic light (Benoit and Assenmacher 1966, Benoit et al. 1966). These experiments were based on the assumption that, at these low intensities, only the retinal receptors would be stimulated. Using this approach, Benoit demonstrated that visible light in the red region (625-647 nm) was most effective in stimulating testis growth. The putative receptors in the retina which mediated photoperiodism would then be separate from the receptors involved in normal vision since the visual receptors, as assayed by the pupillary reflex, were maximally sensitive to yellow light (Benoit et al. 1952).

Subsequent experiments demanded a reevaluation of the role of the eyes in photoperiodic photoreception. Benoit attempted to show a clear dissociation between the retinal and extraretinal receptors by exposing both intact ducks and ducks with sectioned optic nerves to low intensities of monochromatic light. In this experiment, testicular growth in the blind ducks exposed to low intensities (0.045-293 $ergs \cdot cm^{-2} \cdot sec^{-1}$) of monochromatic red light (634-638 nm and 650 nm) was as great as that seen in the intact ducks (Benoit 1970). A careful reconsideration of the published work of Benoit by McMillan et al. (1975) concludes that a retinal participation in photoperiodism in ducks has not been demonstrated. The reason for the greater efficacy of red light in stimulating testis growth was undoubtedly due to the fact that red light penetrates tissue more readily than visible light of shorter wavelengths and could thereby reach and stimulate the receptors located in the brain (Benoit et al. 1954a, 1954b).

The participation of ERRs in testicular responses in a second avian species, the house sparrow (*P. domesticus*) was demonstrated in 1968 (Menaker and Keatts 1968). A series of experiments utilizing the house sparrow showed, by several different experimental approaches, that the eyes were not involved in photoperiodic photoreception; ERRs located in the brain were fully capable of mediating this response (Underwood and Menaker 1970, Menaker et al. 1970, McMillan et al. 1975). An example of one of these experimental approaches is shown in Figure 40.

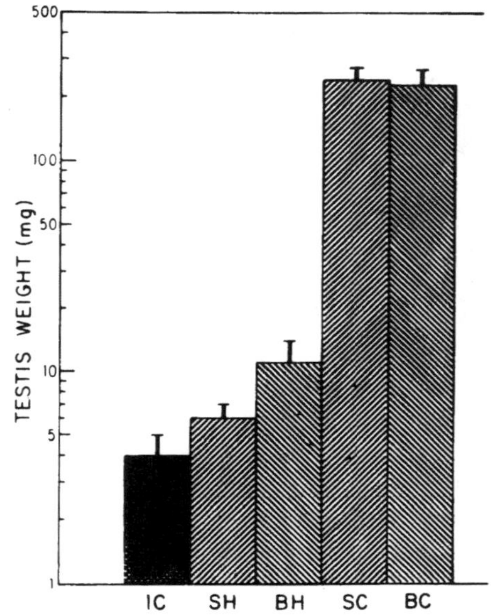

Fig. 40. The demonstration that the eyes are not involved in photoperiodic photoreception in house sparrows. Photosensitive house sparrows were divided into four groups. Feathers were clipped from the heads of both a blind (BC, blind-clipped) and a sighted (SC, sighted-clipped) group, while the heads were covered with an opaque hood in both a blind (BH, blind-hooded) and a sighted (SH, sighted-hooded) group. All four groups were exposed to LD 16:8 of red light (0.15 erg·cm^{-2}·sec, 600 nm-700 nm) for 24 days. Only birds in which the extraretinal receptor was exposed (blind-clipped and sighted-clipped) showed significant growth when compared with birds sacrificed at the beginning of the experiment (IC, initial controls). The hooded birds both blind *and sighted*, in which the brains were shielded from the red light, showed no significant testis growth. (Drawn from data in McMillan et al. 1975.)

The question of the participation of ERRs in other avian species has been pursued by several investigators within the last decade: e.g., in chickens (*Gallus* sp.)

(Harrison 1972); Japanese quail (*Coturnix coturnix japonica*) (Homma and Sakakibara 1971, Oishi and Lauber 1973a, 1973b); and white-crowned (*Zonotrichia leucophrys*) and golden-crowned sparrows (*Z. atricapilla*) (Gwinner et al. 1971, Turek 1975). No clear demonstration of a retinal involvement in the stimulation of gonadal recrudescence in birds has been shown. Birds that are blinded respond as well as intact birds to stimulatory photoperiods. The pineal organ is not necessarily involved since removal of the pineal organ in blinded birds does not impair photoperiodically-significant photoreception. In addition to the work of Benoit, other workers have attempted localization of ERRs. Homma and Sakakibara (1971) implanted orange- or blue-emitting radio-illuminescent discs in various areas of the brain of Japanese quail and obtained testicular growth when the discs were placed near the hypothalamus, optic lobes, or olfactory lobe. Within the basal hypothalamus, implants of radio-illuminescent pellets in the tuberal and dorsal part of the infundibular nuclear complex were effective in eliciting testicular growth in quail, whereas implants in the preoptic and anterior regions were ineffective (Oliver and Baylé 1976).

Although the initiation of testicular growth by long days is mediated extraretinally, the *termination* of sexual activity by short days in Japanese quail depends on their having experienced long days prior to blinding (Homma et al. 1972), suggesting that the eyes may contribute in some fashion to the control of gonadal regression. In the house sparrow, however, a role for the eyes in the control of gonadal regression has been eliminated (Underwood 1975a). A recent study by Yokoyama and Farner (1976) suggests that the eyes may actually suppress plasma levels of luteinizing hormone (LH) in female white-crowned sparrows. Stimulatory photoperiods elicited increases in plasma LH concentrations in both blinded and sighted white-crowned sparrows, but the LH levels in blinded birds were higher than those attained by intact birds.

Extraretinal receptors can mediate photoperiodic photoreception in other vertebrate classes as well. Among the reptiles, ERRs have been shown to mediate photoperiodic photoreception in the iguanid lizard (*Anolis carolinensis*) (Underwood 1975b). Figure 41 shows the testis weights of both blind and sighted anoles exposed to long (14-hour) or short (6-hour) photoperiods in the summer (Fig. 41A) and fall (Fig. 41B). In the summer experiment, long days maintained, and short days caused, testicular regression

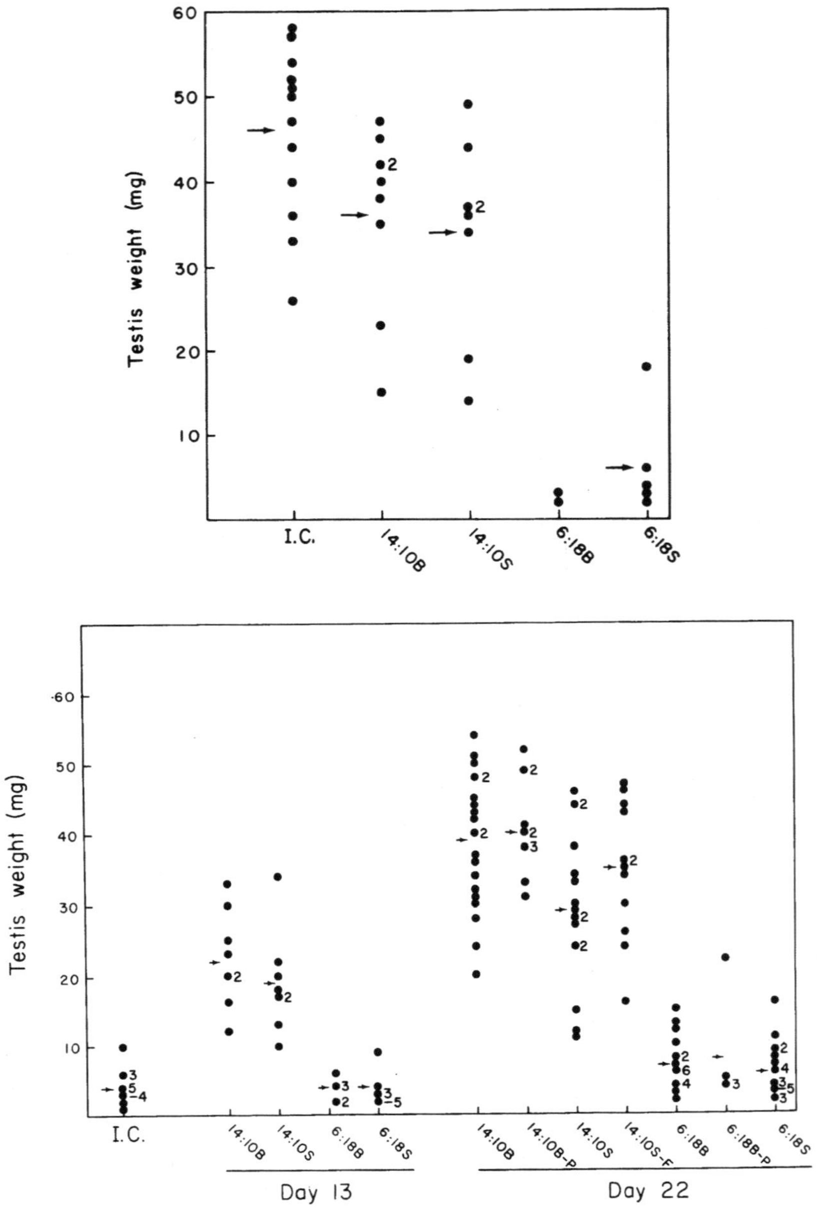

Fig. 41. Effects of long day (LD 14:10) and short day (LD 6:18) photoperiods on testis weights of blinded and sighted *A. carolinensis* in the summer (A) and fall (B). I.C.:

in both blind and sighted lizards. In the fall, long days stimulated testis growth in both blind, blind-parietalectomized, and sighted anoles. These data show that ERRs are fully capable of mediating gonadal responses in lizards but they are not sufficient to completely eliminate a retinal involvement. Blind-parietalectomized anoles responded as well as sighted anoles, showing that the photosensitive parietal eye is not necessarily involved.

In addition to the demonstration of ERRs in birds and reptiles there are a few studies which indicate that ERRs may also be involved in mediating gonadal responses in some fish species (Rasquin and Rosenbloom 1954, Urasaki 1973).

Pineal Biochemical Rhythms

The activities and/or concentrations of various pineal enzymes in higher vertebrates undergo marked daily fluctuations; consequently, the concentrations of biochemicals which are synthesized in the pineal also undergo daily fluctuations (Quay 1974). Some of these daily rhythms are truly circadian--that is, they persist under constant conditions. For example, the enzyme N-acetyltransferase, which is the rate-limiting enzyme in the conversion of tryptophan to melatonin (Fig. 38), undergoes a daily rhythm in activity which persists in DD. The concentration of melatonin in the pineal also shows a circadian rhythm (Quay 1974). On the other hand, a daily rhythm in the activity of the enzyme hydroxyindole-O-methyltransferase (HIOMT) is seen in light-dark cycles but not in DD. Fewer studies have been conducted on the pineals of lower vertebrates, but they also suggest that daily rhythms are present (Wolstenholme and Knight 1971).

In adult mammals, lighting information can reach the pineal only via the eyes. However, the neural pathways mediating the more "tonic" pineal responses to light, such as that of HIOMT activity, are, at least partially,

---

testis weights of lizards sacrificed at the beginning of each experiment; B (blind); B-P (blind-parietalectomized); S (sighted); S-F (sighted, fed *ad lib*). Sighted, fed *ad lib* lizards had food (live mealworms) continuously available; all other groups were hand-fed. The horizontal arrows indicate the means.

separate from the pathways mediating circadian rhythms. Tonic responses are mediated by a pathway involving the retina, the inferior accessory optic tract, the medial forebrain bundle, preganglionic fibers from the cervical spinal cord to the superior cervical ganglia, and post-ganglionic sympathetic fibers from the superior cervical ganglia to the pineal. Pineal circadian rhythms in mammals are driven by a clock or clocks located in the suprachiasmatic nuclei of the hypothalamus (Stephen and Zucker 1972, Stetson and Whatson-Whitmyre 1976, Moore and Eichler 1976). This clock is entrained by light acting via the retina and a direct retinohypothalamic pathway end communicates with the pineal via the superior cervical ganglia.

Hence, in adult mammals blinding abolishes the effects of light on pineal rhythms. In juvenile rats, however, an extraretinal receptor has been implicated in the control of the daily rhythms in pineal serotonin content and HIOMT activity. Machado et al. (1969a, 1969b) demonstrated that the rhythm in serotonin content persists in DD in intact juvenile rats but is abolished in DD after the sympathetic innervation has been interrupted by the administration of nerve growth factor antiserum or by superior cervical ganglionectomy. However, the serotonin rhythm persists *under LD cycles* after sympathetic innervation is abolished. The HIOMT rhythm also persists under LD cycles in blinded juvenile rats (Wetterberg et al. 1970a, 1970b). Wetterberg et al. (1970a, 1970b) suggest that the Harderian glând, a gland found within the orbit of many vertebrates, may be the extraretinal receptor involved, since its removal abolishes the effect of light on serotonin or HIOMT in blinded juvenile rats. If the Harderian gland is involved, however, it must influence the pineal via hormonal rather than neural routes. A direct photosensitivity of the juvenile rat pineal cannot be ruled out.

In chicks a similar situation is seen. Neither blinding nor sympathetic denervation of the pineal prevents a light-induced elevation of HIOMT activity (Lauber et al. 1968) (Fig. 42), suggesting a direct photosensitivity of the chick pineal. A daily rhythm in melatonin content in chick pineals and serum persists in blind birds exposed to light-dark cycles, and the pineal melatonin rhythm can be influenced by light even after nervous information to the pineal has been interrupted by superior cervical ganglionectomy (Ralph 1976). In addition, light can influence N-acetyltransferase activity in blind chicks (Binkley et al. 1975, Ralph et al. 1975). Also, duck pineals in organ

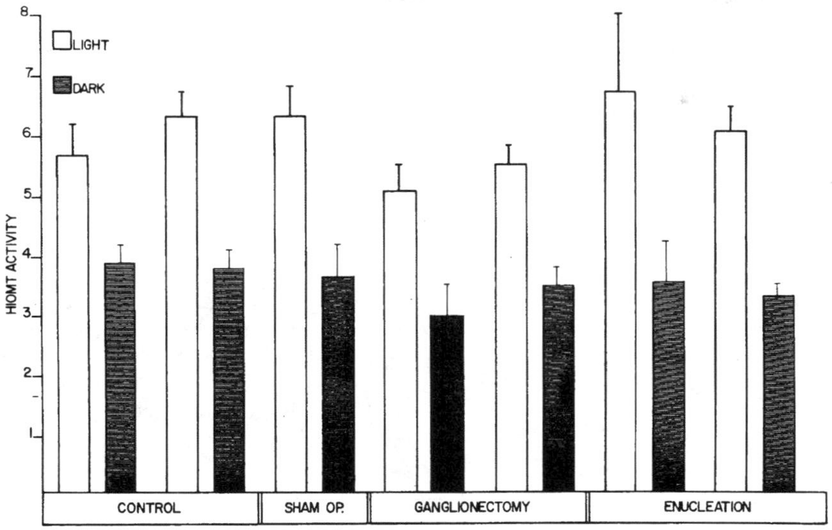

Fig. 42. HIOMT activity in the chick pineal under conditions of constant light or constant darkness and after several surgical procedures. (Redrawn from Lauber et al. 1968. *Science* 161:489-490. Copyright 1968 by the American Association for the Advancement of Science.)

culture maintained for twenty-four hours under continuous light showed significant increases in pineal indole metabolism and incorporation of ^{3}H-uridine by RNA over pineals cultured in DD (Rosner et al. 1971, 1972). Taken together, these studies strongly support a direct photosensitivity of the pineal organ in some birds.

Physiological Color Change

A discussion of the mechanisms of physiological color changes in vertebrates is beyond the scope of the present chapter, but there are a number of observations which show that extraretinal receptors can participate. The mechanism of color change involves concentration or dispersion of melanin granules in dermal chromatophores (Parker 1948). Physiological color changes are generally mediated by hormones and/or the nervous system. The participation of ERRs in the control of physiological color changes is shown by the fact that some blinded fish, amphibians, and reptiles are dark colored when exposed to illumination but become light colored when placed in darkness (von Frisch 1911, Wykes 1937, 1938, Bagnara and Hadley 1970, Kleinholz 1938, Parker 1948). However, many fish, amphibians, and reptiles fail to show any color changes in response to illumination after blinding.

Among lizards, the iguanid species *A. carolinensis* has been extensively utilized in attempts to elucidate the mechanisms of color change. Blinded anoles, when exposed to illumination, are brown but become pale green when placed in the dark, thereby demonstrating the existence of an ERR which can discriminate between conditions of illumination and darkness (Kleinholz 1938). However, blind lizards cannot adapt to the background. Those exposed to illumination on a white background remain dark.

The control of color changes in larval amphibians deserves consideration since the basic mechanisms and sites of photoreception have been more clearly established than those of other vertebrates. Many larval amphibians pass through several stages in the development of color control (Bagnara and Hadley 1970). Fairly early in development, larval amphibians respond to illumination by remaining dark (melanin granules dispersed) and blanch when placed in the dark (melanin granules concentrated). In this stage, the primary chromatic stage, the animals cannot adapt to background (turn pale when illuminated on a white background). In a later stage of larval life, the secondary chromatic stage, these amphibians gain the ability to adapt to the background. In both the primary and secondary stages, blinded animals blanch when placed in the dark. The primary response in *Xenopus* tadpoles may be mediated by the pineal (Bagnara and Hadley 1970). Darkness stimulates the pineal, which is known to be photosensitive, to release melatonin which acts to inhibit the action of melanocyte-stimulating hormone (MSH) at the level of the dermal melanocyte, causing a concentration of melanin granules, and the animal pales. Light inhibits melatonin release by the pineal so the melanophores expand under conditions of illumination. The ability to adapt to background is apparently mediated by the pituitary and does not involve the pineal. The eyes are necessary for the secondary response and presumably mediate the response by inhibition of MSH release by the pituitary. Removal of the eyes tends to make the animals act as if they were in the primary stage.

In adult amphibians, however, the blanching effect is apparently not mediated by the pineal (Bagnara and Hadley 1970). Melatonin does not have much blanching effect in adult frogs. The loss of sensitivity of melanophores to melatonin in adult amphibians appears to be a developmental phenomenon and coincides with the changes from a pineal to a retinal control of melanophore responses. Blinded adult amphibians can still show a slight, but consistent, blanching when placed in darkness (Parker 1948).

Light stimulation of the epithalamus of the blinded minnow (*Phoxinus laevis*) causes expansion of melanophores, and darkness results in melanophore contraction (von Frisch 1911). Removal of the pineal organ does not interfere with the response. Von Frisch suggests that the response in eyeless *Phoxinus* is mediated by photochemical processes in the brain tissue. Eyeless catfish (*Amiurus nebulosus*) show a similar response, which is also unaffected by pinealectomy (Wykes 1938). A melanophore response has also been observed in at least four other species of blinded teleost fish (Wykes 1937). The color changes of larval and adult lampreys (*Lampetra planeri*) show pronounced daily rhythms that persist in DD (Young 1935b). Larval *L. planeri* cannot respond to daily light cycles after removal of the pineal complex (pineal and parapineal). In the adult, however, pinealectomy fails to abolish the response while removal of the eyes abolishes the color response to LD cycles.

Several general conclusions may be drawn regarding the sites of the photoreceptors responsible for mediating physiological color changes in vertebrates: (1) In some vertebrates the eyes are the only route by which light influences color changes, since some animals do not show any color response to illumination after blinding. In others the eyes are involved in adaptation to background but not in the primary chromatic response. (2) In some animals the pineal is involved in the control of color changes and in some cases (e.g., larval amphibians) it seems to serve both a photoreceptive and a secretory function. (3) In other vertebrates (e.g., minnows) neither blinding nor pinealectomy inhibits melanophore responses to illumination or darkness although blinding or pinealectomy may depress the amplitude of the response. In these cases light sensitivity of the skin or of the brain has been suggested.

Phototaxis and Photokinesis

Light stimuli frequently elicit an orienting response in a free-moving animal. The response is said to be a "kinesis" if the direction of locomotion bears no relation to the direction of the stimulus and a "taxis" if the locomotion is oriented either toward (positive phototaxis) or away from (negative phototaxis) the light source (Steven 1963). A number of investigators have shown that extraretinal photoreceptors are involved in these responses in some vertebrates.

Among the lower vertebrates, several investigators have demonstrated that the photokinesis exhibited by normal lamprey larvae and adults is still present after blinding (Parker 1905, Young 1935a, 1935b). The tails of the lampreys *Lampetra planeri* and *L. fluviatilis* are most sensitive to illumination, the head region is less sensitive, and the midbody region the least sensitive (Young 1935a). The sensitivity in the tail region is centered around the lateral line nerves, whereas selective illumination of the head after removal of the eyes, pineal, and parapineal organ still elicits a response (Young 1935b). The spinal cord was also implicated as a light-sensitive area.

A number of freshwater fish appear to be photosensitive after blinding but a similar photosensitivity is almost entirely absent in marine fish (Parker 1909, de la Motte 1963, 1964). Exceptions to the lack of photosensitivity among marine fish are seen in the grouper (*Epinephelus striatus*) (Jordan 1917) and the hagfish (*Myxine glutinosa*) (Newth and Ross 1955). The negative phototaxis exhibited by a normal grouper is also shown by a blinded fish. The head region is most sensitive, followed by the tail region, with the midbody area being the least sensitive in both normal and blinded groupers. However, the reaction time of blinded fish is longer than that of normal fish. Jordan (1917) believes that the integument of these fish is photosensitive. An extensive investigation by Newth and Ross (1955) on the locomotor activity response of the hagfish to localized illumination showed that both the head and the tail regions were responsive to light. Newth and Ross also transected the spinal cords of hagfish and showed that in transectomized hagfish, if the head is illuminated, only that part of the animal anterior to the cut responds; if the caudal region is illuminated, only that part of the animal posterior to the cut responds. They also showed that removal of the skin from the tail eliminated the reaction to selective illumination. Scharrer (1928) trained the teleostean fish *Phoxinus* to give feeding reactions to localized illumination of the brain after blinding and removal of the pineal organ. Localized illumination of other areas of the body was ineffective in producing a reaction. According to Hoar (1955) the phototactic response of the sockeye salmon smolt is dependent upon both the eyes and the pineal organ.

In at least a dozen species of anuran and urodelian amphibians, including both aquatic and terrestrial forms, illumination will elicit a phototaxic response even after removal of the eyes (Parker 1903, Pearse 1910, Adler 1976). The type of phototaxis, either negative or positive, shown by a particular species before blinding was the same as that shown after blinding although the reaction of blinded animals was often slower. These workers suggested that photoreceptors located in the skin mediate the responses of blinded amphibians. Selective illumination of the eyes also caused phototaxic responses indicating that retinal pathways may also be involved. Obreshkove (1921) showed that tadpoles of *Rana clamitans* gave a locomotor response to illumination and the latency in reaction time obeyed the Bunsen-Roscoe Reciprocity Law between 0.3 and 20 lux. The reaction times of blinded tadpoles was identical to that of sighted tadpoles. Ross (1959) showed that, after blinding, both the head and tail of *Ichthyophis glutinosus* (Apoda) are sensitive to localized illumination. The effect of spinal section was similar to that of the hagfish described above; the animals gave responses to light independently in front of and behind the cut.

Among the higher vertebrates, behavioral responses to light have been seen in several species of embryonic or neonatal birds (Heaton and Harth 1974). Shining a light on a neonatal pigeon (*Columba livia*) elicits a stereotyped short latency response: the pigeon raises and moves its head and often shows wing flutterings and leg extensions. The response to light was seen in neonates as well as embryos. In pigeons the response could be blocked by placing an opaque cape over the entire body, except the head, suggesting some form of dermal sensitivity (Fig. 43). However, the responsiveness of chick embryos or ring doves (*Streptopelia risoria*) depends on light reaching the head, suggesting that these two species use either visual or direct brain photoreception.

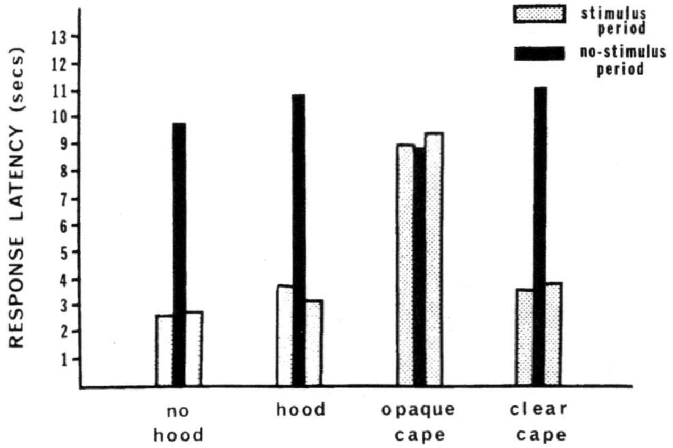

Fig. 43. Latency of overt movements following onset of photic stimulation (stimulus period) compared with latency of spontaneously occurring movements (no stimulus period) in pigeon hatchlings during four experimental conditions (Heaton and Harth 1974).

Threshold light intensities required to elicit a phototaxic or photokinetic response to white light in normal or blinded vertebrates are low. Table 6 lists threshold values for several different species of lower vertebrates.

Action spectra are difficult to obtain for phototaxic and photokinetic responses, due to individual variability and the fact that the locations of photoreceptors are unknown, making it impossible to correct for absorption of light by overlying tissue (if any). However, studies indicate that the maximum sensitivities are generally between 470 and 540 nm, which fall within the limits of the absorption maxima of many visual pigments, and the shapes of the curves are similar to the spectral sensitivity curves obtained from many types of eyes (Steven 1950, 1963, de la Motte 1963, 1964).

These studies clearly indicate the involvement of ERRs in the phototaxic and photokinetic responses of some species of cyclostomes, fish, amphibians, and neonatal birds. The central nervous system has been implicated in some studies as the site of extraretinal photoreception; in others, a light sensitivity of the skin has been

Table 6

Threshold Light Intensities for Phototaxic or Photokinetic Responses

Species	Dark-Adapted Threshold (lux)	Reference
Lampetra planeri	2.7-10.7	Steven (1950)
L. planeri	5.4	Jones (1955)
Phoxinus laevis	< 0.017	Scharrer (1928)
P. laevis	0.0034-0.024	Jones (1956)
Rana clamitans	0.3	Obreshkove (1921)
R. pipiens	1.0	Parker (1903)

suggested. This last suggestion has recently received impetus from the fact that an intense flash of light can elicit electrical responses from isolated skin (Becker and Cone 1966). This light-evoked response was observed in every animal investigated (black mollie, axolotl, frog, rat, and guinea pig) and in both pigmented and albino animals.

Orientation

There is ample evidence of compass orientation in amphibians, that is, the ability to steer in a given direction without the use of landmarks. Compass orientation involves the use of celestial cues and requires the use of an internal biological clock to compensate for the earth's rotation with respect to such cues. The participation of ERRs in compass orientation has been demonstrated in several species of amphibians (Landreth and Ferguson 1967, Taylor and Ferguson 1970, Taylor 1972, Adler and Taylor 1973, Justis and Taylor 1976). Taylor and Ferguson (1970) showed that the cricket frog (*Acris gryllus*) could orient in a predicted direction to the sun even if the eyes were removed (Fig. 44). Covering the skull with opaque plastic abolished orientation in blinded, but not in sighted, frogs. Furthermore, exposing frogs to an artificial LD cycle that was advanced six hours relative to the natural LD cycle caused a 90° counterclockwise shift in orientation outdoors. This shift was observed in blinded frogs as well as in sighted frogs with an opaque skull cap but not in blinded frogs with an opaque skull cap (Fig. 44). Similar kinds of experiments with the tiger salamander (*Ambystoma tigrinum*) yielded the same result (Taylor 1972). Eyeless animals could orient but eyeless animals with an opaque shield on the head could not.

Justis and Taylor (1976) determined the orientational abilities of bullfrog tadpoles (*Rana catesbeiana*) after

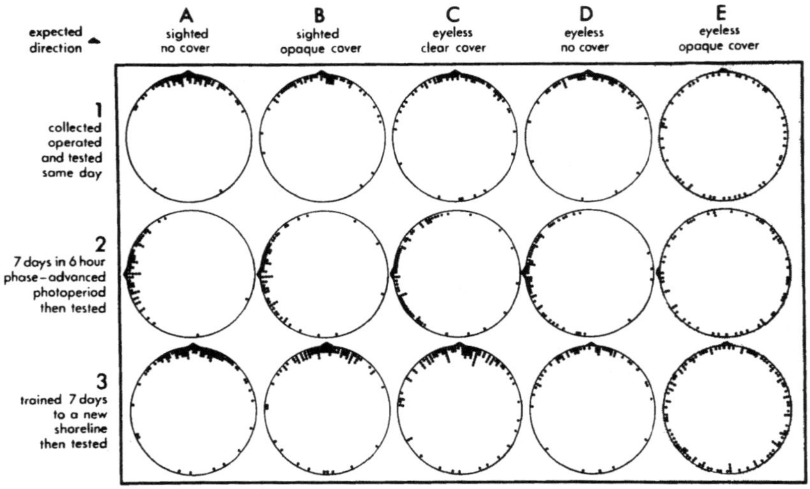

Fig. 44. Directional responses of cricket frogs in outdoor tests. Arrowheads point to expected direction and black dots represent positions of individual frogs at the edge of a circular arena. Note that only frogs which were blinded and had opaque covers on the heads failed to orient (Adler 1976).

various surgical manipulations. These workers showed that predictable orientation responses could be observed in blinded tadpoles, blinded-frontalectomized tadpoles, or blinded-pinealectomized tadpoles. However, if the eyes, frontal organ, and pineal organ were all removed, orientation responses were abolished. Interesting differences were noted in some of the groups with respect to the direction of orientation. For example, eyeless premetamorphic tadpoles shifted their orientation direction 180° from the direction to which they had previously oriented as intact tadpoles. However, eyeless-pinealectomized tadpoles with the frontal organ intact oriented in the same direction as sighted animals. The reasons for these differences are unknown.

The tiger salamander (*A. tigrinum*) can perceive linearly polarized light and use it for purposes of orientation (Adler and Taylor 1973). Salamanders were trained to move to shore along an axis perpendicular to the transmission axis of a linearly polarized filter. Subsequently, they were tested in a circular arena and moved in predictable directions to the polarized light stimuli even when blinded. However, insertion of an opaque shield under the skin of the head abolished orientation even in sighted animals. Adler and Taylor (1973) suggested that the pineal organ is the ERR involved.

Photoreception in Adult Mammals

As discussed previously, extraretinal photoreceptors have been implicated in the control of biochemical rhythms in the pineal organ of juvenile rats (Zweig et al. 1966, Machado et al. 1969a, 1969b, Wetterberg et al. 1970a, 1970b). In adult mammals, however, the eyes are the only photoreceptors involved in the perception of entraining light cycles (Hunt and Schlosberg 1939, Browman 1943, Halberg et al. 1954, Bruss et al. 1958, Richter 1968, Snyder et al. 1965). Of great interest to the present discussion is the possibility that the actual photoreceptors within the eye which are involved in nonvisual light responses may not be the rod or cone receptors which are involved in vision. Albino rats, for example, still retain the ability to discriminate between light and dark and even to discriminate between black and white patterns after their rod photoreceptors have been destroyed by exposure to continuous illumination (Anderson and O'Steen 1972, Bennett et al. 1972). Light can still affect pineal enzyme activities and reproductive states of albino rats which have been visually "blinded" by continuous light exposure (Reiter 1973, Reiter and Klein 1971). Plasma corticosterone levels show circadian variations that can be entrained by light cycles even after exposure to high intensities of LL has destroyed the outer segment, inner segment, and outer nuclear layer of the retina (Dunn et al. 1972). These results suggest that light-sensitive cells, separate from the rods and cones, are present in the retina and can influence both circadian and noncircadian functions. The inferior accessory optic tracts and the direct retinohypothalamic tracts may be routes by which these cells influence pineal activities and entrainment of the biological clock.

Several workers have attempted to determine the nature of the photopigments that (1) mediate photic entrainment of circadian rhythms in adult rats or (2) mediate tonic effects of light on pineal HIOMT activities (Cardinali et al. 1972, McGuire et al. 1973). McGuire et al. (1973) determined the ability of cycles of light of different intensities and color to entrain the circadian body temperature rhythm in rats (Fig. 45). Each experiment consisted of a 7 to 10-day control period during which the animals were entrained to a fluorescent LD 12:12 light cycle, followed by a 14-day experimental period during which a test light cycle was introduced concurrent with a 6-hour phase shift in the lighting regimen. Entrainment to the test cycle was scored as the fraction of animals in each group whose temperature rhythms became entrained. A 50% response dose was estimated from each spectrum studied and is shown in Figure 45 along with the relative spectral sensitivity of rat rhodopsin. Green light (530 nm-545 nm) was most potent as an entraining stimulus; the results are consistent with the hypothesis that rhodopsin mediates the entrainment response.

Cardinali et al. (1972) also determined the magnitude of inhibition of pineal HIOMT activity by light spectra. Groups of rats were housed under one of seven light sources for 96 hours; each group was exposed to the same intensity of irradiation (Fig. 46). Activity of the enzyme was lowest in rats maintained under green light (530 nm), and the results suggest that rhodopsin or another compound with similar absorption properties is involved.

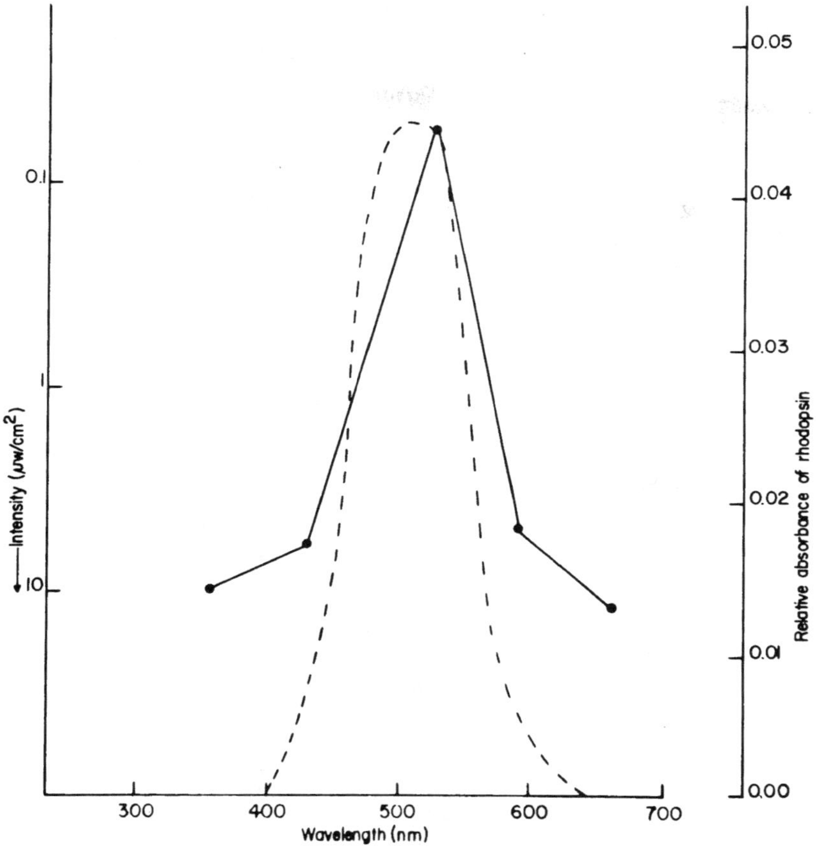

Fig. 45. Action spectrum for entrainment of the body temperature rhythm in rats (solid line). The broken line shows the relative sensitivity of rat rhodopsin. (Redrawn from McGuire et al. 1973. *Science* 181:956-957. Copyright 1973 by the American Association for the Advancement of Science.)

Despite data suggesting that certain responses to light (e.g., circadian rhythms, pineal enzyme activity) occur in the absence of classical rod photoreceptors, the data indicate that the photopigment involved is rhodopsin or a similar compound.

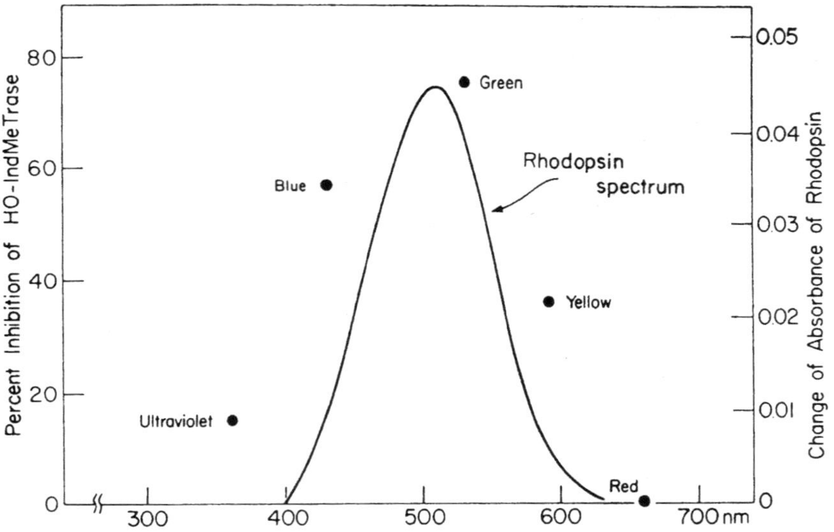

Fig. 46. Action spectrum for photic suppression of pineal HIOMT activity compared with absorption spectrum for rhodopsin. (Redrawn from Cardinali et al. 1972.)

CONCLUSION

Extraretinal photoreceptors mediating a host of different kinds of light-dependent responses have been demonstrated in both vertebrates and invertebrates. It is likely that many extraretinal receptors evolved before the evolution of the lateral eyes of vertebrates or the compound eyes or ocelli of insects. This seems more probable than the alternative hypothesis, that ERRs evolved after organisms already had a perfectly good photoreceptor available to them in the form of the lateral eyes or the compound eyes. The persistence of ERRs in those organisms which have evolved eyes must mean that there is a strong selective advantage to be gained from extracting information from the photic environment by routes that do not necessarily involve the eyes. Once the eyes had evolved they may or may not have been integrated into the photosensory mechanisms already available to the organism. Interestingly, adult mammals possess only a retinal photosensitivity, although the exact photoreceptors within the retina which mediate some responses (such as entrainment of the biological clock or pineal enzyme activities) may be different from those involved in form vision. The reason for the shift in photoreceptive sites from those seen in nonmammalian vertebrates is not certain, but the larger size of mammals, and the thicker skulls and other overlying tissue, may have decreased light penetration to the mammalian brain below critical levels. Mammals may have circumvented this problem by shifting all photoreception to the eye.

In many nonmammalian vertebrates the brain has been identified as the site of extraretinal photoreceptors mediating certain responses. Although it is not known exactly which areas of the brain are involved in many cases, a variety of observations have implicated the hypothalamus as a site of extraretinal photoreception: (1) Benoit et al. (1950a, 1950b), Homma and Sakakibara (1971), and Oliver and Baylé (1976) have elicited photoperiodic responses by localized illumination of the hypothalamus. (2) The diencephalon is also the site of origin of the only other known light-sensitive structures in vertebrates (pineal system and lateral eyes). (3) The hypothalamus is intimately involved in the control of many of the neuroendocrine functions of organisms. And (4) a circadian pacemaker may be located in the suprachiasmatic nuclei of the hypothalamus.

The only light-sensitive structure other than the lateral eyes which has been definitely identified in vertebrates is the pineal system. The pineal system has been implicated as a photoreceptor mediating, at least partly, several kinds of responses, including entrainment and orientation in amphibians, physiological color changes, pineal enzyme activities, and some phototaxic and photokinetic responses. Direct photoreception by the pineal organs of lower vertebrates could, potentially, elicit either hormonal or neural outputs from the pineal. The blanching response in amphibians is an example of the former and orientation to plane-polarized light in amphibians may be an example of the latter. However, participation of pineal systems in photic responses can be complex. The pineal is not only directly photosensitive in lower vertebrates and possibly in juvenile birds and mammals, but the presence of autonomic innervation to the pineal organ in lower vertebrates raises the possibility that extrapineal photoreceptors (such as ERRs in the brain, or the retina) can influence pineal activity. In addition, in some vertebrates there may be mutual interaction between the two components of the pineal system, such as the parietal eye and the pineal of lizards. The frontal organs of amphibians and the parietal eye of lizards can give chromatic responses to light, implying that some extraretinally mediated responses require knowledge of the color as well as the duration and intensity of light. The demonstration of pineal and frontal organ involvement in orientation to celestial cues in amphibians shows that these organs are also capable of determining the direction of incoming light stimuli.

It is clear that many different kinds of ERRs are present in vertebrates and more than one kind of ERR can exist in the same organism. For example, in lizards there are one or more extraretinal receptors located in the brain which are involved in photoperiodic photoreception and entrainment of the biological clock. Whether these two responses are mediated by the same ERR is, at present, unknown. Neither the pineal organ nor the parietal eye is necessarily involved as a photoreceptor in these two responses, but they may be alternate routes of photoreception. The demonstration by neurophysiological means of electrical responses to illumination in the parietal eye and pineal organ of lizards and the presence of afferent nerves leaving these organs show that photic information can be neurally transmitted to the brain. Photic input to the eyes may also modulate pineal activity. The fact that the pineal organ in lizards is part of the time-keeping machinery and the demonstration that melatonin implants mimic some effects of pinealectomy on circadian rhythmicity (at least in birds) suggests that light may affect pineal-dependent circadian rhythmicity by affecting the release of hormones (such as melatonin) from pineal photoreceptive cells. Even in a single organism, such as a lizard, light undoubtedly has multiple inputs and multiple effects.

Spectral sensitivity studies have been most fruitful in elucidating the nature of extraretinal photopigments in insects. In more advanced insects, entrainment of circadian rhythms is accomplished solely by ERRs, and action spectra have shown that the photopigments involved are different from those present in the insects' eyes. The persistence of light-dependent phase shifts in the eclosion rhythm of carotenoid-depleted flies raises the intriguing possibility that the photopigment involved is different from the other known photopigments. Photoperiodic photoreception in insects is entirely mediated by ERRs; and action spectra show that, in the majority of insects, ERRs are mainly sensitive to blue-green light. In advanced insects the receptors involved in entrainment and those mediating photoperiodic photoreception are located in the cerebral lobe area of the brain; however, there is no conclusive evidence that they are identical.

In vertebrates, spectral sensitivity studies on extrapineal ERRs are virtually nonexistent. In fact, such studies would probably not be fruitful until more is known about the exact location of the ERRs. The lack of knowledge about location makes it impossible to correct for the filtering effects of overlying tissue and any action spectra generated would be distorted.

The threshold sensitivities of ERRs in both insects and vertebrates are very low. Threshold sensitivities for achromatic responses from vertebrate pineal systems in intact animals (taking into account the opacity of overlying tissue) are similar to the sensitivities of some other brain ERRs, such as the nonpineal brain receptors mediating entrainment (0.05-0.1 lux in intact animals). This comparison shows that nonspecialized neural tissue can be as sensitive to light as the more specialized receptors seen in vertebrate pineal systems.

Extraretinal photoreception is practically ubiquitous in the animal kingdom. Any attempts to define a response to light, whether it is an action spectrum, a phototaxic response, or even an enzyme activity, must take into account the possibility that it may be influenced by more than one kind of photoreceptor. Investigations of ERRs have revealed the obvious and, in many cases, overriding importance of these receptors in mediating major physiological responses to light. The stage is set for rapid advances in our understanding of the anatomical locations, the neural and hormonal outputs, and the functional and phylogenetic interrelationships of these photoreceptors.

ACKNOWLEDGMENTS

Part of the work described in this chapter was supported by NSF grant PCM76-06842.

REFERENCES

Adler, K. 1971. Pineal end organ: Role in extraoptic entrainment of circadian locomotor rhythm in frogs. In *Biochronometry*, M. Menaker (ed.). Washington, D.C.: Nat. Acad. Sci., pp. 342-350.

Adler, K. 1976. Extraocular photoreception in amphibians. *Photochem. Photobiol.* 23:275-298.

Adler, K., and Taylor, D. H. 1973. Extraocular perception of polarized light by orienting salamanders. *J. Comp. Physiol.* 97:203-212.

Anderson, K. V., and O'Steen, W. K. 1972. Black-white and pattern discrimination in rats without photoreceptors. *Exp. Neurol.* 34:446-454.

Ariëns-Kappers, J. 1965. Survey of the innervation of the epiphysis cerebri and the accessory pineal organs in vertebrates. *Progr. Brain Res.* 10:87-153.

Bagnara, J. T., and Hadley, M. E. 1970. Endocrinology of the amphibian pineal. *Amer. Zoologist* 10:201-216.

Becker, H. E., and Cone, R. A. 1966. Light-stimulated electrical responses from skin. *Science* 154:1051-1053.

Bennett, M. H.; Dyer, R. F.; and Dunn, J. D. 1972. Light-induced retinal degeneration: effect upon light-dark discrimination. *Exp. Neurol.* 34:434-445.

Benoit, J. 1935. Stimulation par la lumière artificielle du développement testiculaire chez des canards aveugles par section du nerf optique. *C. R. Soc. Biol.* (Paris) 120:133-136.

Benoit, J. 1938. Rôle des yeux et de la voie nerveuse oculo-hypophysaire dans la gonadostimulation par la lumière artificielle chez le canard domestique. *C. R. Soc. Biol.* (Paris) 129:231-234.

Benoit, J. 1970. Étude de l'action des radiations visibles sur la gonadostimulation et de leur pénétration intracranienne chez les oiseaux et les mammifères. In *La photorégulation de la reproduction chez les oiseaux et les mammifères*, J. Benoit and I. Assenmacher (eds.). *Coll. Int. C.N.R.S.*, No. 172, Paris. pp. 121-146.

Benoit, J., and Assenmacher, I. 1954. Sensibilité comparée des récepteurs superficiels et profonds dans le réflexe opto-sexual chez le canard. *C. R. Acad. Sci.* (Paris) 239:105-107.

Benoit, J., and Assenmacher, I. 1966. Recherches sur la photosensibilité des récepteurs nerveux superficiels et profonds dans la gonadostimulation par les radiations visibles chez le Canard Pékin impubère. *C. R. Acad. Sci.* (Paris) 262:2750-2752.

Benoit, J.; Assenmacher, I.; DeLage, C.; Muel, B.; and Kordon, C. 1966. Réflexe photosexuel du canard mâle et sensibilité de la rétine à différentes radiations rouges monochromatiques. *J. Physiol.* (Paris) 58:463-464.

Benoit, J.; Assenmacher, I.; and Walter, F. X. 1952. Différences de sensibilité de la rétine du canard aux radiations colorées dans le réflexe pupillaire et dans le réflexe optosexuel. *C. R. Soc. Biol.* (Paris) 146:1027-1030.

Benoit, J.; Assenmacher, I.; and Walter, F. X. 1953. Dissociation expérimentale des rôles des récepteurs superficiels et profonds dans la gonadostimulation hypophysaire par la lumière chez le canard. *C. R. Soc. Biol.* (Paris) 147:186-191.

Benoit, J., and Ott, L. 1944. External and internal factors in sexual activity. Effect of irradiation with different wave lengths on the mechanisms of photostimulation of the hypophysis and on testicular growth in the immature duck. *Yale J. Biol. Med.* 17:22-46.

Benoit, J.; Tauc, L.; and Assenmacher, I. 1954a. Mesure photoélectrique de la pénétration transorbitaire des radiations visibles jusqu'au cerveau, chez le canard domestique. *C. R. Acad. Sci.* (Paris) 239:451-453.

Benoit, J.; Tauc, L.; and Assenmacher, I. 1954b. Nouveaux résultats de mesure photoélectrique de la pénétration de radiations lumineuses visibles jusqu'au cerveau, par le côté et le sommet de la tête, chez des canards blancs et pigmentés. *C. R. Acad. Sci.* (Paris) 239:508-510.

Benoit, J.; Walter, F. X.; and Assenmacher, I. 1950a. I. Nouvelles recherches relatives à l'action de lumières de différentes longueurs d'onde sur la gonadostimulation du canard mâle impubère. *C. R. Soc. Biol.* (Paris) 144: 1206-1213.

Benoit, J.; Walter, F. X.; and Assenmacher I. 1950b. I. Contribution à l'étude du réflexe optohypophysaire.

Gonadostimulation chez le canard soumis à des radiations lumineuses de diverses longueurs d'onde. *J. Physiol.* (Paris) 42:537-541.

Binkley, S.; MacBride, S. E.; Klein, D. C.; and Ralph, C. L. 1975. Regulation of pineal rhythms in chickens: refractory period and nonvisual light perception. *Endocrinology* 96:848-853.

Browman, L. G. 1943. The effect of bilateral optic enucleation upon the activity rhythms of the albino rat. *J. Comp. Psychol.* 36:33-46.

Bruce, V. G., and Minis, D. H. 1969. Circadian clock action spectrum in a photoperiodic moth. *Science* 163:583-585.

Bruss, R. T.; Jacobson, R.; Halberg, F.; Zander, H. A.; and Bittner, J. J. 1958. Effects of lighting regimen and blinding upon gross motor activity of mice. *Fed. Proc.* 17:21.

Cardinali, D. P.; Larin, F.; and Wurtman, R. J. 1972. Control of the rat pineal gland by light spectra. *Proc. Nat. Acad. Sci. U.S.* 69:2003-2005.

Claret, J. 1966a. Recherche du centre photorécepteur lors de l'induction de la diapause chez *Pieris brassicae*. *C. R. Acad. Sci.* (Paris) 262:1464-1465.

Claret, J. 1966b. Mise en évidence du rôle photorécepteur du cerveau dans l'induction de la diapause chez *Pieris brassicae*. *Annls. Endocr.* 27:311-320.

de la Motte, I. 1963. Untersuchungen zur vergleichende Physiologie der Lichtempfindlichkeit geblendeter Fische. *Naturwissenchaften* 50:363.

de la Motte, I. 1964. Untersuchungen zur vergleichende Physiologie der Lichtempfindlichkeit geblendeter Fische. *Z. Vergl. Physiol.* 49:58-90.

Dodt, E. 1963. Photosensitivity of the pineal organ in the teleost, *Salmo irideus* (Gibbons). *Experientia* 19:642-643.

Dodt, E., and Heerd, E. 1962. Mode of action of pineal nerve fibers in frogs. *J. Neurophysiol.* 25:405-429.

Dodt, E., and Jacobson, M. 1963. Photosensitivity of a localized region of the frog diencephalon. *J. Neurophysiol.* 26:752-759.

Dodt, E., and Scherer, E. 1968. The electroretinogram of the third eye. In *Advances in Electrophysiology and Pathology of the Visual System*, 6th ISCERG Symposium. Leipzig: VEB G. Thieme, p. 231.

Dumortier, B. 1972. Photoreception in the circadian rhythm of stridulatory activity in *Ephippiger* (Ins., Orthoptera). *J. Comp. Physiol.* 77:80-112.

Dunn, J.; Dyer, R.; and Bennett, M. 1972. Diurnal variation in plasma corticosterone following long-term exposure to continuous illumination. *Endocrinology* 90:1660-1663.

Engbretson, G. A., and Lent, C. M. 1976. Parietal eye of the lizard: Neuronal photoresponses and feedback from the pineal gland. *Proc. Nat. Acad. Sci. U.S.* 73:654-757.

Engelmann, W., and Honegger, H. W. 1966. Tagesperiodischer Schlüpfrhythmik einer augenlosen *Drosophila melanogaster* Mutante. *Z. Naturforsch.* 22B:1-2.

Eriksson, L. O. 1972. Tagesperiodik geblendeter Bachsaiblinge. *Naturwissenschaften* 59:219-220.

Gaston, S., and Menaker, M. 1968. Pineal function: the biological clock in the sparrow? *Science* 160:1125-1127.

Gwinner, E. G.; Turek, F. W.; and Smith, S. D. 1971. Extraocular light perception in photoperiodic responses of the White-crowned Sparrow (*Zonotrichia leucophrys*) and of the Golden-crowned Sparrow (*Z. atricapilla*). *Z. Vergl. Physiol.* 75:323-331.

Harrison, P. C. 1972. Extraretinal photocontrol of reproductive responses of Leghorn Hens to photoperiods of different length and spectrum. *Poultry Sci.* 51:2060-2064.

Halberg, F.; Visscher, M. B.; and Bittner, J. J. 1954. Relation of visual factors to eosinophil rhythm in mice. *Amer. J. Physiol.* 179:229-235.

Hamasaki, D. I. 1969. Spectral sensitivity of the parietal eye of the green iguana. *Vision Res.* 9:515-523.

Hamasaki, D. I., and Dodt, E. 1969. Light sensitivity of the lizard's epiphysis cerebri. *Pflügers Arch.* 313:19–29.

Hamasaki, D. I., and Streck, P. 1971. Properties of the epiphysis cerebri of the small-spotted dogfish shark, *Scyliorhinus caniculus, L. Vision Res.* 11:189–198.

Heaton, M. B., and Harth, M. S. 1974. Non-visual light responsiveness in the pigeon: developmental and comparative considerations. *J. Exp. Zool.* 188:251–264.

Hoar, W. S. 1955. Phototactic and pigmentary responses of the sockeye salmon smolts following injury to the pineal organ. *J. Fish. Res. Board. Can.* 12:178–185.

Homma, K., and Sakakibara, Y. 1971. Encephalic photoreceptors and their significance in photoperiodic control of sexual activity in Japanese quail. In *Biochronometry*, M. Menaker (ed.). Washington, D.C.: Nat. Acad. Sci., pp. 333–341.

Homma, K.; Wilson, W. O.; and Siopes, F. D. 1972. Eyes have a role in photoperiodic control of sexual activity of *Coturnix. Science* 178:421–423.

Hunt, J. M., and Schlosberg, H. 1939. The influence of illumination upon general activity in normal, blinded, and castrated male white rats. *J. Comp. Psychol.* 28: 285–298.

Jones, F. R. H. 1955. Photo-kinesis in the ammocoete larva of the brook lamprey. *J. Exp. Biol.* 32:492–503.

Jones, F. R. H. 1956. The behaviour of minnows in relation to light intensity. *J. Exp. Biol.* 33:271–281.

Jordan, H. 1917. Integumentary photosensitivity in a marine fish, *Epinephelus striatus* Bloch. *Amer. J. Physiol.* 44: 259–274.

Justis, C. S., and Taylor, D. H. 1976. Extraocular photoreception and compass orientation in larval bullfrogs, *Rana catesbeiana. Copeia* 1976:98–105.

Kelly, D. E. 1962. Pineal organs: photoreception, secretion and development. *Amer. Sci.* 50:597–625.

Kleinholz, L. H. 1938. Studies in reptilian color changes. II. The pituitary and adrenal glands in the regulation of the melanophores of *Anolis carolinensis*. *J. Exp. Biol.* 15:474-491.

Landreth, H. F., and Ferguson, D. E. 1967. Newts: sun-compass orientation. *Science* 158:1459-1461.

Lauber, J. K.; Body, J. E.; and Axelrod, J. 1968. Enzymatic synthesis of melatonin in avian pineal body: extraretinal response to light. *Science* 161:489-490.

Lees, A. D. 1960. Some aspects of animal photoperiodism. *Cold Spring Harb. Symp. Quant. Biol.* 25:261-268.

Lees, A. D. 1964. The location of the photoperiodic receptors in the aphid *Megoura viciae*. *J. Exp. Biol.* 41:118-133.

Lees, A. D. 1971. The relevance of action spectra in the study of insect photoperiodism. In *Biochronometry*, M. Menaker (ed.). Washington, D.C.: Nat. Acad. Sci., pp. 372-380.

Lickey, M. E.; Block, G. D.; Hudson, D. J.; and Smith, J. T. 1976. Circadian oscillators and photoreceptors in the gastropod. *Aplysia*. *Photochem. Photobiol.* 23:245-251.

Loher, W. 1972. Circadian control of stridulation in the cricket *Teleogryllus commodus* Walker. *J. Comp. Physiol.* 79:173-190.

Machado, C. R. S.; Wragg, L. E.; and Machado, A. B. H. 1969a. Circadian rhythm of serotonin in the pineal body of immunosympathectomized immature rats. *Science* 164:442-443.

Machado, C. R. S.; Machado, A. B. H.; and Wragg, L. E. 1969b. Circadian serotonin rhythm control: sympathetic and nonsympathetic pathways in rat pineals of different ages. *Endocrinology* 85:846-848.

McGuire, R. A.; Rand, W. M.; and Wurtman, R. J. 1973. Entrainment of the body temperature rhythm in rats: effect of color and intensity of environmental light. *Science* 181:956-957.

McMillan, J. P.; Underwood, H. A.; Elliott, J. A.; Stetson, M. H.; and Menaker. M. 1975. Extraretinal light perception in the sparrow, IV. Further evidence that the eyes do not participate in photoperiodic photoreception. *J. Comp. Physiol.* 97:205-213.

Menaker, M. 1968. Light perception by extraretinal receptors in the brain of the sparrow. *Proc. Amer. Psychol. Assn. 76th*: 299-300.

Menaker, M., and Keatts, H. 1968. Extraretinal light perception in the sparrow. II. Photoperiodic stimulation of testis growth. *Proc. Nat. Acad. Sci.* (Wash.) 60: 146-151.

Menaker, M., and Underwood, H. 1976. Extraretinal photoreception in birds. *Photochem. Photobiol.* 23:299-306.

Menaker, M.; Roberts, R.; Elliott, J.; and Underwood, H. 1970. Extraretinal light perception in the sparrow. III. The eyes do not participate in photoperiodic photoreception. *Proc. Nat. Acad. Sci.* (Wash.) 67:320-325.

Moore, R. Y., Eichler, V. B. 1976. Central neural mechanisms in diurnal rhythm regulation and neuroendocrine responses to light. *Psychoneuroendocrinology* 1:265-279.

Morita, Y., and Bergmann, G. 1971. Physiologische Untersuchungen und weitere Bemerkungen zur Struktur des lichtempfindlichen Pinealorgans von *Pterophyllum scalare* Cuv et Val (Cichlidae, Teleostei). *Z. Zellforsch. Mikrosk. Anat.* 119:289-294.

Newth, D. R., and Ross, D. M. 1955. On the reaction to light of *Myxine glutinosa*. *L. J. Exp. Biol.* 32:4-21.

Nishiitsutsuji-Uwo, J., and Pittendrigh, C. S. 1968b. Central nervous system control of circadian rhythmicity in the cockroach. III. The optic lobes, locus of the drawing oscillator? *Z. Vergl. Physiol.* 58:14-46.

Nishiitsutsuji-Uwo, J., and Pittendrigh. 1968a. Central nervous system control of circadian rhythmicity in the cockroach. II. The pathway of light signals that entrain the rhythm. *Z. Vergl. Physiol.* 58:1-13.

Obreshkove, V. 1921. The photic reactions of tadpoles in relation to the Bunsen-Roscoe law. *J. Exp. Zool.* 34: 235-279.

Oishi, T., and Lauber, J. K. 1973a. Photoreception in the photosexual response of quail. I. Site of photoreceptor. *Amer. J. Physiol.* 225:155-158.

Oishi, T., and Lauber, J. K. 1973b. Photoreception in the photosexual response of quail. II. Effect of intensity and wave length. *Amer. J. Physiol.* 225:880-886.

Oliver, J., and Baylé, J. D. 1976. The involvement of the preoptic-suprachiasmatic region in the photosexual reflex in quail: effects of selective lesions and photic stimulation. *J. Physiol.* (Paris) 72:627-637.

Page, T. L., and Larimer, J. L. 1976. Extraretinal photoreception in entrainment of crustacean circadian rhythms. *Photochem. Photobiol.* 23:245-251.

Parker, G. H. 1903. The skin and the eyes as receptive organs in the reactions of frogs to light. *Amer. J. Physiol.* 10:28-36.

Parker, G. H. 1905. The stimulation of the integumentary nerves of fishes by light. *Amer. J. Physiol.* 14:413-420.

Parker, G. H. 1909. The integumentary nerves of fishes as photoreceptors and their significance for the origin of the vertebrate eye. *Amer. J. Physiol.* 25:77-80.

Parker, G. H. 1948. *Animal Colour Changes and Their Neurohumours.* Cambridge, England: Cambridge Univ. Press.

Pearse, A. S. 1910. The reactions of amphibians to light. *Proc. Amer. Acad. Arts. Sci.* 45:161-208.

Pittendrigh, C. S. 1972. Circadian surfaces and the diversity of possible roles of circadian organization in photoperiodic induction. *Proc. Nat. Acad. Sci. U.S.* 69: 2734-2737.

Pittendrigh, C. S., and Minis, D. H. 1964. The entrainment of circadian oscillations by light and their role as photoperiodic clocks. *Amer. Nat.* 98:261-294.

Pittendrigh, C. S., and Minis, D. H. 1971. The photoperiodic time measurement in *Pectinophora gossypiella* and its relation to the circadian system in that species. In *Biochronometry*, M. Menaker (ed.). Washington, D.C.: Nat. Acad. Sci., pp. 212-250.

Pittendrigh, C. S.; Eichhorn, J. H.; Minis, D. H.; and Bruce, V. G. 1970. Circadian systems VI. Photoperiodic time measurement in *Pectinophora gossypiella*. *Proc. Nat. Acad. Sci. U.S.* 66:758-764.

Quay, W. B. 1974. Pineal chemistry in cellular and physiological mechanisms. Springfield, Ill.: Charles C Thomas.

Ralph, C. L. 1976. Correlations of melatonin content in pineal gland, blood, and brain of some birds and mammals. *Amer. Zoologist* 16:35-43.

Ralph, C. L.; Binkley, S.; MacBride, S.; and Klein, D. 1975. Regulation of pineal rhythms in chickens: effects of blinding, constant light, constant dark, and superior cervical ganglionectomy. *Endocrinology* 97:1373-1378.

Rasquin, P., and Rosenbloom, L. 1954. Endocrine imbalance and tissue hyperplasia in teleosts maintained in darkness. *Bull. Amer. Mus. Nat. Hist.* 104:359-426.

Reiter, R. J. 1973. Comparative effects of continual·lighting and pinealectomy on the eyes, the Harderian glands and reproduction in pigmented and albino rats. *Comp. Biochem. Physiol.* 44A:503-509.

Reiter, R. J., and Klein, D. C. 1971. Observations on the pineal gland, the Harderian glands, the retina, and the reproductive organs of adult female rats exposed to continuous light. *J. Endocr.* 51:117-125.

Relkin, R. 1976. *The Pineal*. Montreal: Eden Press.

Richter, C. P. 1968. Inherent twenty-four hour and lunar clocks of a primate--the squirrel monkey. *Communications Behav. Biol.* 1:305-332.

Roberts, S. K. 1965. Photoreception and entrainment of cockroach activity rhythms. *Science* 148:958-959.

Rosner, J. M.; Declerq de Perez Bedes, G.; and Cardinali, D. P. 1971. Direct effect of light on duck pineal explants. *Life Sci.* 10:1065-1069.

Rosner, J. M.; Denari, J. H.; Nagle, C. A.; Cardinali, D. P.; Declerq de Perez Bedes, G.; and Orsi, L. 1972. Direct action of light on serotonin metabolism and RNA biosynthesis in duck pineal explants. *Life Sci.* 11:829-836.

Ross, D. M. 1959. The response to light in *Ichthyophis* (Amphibia-Apoda) from Ceylon. *Proc. Zool. Soc.* (Lond.) 132:83-98.

Saunders, D. S. 1976. *Insect Clocks*. New York: Pergamon Press.

Scharrer, E. 1928. Die Lichtempfindlichkeit blinder Elritzen (Untersuchungen über das Zwischenhirn der Fische). *Z. Vergl. Physiol.* 7:1-38.

Snyder, S. H.; Zweig, M.; Axelrod, J.; and Fischer, J. E. 1965. Control of the circadian rhythm in serotonin content of the rat pineal gland. *Proc. Nat. Acad. Sci. U.S.* 53:301-305.

Sokolove, P. G. 1975. Localization of the cockroach optic lobe circadian pacemaker with microlesions. *Brain Res.* 87:13-21.

Sokolove, P. G., and Loher, W. 1975. Role of the eye, optic lobes, and pars intercerebralis in locomotory and stridulatory circadian rhythms of *Teleogryllus commodus*. *J. Insect. Physiol.* 21:785-799.

Stephan, F. K., and Zucker, I. 1972. Circadian rhythms in drinking behavior and locomotor activity of rats are eliminated by hypothalamic lesions. *Proc. Nat. Acad. Sci. U.S.* 69:1583-1586.

Stetson, M. H., and Whatson-Whitmyre, M. 1976. Nucleus suprachiasmaticus: the biological clock in the hamster? *Science* 191:197-199.

Steven, D. M. 1950. Some properties of the photoreceptors of the brook lamprey. *J. Exp. Biol.* 27:350-364.

Steven, D. M. 1963. The dermal light sense. *Biol. Rev.* 38: 204-240.

Taylor, D. H. 1972. Extraoptic photoreception and compass orientation in larval and adult salamanders. *Anim. Behav.* 20:237-240.

Taylor, D. H., and Ferguson, D. E. 1970. Extraoptic orientation in the southern cricket frog, *Acris gryllus*. *Science* 168:390-392.

Truman, J. W. 1972. Physiology of insect rhythms. II. The silkworm brain as the location of the biological clock controlling eclosion. *J. Comp. Physiol.* 81:99-114.

Truman, J. W. 1974. Physiology of insect rhythms. IV. Role of the brain in the regulation of the flight rhythm of the giant silkmoths. *J. Comp. Physiol.* 95:281-296.

Truman, J. W. 1976. Extraretinal photoreception in insects. *Photochem. Photobiol.* 23:215-225.

Truman, J. W., and Riddiford, L. M. 1970. Neuroendocrine control of ecdysis in silkmoths. *Science* 167:1624-1626.

Turek, F. W. 1975. Extraretinal photoreception during the gonadal photorefractory period in the Golden-crowned sparrow. *J. Comp. Physiol.* 96:27-36.

Turek, F. W.; McMillan, J. P.; and Menaker, M. 1976. Melatonin: effects on the circadian locomotor rhythm of sparrows. *Science* 194:1441-1443.

Underwood, H. 1973. Retinal and extraretinal photoreceptors mediate entrainment of the circadian locomotor rhythm in lizards. *J. Comp. Physiol.* 83:187-222.

Underwood, H. 1975a. Retinally perceived photoperiod does not influence subsequent testicular regression in house sparrows. *Gen. Comp. Endocrinol.* 27:475-478.

Underwood, H. 1975b. Extraretinal light receptors can mediate photoperiodic photoreception in the male lizard *Anolis carolinensis*. *J. Comp. Physiol.* 99:71-78.

Underwood, H. 1977. Circadian organization in lizards: the role of the pineal organ. *Science* 195:587-589.

Underwood, H., and Menaker, M. 1970. Photoperiodically significant photoreception in sparrows: is the retina involved? *Science* 167:198-301.

Underwood, H., and Menaker, M. 1976. Extraretinal photoreception in lizards. *Photochem. Photobiol.* 23:227-243.

Urasaki, H. 1973. Effect of pinealectomy and photoperiod on oviposition and gonadal development in the fish *Oryzias latipes*. *J. Exp. Zool.* 185:241-246.

van Veen, T.; Hartwig, H. G.; and Müller, K. 1976. Light-dependent motor activity and photonegative behavior in the eel (*Anguilla anguilla L.*) *J. Comp. Physiol.* 111: 209-219.

von Frisch, K. 1911. Beiträge zur Physiologie der Pigmentzellen in der Fischhaut. *Pflügers Arch. Ges. Physiol.* 138:319-387.

Wetterberg, L.; Geller, E.; and Yuwiler, A. 1970a. Harderian gland: an extraretinal photoreceptor influencing the pineal gland in neonatal rats? *Science* 167:884-885.

Wetterberg, L.; Yuwiler, A.; Ulrich, R.; Geller, E.; and Wallace, R. 1970b. Harderian gland: influence on pineal hydroxyindole-O-methyltransferase activity in neonatal rats. *Science* 170:194-196.

Williams, C. M. 1969. Photoperiodism and the endocrine aspects of insect diapuase. *Symp. Soc. Exp. Biol.* 23:285-300.

Williams, C. M., and Adkisson, P. L. 1964. Physiology of insect diapause. XIV. An endocrine mechanism for the photoperiodic control of pupal diapause in the oak silkworm, *Antheraea pernyi*. *Biol. Bull.* 127:511-525.

Wolstenholme, G. E. W., and Knight, J. (eds.). 1971. *The Pineal Gland*. Edinburgh and London: Churchill Livingstone.

Wurtman, R. J.; Axelrod, J.; and Kelly, D. E. 1968. *The Pineal*. New York: Academic Press.

Wykes, U. 1937. The photic control of pigmentary responses in teleost fishes. *J. Exp. Biol.* 14:79-87.

Wykes, U. 1938. The control of photo-pigmentary responses in eyeless catfish. *J. Exp. Biol.* 15:363-370.

Yokoyama, K., and Farner, D. S. 1976. Photoperiodic responses in bilaterally enucleated female white-crowned sparrows, *Zonotrichia leucophrys gambelii*. *Gen. Comp. Endocrinol.* 30:528-533.

Young, J. Z. 1935a. The photoreceptors of lampreys. I. Light sensitive fibres in the lateral line nerves. *J. Exp. Biol.* 12:229-238.

Young, J. Z. 1935b. The photoreceptors of lampreys. II. The function of the pineal complex. *J. Exp. Biol.* 12:254-270.

Zweig, M.; Snyder, S. H.; and Axelrod, J. 1966. Evidence for a nonretinal pathway of light to the pineal gland of newborn rats. *Proc. Nat. Acad. Sci. U.S.* 56:515-520.

Zimmerman, N. H., and Menaker, M. 1975. Neural connections of sparrow pineal: role in circadian control of activity. *Science* 190:477-479.

Zimmerman, W. F., and Ives, D. 1971. Some photophysiological aspects of circadian rhythmicity in *Drosophila*. In *Biochronometry*, M. Menaker (ed.). Washington, D.C.: Nat. Acad. Sci., pp. 381-391.

Zimmerman, W. F., and Goldsmith, T. H. 1971. Photosensitivity of the circadian rhythm and of visual receptors in carotenoid depleted *Drosophila*. *Science* 171:1167-1168.

Extraretinal Photoreception: Words of Caution: Discussion

C. Richard Tracy

The study of extraretinal photoreceptors, and their involvement in endocrine processes, is one of the more exciting frontiers of biological science today. This is the case in part because so little is known about such systems, and in part because the animal kingdom is replete with a diversity of adaptations involving extraretinal photoreceptors which may be of considerable importance, but which we (humans) find hard to identify with because humans generally do not have similar adaptations.

I personally find this area of science also one of the most frustrating areas of biology. Far too often, the methods of study do not clearly test hypotheses; i.e., the exclusivity of results, and/or conclusions based on experimental results, are often not well established. Even more importantly, rarely are true "adaptations" (in the evolutionary sense) separated from spurious physiological effects. Let me discuss an example at length.

The pineal complex (as Herb Underwood has told us) has been implicated as a major light-sensitive organ in most vertebrates. It can be implicated in a number of adaptive responses of vertebrates (entrainment, orientation in amphibians, color change, phototactic responses, and others), but do pineal processes naturally function in these responses? Indeed, do we even know that the pineal is the principal organ involved? In essentially every experiment on amphibians in which the pineal organ has been excised, the underlying brain is also inevitably damaged. The paraphysis and habenula are prominent structures in the same region and can be mistaken for the pineal organ, which is quite inconspicuous (Charles Ralph, personal communication). Thus, we have not eliminated involvement of the paraphysis in the processes attributed to the pineal. The pineal is an enormously mysterious organ which is apparently very ancient (perhaps preceding lateral eyes, phylogenetically, see p. 162). It appears to produce literally dozens of hormones, but only one is known to "escape" from the organ--melatonin. Yet, melatonin is produced in other parts of the body as well.

We know that in amphibians melatonin inhibits the production of melanocyte-stimulating hormone (MSH), which is produced in the pars intermedia of the pituitary. MSH functions to disperse melanin in dermal melanophores, thus causing the skin to become dark. The question I would like to pose is: "Are there times in which this process functions not as an adaptation which has evolved by the process of natural selection, but rather, as a physiological effect that is apparent in laboratory experiments but has no adaptive significance?" Let me give an extreme (ridiculous?) example of how one can perform an experiment and conclude from the results of that experiment that the organism studied has an adaptation which actulaly has no adaptive significance.

Suppose we submerse a treatment group of naked humans in a cold water bath for two hours. When we remove the people, we notice that they are blue (and wrinkled). Then we conclude that this color change is an adaptation for reflecting blue light as part of the physiological thermoregulation of the animal. Perhaps skin darkening in amphibians subjected to cold environments is analogously irrelevant in the evolutionary sense.

Consider a portion of the physiology of color change in frogs. The skin contains dermal melanophores, which disperse or condense melanin in response to the relative presence or absence (respectively) of MSH. The amount of MSH secreted from the pars intermedia appears to be controlled by two hormones: melatonin (presumably of pineal origin) and MSH Release Inhibitory Hormone (MSH-RIH), a chemical that has not been isolated but has been found in hypothalamic preparations (William Gern, personal communication). Thus, MSH is under inhibitory control by at least one (and perhaps more) hormone(s), such that if the inhibitor(s) of MSH are somehow blocked, MSH will act to disperse melanin, thus making the animal darker.

Suppose some of the known environmental "cues" that cause darkening in frogs (e.g., cold ambient conditions) actually act to create an abnormal inhibition of melatonin and/or MSH-RIH? Then cold "toxicity" would result in skin darkening in frogs in much the same way that humans turn blue when subjected to cold. In this case we would observe a physiological response which is not the result of natural selection (i.e., not an adaptation).

The conservative "words of caution" that I have developed here--that conceptual models of biological processes sometimes may be the result of imprecise conclusions based on the results of some kinds of experiments--do not constitute a new message. Heward and Hadley (1975) have suggested that all of the observed involvement of melatonin in biological systems may not represent naturally occurring physiological phenomena, but instead may reflect "pharmacological consequences of melatonin toxicity."

Underwood: As Tracy points out, the study of extraretinal photoreception is an exciting undertaking but one which can be fraught with difficulties--not the least of which is the fact that extraretinal photoreceptors have only rarely been localized and some responses clearly have more than one photoreceptive input. The pineal "system" stands out as an extraretinal receptor because of its proven photosensory capacity; however, it has been, in a sense, a system in search of a function. Consequently, most of the work in this area has involved the classical procedures of removal of the system, or injection of a putative pineal hormone (usually melatonin), with observation of an effect on a particular target organ. These experiments have implicated a role for the pineal system in a host of functions. Tracy points out that the observed effects of pinealectomy may have no real adaptive significance or may be the result of damage to adjacent brain areas (such as the paraphysis). Furthermore, he suggests that the effects of melatonin injections may be pharmacological rather than physiological. I concur that alternative explanations are possible in some cases--as they are in any area of biology--(see discussion following Chapter 3)--but the weight of evidence suggests that the pineal system is an important component of the photo-neuro-endocrine system. I feel that continued investigations will show that the pineal system will rival in importance other major control systems, such as the hypothalamo-hypophysial system.

ACKNOWLEDGMENTS

I could not have produced portions of this discussion without extensive discussions with Bill Gern, Scott Turner, and Charles Ralph (all of Colorado State University). However, since the ideas that I have presented occasionally run counter to accepted dogma, I must accept blame for incorrect, unfair, and/or naive statements.

REFERENCES

Heward, C. B., and Hadley, M. E. 1975. Structure-activity relationships of melatonin and indoleamines. *Life Sci.* 17:1167-1178.

Chapter 5

Mechanisms of Color Vision: An Ethologist's Primer

Samuel H. Gruber

Introduction and Definition of Color
Theories of Color Vision
- Duplexity Theory of Vision
- Minimum Requirements for Color Vision

Visual Pigments and Their Relation to Color Vision
Functional Mechanisms Underlying Color Vision
- Electrical Recording from the Retina
- Responses of the Photoreceptors
- Responses of the Horizontal, Bipolar, and Amacrine Cells
- Responses of the Ganglion Cells

Methods for Assessing Color Vision of Animals
Phylogeny of Color Vision and Concluding Remarks

INTRODUCTION AND DEFINITION OF COLOR

Our understanding of the mechanisms subserving color vision has increased to such an extent during the past few years that many of the basic phenomena have been adequately demonstrated and explained. These data have been reviewed and interpreted in several clearly written, comprehensive articles, and consequently much of the information to be presented here can be found in greater detail in these articles (see References). Nevertheless, it seems useful to present, under one cover, the basic facts and concepts of color vision along with the more specialized contributions dealing with the significance of color in behavior. Hence this chapter includes a review of color vision theories and their history, the anatomical, biochemical, and physiological bases of color vision, and brief discussions on methodology, psychophysics, and phylogenetic aspects of color.

Color and its appreciation are so important in human perception that hue is often considered a direct physical attribute of an object, much like texture or hardness (Rodieck 1973, Dartnall 1975). While this is not quite true, the reader is directed to Wright (1967) for an extremely thought-provoking discussion of the "objectivity" of color. In any case, for us and probably for a number of Old World primates as well, color dominates the daytime visual world and can directly affect emotions and thus behavior (Sheppard 1968). A simple list of human endeavors in which color is of primary importance would fill pages. As Hurvich and Jameson (1969) put it, color is in the public domain. It follows that scientists have long been interested in color and have produced a voluminous and complicated literature on nearly every facet of that subject.

For ethologists, color has several important and specific implications: for example, in predatory-prey relations, intra- and interspecific communications (see Chapters 8 and 9), and orientation (see Chapter 4). Also, color assumes importance for us because of the essentially observational basis of ethology. Tinbergen (1951) understood this well when he wrote that "each animal has its own *Merkwelt* (perceptual world) and this world differs from its environment as we perceive it, that is to say, from our own *Merkwelt*" (p. 16). Thus, as an observer the ethologist can easily be seduced into believing that an animal's appreciation of colors is the same as his. This is a pitfall which must be guarded against. It should be understood that no matter how similar the peripheral mechanisms may be, an animal must be shown by behavioral tests to make discriminations similar to ours if we are to begin to believe that it has similar color vision. This is another reason that Tinbergen (1951) stressed the role of sensory physiology as a starting point in behavioral observations.

Clearly, the perception of color is a sensation, and its objective and subjective aspects have made the definition of color very difficult. Many authors (Tansley 1965, Wyszecki and Stiles 1967, Abramov 1972) believe that the simple discrimination of wavelength provides an organism with color vision. Others, perhaps with a more perceptual background, argue that color, especially color appearances, must be specified by at least three variables: hue, saturation or colorimetric purity, and brightness. How then can color be defined?

Perhaps the most widely accepted definition of color in the visual sciences, encompassing ideas of both the Optical Society of America and the Commission Internationale d'Eclairage (CIE), is that color is that aspect of vision which includes everything but spatial and temporal inhomogeneities of light. But as Boynton (1971) points out, this extremely broad concept is clearly not what most people understand as color. For example, under this definition a black-and-white television receiver could be sold as a color set.

Conversely, color can be narrowly defined as that aspect of the complete visual experience abstracted from (1) the spectral characteristics of the stimulus energy, (2) the spectral match functions of the observer, (3) the subject's color memory, (4) state of adaptation, (5) expectations, (6) emotional state, and (7) the appearance of nearby objects--and so on (Burnham et al. 1963). As generally understood, however, the concept of color includes perceptions of hue, saturation, and brightness abstracted from the total visual experience and scaled along a specific dimension of color. However, Burnham et al. (1963) noted that even with a rigorous definition, the term color can take on different shades of meaning according to the sense in which it is used. Therefore, any attempt to give the word color a single meaning is extremely pedantic. Le Grand (1957) suggests that if one is in doubt about context, another term such as "chromatic" or "hue" vision might be preferable.

The relation between color appearance and stimulus wavelengths is very well known (incidentally, Boynton [1966] correctly pointed out that wavelength was an exceedingly poor choice of unit). The implication is that

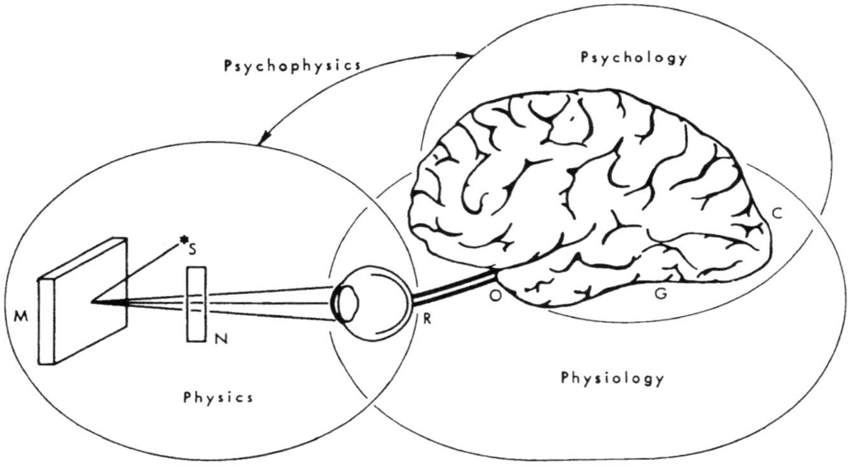

Fig. 47. The three domains of color vision. The physical stimulus (S) consists of reflected quanta from matter (M) which pass through a transmitting substance (N) and into the eye, where they are absorbed in the photoreceptors. The physical stimulus is transformed in the retina (R) to a physiological stimulus, which is transmitted to the brain via the optic nerve (O), where it is further processed physiologically at the geniculate nucleus (G) and the striate cortex (C). The locale where physiology grades into awareness (i.e., psychological stimulus) is not precisely known. However, as shown, psychophysics is the systematic attempt to relate the physical stimulus to perception, with the goal of understanding underlying functional mechanisms. (Sheppard 1968. Reproduced with the permission of the author and publisher. © 1968 American Elsevier, New York.)

the appearance of a particular color, say red, is physically determined, but this can be very misleading. In fact, color depends not only on physical factors, such as wavelength and intensity, but on physiological mechanisms and even subtle perceptual factors as well (Fig. 47). That is why the definition of color presented above included such a variable as the observer's expectations. This means that, under *identical* physical conditions, an object may have different appearances (Burnham et al. 1963). Conversely, when the physical intensity of a monochromatic stimulus is changed, while the wavelength is held constant, the color appears to change (Fig. 48). This is the well-known Bezold-Brücke effect (Bezold 1873).

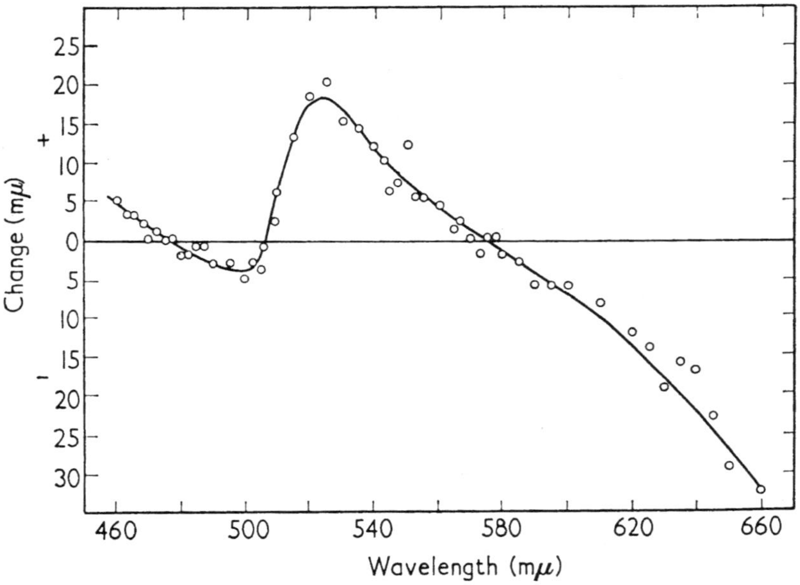

Fig. 48. The Bezold-Brücke effect. The curve shows how much an observer must change the wavelength of the physical stimulus to counteract the change in perceived hue which accompanies an increase from 100 to 1000 trolands. The straight horizontal line represents a hypothetical condition of no change in hue. (Marriott 1962a. Reproduced with the permission of the author and publisher. © 1962 Academic Press, New York.)

Finally, the importance of brain mechanisms in color vision is often overlooked. In man, the final coding which produces the appreciation of color apparently takes place in area 18 of the visual cortex, and appears to be quite localized. Pearlman (1977) reported a case in which a patient with normal color vision suffered a vascular accident and reported that his visual world was no longer colored. The localized brain lesions apparently destroyed an important color "decoding" center, while leaving the rest of his visual functions essentially intact.

Thus, while physiological and psychological studies of animal vision might demonstrate that the visual system is capable of wavelength discrimination, we cannot, from this evidence, conclude that the animal perceives any particular color. Cornsweet (1970) put it another way: if a totally color-blind person tells you he sees colors, you cannot argue. You can merely note that his color names are not reliably related to wavelength and thus his visual system has lost all the information contained in that physical dimension.

I have presented this unsystematic sampling of some objective aspects of color to provide not only an awareness of the complex nature of color vision, but to reinforce the care which one must take in interpreting chromatic events in behavior.

THEORIES OF COLOR VISION

A theory of color vision is any systematic attempt to explain how color responses are produced and to account for all the well-established facts of color vision such as color mixtures, afterimages, contrast effects, color blindness, and the like. While many such theories exist today, most are basically variations on two themes--the Young-Helmholtz and the Hering-opponent schemes.

The great masters knew very well that a mixture of three bright, primary pigments could produce an entire gamut of colors, but it was not until the studies of Newton (1672) that the science of color was put on a modern footing (Marriott 1962a). In his famous prism experiments, Newton showed that white sunlight was not homogeneous but rather a continuously variable mixture of radiations. Once the rays were separated into a spectrum, the individual color bands could not be further broken down and were thus monochromatic. Newton also proved that objects take their colors by absorbing certain rays and reflecting others (see Chapter 1). Interestingly, by superimposing pairs of spectral colors, he was able to formulate an essentially correct center-of-gravity law (Rushton 1969). For example, if spectral yellowish-red were mixed with some spectral yellowish-green, the result was a pure yellow indistinguishable from spectral yellow (with a bit of white added). However, Newton demonstrated these yellows to be physically different by again passing them through a prism. By arranging the spectral colors in a circle and assigning each color a mass proportional to its intensity, he assumed that the resultant position of any mixture of spectral lights within the color circle would lie at their center of gravity. The logical conclusion of this finding is that color vision is trivariant, i.e., fully specified by only three variables. Yet Newton did not draw this conclusion. Instead, in a series of queries, he asked if there could not exist great numbers of visual receptors each tuned to a different frequency of light (Marriott 1962a). Still, Newton's essential contribution to color vision was his recognition of the domain of color as more restricted than that of light (Rodieck 1973).

Gradually throughout the eighteenth century, the trivariance of color vision became accepted fact. Lomonsov (1757) even suggested that there were three sorts of light. In 1777, Palmer explicitly outlined a trichromatic theory of color vision, although Young (1802) is usually given the credit for this formulation (Wasserman 1973).

It was in the same lecture in which he established that light is propagated by wave motion that Young (1802) briefly commented on color vision, thus answering Newton's one hundred-year-old query. In an often-quoted passage, he introduced trichromacy as follows: "Now, as it is almost impossible to conceive each sensitive point of the retina to contain an infinite number of particles, each capable of vibrating in perfect unison with every possible undulation, it becomes necessary to suppose the number limited, for instance, to the three principal colors, red, yellow, and blue. . . ." (p. 20). A modern restatement of Young's hypothesis is that from any local region of the visual field, and hence the retina, there are but three independent signals--particularly when rod signals make no contribution (Rodieck 1973).

With this statement Young resolved a paradox that had puzzled scientists for over one hundred years: how to reconcile the continuum of spectral radiations with the trivariance of vision. With clear simplicity, Young assigned the origins of trichromacy not to the physics of light but rather to the physiology of vision. Young, of course, did not know what sort of resonators were vibrating in the retina, but using his own measurement of wavelength, and the velocity of light as previously determined by Römer and Bradley, he calculated the frequency of vibration at 5×10^{14} Hz. The resonators thus could not be material objects. We now know that they are the π orbital electrons of the visual pigments (Rushton 1969, 1972a).

Whereas Young's ideas fitted well with Müller's doctrine of specific nerve energies (for review, see Boring 1942), it was not until the studies of Maxwell (1860) and Helmholtz (1866) that the trichromatic theory was given a firm mathematical basis.

The theory is actually based on experiments involving mixtures of colored lights presented in pairs to a subject (Marriott 1962b). If the mixtures are physically different yet appear identical, they are called metamers (Boynton 1971). In general, if a subject is given any four spectral (pure) colors and permitted to mix them in two patches (i.e., λ_1 and λ_2 in one patch; λ_3 plus λ_4 in the other) and allowed to adjust the intensities of any *three* of them, he will be able to get a perfect match between the two patches, that is, the patches will be metamers. This result leads directly to the conclusion that the subject's visual system contains three and only three color channels (Cornsweet 1970). The fundamental ideas of this stimulus-based theory are that the (human) visual system contains three color systems based on three types of photochemically decomposable substances found in three types of cone receptors. Each of these visual pigments has a peak sensitivity in different parts of the spectrum but nevertheless absorbs some light across the spectrum. In addition, each of the three cone types is associated with its own neural connections and all color sensations are considered as compounded of varying amounts of the three *excitatory* systems. For example, white arises from equal stimulation of all three systems and black from the condition of no stimulation. Yellow presumably arises from equal stimulation of the "red" and "green" systems (Marriott 1962b, Hurvich and Jameson 1969).

Upon close scrutiny, the Young-Helmholtz theory has several important defects and fails to account for such phenomena as the Bezold-Brücke effect, the apparent linkage between specific color pairs, and certain rare forms of color blindness (Hurvich 1960). This lack has prompted the formulation of alternative theories, the most successful being the Hering- or opponent-mechanism scheme (Hering 1878).

Probably the most compelling observation that led Hering to propose a new theory was that there seemed to be four (not three) fundamental or unitary colors--blue, green, yellow, and red--with the other colors appearing as mixtures. Because of this, the Hering formulation is often said to be a four-variable theory, but this is not so. Helmholtz (1896) realized this and even presented linear equations transforming Hering's data to trichromatic data (Hurvich and Jameson 1969). The opponent theory is actually a trivariant theory and Marriott (1962b) has even called it a variation of the trichromatic theory. However, the Young-Helmholtz and Hering viewpoints differ fundamentally in their concepts of the structure and functions of the three-variable system (Hurvich 1960). Hering conceived of three pairs of physiological processes: red-green, yellow-blue, and black-white. The members of each pair are opposite and antagonistic, i.e., they do not blend--no color can be called yellow-blue. Conversely, each component of the pair seems to demand the other; white surrounded by blue will always appear slightly yellow (Linksz 1964). Thus, Hering's system is response-based, that is, based upon the appearance of colors. The Young-Helmholtz theory, in contrast, is stimulus-based, and, especially in its modern form, does not specify or predict the colors of metamers (Hurvich and Jameson 1969).

Hering originally postulated a retinal substance for each opponent mechanism--one decomposed in, for instance, red light by catabolic action and regenerated anabolically in green light (Marriott 1962b). Although no such substances actually exist, the excitatory-inhibitory nature of nervous transmissions, one of the most significant findings of twentieth-century sensory physiology, could form the basis of Hering-type signal processing in the visual system. As Granit (1955) remarked: "these results are a belated vindication of the essential truth of Hering's contention that there are two fundamental processes of opposite character in the retina, even though he could never have foreseen in what way his idea would come true" (p. 78).

Duplexity Theory of Vision

Before discussion of some of the evidence supporting the above two formulations, one other theory should be considered because it bears directly on the anatomical substrates of color vision. After years of study, Schultze (1866) proposed that the vertebrate retina contains two very different end organs, which were called rods and cones (because of their shapes). He also claimed that the habits of an animal could be predicted from the type of receptors found in its retina. For example, animals with cone-dominated retinas were almost certain to be active in daylight, whereas nocturnal animals were found to possess rod-dominated retinas. These observations have come down to us today in the form of the duplexity theory of vision (Shipley 1964), in which certain physiological attributes have been added to these ecological factors. For example, rods are said to form a high-sensitivity visual system with a relatively slow response time. Cones, on the other hand, provide for high acuity and, more importantly for this discussion, form the anatomical substrate of color vision. In other words, when we see with our rods under conditions of dim illumination, colors are not perceived. As the intensity is increased above the threshold for cone activity, colors appear. The intensity variation between rod and cone thresholds is called the photochromatic interval (Graham 1965).

Minimum Requirements for Color Vision

Before the underlying mechanisms of color vision are considered, one final discussion, drawn mainly from Cornsweet (1970), is presented to provide a basis for understanding the minimum requirements for making discriminations among wavelengths. The first requirement of vision is the absorption of photons, and there are two sensitive ways in which photons interact with matter: photochemically as with photographic film and electronically as in a television tube. The eye uses the photographic method; vision depends upon the bleaching and regeneration of an organic dye (Rushton 1969). The best known of these is rhodopsin. More will be said about visual pigments later. The point is that vision and its spectral limits depend on the way visual pigments absorb light.

Figure 49 is the absorption spectrum of rhodopsin, the light-absorbing pigment found in rods. Consider an

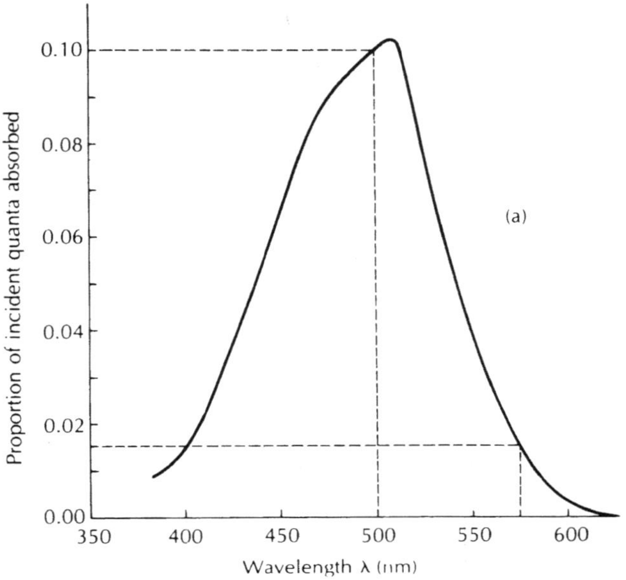

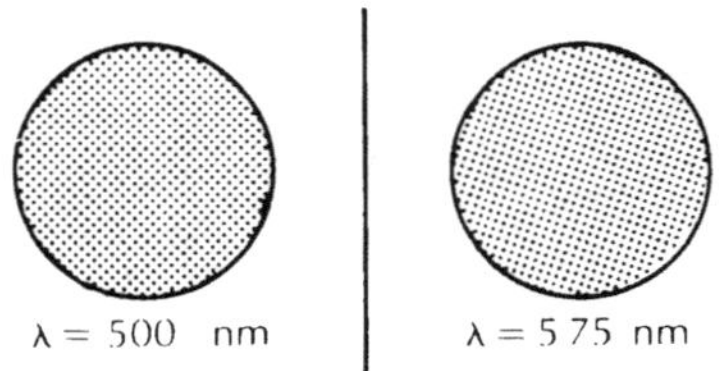

Quanta incident	Quanta absorbed	Quanta incident	Quanta absorbed
1000	100	1000	15
1000	100	6667	100
2000	200	13,334	200

(b)

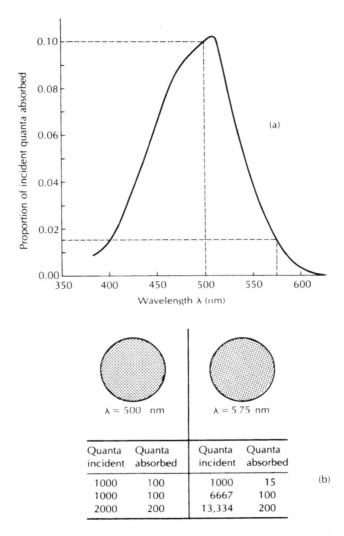

Fig. 49. (a) Absorption spectrum of rhodopsin plotted on a linear scale. Curve shows the relation between stimulus wavelength and relative number of quanta absorbed. (b) The table gives the number of quanta absorbed as a result of stimulating the eyes with patches of light at λ = 500 and λ = 575. See text for further details. (Cornsweet 1970. Reproduced with the permission of the author and publisher. © 1970 Academic Press, New York.)

animal with a single class of receptors all containing rhodopsin. If such a subject is presented with two patches of monochromatic light, at 500 and 575 nm, as shown in Figure 49, and 1000 quanta of each are incident on its retinas, 100 quanta at 500 nm will be absorbed by the visual pigment while only 15 absorptions will occur at 575 nm. Since the stimulus patches produce different retinal effects (even though the quantum intensities are identical), the animal might discriminate between them. However, by merely increasing the quantum intensity of the 575-nm patch to 6667 photons, the effect on the retina will be identical for both; namely, 100 absorptions at 500 nm and 100 at 575 nm. Now, even though the stimuli are physically quite different, they produce the same effect and thus must appear the same no matter how much signal processing takes place downstream in the visual system.

In general, a subject whose visual system is composed of a single class of receptors containing but one visual pigment cannot discriminate between two patches of monochromatic light when their quantum intensities are adjusted to the inverse ratio of the absorption spectrum of the visual pigment. Such a condition (single receptor/pigment) is termed monochromacy. The visual system of a monochromat loses all information contained in wavelength and only discriminates on the basis of perceived brightness differences. In a word, the monochromat is completely color-blind.

There is one crucial assumption: though the wavelength of a quantum sets the probability of whether the pigment absorbs it, once absorbed it is assumed to produce the same effect, namely, isomerization of the pigment molecule regardless of wavelength. Put another way, the output of a photoreceptor depends upon its quantum catch, not which quanta are caught (Rushton 1972a). Thus, once a quantum is absorbed there is no information about energy, frequency, or wavelength available to the receptor (Boynton 1966). This is the principle of univariance (Naka and Rushton 1966), a very important concept which is frequently misunderstood.

Consider another animal whose retina contains two classes of receptors, each with its own visual pigment (whose absorption spectra are shown in Fig. 50). As in the last example, two monochromatic patches are flashed at 1000 quanta each incident on the retina. This time, the actual wavelengths, shown by arrows at λ_1 and λ_2 (Fig. 50), have not been specified since absorption at any point along the abscissa simply depends upon the shape of the curve. Under these conditions, receptor system *A* will absorb

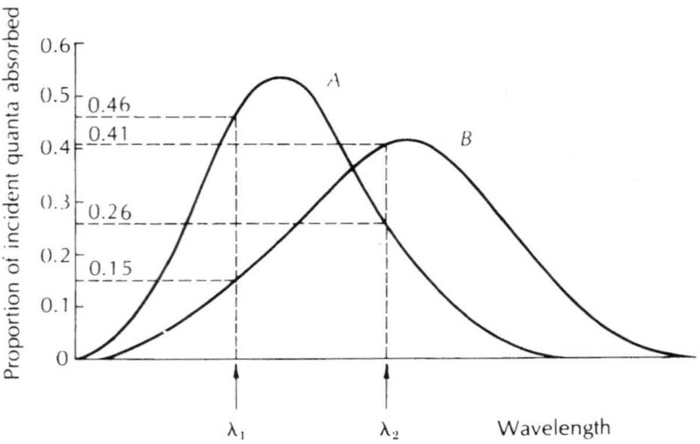

(a)

Condition	Quanta incident	Quanta absorbed by *A*	Quanta absorbed by *B*	Quanta incident	Quanta absorbed by *A*	Quanta absorbed by *B*
1	1000	460	150	1000	260	410
2	1000	460	150	1770	460	725
3	1000	460	150	366	95	150

(b)

Fig. 50. (a) Absorption spectra of two hypothetical pigments found in the retina. (b) The table shows the effects on the visual system of three experiments in which the intensities of patches λ_1 and λ_2 were adjusted in an attempt to stimulate equally both A and B systems at the same time. Details of the three experiments are given in the text. (Cornsweet 1970. Reproduced with the permission of the author and publisher. © 1970 Academic Press, New York.)

460 quanta at λ_1, while *B* absorbs 150. At the same time system *A* absorbs only 260 at λ_2 and *B* absorbs 410. Clearly, patches λ_1 and λ_2 produce different effects on the subject's visual system and are thus discriminable. Now let us attempt to adjust the quantum intensities of the patches so as to produce identical effects on the visual system as we

did for the monochromat. By increasing the intensity of λ_2 to 1770 incident quanta, we are indeed able to produce the same effect from both patches on system *A*: namely, 460 quanta absorbed. However, system *B* will absorb only 150 quanta at λ_1 compared with 725 at λ_2. Condition 3 (Fig. 50) shows our attempt with system *B*. We were not successful in adjusting the quantum output of the patches to produce the same effects and, in general, we cannot make any adjustment in the intensity of any two monochromatic patches so they will produce, at the same time, identical effects on the *A* and *B* receptor systems. Thus the subject's visual system does not lose the information that patches λ_1 and λ_2 contain wavelength differences.

This system is capable of color vision, provided the information is not lost in a higher center. The condition of two receptor systems/pigments is called dichromacy (which is strictly defined on the basis of color mixture experiments). However, both dichromacy and trichromacy can theoretically exist in a retina with only one visual pigment. For example, the pigeon (probably a trichromat) was reported to have only a single visual pigment (Daw 1973) whose absorption characteristics are altered by the colored oil droplets interposed between the receptor inner and outer segments. Such a receptor's final absorption spectrum would be a product of the nonvisual pigment, in the oil droplets, and the visual pigment (Rodieck 1973). If the neural system could keep the receptor signals separate, color vision would then be possible with only one pigment. In actual fact, pigeons are now known to have a multiplicity of visual pigments in addition to oil droplets (Jacobs 1976).

For an extremely lucid discussion of mono-, di-, and trichromacy, including the logic behind color mixture experiments and many other basic aspects of color vision, the reader is directed to Cornsweet (1970).

VISUAL PIGMENTS AND THEIR RELATION TO COLOR VISION

Just over one hundred years ago, Boll (1876) discovered that the purple color of a dark-adapted frog retina first fades to yellow, then becomes clear, when placed in daylight. Almost simultaneously, Kühne's (1877) papers began to appear, in which he described how this photosensitive material was eventually isolated and characterized.

Kühne demonstrated that *Sehpurpur* (or rhodopsin) was a protein which could be extracted from the retina in bile salts, and after bleaching in light would regenerate in darkness in the intact retina. Kühne described the discovery of rhodopsin as "nothing less than the key to the secret of how a nerve can be excited by light" (quoted by Bridges and Ripps 1977, p. 90).

In the intervening one hundred years the precise structure of this molecule and the bleaching cycle have come to be known in detail. Kühne was right: visual pigments mediate the transduction of light (electromagnetic energy) to nerve signals (electrochemical energy). But we still do not know the precise manner in which this transformation takes place. We do know that rhodopsin is a visual pigment, i.e., its quantum catch is the basis of visual information (Rushton 1969). In fact, one of the clearest and most fully supported observations in the visual sciences is the relation between the dark-adapted spectral sensitivity of the human eye and the absorption spectrum of rhodopsin (Graham 1965). Yet for all of this, rhodopsin tells us little about color vision. This is because rhodopsin is the visual pigment associated with rod photoreceptors and thus is responsible for achromatic scotopic vision (as explained earlier).

However, rod pigments have provided some insight, especially into the structure of cone pigments. Extraction of rhodopsin from the retina has demonstrated, from *in vitro* studies, that the effect of light on the visual pigment isomerizes the 11-*cis* chromophore to the all-*trans* configuration (Fig. 51). Unfortunately, the low concentration of cone pigments in a duplex retina has not permitted comparable *in vitro* studies. However, indirect evidence leads to the conclusion that the basic structure and activity of cone pigments are exactly the same as those of rods (Abramov and Gordon 1973).

All known visual pigments are complex molecules consisting of a species-specific protein, opsin (molecular weight *ca* 40,000), onto which is complexed a polyene structure known as a chromophore (Fig. 51). If the chromophore is based on vitamin A_1 (retinal), the molecule is called rhodopsin; that based on vitamin A_2 (3-dehydroretinal) is called porphyropsin. Retinal and 3-dehydroretinal are the only visual chromophores yet isolated. Despite the ubiquity of retinal and 3-dehydroretinal, visual pigments vary considerably in their point of maximum absorption, from 345 nm (ultraviolet) in an insect to 640 nm (deep red) in the chicken pigment.

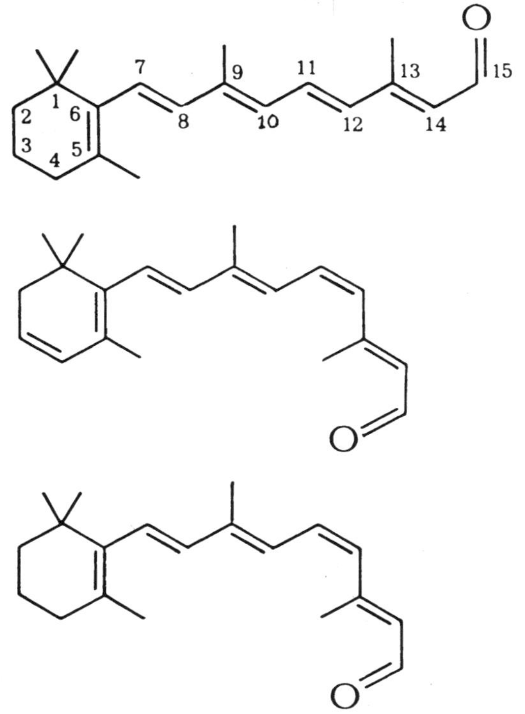

(a)

(b)

(c)

Fig. 51. Molecular structures of the light-absorbing portion of the visual pigment molecule known as the chromophore. (a) All *trans*-retinal, which is the geometric isomer taken by the molecule in the bleached state *after* absorption of a quantum. Numbers 1-15 show the position of the carbon atoms. (b) 11-*cis*-3-dehydroretinal, the vitamin A_2-based chromophore in the unbleached state. This chromophore complexed onto opsin forms porphyropsin. Note the extra double bond between carbon atoms 3 and 4. (c) Unbleached 11-*cis* retinal. This is the vitamin A_1-based chromophore associated with rhodopsin. (Abrahamson and Wiesenfeld 1972. The structure, spectra, and reactivity of visual pigments. In *Handbook of Sensory Physiology. Photochemistry of Vision*, Vol. VII/1, H. J. Dartnell (ed.), pp. 69-121. Reproduced with the permission of the authors and publisher. © 1972 Springer-Verlag, Berlin.)

This means that the biochemical elaboration of visual pigments with variable absorption spectra is possible using the same underlying structure. Thus, many authors believe that cone pigments utilize the basic 11-*cis* chromophore structure to capture photons, but vary their absorption spectra by subtle changes in the opsin portion of the molecule (Alpern 1968, Abramov and Gordon 1973, and MacNichol et al. 1973).

There are several basic questions about cone pigments which bear directly on color vision and have remained unanswered until the relatively recent development of two analytical techniques: reflection densitometry (Campbell and Rushton 1955) and microspectrophotometry (Hanaoka and Fujimoto 1957). Such questions include the number of cone pigments underlying color vision, the shape of their absorption spectra, whether they are combined together in the cones or segregated, and what values their photosensitivity, quantum efficiency, and optical densities assume.

One of the basic tenets of trichromacy is the existence of three retinal "resonators." The evidence supporting this prior to the 1960s was based primarily on psychophysical experiments such as color mixture and chromatic adaptation (Marriott 1962b). Then in 1955 and continuing through the 60s, Rushton's laboratory announced positive identification of at least two cone pigments in the living human eye (reviewed in Rushton 1972a). His method, reflection densitometry, is based on the principle of the ophthalmoscope. This powerful technique established that there were red and green "catching" pigments in the (rod-free) human fovea, which have a time course of bleaching and regeneration much faster than that of rod pigments. Rushton called these erythrolabe and chlorolabe, respectively. Technical limitations did not permit him to explore the shorter wavelength portion of the spectrum. However, Rushton (1963, 1965) was able to prove that dichromat color defectives known as protanopes and deuteranopes (both are red-green defectives) lack erythrolabe and chlorolabe, respectively. Yet his studies left open the questions of a blue "catching" pigment, whether the pigments are segregated into individual receptors, the precise density and absorption spectra of cone pigments, and such effects as the waveguide properties of cones on color vision.

Microspectrophotometry (MSP) has to a large extent provided answers to these questions. The basic method consists of placing a bit of living retina on a microscope stage, receptor side up, and shining a minute column of monochromatic light first through a clear portion of the slide, then through the receptor outer segment. This produces sample and reference beams which contain information

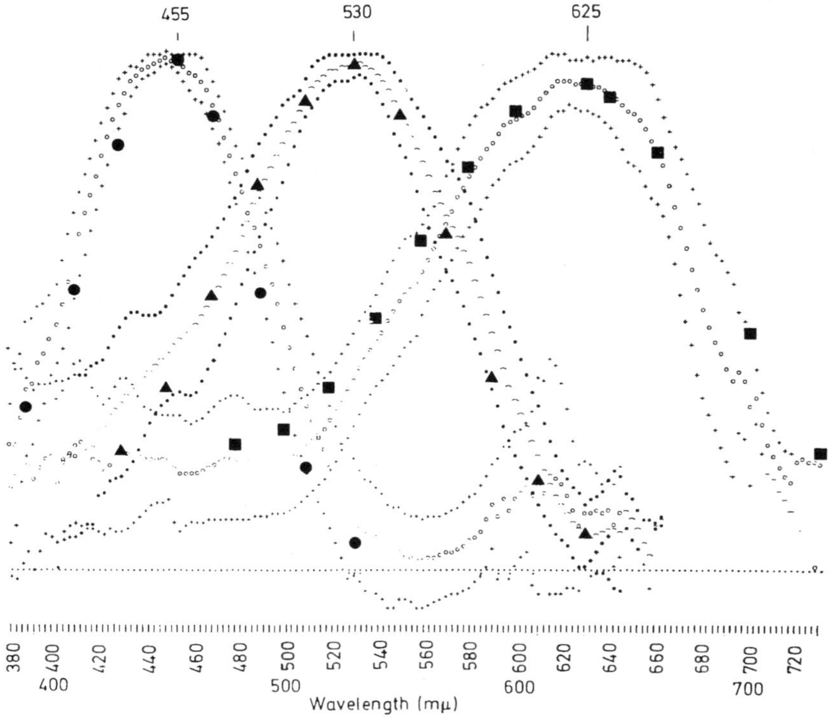

Fig. 52. MSP data from individual cone cells of the goldfish. The three curves represent computer printouts of the different spectra caused by bleaching away the pigment contained in each of the three cone types as explained in the text. The horizontal dotted line represents the condition of zero difference upon bleaching. The large symbols represent the theoretical shape of a visual pigment with peaks as shown (455, 530, and 625). The medium wavelength pigment was later adjusted slightly to 535 nm. (After Marks 1965. Figure taken from Abramov 1972 and reproduced with the permission of the author and publisher. ©1972 Springer-Verlag, Berlin.)

about the ratio of their intensities and thus about the fraction of light transmitted by the receptor. When this is plotted for each wavelength, it gives the receptor's absorption spectrum. MSP has finally and unequivocally identified Young's three resonators (at least in the goldfish) as three bleachable visual pigments not mixed but contained each in its own cone type. The peak absorptions seen in Figure 52 were placed at 455, 535, and 625 nm (Marks 1965). The results from primate (including human) receptors have been less convincing because of technical difficulties. However, the MSP data reviewed by Liebman (1972) indicate peak absorptions at 455, 535, and 570 nm. These strongly support but do not fully confirm the hypothesis that human color perception is mediated by three cone types (MacNichol et al. 1973, Rodieck 1973).

In summary, the human retina contains, besides the rod pigment rhodopsin, three other types of bleachable substances: cyanolabe, chlorolabe, and erythrolabe, with maximum absorption at about 455, 535, and 570 nm. These are the cone pigments subserving color vision. All four retinal pigments have identical chromophores--11-*cis* retinal--which isomerize to all-*trans* retinal upon absorption of a quantum. The differences in point of peak absorption are thus related to differences in the protein opsin. Human color defectives have been shown to lack either chlorolabe or erythrolabe. Other trichromatic animals such as teleosts and primates also have three cone pigments. Thus, Young's three resonators have been identified as the cone pigments and the pigment data clearly support the Young-Helmholtz formulation.

FUNCTIONAL MECHANISMS UNDERLYING COLOR VISION

Before physiological mechanisms of color vision are discussed, a brief description of the structure of the retina will be given for orientation purposes. Further details on the vertebrate retina can be found in Dowling (1970) and Stell (1972).

The vertebrate retina is bounded distally by a nutritive layer, the pigment epithelium, and proximally by the posterior extent of the inner limiting membrane of the vitreous body. Between these lie three cellular and two synaptic layers containing five types of neurons (Fig. 53).

Photoreceptors are found in the most distal retinal layer, which in animals with duplex retinas contains two distinct populations--the rods and cones. It should be

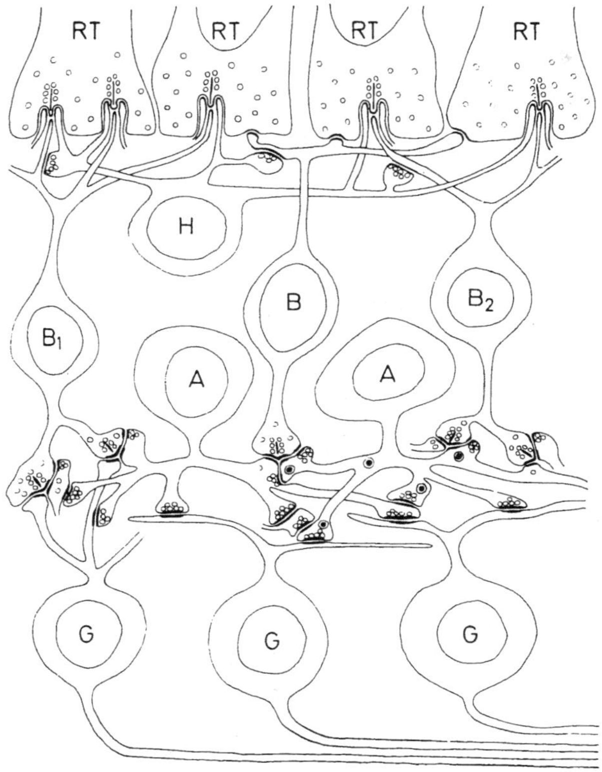

Fig. 53. Structural organization of the vertebrate (frog) retina. Diagram shows the different neurons and their patterns of synaptic interconnection. RT = receptor terminals; H = horizontal cell; B = bipolar cells (B_1 suggests a more direct route to ganglion cells, B_2 an indirect route via amacrine cells); A = amacrine cells; and G = ganglion cells. The possibility for interaction in such a system (consisting of hundreds of millions of cells) is enormous. (Dowling 1968. Synaptic organization of the frog retina: an electron microscope analysis comparing the retinas of frogs and primates. *Proc. Roy. Soc. B.* 170:205-228. Reproduced with the permission of the author and publisher. © 1968 Royal Society of London.)

understood that the criteria for separating these receptor types are not satisfied in all cases. That is, both cone-like rods and rodlike cones can be observed in various animals (Pedler 1965). Within individual species, the distribution of rods and cones across the retina is often uneven. For example, in man, the central retina contains a rod-free pit known as the fovea centralis. There are about 100 million rods but only 6 million cones in the human retina (Graham 1965). Photoreceptors are composed of two parts, the outer segment or input portion containing the visual pigment, and the inner segment or output portion. The inner segment contains the nucleus, energy supply, presynaptic membranes, and neurotransmitter. The level of cell bodies and nuclei of the receptors is known as the outer nuclear layer.

The first synaptic, or outer plexiform, layer contains synaptic processes of the receptor, and horizontal and bipolar cells.

Between the first and second synaptic layers lies the second cellular layer of intermediate neurons, consisting of the cell bodies of the horizontal bipolar and amacrine cells. This level is known as the inner nuclear layer. Bipolar cells appear to conduct information vertically in the retina, while horizontal and amacrine cells send their processes laterally. The second synaptic layer contains interconnections between bipolar, amacrine, and ganglion cells and is termed the inner plexiform layer.

The most proximal cellular layer--the nerve fiber layer--is composed of the ganglion cell bodies and their axons. This layer represents the output station of the retina, since the ganglion cell axons coalesce to form the optic nerve, which leaves the eye and communicates directly with the brain.

One final cell type regularly seen in the retina is the Müller cell, which is a structural or glial cell. These run the entire vertical extent of the retina from outer nuclear to nerve fiber layer. The layered arrangement of the vertebrate retina is extremely regular, and homologous elements can be recognized from fish to man. However, in many animals there are a number of cell types which are difficult to classify, including displaced and "interplexiform" cells (Stell 1972).

Electrical Recording from the Retina

One of the most important and presently troublesome questions for the Young-Helmholtz scheme is the shape of the fundamental response curves of the three receptor systems. Through the years a number of these curves, said to represent cone receptor sensitivities, have been published, starting with those of Helmholtz (1866; Fig. 54). Perhaps the most elaborate and successful attempt to isolate and specify these mechanisms is the two-color threshold technique of Stiles (1939); see Marriott (1962b) for review. His five π-mechanisms are shown in Figure 55. Stiles (1939) suggested that the short-, medium-, and long-wavelength cone sensitivities are represented by π_1, π_4, and π_5. However, the curves are probably conditioned by interactions within the visual system. The dozens of experiments of

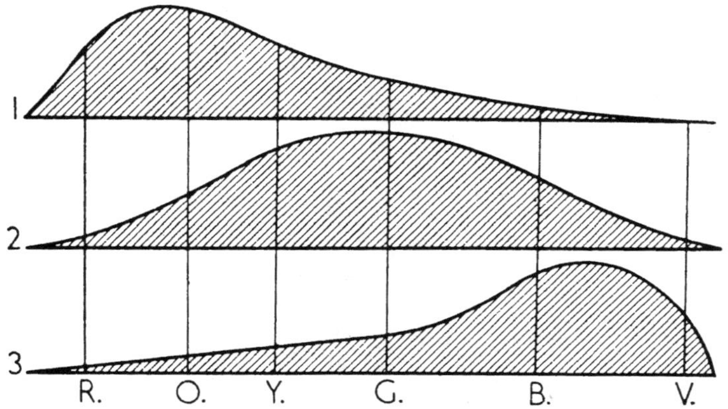

Fig. 54. Fundamental response curves of Helmholtz (1866). These purely theoretical curves illustrate Helmholtz's belief that photochemical substances mediating vision were broadly tuned. Given an intense enough monochromatic light, all three response mechanisms would respond to some extent. Letters on the abscissa represent the appearance of the spectrum (red-violet). (Marriott 1926b. Reproduced with the permission of the author and publisher. © 1962 Academic Press, New York.)

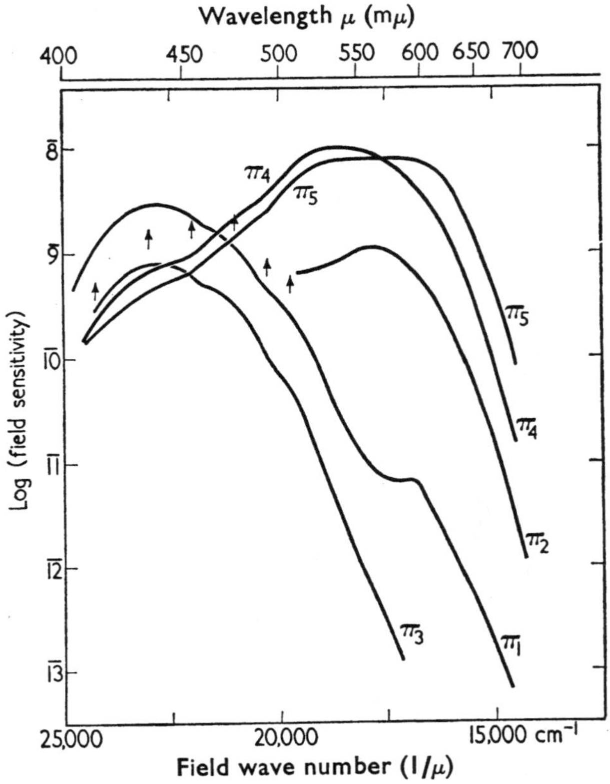

Fig. 55. A modern example of the fundamental response curves; the so-called π-mechanisms of Stiles (1939). The experimental conditions of this psychophysical test were: subject was preadapted to a large (10°) colored field and tested with a smaller (1°) monochromatic test stimulus. The spectral sensitivities shown were calculated from threshold vs. intensity curves. The five π-mechanisms are thought to derive from cones since the stimuli fell entirely on rod-free fovea. π_1, π_4, and π_5 were called the "blue, green, and red" mechanisms, respectively. (After Stiles, taken from Marriott 1962b. Reproduced with the permission of the author and publisher. © 1962 Academic Press, New York.)

this sort, while extremely important, involve psychophysical testing of human observers and thus infer physiological mechanisms from behavioral data.

With the advent of sophisticated electrophysiological techniques in the early 1960s, a more direct, objective approach became available. Electrical recording from the retina was attempted in the mid-nineteenth century (Holmgren 1865) and rod and cone electroretinograms were differentiated as early as 1911 by Piper (Granit 1962). Later, receptor potentials were recorded with gross electrodes by treating the isolated retina with sodium aspartate (Furukawa and Hanawa 1955).

However, the most important results, from the standpoint of color vision, have come from single units recorded with the aid of microelectrodes made by pulling heated glass capillary tubes. Using glass capillaries with a tip diameter of 5 μm, Svaetichin (1953) claimed to have penetrated and recorded directly from individual cone cells. He did not obtain all-or-nothing spikes, but rather graded potentials whose amplitude increased with increasing stimulus intensity. Such response characteristics agreed with the theory of generator potentials (Granit 1947), so Svaetichin was justified in believing he had recorded receptor potentials. However, this was not the case since his electrode was actually proximal to the receptor layer (see below).

Responses of the Photoreceptors

Finally, in 1956 Tomita developed a Gerard-Ling type microcapillary tip with a diameter of less than 0.5 μm (Granit 1962). A second technical advance, which enabled Tomita (1965) to successfully record from individual receptors, was a jolter device that pitched the retina with high acceleration against the slowly advancing micropipette (tip less than 0.1 μm).

The most successful of Tomita's spectral response curves was taken from the carp, a cyprinid fish with rather large cones. Happily, more is known about vision in the Cyprinidae than in any other group of teleosts. For example, several studies have conclusively demonstrated that these fish have trivariant color vision (Northmore and Yager 1975). Also, cone pigments of this group are well known from the MSP work described above.

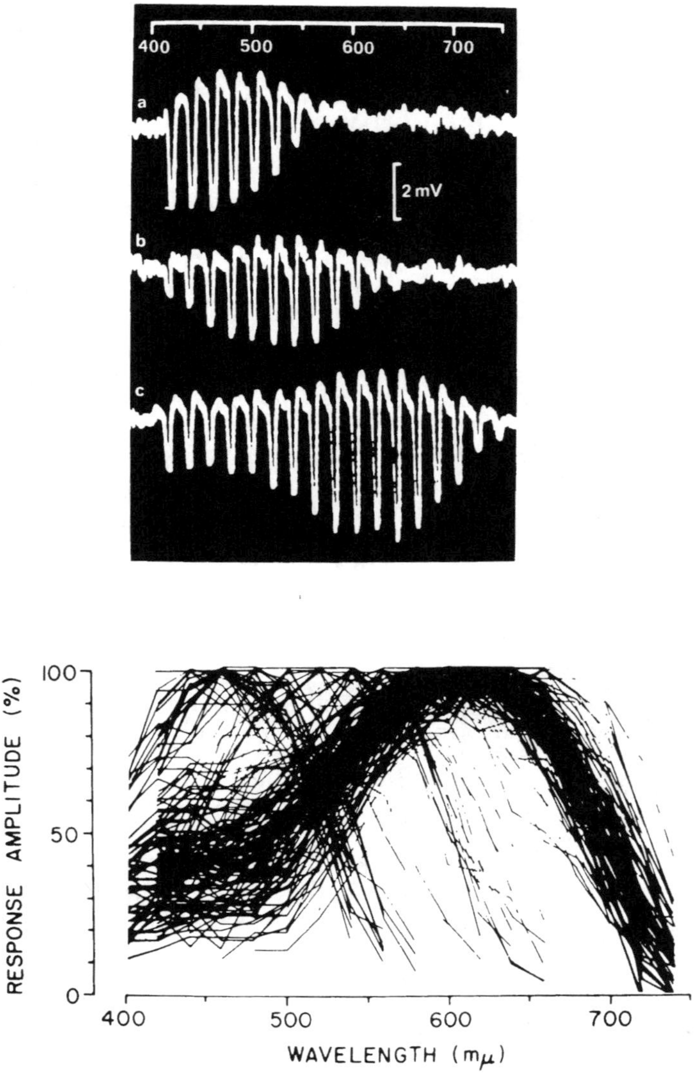

Fig. 56. (Above) Individual responses from short- (a), medium- (b), and long-wavelength (c) sensitive cones in the retina of the carp. Spectral scale above is in nanometers. The records represent negative (hyperpolarizing) graded responses to a constant number of quanta at each wavelength tested. Amplitude

Tomita scanned the spectrum from 400 to 750 nm in 20-nm steps to obtain the results for the three different cone mechanisms that are shown in Figure 56. The retina was presented with an equal quantum flux at each monochromatic step, revealing three different cones with dominant peaks in the short-, medium-, and long-wavelength portion of the spectrum (Fig. 56) (Tomita et al. 1967). Note that the responses in Figure 56 are negative-going and thus hyperpolarizing potentials. This was an unexpected result since photoreceptors from several invertebrate species, as reported from much earlier work, depolarize when illuminated (Fuortes and O'Bryan 1972).

However, DeValois and DeValois (1975) correctly noted that since the visual world consists of light and dark objects, the response of receptors to a decrement is just as important as the response to an increment. So vertebrate receptors apparently release a chemical transmitter when the light level falls, whereas invertebrates release a transmitter when there is an increase in illumination. For both systems, the light falling on a given receptor is continuously modulated as the eye moves, and thus both receptor types respond with fluctuating membrane potentials of opposite sign.

Receptor potentials have been recorded from a number of lower vertebrates (frog, turtle, mud puppy) and all are graded and hyperpolarized (Tomita 1972, Daw 1973, Rodieck 1973). Direct recordings from photoreceptors of higher vertebrates, especially primates, have not yet been reported. Eventually such recordings should provide much-needed independent confirmation of the few MSP results from primate receptors (MacNichol et al. 1973).

Clearly the receptor sensitivities of cyprinid fish agree very well with their absorption spectra (Table 7), and this strongly supports the Young-Helmholtz theory at the receptor level.

---

of the response is thus proportional to the sensitivity of the receptor. (Below) One hundred forty-two such curves replotted as spectral sensitivity and superimposed. (Tomita et al. 1967. Reproduced with the permission of the authors and the editor of *Vision Research*. © 1967 Pergamon Press, London.)

Table 7

Correspondence Between the Maximum Absorption (λ_{max}) of Single Goldfish Cones as Determined by MSP and the Peak Spectral Sensitivity of Individual Cone Receptors in the Closely Related Carp. The Small Differences Can Easily Be Accounted for by Species Differences and Experimental Error

B-type	G-type	R-type	
462 ± 15 nm	529 ± 14 nm	611 ± 23 nm	Tomita et al. (1967) (carp)
455 ± 15	530 ± 5	625 ± 5	Marks (1965) (goldfish)

Source: Tomita (1972). Reproduced with the permission of the author and publisher.

These studies also support the duplexity theory, since individual rods were shown to be ten times more sensitive than cones but much slower than cones in returning to voltage baselines following stimulation (Jacobs 1976). This result correlates well with the relatively higher sensitivity but lower temporal resolution of the scotopic (rod) system.

One final question about individual receptors concerns the role of rods in color vision. The literature on this old controversy is still confusing and contradictory. For example, rods have occasionally been considered as the blue receptor, but the evidence against this is overwhelming (Marriott 1962b, Rushton 1972). In fact, rod vision is colorless. However, Daw (1973) reported that humans see colors when only rods and "red cones" are active. Naturally, colors are not seen when the intensity falls completely below cone threshold, since only one receptor system is in operation, as explained on page 196. More recently, Jacobs (1976) noted increasing evidence of rod cone interaction at various levels in the visual system and under a variety of conditions. Opinion on the contributions that rod signals make to color vision varies from desaturation, i.e., dilution of the color by addition of white (Rushton 1972), to rods mimicking the "blue" receptor (Ambler 1974). With the present popularity of such investigations, we may soon expect to understand the role of rods in color vision.

Responses of the Horizontal, Bipolar, and Amacrine Cells

Up to this point, all the evidence has agreed with the Young-Helmholtz theory of color vision. By placing micropipettes into fish retinas, Svaetichin (1953) provided the first physiological evidence that opponent mechanisms at the retinal level were not a figment of Hering's imagination.

Horizontal cells (Fig. 53) are quite variable; in sharks they form up to three distinct rows of huge, block-like, axonless cells whose processes connect with receptors and bipolar cells. Stell and Witkovsky (1973) observed that rod and cone connections were morphologically segregated in different layers of horizontal cells. The horizontal cells of mammals are quite different: they do not form obvious layers, they possess an axon, and both rods and cones can terminate on a single horizontal cell (Stell 1972). With such anatomical variability, it is not surprising that the horizontal cell responses of different vertebrates differ greatly.

As mentioned, Svaetichin (1953) was the first investigator to report graded intracellular potentials from the retina. Subsequent studies (e.g., Kaneko 1970) demonstrated by dye marking that Svaetichin's responses probably originated in the horizontal cells. However, receptor, bipolar, and possibly amacrine, as well as horizontal cells, all respond with graded hyperpolarizing potentials. Thus, Motokawa termed these large (10–50 mV), negative voltage changes "S-potentials," both in honor of Svaetichin and to be neutral as to site of origin (Gouras 1972).

S-potentials come in two variations: luminosity (L)-type, which is purely hyperpolarizing, and chromaticity

(C)-type, which depolarizes to some wavelengths and hyperpolarizes to others (Fig. 57).

It is possible to determine which type of photoreceptor is feeding information to a particular horizontal cell by measuring the spectral sensitivity of that cell after the retina has been selectively adapted to particular wavelengths of light. This technique--chromatic adaptation--adapts the receptors which capture photons best at the color of the adapting light while leaving the responses of other receptor-types virtually intact. Thus, Laufer and Milan (1970), using L-type potentials, were able to demonstrate input to horizontal cells from three different cone types whose spectral sensitivities agreed very well with MSP data from the same species, a marine teleost. These data further support the Young-Helmholtz scheme. But L-potentials were so named because they were thought to form part of the brightness or luminosity-sensing channel. C-potentials are perhaps more interesting to us since they appear to have some relation to color channels. Most interesting is the antagonism shown by such a cell to different wavelengths of light (Fig. 57). This is precisely what Hering predicted: a physiological mechanism which responds in one direction, say positively, to one part of the spectrum, and in the opposite direction, that is negatively, to another part.

There are actually three types of C-potential: R/G (cell depolarized by red, hyperpolarized by green) and G/R (its mirror image); G/B and B/G; and R,B/G (cell depolarized by red and blue, hyperpolarized by green, but not vice versa). R/G and R,B/G are shown in Figure 57.

These responses probably do not represent color processing on the main visual pathway since the relation of S-potentials to vision remains unclear. Horizontal cells are electrically coupled one to the other by low-resistance gap junctions (Kaneko 1970) and integrate information from virtually the entire retina (Daw 1973). Thus, many authors have suggested that this system measures the average retinal brightness and scales down signals, thus allowing the retina to function over a greater dynamic range. In other words, this may be the retina's automatic gain control system (Rushton 1972a, Gouras 1972, MacNichol et al. 1973).

Finally, it appears that horizontal cells in the turtle retina feed back information to their photoreceptors (Fuortes and Simon 1974). This means that the individual responses of a turtle cone not only depend on the number of quanta absorbed, but are also influenced by activity of neighboring cones via a receptor-horizontal cell-receptor

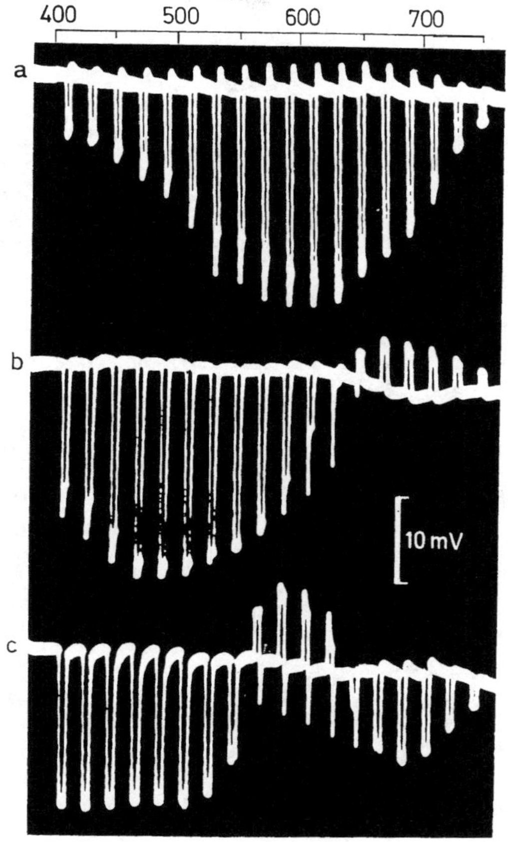

Fig. 57. Spectral response of the S-potential originating in the horizontal cells of the carp retina. (a) Luminosity (L-type), S-potential hyperpolarizes to all wavelengths of the equal quantum spectrum. The sensitivity of this cell peaks near 620 nm, indicating input from the long-wavelength cones. (b) A spectrally opponent, chromaticity (C-type) S-potential from a horizontal cell receiving inhibition from some cones and excitation from others. (c) A triphasic C-type response, the so-called R,B/G response, receiving input from all three cone types. Scales are in nanometers. (After Tomita, taken from Abramov 1972. Reproduced with the permission of the author and publisher. © 1972 Springer-Verlag, Berlin.)

feedback loop. Thus, the principle of univariance must be questioned, at least in the turtle retina (Jacobs 1976).

Bipolar cells, on the direct path from receptor to brain, are extremely small and thus are difficult to record from. Nevertheless, the few successful recordings demonstrate that the system of lateral inhibition and antagonism in the receptive field, found at so many levels in the visual system, starts with the bipolar cell (Dowling and Werblin 1969, Kaneko 1971, Rushton 1972a). The receptive field of a retinal neuron consists of all the other cells which directly or indirectly influence its electrical activity. Both receptors and horizontal cells converge on the bipolar cell and thus form its receptive field.

As with horizontal cells, bipolars display color-coded and noncolor-coded responses. For example, if a spot of light shines in the center of a group of photoreceptors hooked up to a particular bipolar cell, i.e., in its receptive field center, that bipolar may depolarize. For many bipolars, light that appears red to us seems the most effective stimulus. However, the same stimulus irrespective of the wavelength would hyperpolarize the cell if it fell on the periphery of its concentric receptive field. Such a cell behaves in a spatially opponent but spectrally nonopponent manner. A few bipolar cells have been found in which the center response was activated by red and the peripheral response by wavelengths that appear green (Daw 1973). Such cells clearly code the information contained in the wavelength and show spatial as well as chromatic opponent activity.

Very little is known of the physiology of amacrine cells (for review, see Naka and Chan 1976). Like horizontal cells, amacrines send their processes laterally into the retina and are therefore in a position to integrate information over large areas. Amacrine cells fire spike action potentials but code information in other ways as well. For example, a transient-type amacrine cell might depolarize at onset and offset of illumination and fire one or more spikes. Such a cell does not code for colors. In contrast, Kaneko (1971) found a sustained-type (i.e., cell responds for the duration of illumination) amacrine cell in the retina of the goldfish which hyperpolarized to red and depolarized to green stimuli. Such a cell showed chromatic opponent responses only, with no evidence for spatial separation of red and green input (Daw 1973).

Responses of the Ganglion Cells

The final result of signal processing in the retina can be seen in the activity of the ganglion cells. Unlike the receptors and intermediate neurons that code by amplitude-modulated (i.e., graded) hyperpolarizing and depolarizing potentials, ganglion cells transmit information to the brain by self-propagating all-or-none spikes which form a time-variant, frequency-coded message. That retinal ganglion cells fire spikes has long been known from the early work of Adrian, Hartline, Granit, and others (for review, see Granit 1955). However, it was Kuffler (1953) and Barlow (1953) who independently discovered that the activity of ganglion cells is organized into concentric center-surround receptive fields, which are shown in Figure 58. This was an important finding, since the coding of color information in certain ganglion cells depends on a knowledge of these spatially antagonistic receptive fields. The situation is potentially complicated: considering three cone types, each possibly contributing excitation or inhibition to a ganglion cell, there are 702 possible receptive field organizations, of which about 20 have been discovered (Rodieck 1973).

The most comprehensive results on color coding by ganglion cells have come from the retinas of the goldfish (Daw 1968) and the macaque monkey (DeValois and Jacobs 1968). Actually, most of the primate recordings were obtained from the next neuronal station in the visual path, the lateral geniculate nucleus. The studies of Gouras (review: 1971) are an exception. He recorded directly from ganglion cells in the monkey retina. However, most authors believe that little transformation of the ganglion cell code, if any, takes place at the lateral geniculate nucleus, and so results are practically the same as those from the retina.

The firing pattern of ganglion cells can be divided into two types: tonic (sustained) "on" or "off" responses, firing a burst of spikes which is maintained at some level during stimulation; and phasic (transient) responses, firing a short burst at the beginning and end of stimulation--the so-called "on-off" response. Ganglion cells of many vertebrate retinas have a spontaneous or resting rate of firing and thus can respond by excitation, i.e., an increase in firing level, or inhibition, i.e., a decrease compared with the spontaneous rate. Finally, there are two general types

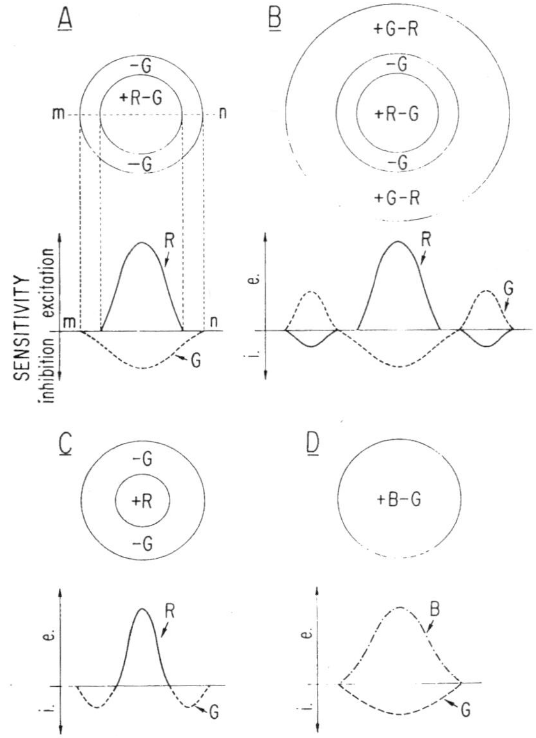

Fig. 58. Receptive field organization (spatial and chromatic) of opponent ganglion cells in the retinas of goldfish (A, B) and lateral geniculate nucleus of the macaque (C, D). B, G, and R represent stimuli which appear blue, green, and red, respectively. + or e and - or i represent excitation (increase in firing rate) and inhibition. The graphs below the concentric diagrams approximate the cell's responses as a stimulus is moved across the diameter of its receptive field. A represents the organization of a ganglion cell's responses when the retina is explored with small spots of light. Addition of an annulus brings out the "true" complexity shown in B. This is the double opponent cell described in the text. C and D are typical responses of the macaque LGN cells. This organization is still open to interpretation. (Abramov 1972. Reproduced with the permission of the author and publisher. © 1973 Springer-Verlag, Berlin.)

of interactions which take place at the ganglion cell level: (1) comparison by various neurons of receptor activity from different retinal locations, giving rise to the spatially opponent organization of the receptive field shown in Figure 58; and (2) comparison of the activity of the different cone types to form chromatic or spectrally opponent organization. Most ganglion cells exhibit both characteristics (DeValois and DeValois 1975).

Spatially opponent but noncolor opponent ganglion cells that respond with either excitation or inhibition at all wavelengths have been found in the goldfish and monkey retina. Both the center and surround of the receptive field have the same spectral sensitivity, which means that they are fed by the same type of receptor. Thus in the goldfish, many spectrally nonopponent ganglion cells have excitatory input to the receptive field center from the "red" cones (peak absorption at 625 nm) and inhibitory input to the receptive field periphery also from the 625 cones. DeValois and DeValois (1975) term such cells, which respond by excitation to incremental stimuli (i.e., a tiny white spot on a black background), +Wh-Bl cells. Mirror image responses, -Wh+Bl, are found with equal frequency. Such cells roughly correspond to Hering's black/white opponent mechanism although luminosity information is not exclusively carried by these cells (DeValois 1972).

The situation with spectrally opponent cells is somewhat more complicated, but the basic response is that the cell is excited by some wavelengths and inhibited by others. DeValois and colleagues recognize only four types of spectrally opponent ganglion cells: the red-green system, which consists of +R-G cells that fire maximally to the spectral region that appears red and inhibit to the spectral region that appears green; their mirror image -R+G; and the yellow-blue system composed of +Y-B and -Y+B cells (Fig. 59). These authors believe that the interaction of cone types which gives rise to the RG, YB, and BlWh systems are represented by the model shown in Figure 60. In this scheme, the long-wavelength cone receptor (λ_{max} 565 nm in the rhesus macaque) is central to this scheme. The short-wavelength cone is involved in the least number of interactions, which might account for its relatively poor representation in various electrophysiological and MSP studies.

A further complication is that most spectrally opponent cells also show spatial opponency. Daw (1973) discovered doubly opponent ganglion cells in the goldfish retina (Fig. 58) which were excited when the receptive field center was stimulated by red but inhibited by green.

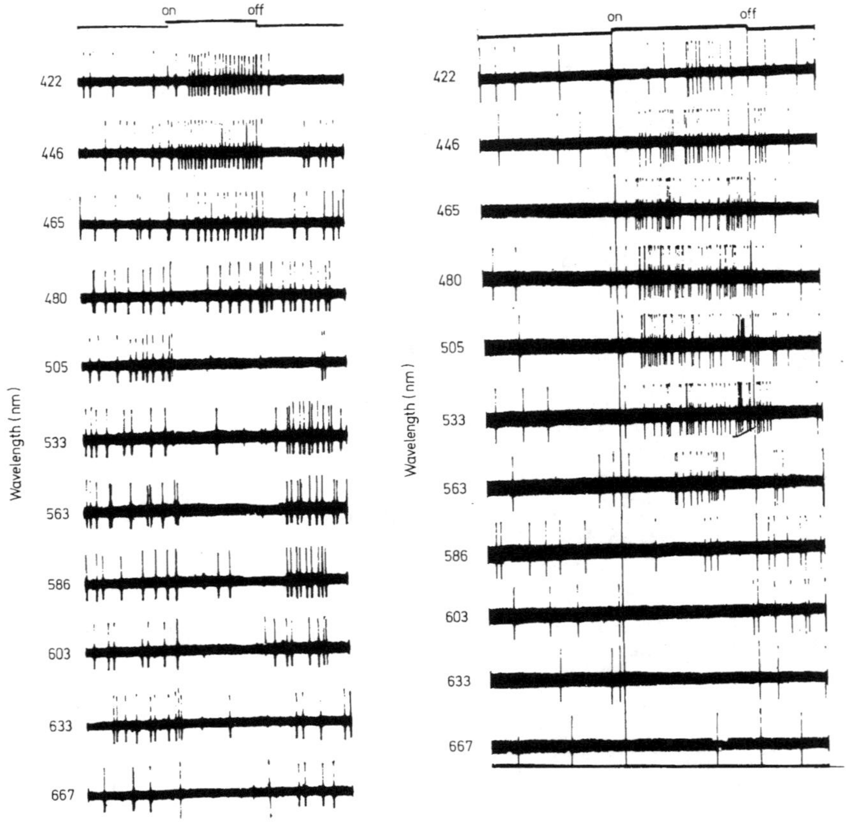

Fig. 59. Chromatic-opponent responses from the LGN of the macaque monkey. Left-hand records are from a +G-R cell and right-hand data are from a +B-Y cell. The thick black horizontal traces are the base lines and the numerous vertical traces represent depolarizing all-or-none spike potentials from LGN cells. "On-off" represents the one-second duration of a monochromatic stimulus. Note that maximum excitation for the +G-R cell is between 480 and 585 nm (the green region of the spectrum), compared with 422-446 nm for the +B-Y cell. (Modified from DeValois 1973. Reproduced with the permission of the author and publisher. © 1973 Springer-Verlag, Berlin.)

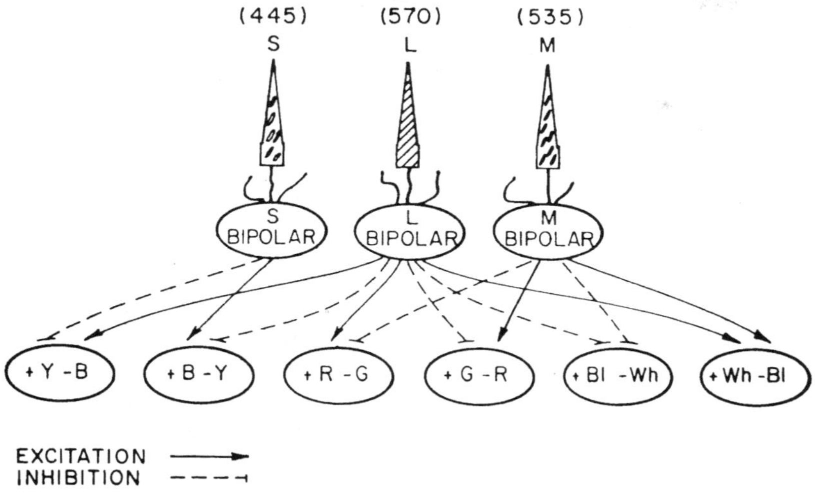

Fig. 60. Model of hypothetical connections of the three Young-Helmholtz-type receptors in the macaque which transform to Hering-type responses before the level of the LGN. Spatial organization in this model is ignored. The long-wavelength cone (570) is central to this scheme. (DeValois 1973. Reproduced with the permission of the author and publisher. © 1973 Springer-Verlag, Berlin.)

The same response occurred in the periphery, except the signs of red and green were reversed. Such cells, which have also been found in the primate cortex, would be capable of signaling simultaneous color contrast.

DeValois (1966), Abramov (1972), and DeValois and DeValois (1975) have attempted to relate the functional organization of ganglion and geniculate cells to some psychophysical results in color vision. For example, they show how ganglion cells are capable of wavelength discrimination and that the minimum change in wavelength across the spectrum that produces a criterion change in firing rate of some ganglion cells gives a curve very similar to that of the classical wavelength-discrimination function of man. They also discuss saturation, contrast effects, and color naming.

Only a few studies on color-coded responses in higher brain centers have been reported. Accordingly, it is premature to attempt a discussion of this subject (for recent review, see DeValois 1973). The direction of signal processing in the cortex seems to be toward separation of chromatic and achromatic information carried on the opponent cell signals, and narrower tuning of the spectral sensitivities.

Because of space and time limitations, I have presented an abbreviated and simplified view of the physiology of color vision. We have seen that trichromatic vision in man and other animals is mediated by three types of cones that have overlapping but different spectral sensitivities based upon three different photopigments (λ_{max} 445, 535, and 565 nm in man). Scotopic (achromatic) vision is mediated by rods that contain rhodopsin (λ_{max} 505 nm). These broad-band receptors feed into a circuit that differences the receptor output to extract narrow-band information, a characteristic of signal processing in other nervous systems. Thus, cones should not be considered color receptors since they certainly function in acuity and all other aspects of photopic vision. Rather, they should be considered light receptors that respond to increments and decrements. It is thus neural processing of comparison and differencing by opponent cells that underlies color vision.

The information about colors passed to the central nervous system is derived from neural processing of cone signals, not from the raw cone signals themselves. Processing by the retinal neurons involves transformation of essentially negative cone signals to antagonistic, graded responses at the horizontal, bipolar, and amacrine cell layers. Color-opponent responses are characterized by a cell depolarizing for some wavelengths and hyperpolarizing for others. In addition to chromatic responses, some cells have spatially opponent responses, in which the cell is hyperpolarized by a small spot of white light falling in the center of its receptive field and depolarized by an annulus of light in the periphery. The mirror image of this arrangement is also seen. Finally, the responses of ganglion and LGN cells are entirely different: when these cells discharge, the amplitude of the response is always the same. Information is coded in terms of some transform of an increase or decrease in rate of firing of all-or-none spike potentials. Ganglion cells show, at the same time, spatial as well as chromatic-opponent organization of their receptive fields. Thus they appear to multiplex both color and luminance information in their signal transformation. There is reasonably good correlation between the complexity of response of a chromatic-opponent ganglion cell and the type of behaviorally determined color vision that an animal possesses. In the poorly known higher brain centers, the concentric receptive fields are transformed to bars, and color information is extracted by highly color-specific cells. Other brain cells generalize across colors to extract spatial information about figure and forms.

METHODS FOR ASSESSING COLOR VISION OF ANIMALS

While it is unlikely that an animal that possesses all the machinery described above would be color-blind, there is no way to demonstrate that such an organism actually discriminates between wavelengths without a behavioral test of some sort. The classical example of this problem is the visual system of the cat, which has cones and opponent responses, but only the most rudimentary color vision, which can play little if any role in its behavior. Yet, from the physiological evidence, one might expect this animal to have reasonable color vision. In fact, cats were thought to be color-blind for years until a minimal color sense was eventually demonstrated (Sechzer and Brown 1964). This raises another problem with color vision investigations: it is logically impossible to prove that an animal is color-blind. Negative evidence is not compelling. Just as in the cat, with enough data or a new behavioral technique, color vision might be found in a supposedly color-blind animal. In fact, it appears that many domestic animals that were once regarded as completely color-blind have recently been shown to have some color sensitivity (DeValois and DeValois 1975).

How have nonhuman animals been reliably tested for color vision? Walls (1942) outlined a sample ideal procedure after noting that some earlier techniques were ingenious and some were very stupid. Actually, Walls correctly noted that the major pitfall in a color vision test is inadequate control over brightness cues. Situations in which brightness cues covary with color cues must be completely eliminated in all color discrimination tests, and he suggested a technique that is now known as heterochromatic brightness matching with randomization. Before I give details on this technique, an outline of the general sorts of tests that have been used to "prove" color vision in animals and a brief comment on the validity of these is given.

There are two behavioral techniques for testing color vision: reflex methods, and methods that require some form of training. Reflex methods depend upon an unlearned, orienting photic response that must be resistant to habituation or fatigue. Such behavior includes the dorsal light reaction (Silver 1974), optokinetic and optomotoric responses (Cronley-Dillon and Sharma 1968), positive and negative phototaxis and photokinesis (Muntz 1962), and even the adaptation of body coloration to different backgrounds (Kühn 1950; see also Chapter 4).

While these methods are convenient and their responses relatively easy to elicit, the behavior and resultant data are often described as capricious. This is because the experimenter is at the mercy of the particular response mechanism, which often depends upon uncontrolled intervening variables. For example, a species might be positively phototactic during one part of the lunar cycle and then become negatively phototactic, thus throwing the results into turmoil. One of the most commonly used reflex methods involves the unconditioned optomotor response in which an organism, placed in the center of a rotating striped cylinder, either aligns itself like a magnetic pointer toward one of the stripes or moves around at the same rate as the cylinder. When the speed of rotation is increased, a critical point is reached when the subject cannot follow and either falls off "the mark" or, more commonly, gives a sharp reflexive movement at the end point. Schlieper (1927) used this technique for color vision studies in several animals but the results were curious: even though some of the subjects were previously shown by other methods to have color vision, when tested in Schlieper's chamber with alternating colored and gray stripes, there was always some intensity of gray which abolished the response, falsely indicating a lack of color vision. Thus, the optokinetic method has been criticized because several cues are operating simultaneously, i.e., spatial and temporal cues superimposed on chromatic cues. In general, the reflexive technique is convenient, but it is fraught with difficulty in interpretation as well as response measurement and experimental repeatability (Blough and Yager 1972, Northmore and Yager 1975).

Training methods fall into three categories: classical conditioning, operant conditioning, and techniques with elements of both, such as avoidance conditioning (for review, see Stebbins 1970). The method suggested by Walls (1942), mentioned earlier, belongs to operant conditioning and is perhaps the most common and unambiguous technique for testing wavelength discrimination. The apparatus consists of a runway with a starting point, then a point where the subject chooses one of two colored stimuli, and a reinforcement point where appropriate reward is given for the response. Figure 61 shows a lemon shark having just chosen

Fig. 61. Photograph of a young lemon shark (*Negaprion*) choosing one of two stimuli in a color vision test involving two-choice heterochromatic brightness matching with randomization (see text for explanation). This is the "standard" training method for deciding whether an animal can discriminate between visual stimuli (in this case an array of illuminated optical fibers) on the basis of wavelength only. (Gruber 1977. Reproduced with the permission of the editor of *American Zoologist*. © 1977 American Society of Zoologists.)

the right-hand door in a color vision test of this type. Several variations of the two-choice method have been developed, including the use of more than two stimuli, which reduces the level of random correct choice from 50% to 1/n (where n is number of stimuli) (DeValois 1965). However, the important point in all color vision tests of this sort is that, as stated, controls must insure that the subject is not choosing on the quantitative basis of brightness differences but rather on qualitative differences between the wavelengths of the two stimuli. Typically, the experimenter chooses chromatic test and comparison stimuli from the subject's previously determined spectral sensitivity curve. These are adjusted in brightness so that the experimenter feels reasonably assured that they are close or equal in perceived brightness (to the subject). The animal is then trained to associate food with the comparison hue whose position is randomly varied with the test hue. For the color vision test, a trained animal is asked to pick out the comparison hue when the test hue is varied both in position and over a two-to-three log (100- to 1000-fold difference) range of intensities. If the subject can successfully discriminate over the entire range of intensities, it is said to have color vision.

Several variations in this color vision test have been devised, including a monochromatic vs. gray discrimination test (McCleary and Bernstein 1959). Kickleiter and Loop (1976) have criticized the traditional controls for brightness cues as more complicated than necessary and have presented a simple and valid alternative, using broad band stimuli whose quantal fluxes do not overlap at any point.

Classical conditioning involves an entirely separate training paradigm and has been used infrequently for color vision testing. This method depends upon the sensory association of a previously neutral stimulus with a stimulus effective in eliciting some motor response. For example, the subject could be trained to associate a neutral flash of light with an electric shock which always evokes a reflex movement of the nictitating membrane (Gruber and Schneiderman 1975). Such associative learning trials eventually produce a conditioned response between light and shock; the subject now moves its nictitating membrane in response to the light, in anticipation of the shock.

For a test of color vision, the technically difficult method of "silent substitution" is used (Boynton 1971). The animal is trained to respond when one color is silently substituted for another which is equated as closely as possible in brightness to the first color. Once the response is established, color vision is tested by varying the brightness of the substitution stimulus above and below the adapting stimulus. Application of this method to color vision in the lemon shark is described by Gruber (1975).

Two relatively newer techniques, conditioned suppression and avoidance conditioning, are achieving a certain popularity in studies of animal psychophysics (Stebbins 1970, Blough and Lipsitt 1971, Blough and Yager 1972, Northmore and Yager 1975) and could be modified for color vision tests.

PHYLOGENY OF COLOR VISION AND CONCLUDING REMARKS

The phylogenetic development of color vision is rather discontinuous. It is best developed in those animals with well-organized eyes, where vision plays an important role in behavior, but this is not always so. For example, a color sense has been claimed for some minute planktonic arthropods, such as copepods and cladocerans. The eye of such animals is composed of a few hundred cells at most. However, vision may be relatively important for these animals both in feeding and in diurnal, vertical migrations.

Color vision has been tested in the arthropod, mollusc, and chordate phyla. There are surprising similarities between the physiology and psychophysics of color vision in such diverse forms as man and honey bee (Autrum 1968). The evidence for color vision in the Mollusca is not compelling. Color discrimination was apparently demonstrated in the octopus by training experiments. However, Orlov and Byzov (1961) found only a single receptor type, which was confirmed physiologically by Hamasaki (1968). Experiments on the well-developed eyes of lamellibranch molluscs have not demonstrated a color sense.

Of the arthropods, insects have the best color vision. A color sense has been found in representatives of all orders of Insecta. The most intensively studied are the honey bees (Autrum and Thomas 1973), which have highly developed trichromatic vision, similar in many respects to that of fishes, birds, and higher mammals. One interesting fact emerging from the insect studies is that ultraviolet may be a primary color for them. Ultraviolet sensitivity in the insects has apparently coevolved with the so-called "honey guides," which are highly ultraviolet-reflecting patterns found in flowers.

Color sensitivity is suspected in various crustacea and arachnids. The horseshoe "crab" *Limulus* has two receptor types with differential absorption spectra, which suggests color sensitivity.

Color vision is represented to a greater or lesser degree in all orders of the vertebrates. It is especially prominent in the teleost fishes, lizards, turtles, birds, and higher mammals. Reviews of the occurrence of color vision in various taxa can be found in the following: *General*--Viaud (1960), Autrum and Thomas (1973); *Insecta*--von Frisch (1960), Burkhardt (1962); *Vertebrates*--Walls (1942), Jacobs (1976); *Fishes*--Herter (1952); and *Primates*--DeValois and Jacobs (1968).

As we have seen, color vision has been convergently evolved in many unrelated phyla from unrelated anatomical substrates but often with a common biochemical basis. Clearly, the analysis of wavelength variations of light must be valuable for the possessor of color vision, but the value is not always obvious. The "purpose" of sensory systems is to provide the organism with up-to-the minute information on environmental conditions. Because of the high speed of light and its rectilinear propagation, an image-forming photoreceptive system is ideal for this purpose. The main function of such a visual system is to analyze the pattern of environmental radiation in spatiotemporal terms, thereby informing the organisms about type, number, and changes of significant objects in visual space. Naturally the evolution of color vision provides its possessor with some selective advantage. But what might that advantage be? At least part of it has to do with the perception of contrast, an extremely important visual process. Hartline long ago demonstrated, when he discovered the process of lateral inhibition, that the visual system is set up to promote contrast (for review, see Hartline and Ratliff 1972). The opponent receptive fields discussed above also reflect the importance of contrast. Walls (1942) used the analogy of a color vs. black-and-white moving picture to explain how color vision enhances visibility, a perceptual correlate of contrast. An actress, he said, might report to work wearing a highly discriminable blue skirt and red blouse. But if the pigments were improperly matched to the sensitivity of the black-and-white film, she would appear to be wearing a uniform. So it is with animals. Color vision to a pelagic predatory fish might mean the difference between discriminating its prey against the monotonous blue haze and completely missing it. On the other hand, it is equally important for the prey to detect the predator. The interplay between color vision, animal coloration, and predatory as well as social activity provides us with a wealth of examples of how color apparently relates to behavior. Many of the ideas on the selective value of color vision originated with Wallace (1891), and were discussed by Walls (1942). More recently, they have been developed and clearly explained by McFarland and Munz (1975).

The value of human color vision clearly resides in the approximately 160 new qualities which can be used to characterize man's external world. These 160 qualities translate out to several million discriminable colors if all levels of saturation and intensity are included. This provides us with a powerful analytical mechanism, not only to aesthetically appreciate a beautiful sunset, but to predict whether it portends fair weather or foul.

ACKNOWLEDGMENTS

This chapter is dedicated to Drs. Arnold Blaustein, Jacob Neber, and Daniel Nixon, whose efforts made the production of this work possible. The writing of this chapter was entirely supported by Office of Naval Research Contract N0014-75-C-0173/sub. 1. I gratefully acknowledge travel support from the Biomedical Sciences Support Grant FR-07022-10, General Research Support Branch, Division of Research Resources, Bureau of Health Professions Education and Manpower Training, N.I.M. (to E. H. Man) and the RSMAS General Operations Account (W. Hay, Dean). I thank T. Shipley for loan of personal reference materials and Marie Gruber for the artwork.

REFERENCES

Abramov, I. 1972. Retinal mechanisms of colour vision. In *Handbook of Sensory Physiology. Physiology of Photoreceptor Organs*, Vol. VII/2, M. G. Fuortes (ed.). Berlin: Springer-Verlag, pp. 567-607.

Abramov, I., and Gordon, J. 1973. Vision. In *Handbook of Perception*, Vol. 3, E. C. Carterette and M. P. Friedman (eds.). New York: Academic Press, pp. 327-357.

Alpern, M. 1968. Distal mechanisms of vertebrate color vision. *Ann. Rev. Physiol.* 30:279-318.

Ambler, M. 1974. Hue discrimination in peripheral vision under conditions of dark and light adaptation. *Percept. Psychophysics* 15:586-590.

Autrum, H. 1968. Color vision in man and animals. *Naturwissenschaften* 55:10-18.

Autrum, H., and Thomas, I. 1973. Comparative physiology of color vision in animals. In *Handbook of Sensory Physiology. Central Visual Information A*, Vol. VII/3, R. Jung (ed.). Berlin: Springer-Verlag, pp. 662-692.

Barlow, H. B. 1953. Summation and inhibition in the frog's retina. *J. Physiol.* (Lond.) 119:69-88.

Bezold, W. von. 1873. Uber das Gesetz der Farbenmischung die physiologischen Gründ farben. *Ann. Phys. Lpz.* 150: 221-247.

Blough, D. S., and Lipsitt, L. P. 1971. The discriminative control of behavior. In *Woodworth and Schlosberg's Experimental Psychology*, J. W. Kling and L. A. Riggs (eds.)., 3rd Ed. New York: Holt, Rinehart, pp. 743-789.

Blough, D. S., and Yager, D. 1972. Visual psychophysics in animals. In *Handbook of Sensory Physiology. Visual Psychophysics*, Vol. VII/4, D. Jameson and L. M. Hurvich (eds.). Berlin: Springer-Verlag, pp. 732-763.

Boll, F. 1876. Zur Anatomie und Physiologie der Retina. *Mber. Berl. Akad. Wiss.* 12:783-788.

Boring, E. G. 1942. *Sensation and Perception in the History of Experimental Psychology*. New York: Appleton.

Boynton, R. M. 1966. Vision. In *Experimental Methods and Instrumentation in Psychology*, J. B. Sidowski (ed.). New York: McGraw-Hill, pp. 273-330.

Boynton, R. M. 1971. Color vision. In *Experimental Psychology*, J. W. Kling and L. A. Riggs (eds.). New York: Holt, Rinehart, pp. 567-608.

Bridges, C. D., and Ripps, H. 1977. Rhodopsin: How a nerve is excited by light. *Invest. Ophth. Visual Sci.* (ARVO Supplement). 90 pp.

Burkhardt, D. 1962. Colour discrimination in insects. In *Advances in Insect Physiology*, Vol. II, J. W. Beament, J. E. Treherne, and V. B. Wigglesworth (eds.). New York: Academic Press, pp. 131-173.

Burnham, R. W.; Hanes, R. M.; and Bartelson, J. C. 1963. *Color: A Guide to Basic Facts and Concepts*. New York: Wiley.

Campbell, F. W., and Rushton, W. A. 1955. Measurement of the scotopic pigment in the living human eye. *J. Physiol.* (Lond.) 187:427-436.

Cornsweet, T. N. 1970. *Visual Perception*. New York: Academic Press.

Cronley-Dillon, J. R., and Sharma, S. C. 1968. Effect of season and sex on the photopic spectral sensitivity of the three-spined sticleback. *J. Exp. Biol.* 49:679-687.

Dartnall, H. J. 1975. Assessing the fitness of visual pigments for their photic environment. In *Vision in Fishes: New Approaches in Research*, M. A. Ali (ed.). New York: Plenum Press, pp. 543-564.

Daw, N. 1968. Colour-coded ganglion cells in the goldfish retina: extension of their receptive fields by means of new stimuli. *J. Physiol.* (Lond.) 197:567-592.

Daw, N. 1973. Neurophysiology of color vision. *Physiol. Rev.* 53:571-611.

DeValois, R. L. 1965. Behavioral and electrophysiological studies of primate vision. In *Contributions to Sensory Physiology*, Vol. I, W. Neff (ed.). New York: Academic Press, 137-178.

DeValois, R. L. 1966. Analysis of response patterns of LGN cells. *J. Opt. Soc. Am.* 56:966-977.

DeValois, R. L. 1972. Processing of intensity and wavelength information in the visual system. *Invest. Ophthal.* 11:417-426.

DeValois, R. L. 1973. Central mechanisms of color vision. In *Handbook of Sensory Physiology. Central Visual Information A*, Vol. VII/3, R. Jung (ed.). Berlin: Springer-Verlag.

DeValois, R. L., and DeValois, K. K. 1975. Neural coding of color. In *Handbook of Perception. Seeing*, Vol. V, E. C. Carterette and M. P. Friedman (eds.). New York: Academic Press, pp. 117-166.

DeValois, R. L. and Jacobs, G. H. 1968. Primate color vision. *Science* 162:533-540.

Dowling, J. E. 1970. Organization of vertebrate retinas. *Invest. Ophthal.* 9:655-680.

Dowling, J. E., and Werblin, F. 1969. Organization of the retina of the mud puppy, *Necturus maculosus*. I. Synaptic structure. *J. Neurophysiol.* 32:315-388.

Frisch, K. von. 1960. Über den Farbensinn der Insekten. In *Mechanisms of Colour Discrimination*, Y. Galifret (ed.). New York: Academic Press, pp. 19-40.

Fuortes, M. G., and O'Bryan, P. M. 1972. Generator potentials in invertebrate photoreceptors. In *Handbook of Sensory Physiology. Physiology of Photoreceptor Organs*, Vol. VII/2, M. G. Fuortes (ed.). Berlin: Springer-Verlag, pp. 321-338.

Fuortes, M. G., and Simon, E. J. 1974. Interactions leading to horizontal cell responses in the turtle retina. *J. Physiol.* (Lond.) 240:177-198.

Furukawa, T., and Hanawa, I. 1955. Effects of some common cations on the electroretinogram of the toad. *Jap. J. Physiol.* 5:289-300.

Gouras, P. 1971. The function of the midget cell system in primate color vision. *Vision Res. Suppl.* 3:397-410.

Gouras, P. 1972. S-potentials. In *Handbook of Sensory Physiology. Physiology of Photoreceptor Organs*, Vol. VII/2, M. G. Fuortes (ed.). Berlin: Springer-Verlag, pp. 513-529.

Graham, C. H. 1965. *Vision and Visual Perception*. New York: Wiley.

Granit, R. 1947. *Sensory Mechanisms of the Retina*. London: Oxford Univ. Press.

Granit, R. 1955. *Receptors and Sensory Perception*. New Haven: Yale Univ. Press.

Granit, R. 1962. Neurophysiology of the retina. In *The Eye*, Vol. II, H. Davson (ed.). New York: Academic Press, pp. 575-691.

Gruber, S. H. 1975. Duplex vision in the elasmobranchs: histological, electrophysiological and psychophysical evidence. In *Vision in Fishes: New Approaches to Research*, M. A. Ali (ed.). New York: Plenum Press, pp. 525-542.

Gruber, S. H. 1977. Visual system of the elasmobranchs: adaptations and capability. *Amer. Zoologist* 17:453-469.

Gruber, S. H., and Schneiderman, N. 1975. Classical conditioning of the nictitating membrane response of the lemon shark (*Negaprion brevirostris*). *Behav. Res. Methods Instr.* 7:430-434.

Hamasaki, D. I. 1968. The electroretinogram of the intact anesthetized octopus. *Vision Res.* 8:247-258.

Hanaoka, T., and Fujimoto, K. 1957. Absorption spectrum of a single cone in carp retina. *Jap. J. Physiol.* 7:276-285.

Hartline, H. K., and Ratliff, F. 1972. Inhibitory interaction in the retina of Limulus. In *Handbook of Sensory Physiology. Physiology of Photoreceptor Organs*, Vol. VII/2, M. G. Fuortes (ed.). Berlin: Springer-Verlag, pp. 381-448.

Helmholtz, H. von. 1866. *Handbuch der Physiologischen Optik*, 1st ed. Leipzig: Voss.

Helmholtz, H. von. 1896. *Handbuch der Physiologischen Optik*, 2nd ed. Hamburg: Voss.

Hering, E. 1878. *Zur Lehre vom Lichtsinn*. Vienna: Carl Gerold's Sohn.

Herter, K. 1953. *Die Fischdressur und Ihre sinnesphysiologische Grundlage*. Berlin: Akademie-Verlag.

Holmgren, F. 1865. Method att objectivera effecten av ljustintryck på rètina. *Upsala Läk.-Fören Förh.* 1:177-191.

Hurvich, L. M. 1960. The opponent-pairs scheme. In *Mechanisms of Colour Discrimination*, Y. Galifret (ed.). New York: Pergamon Press, pp. 199-219.

Hurvich, L. M., and Jameson, D. 1969. Human color perception. An essay review. *Amer. Scientist* 57:143-166.

Jacobs, J. H. 1976. Color vision. *Ann. Rev. Psychol.* 27:63-89.

Kaneko, A. 1970. Physiological and morphological identification of horizontal bipolar and amacrine cells in the goldfish retina. *J. Physiol.* (Lond.) 207:623-633.

Kaneko, A. 1971. Physiological studies of single retinal cells and their morphological identification. *Vision Res. Suppl.* 3:17-26.

Kickleiter, E., and Loop, M. S. 1976. A test of wavelength discrimination. *Vision Res.* 16:951-956.

Kuffler, S. W. 1953. Discharge patterns and functional organization of the mammalian retina. *J. Neurophysiol.* 16:37-68.

Kühn, A. 1950. Über den Farbwechsel und Farensinn von Cephalopoden. *Z. Vergl. Physiol.* 32:572-598.

Kuhne, W. 1877. Über den Sehpurpur. *Untersuchungen Physiol. Inst. Univ. Heidelburg* 1:15-103.

Laufer, M., and Milan, E. 1970. Spectral analysis of L-type S-potentials and their relation to photopigment absorption in a fish (*Eugerres plumeri*). *Vision Res.* 10:237-251.

Le Grand, Y. 1957. *Light, Colour and Vision.* New York: Wiley.

Liebman, P. A. 1972. Microspectrophotometry of photoreceptors. In *Handbook of Sensory Physiology. Photochemistry of Vision*, Vol. VII/1, H. J. Dartnall (ed.). Berlin: Springer-Verlag, pp. 481-528.

Linksz, A. 1964. *An Essay on Color Vision.* New York: Grune and Stratton.

Lomonsov, M. V. 1757. *Lectures on the Origin of Light, Presenting a New Theory of Colors*. 1952 Edition of Lomonsov's collected works. Moscow.

McCleary, R., and Bernstein, J. J. 1959. A unique method for control of brightness cues in the study of color vision in fish. *Physiol. Zool.* 32:284-292.

McFarland, W. N., and Munz, F. W. 1975. Part III: The evolution of photopic visual pigments in fishes. *Vision Res.* 15:1071-1080.

MacNichol, E. F., Jr.,; Fineberg, R.; and Harosi, F. I. 1973. Colour discrimination processes in the retina. In *Color, 72*, International Color Society (ed.). New York: Wiley, pp. 191-251.

Marks, W. B. 1965. Visual pigments of single goldfish cones. *J. Physiol.* (Lond.) 178:14-32.

Marriott, F. H. 1962a. Color vision: introduction. In *The Eye*, Vol. II, H. Davson (ed.). New York: Academic Press, pp. 219-230.

Marriott, F. H. 1962b. Color vision: theories. In *The Eye*, Vol. 2, H. Davson (ed.). New York: Academic Press, pp. 299-322.

Maxwell, J. C. 1860. On the theory of compound colors and the relations of colors to the spectrum. *Philosophical Trans.* 150:57-84.

Muntz, W. R. 1962. Effectiveness of different colors of light in releasing the positive phototactic behavior of frogs, and a possible function of the retinal projection to the diencephalon. *J. Neurophysiol.* 25:712-720.

Naka, K-I., and Chan, R. 1976. The amacrine cell. *Vision Res.* 16:1119-1130.

Naka, K-I., and Rushton, W. H. 1966. S-potentials from color units in the retina of fish (Cyprinidae). *J. Physiol.* (Lond.) 185:536-555.

Newton, I. 1672. New theory about light and colors. *Phil. Trans.* 80:3705-3787.

Northmore, D. P., and Yager, D. 1975. Psychophysical methods for investigations of vision in fishes. In

Vision in Fishes: New Approaches to Research, M. A. Ali (ed). New York: Plenum Press, pp. 689-704.

Orlov, D. Y., and Byzov, A. L. 1961. Colorimetric investigation of sight in cephalopod molluscs. *Dokl. Akad. Nauk.* 139:723-725. (In Russian.)

Palmer, G. 1777. *Theory of Colours and Vision.* London: Leacroft.

Pearlman, A. L. 1977. Cerebral color blindness: an acquired defect in hue discrimination. *Invest. Ophthal. Visual Sci.* (ARVO Supplement, Abstract only.)

Pedler, C. 1965. Rods and cones--a fresh approach. In *Colour Vision Physiology and Experimental Psychology.* A. V. DeReuk and J. Knight (eds.). Boston: Little Brown, pp. 52-82.

Purdy, D. M. 1931. Spectral hue as a function of intensity. *Amer. J. Psych.* 43:541-599.

Rodieck, R. W. 1973. *The Vertebrate Retina: Principles of Structure and Function.* San Francisco: W. H. Freeman.

Rushton, W. A. 1963. A cone pigment in the protanope. *J. Physiol.* (Lond.) 168:345-359.

Rushton, W. A. 1965. A foveal pigment in the deuteranope. *J. Physiol.* (Lond.) 176:24-37.

Rushton, W. A. 1969. Colour perception in man. In *Processing of the Optical Data by Organisms and by Machines* (Proc. Intl. School Phys. "Enrico Fermi"), Course XVIII. New York: Academic Press, pp. 565-579.

Rushton, W. A. 1972a. Review lecture. Pigments and signals in color vision. *J. Physiol.* (Lond.) 220:1-31.

Rushton, W. A. 1972b. Visual pigments in man. In *Handbook of Sensory Physiology. Photochemistry of Vision*, Vol. VII/1, H. J. Dartnall (ed.). Berlin: Springer-Verlag, pp. 364-394.

Schlieper, C. 1927. Farbensinn der Tiere und optomotorische Reaktionen der Tiere. *Z. Vergl. Physiol.* 6:453-472.

Schultze, M. 1866. Zur Anatomie und Physiologie der Retina. *Arch. Mikroskop. Anat.* 2:175-286.

Sechzer, J. A., and Brown, J. L. 1964. Color discrimination in the cat. *Science* 144:427-429.

Sheppard, J. J., Jr. 1968. *Human Color Perception*. New York: American Elsevier.

Shipley, T. 1964. Rod-cone duplexity and the autonomic action of light. *Vision Res.* 4:155-177.

Silver, P. H. 1974. Photopic spectral sensitivity of the neon tetra (*Paracheirodon innesi* Myers) found by the use of a dorsal light reaction. *Vision Res.* 14:329-334.

Stebbins, W. C. 1970. *Animal Psychophysics: the Design and Conduct of Sensory Experiments*. New York: Appleton.

Stell, W. K. 1972. The morphological organization of the vertebrate retina. In *Handbook of Sensory Physiology: Physiology of Photoreceptor Organs*, Vol. VII/2, M. G. Fuortes (ed.). Berlin: Springer-Verlag, pp. 111-214.

Stell, W. K., and Witkovsky, P. I. 1973. Retinal structure in the smooth dogfish, *Mustelus canis*: light microscopy of receptor and horizontal cells. *J. Comp. Neurol.* 148: 1-32.

Stiles, W. S. 1939. The directional sensitivity of the retina and the spectral sensitivities of the rods and cones. *Proc. Roy. Soc. B.* 127:64-105.

Svaetichin, G. 1953. The cone action potential. *Acta Physiol. Scand.* 29:565-600.

Tansley, K. 1965. *Vision in Vertebrates*. London: Chapman and Hall.

Tinbergen, N. 1951. *The Study of Instinct*. Oxford: Clarendon Press.

Tomita, T; Murikami, H.; and Paulter, E. L. 1967. Spectral response curves of single cones in the carp. *Vision Res.* 7:519-531.

Tomita, T. 1965. Electrophysiological study of the mechanisms subserving color coding in the fish retina. *Cold Spr. Harbor Symp. Quant. Biol.* V 30:559-566.

Tomita, T. 1972. Light-induced potential and resistance changes in vertebrate photoreceptors. In *Handbook of*

Sensory Physiology. Physiology of Photoreceptor Organs, Vol. VII/2. M. G. Fuortes (ed.). Berlin: Springer-Verlag, pp. 483-511.

Viaud, G. 1960. La vision chromatique chez les animaux (sauf les insectes). In *Mechanisms of Colour Discrimination*, Y. Galifret (ed.). New York: Academic Press, pp. 41-57.

Wallace, A. R. 1891. *Natural Selection and Tropical Nature*, 2nd ed. London: Macmillan.

Walls, G. L. 1942. *The Vertebrate Eye and its Adaptive Radiation*. Bloomfield Hills, Mich.: Cranbrook Inst. of Sci.

Wasserman, G. S. 1973. Invertebrate color vision and the tuned receptor paradigm. *Science* 18:268-276.

Wright, W. D. 1967. *The Rays Are Not Coloured*. London: Adam Hilger.

Wyzecki, G., and Stiles, W. S. 1967. *Color Science: Concepts and Methods. Quantitative Data and Formulas*. New York: Wiley.

Young, T. 1802. The Bakerian lecture. On the theory of light and colours. *Phil. Trans. Roy. Soc.* 12:12-48.

Chapter 6

Visual Discriminations Encountered in Food Foraging By a Neotropical Primate:

Implications for the Evolution of Color Vision

D. Max Snodderly

Introduction
Methods
  Study Group and Locale
  Plant Specimens
  Photographic Documentation
  Reflectance Measurements
Callicebus torquatus and Its Food Sources
  Evidence for Coevolution
  Visual Appearance and Reflectance Spectra of Fruit
  Reflectance Spectra Grouped by Color
  Importance of Fruit Size
Plant Adaptations and Primate Foraging Behavior
Relationship of Foraging Behavior to Color Vision
  Environmental Selection
  Mechanistic Considerations
  Theoretical Issues
  Refining the Approach
  The Need for Habitat Conservation

INTRODUCTION

Vision is one of the principal senses of primates. It plays such a dominant role that the morphology of the visual apparatus is one criterion for distinguishing primates from other mammalian forms (Napier and Napier 1967). Small wonder that a great deal of effort has gone into laboratory measurement of the visual capacities of primates (DeValois and Jacobs 1971). Paradoxically, field studies have done little to specify the visual discriminations a primate makes in its natural environment. This is especially true in the realm of color vision.

Classical tests of color vision include sensitivity to light of different wavelengths (spectral sensitivity), ability to distinguish differences between two similar wavelengths (wavelength discrimination), and ability to distinguish a faintly colored light from an achromatic, white light (saturation discrimination) (see Chapter 5 for further discussion). Several primate species have been studied, using one or more of these tests as a means of describing their color vision. The results show that characteristic differences exist among species, and perhaps even between the two sexes of certain species.

Although the data are not comprehensive, they suggest a division between the performance of New World and Old World primates on standard color discriminations. Old World primates (*Macaca*, *Pan*, and *Papio*) have normal human-type color vision with acute wavelength discrimination all across the visible spectrum. New World primates (*Saimiri*, *Cebus*, and *Lagothrix*[1]) have lower sensitivity to light of long wavelengths and poorer wavelength discrimination in the red end of the spectrum. The evidence for these summary statements has been reviewed by DeValois and Jacobs (1971), and recent additional data have reinforced this view (DeValois et al. 1974, DeValois and Morgan 1974, Ptito et al. 1973). The best documented comparison is that between *Macaca* and *Saimiri*, where fourteen to fifteen individuals of each species have been tested. If there are differences among the

---

[1]There is confusion about the species identification in this case because the author equates *Lagothrix* with *Ateles*, which is a separate genus of New World monkey.

macaques, they are so small as to be negligible in the present context, so I shall not attempt to differentiate within the genus. The difference between the macaques and the squirrel monkeys, on the other hand, is large and functionally important. Figure 62 summarizes the performance of five macaques and four squirrel monkeys tested in the same apparatus on a wavelength discrimination problem.

Two points are of special interest: (1) the squirrel monkeys require a larger wavelength difference for detection

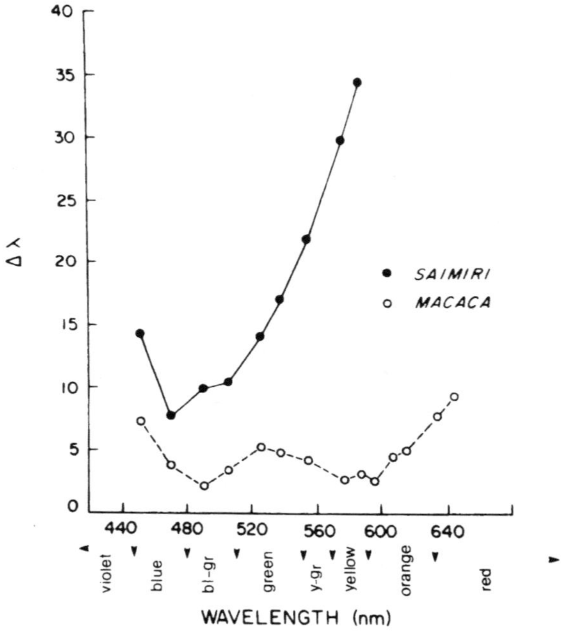

Fig. 62. The difference in wavelength between equally luminous (i.e., approximately equally bright) lights that can be detected by macaques and by squirrel monkeys. During the test, the monkey saw a panel of four lights, one of which was different in wavelength from the other three. It had to identify the panel that was different. (Data from DeValois and Morgan 1974. Color names assigned to wavelength ranges by normal human observers are indicated for reference.)

in all regions of the spectrum, and (2) their performance is especially poor at the long wavelengths which we see as yellow to red. In the region around 580 to 600 nm, the squirrel monkeys require approximately ten times as great a wavelength difference for discrimination as macaques or normal humans.

This poses the problem that stimulated my investigations: if primates are so dependent on vision, and New World monkeys have relatively poor color vision, why has natural selection not eliminated the New World monkeys, or at least improved their vision? The logical place to look for the answer is in the monkey's environment, where the selection pressures are found. The challenge is how to characterize the selection pressures in some way that is meaningful from a physical or psychobiological point of view. In this case it means specifying the color discriminations that are posed by the environment.

Students of predator-prey relationships have long recognized the importance of color in the environment in relation to animal camouflage and animal warning signals (Cott 1957, Edmunds 1974). Here I extend this line of thinking to include the monkey as a predator, preying on fruits that have a cryptic or conspicuous appearance. This places the problem in the larger context of the coevolution of animals (monkeys) and plants (Gilbert and Raven 1975). Hence the relevant color discrimination is finding the fruit amid a background of foliage. As a first step toward specifying this discrimination in physical terms, I present reflectance spectra for fruits and leaves of major food sources of a neotropical primate.

METHODS

Study Group and Locale

Behavioral observations of a troop of *Callicebus torquatus* were made by Warren Kinzey and his associates during June, July, and August 1974; June and July 1975; January 1976; and January 1977, at Estacion Biologica Callicebus in northern Peru. I participated in the 1975 expedition and I analyzed food plant samples collected during the subsequent years. The troop consisted of three animals in 1974, four in 1975, and five in 1976, as infants were born into the family unit.

The study area is near Mishana, about 30 km southwest of the Amazon port city of Iquitos in closed-canopy, tropical evergreen forest. Although it is difficult to be certain of the history of the area, we believe the plants are native and that *Callicebus torquatus* is stably adapted to this habitat.

The terrain is gently undulating, with slight variations in elevation that establish drainage patterns and variations in plant populations. This is an area of blackwater streams, where the soil is nutrient-poor and sandy, with only a thin layer of humus on top (cf. Janzen 1974). Vegetation types vary systematically, with palms numerous in lower, wetter areas, but virtually absent in the drier zones near the hilltops. Underbrush is thick in the low-lying areas, whereas the hilltops are relatively open and the forest there is dominated by taller and more widely spaced trees. More detailed descriptions of the habitat and the time spent in various areas by the monkeys are available elsewhere (Kinzey et al. 1977, Kinzey 1977a).

Observation conditions are difficult, especially during heavy rains, and we were sometimes out of contact with the animals for periods of several days. When the animals were in view, activities of all members of the troop were sampled every five minutes. An animal was "feeding" if it was reaching for a food item, ingesting food, or obviously searching for additional morsels. Food trees, vines, and shrubs were individually marked and numbered and their locations were recorded on a map of the troop's home range.

Plant Specimens

Samples of leaves and fruit were collected in 1975, 1976, and 1977 from the food plants, taking care to select fruit specimens like those eaten by the monkeys. Since color is one of the most labile properties of vegetation, it was not possible to use chemical preservatives, nor to freeze most samples without altering the property that we wished to study. The samples had to be collected on the day before leaving camp and placed in an ice-cooled chest the next day for air transport to the laboratory. On the last two expeditions, the samples were under refrigeration within one day and were being measured in my laboratory within three days of being plucked from the Amazon jungle. Dehydration of the samples was retarded as much as possible by storing each specimen in a sealed plastic bag until its reflectance was measured. After optical measurements were completed, the plant specimens were frozen and stored until more detailed examination of fruit structure and dimensions could be made. Freezing also destroyed any plant pests that might have been present.

Photographic Documentation

When possible, fruits being fed upon by the monkeys were photographed *in situ* to record the appearance of the fruit when viewed against the natural background of the forest. This required a telephoto lens with a focal length of 600 mm (300 mm lens with 2 × extender) mounted on a tripod for good resolution. Kodachrome 25 color transparency film (Kodak) was used when light levels were adequate because it is fine grained and stable. When a breeze was blowing, it was sometimes necessary to use high-speed Ektachrome (Kodak) in order to increase the shutter speed enough to prevent blurring of the photograph.

Closeup photographs were taken with a 50 mm Macro lens, both in the field and in the laboratory, usually with Kodachrome 25 film. Since exposure conditions and ambient illumination affect color reproduction, it is best to standardize these when possible. Flash illumination with a unit that has a standard daylight energy spectrum was always used in the laboratory and was also used in the field in most cases. As a further aid, laboratory photographs included a gray scale and standard color patches (Kodak gray scale and color separation guides) so that the degree of exposure could be judged and any imbalance in the color film could be corrected in later photographic processing such as color printing.

The background in the laboratory closeup photos was a neutral gray with a nominal 18% reflectance (Kodak Neutral Test Card or a flannel cloth). This prevented visual color contrast effects between the plant specimen and the background and assured that commercial automated printing techniques would produce a color print of acceptable quality from color negative film.

Reflectance Measurements

Light reflected from the surface of vegetation consists of two main components. (For illustration see Wright

1969, Plate I.) At the outermost surface, which may be smooth and waxy, specular reflection of all wavelengths of light occurs. This is a mirror-like reflection that appears white to the observer and imparts an impression of glossiness. Light that penetrates deeper into the surface tissue encounters cellular structures containing plant pigments that absorb some wavelengths of light and scatter others widely. Such diffusely reflected light appears colored to an observer (see Chapter 1 for a discussion of reflectance).

Specular reflection cannot be entirely isolated from diffuse reflection, even when studying flat, man-made samples (Hunter 1937). Measurements are still more difficult when studying natural objects that have complex surfaces (Snodderly 1978). For present purposes the more important component to specify is diffuse reflection, since specular reflection is usually not colored and is prominent only when illuminating and viewing angles are nearly equal.

The curves in Figure 63 illustrate that diffuse reflection is the predominant component when an integrating sphere is used to collect the reflected light. A locally grown, shiny tomato (*Lycopersicon*) was illuminated so as to maximize the specular reflection (S) or maximize diffuse reflection (D). The same tomato was then illuminated with a light beam incident normally on the surface while reflected light was collected in an integrating sphere (I) in a Beckman DK 2A spectrophotometer in the "diffuse mode" (for illustration of the geometry see Lavin 1971, Fig. 43, or Wright 1969, Fig. I, II).

Part of the specular reflection is directed out of the sphere, but with a curved object such as a fruit, some of the specularly reflected light will inevitably contaminate the intended measure of diffuse reflectance. However, my earlier measurements (Snodderly 1978) with commercial glossy paint samples indicated that only about 3% of additional reflectance could be attributed to the specular component when it was deliberately included in the measurement. Since natural fruits are considerably less glossy than these paints, the errors introduced in the diffuse reflectance by including some specularly reflected light are probably smaller than the variation in diffuse reflectance from sample to sample.

The measurement with the most specular reflection (S) shows the least variation of reflectance with wavelength,

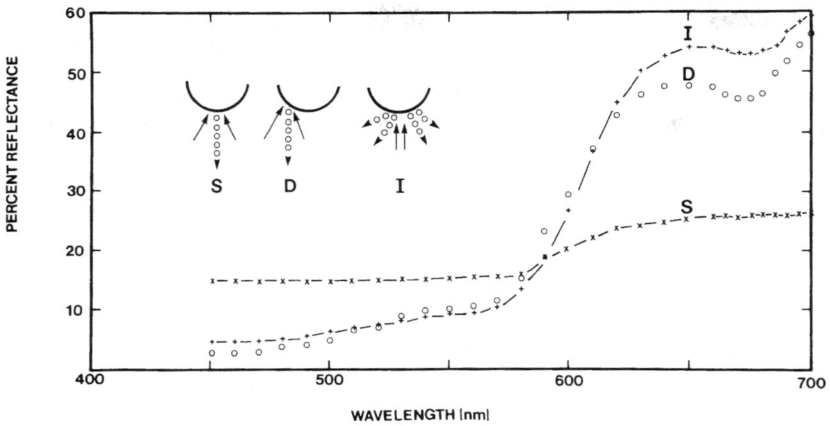

Fig. 63. Reflectance spectra of the same specimen measured in Beckman DK 2A spectrophotometer with integrating sphere (I). Reflectance with strong specular component (S) measured with axis of the illuminating beam approximately normal to the tomato's surface and the reflected beam collected on the same axis. The illuminating beam converged in a 30° angle and the reflected beam was collected over an angle of 1.5°. Diffuse component (D) of reflectance measured with fruit at acute angle to axis of the illuminating beam and reflected beam collected on the same axis. The inset in the upper left illustrates these three conditions. Solid arrows indicate incident light. Open circles indicate reflected light collected for measurement. All values are relative to a barium sulfate reference plate normal to the incident beam.

as would be expected. Since it includes some diffusely reflected light, the form of the curve is similar to the other two, but the ratio of maximum to minimum reflectance is only about 1.8, whereas the same ratio for the diffuse component (D) is about 25 and the variation of reflectance with wavelength is very similar to that found with the integrating sphere (I).

All other reflectance spectra in this article were measured with the spectrophotometer and integrating sphere in the "directional-hemispherical" mode described above (Judd 1967). With this instrument, measurements are reproducible to at least + 2 nm on the wavelength scale and about ± 1% in reflectance. Half bandwidth for my measurements was less than 2 nm between 400 and 600 nm; above 600 nm it increased to 3 nm at 630 nm, 5.5 nm at 670 nm, and 9.5 nm at 700 nm. Barium sulfate was used as the reference surface and the integrating sphere was coated with magnesium oxide.

In the standard configuration, the sample and reference beams impinge on surfaces placed behind 20 mm circular ports in the integrating sphere. The light beams are rectangular, about 7 x 8 mm in extent. For small fruits and for local areas of larger fruits these dimensions are too large. Consequently, in the last series of measurements, the sample beam aperture was reduced by covering the sample port with a magnesium oxide-coated metal plate with a rectangular aperture only 8 x 10 mm. The small samples were taped on an even smaller, 5 x 7 mm rectangular aperture cut from a Kodak neutral test card of 90% reflectance. The sample and reference beams were demagnified to 3 x 6.5 mm by inserting two lenses into each beam in a telescopic arrangement. Zero and full-scale settings were readjusted to account for these modifications, which enabled me to measure single small berries such as *Psychotria axillaris*, as well as discrete local areas of larger specimens.

CALLICEBUS TORQUATUS AND ITS FOOD SOURCES

Evidence for Coevolution

The major food sources of *Callicebus torquatus* have been identified by Kinzey and his associates (1977b) on the basis of four hundred hours of field observations in 1974, 1975, and 1976. Their studies have shown that fruit is the principal component of the diet, accounting for about 70% of the total feeding time. The selection of fruits eaten is quite restricted, with 80% of the time spent feeding on fruit devoted to only sixteen species of trees and shrubs.

Characteristics of these major food sources are listed in Table 8. Additional data gathered in 1977 confirm that these plant species are of major importance (Kinzey, personal communication). A few other species with interesting visual properties are described in Table 9, and photographs of several species are shown in Figures 64 and 65.

TABLE 8

Fruits Serving as Major Food Sources for *Callicebus torquatus*

Plant	Fruit Characteristics				External Fruit Color		Fruit Part Eaten
	Shape; Size	Fruit Wall	Inner Structure	Seeds	When Mature	When Eaten	
Clarisia racemosa (64)[a]	Spherical; 19-mm diam.	Tough; 2 mm thick	Single large seed	Thin coat; nutlike	Yellow/black	Light yellowish-green	Seed
Pithecellobium[b] (64)	Curved strip 12 mm wide; up to 45 mm long	Pod	Legume, up to 10 seeds	Soft when immature	--	Green	Seed
Alchornea (66, 70, 71)	3-lobed, 11-mm max. dimension	Thin epidermis; hard, brittle parenchyma	Thin aril around single seed in each lobe	Brittle coat but thin	Yellow near stem, red at apex	Yellow/red	Aril and seed
Maripa[b] (72)	Spherical, 16-mm diam.	Hard, brittle	Several large seeds	Soft	Brown	Brown	Seed, perhaps also insect larvae
Jessenia polycarpa[c] (64, 70)	Oblong, 35 x 21 nm	Thin, tough epidermis; fleshy parenchyma	Single large seed	Stony coat (endocarp)	Black	Black, slight purple tint	Fleshy fruit wall

Table 8 (continued)

Psychotria axillaris (66, 67, 69, 70)	Oblong, 5 x 9 mm	Thin epidermis; fleshy parenchyma	Single seed, 3 x 6 mm	Hard coat	Purple	Usually light yellowish-green	Entire fruit
Guatteria elata	Oblong, 7 x 11 mm	Thin epidermis; fleshy parenchyma	Single seed, 5 x 9 mm	Stony coat	Purple	Purple	Entire fruit
Gavarretia (67, 68)	Oval, 20 x 20 x 13 mm	Tough; 2 mm thick	2 cells, 2 large seeds	Soft upper half, hard lower half	--	Green	Seed
Virola	Round	--	Single seed	--	--	Brownish-green	--
Coccoloba	--	--	--	--	--	--	--
Unidentified Tree 269	--	--	--	--	--	Red	--
Pourouma tessmanii (64, 67, 70, 72)	Spherical, 13-mm diam.	Tough; 2 mm thick	Single large seed	Thin coat; nutlike	--	Light yellowish-green	Seed
Duroia longifolia (64, 65, 68)	Oblong, 6 x 8 cm	Leathery hesperidium; 5 mm thick	Many seeds in syrupy brown matrix	Small	Yellow	Green	Syrupy interior

Table 8 (continued)

Iryanthera[b] (66, 67, 68, 69, 71)	Spherical, 15–25-mm diam.	Tough; 3–5 mm thick	Single seed	Aril and thin coat, or pulpy (2 species)	One species dehiscent with red aril	Light yellowish-green (both species)	Aril and seed; or pulpy seed alone
Brosimum	Spherical, knobby, 23-mm diam.	Tough; 3 mm thick	Aril covering single seed	--	--	Brown	Aril and possibly seed
Tovomita (67, 68, 71)	Pyriform, 25 x 25 mm	Tough; 2 mm thick	4 cells	Thin coat, soft	Dehiscent red interior; orange seeds	Green	Seed

Note: The above species account for 80% of the time spent feeding on fruit in 400 hours of observation. Species are listed in order of decreasing utilization. Dashes indicate that the information is unknown. Unidentified species are labeled by the number assigned to the tree(s) on the map of the monkeys' home range.

[a]Numbers in parentheses refer to figures that contain photographs or reflectance spectra.

[b]More than one species.

[c]Also known as *Jessenia bataua*.

TABLE 9

Fruits Serving as Additional Food Sources for *Callicebus torquatus*

Plant	Fruit Characteristics				External Fruit Color		Fruit Part Eaten
	Shape; Size	Fruit Wall	Inner Structure	Seeds	When Mature	When Eaten	
Unidentified--trees 161, 217, 220, 221 (70)	Spherical; 11-mm diam.	Hard; 2 mm thick	Single seed, gelatinous arilloid	Stony coat	Purple	Purple	Aril and seed
Unidentified--trees 169, 192, 239, 241 (65)	Oblong; 28 x 18 mm	Thin epidermis; fleshy parenchyma	Single large seed	Stony coat	Orange	Orange	Fleshy fruit wall
Salacia (liana) (66, 71)	Spherical; 31-mm diam.	Tough; 2 mm thick	Spongy yellow matrix with several large seeds	Thin coat, soft	--	Green	Seed
Mendoncia (liana)	42 x 21 mm	Flat pod	Legume, several seeds	Soft	--	Light yellowish-green	Seed

Note: The first two entries are species of which at least four different individual trees were fed upon. The last two entries are minor food sources whose reflectance spectra were measured. Other contentions same as Table 8.

I have measured the reflectance of fruits and/or leaves of 70% of the species listed in Tables 8 and 9. The results are so consistent that the major patterns are well delineated and they correlate well with the perceptual judgments of a human observer. Therefore, fruits are categorized by their appearance as a starting point for the analysis.

Fruits can be either cryptically or conspicuously colored. Light, yellowish-green fruits are particularly cryptic when viewed against the undersides of leaves. When the fruit is a darker green, it is more cryptic if viewed against the top sides of leaves. About half the major food sources of *C. torquatus* are eaten when the fruit is a cryptic light or dark green. The other fruits take on a variety of colors that are noticeably different from the green background.

Botanists regard visually conspicuous fruit as an adaptation to facilitate dispersal of plant seeds by animals (van der Pijl 1969, Halle 1974, Snow 1971). This implies that seeds of cryptic fruits may *not* be dispersed by animals. Data in the tables demonstrate that the monkeys are specifically chewing and eating the *seeds* of many cryptic green fruits. Since the seed is destroyed, the plant gains nothing from being fed upon by the monkeys, and the evolutionary selection pressure is to make the fruit as difficult to find as possible.

The rule that the fruit should be green, and thus cryptic if the monkey destroys the seed, holds for all cases except *Maripa*. This is an interesting exception, because *Maripa* is a liana that grows on large trees and its brown fruit may be relatively inconspicuous against the bark of the tree trunk when seen from the monkeys' viewpoint.

Several fruits are eaten when green, even though they change color when allowed to mature (e.g., *Psychotria axillaris*, *Duroia*, and *Tovomita*); hence, *C. torquatus* is feeding on unripe fruits, which increases the number of discriminations among subtle shades of green that the animals must make in order to survive. The advantage gained by eating green fruits may be priority over other animals that would compete for the same plant species when the fruit ripens. Some of the fruits would be conspicuously dehiscent if left to ripen (e.g., *Tovomita*, one species of *Iryanthera*). Others would probably dehise, but were so efficiently harvested by the monkeys that we never had the opportunity to observe a fully ripe fruit. In particular, the *Pithecellobium* trees had fruit so cryptic that

Fig. 64. Native fruits *in situ*: Je: *Jessenia polycarpa*. The large cluster of fruits is attached to the side of the trunk at the base of the palm fronds. Pi: *Pithecellobium* pod. Po: *Pourouma tessmanii*

viewed from immediately beneath the tree looking nearly vertically up the trunk. Du: *Duroia longifolia*. Cl: two fruits of *Clarisia racemosa*, the most preferred food from one of the tallest trees in the forest. All of the above-named fruits are major food sources for *Callicebus torquatus*. Psk: *Psychotria klugii* berries, a conspicuous fruit not eaten by the monkeys. These photographs demonstrate the difficulty of loacting many of the fruits when color cues are absent. Shape and brightness contrasts are more subtle than color contrasts.

the pods were practically undetectable by a human observer standing on the ground (see Fig. 64). Yet when the pod was opened, its inside surfaces turned a bright, conspicuous orange. This color change may be an adaptation for dispersal by birds (van der Pijl 1969), a system that the monkeys have aborted by eating the seeds before dehiscence can occur. Other fruits (*Alchornea*, *Gavarretia*) with prominent sutures would eventually open and expose seeds for dispersal but they, too, are usually eaten before dehiscence.

At this point we cannot quantify how effective a dispersal agent *C. torquatus* is for the more conspicuous fruits. However, it seems reasonable to assume that when the monkeys eat the whole fruit or some part other than the seed, a fraction of the seeds survive to be defecated and dispersed. Consistent with the above assumption, the tables show that some part of the fruit other than the seed must be edible in order for the fruit to be visually conspicuous. Since there appears to be no universally accepted system of nomenclature for fruit structures, I have elected to use simple descriptive terms in the tables. I have been guided by the terminology chosen by Esau (1965), van der Pijl (1969), and Harrington and Durrell (1957).

In many cases the noncryptic fruits have fleshy walls and/or arils that the monkeys eat, and the seed is only incidentally and nondestructively ingested. Since *C. torquatus* rarely sleeps in feeding trees, it transports the ingested seed to a new location and defecates it along with some fertilizer where the seedling does not have to compete with the parent plant. This is an excellent dispersal method for those seeds that survive.

There are several reasons why this coevolutionary relationship between the monkeys and their food sources should exert an especially strong selection pressure on visual discrimination capacities as compared with other sensory and cognitive abilities. For example, a competing hypothesis is that the monkeys could learn the location and fruiting cycles of preferred trees and exploit them on the basis of spatial and temporal memories. This is unlikely because many of the plants in this area, like those in other tropical regions (e.g., Janzen 1975, Smythe 1970, Struhsaker 1975), do not appear to have a tightly synchronized annual fruiting cycle. During July of 1975, I inspected twenty-two trees and lianas that the troop had fed upon at about this time of year in 1974. Only one tree, a *Clarisia*, was fed upon at this time of year in 1975. Two other trees had unripe fruit, and none of the other plants had any fruit at all. This would make it very difficult for the animals to rely on memory alone.

Olfactory cues, which are probably of great importance for nocturnal animals, appear to be virtually absent from the fruits eaten by *C. torquatus*. None of the fruits had distinctive odors for a human observer and only one (*Duroia*) had a sweet taste. Most of the fruits tasted starchy or slightly bitter when they were sampled.

Observation of the monkeys during feeding strongly supports the idea that locating of fruits relies predominantly on visual search (Fig. 65). Frequently a monkey sits in the fork of a tree branch and looks intently around the surrounding foliage before moving quickly to the end of a branch to pluck a fruit. Often the fruit is plucked, placed in the mouth, and bitten in one continuous motion, but sometimes the monkey clearly smells and inspects the fruit closely before eating. This behavior indicates that the chemical senses may not play a large role in locating the fruit, although they may influence the acceptance of particular specimens according to the state of ripeness.

Visual Appearance and Reflectance Spectra of Fruit

The visual configuration assumed by fruits and leaves of several major food sources are illustrated in Figures 64 and 66. Some fruits occur singly (e.g., *Clarisia*, *Duroia*) while others are clustered in large (e.g., *Jessenia*) or small (e.g., *Iryanthera*) aggregations. In the case of the conspicuous fruit of *Alchornea* (Fig. 66), the aggregation creates a pattern of alternating red and yellow regions that is strikingly similar to the color-color figures sometimes used in laboratory experiments (van der Horst et al. 1967, Hilz and Cavonius 1970, DeValois et al. 1977). The cryptic green fruits, on the other hand, do not generate notable patterns by their aggregation geometry.

Reflectance spectra for several of the yellowish-green fruits are compared in Figure 67. A single fruit can have both light and dark areas, and fruits from different species can be lighter or darker, but the reflectance spectra are so similar that different concentrations of pigment could possibly account for the variations observed. The reflectance increases still more in the infrared and for most

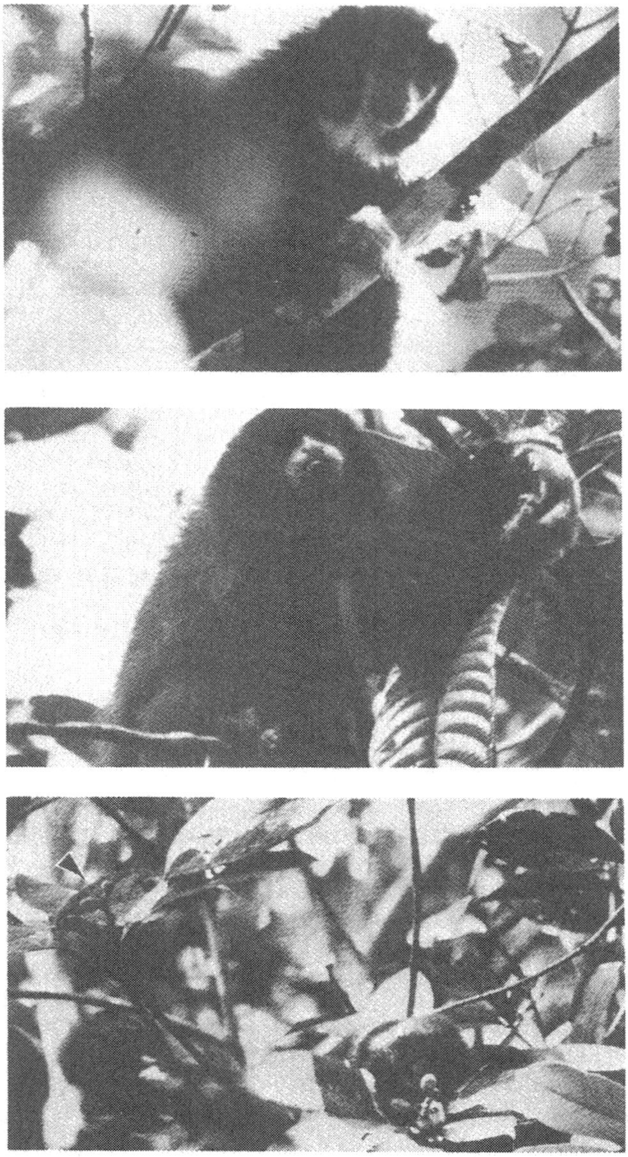

Fig. 65. Top panel: Juvenile *Callicebus torquatus* perched quietly on a limb. These monkeys are not familiar to most primatologists because they live in remote regions and they are not exported from their home

vegetation it reaches a maximal plateau between about 750 and 800 nm (see Nickerson et al. 1945).

In absorption spectrophotometry, spectra can be plotted on a logarithmic scale and slid vertically for comparison, as is done in the bottom panel. If the spectrum is determined only by different concentrations of a single pigment, the curves should superimpose. The situation is somewhat more difficult to interpret in reflectance measurements, because the physical structure containing the pigments can also reflect light nonselectively (i.e., approximately constant across the spectrum). This tends to broaden the spectrum without displacing the peak when it is plotted logarithmically, and it probably is responsible for much of the spread among the points shown. There may also be some minor contribution to light absorption by other pigments, especially at the short wavelengths.

As mentioned above, the lightness or darkness of the green fruits has a substantial influence on their visibility when viewed against the leaves of the plant. All of nineteen plants sampled had leaves with a more reflective underside than topside, and visual observation of many other plant species suggests that this is a general rule (see Chapter 7). Consequently, the most cryptic pattern for a green fruit is a dark topside and a light underside. Many of the green fruits do have this shaded pattern, which probably results from a corresponding distribution of chlorophyll pigmentation. In treatments of animal camouflage this is known as countershading, because the darker surface is oriented toward the principal source of illumination and it tends to give the object a uniform, inconspicuous appearance (e.g., Cott 1957, Edmunds 1974).

countries. Middle panel: An adult female *C. torquatus* feeding on *Duroia longifolia*. The vertical smear in front of her body is a piece of the fruit wall that she has bitten off and spat out. Note that the fruit being grasped with both hands is about as large as the monkey's head. Bottom panel: *C. torquatus* feeding on unidentified orange fruit. Like many fruits, these grow at the very tip of small branches (arrow), where they are difficult to reach unless the animal is small enough to crawl out to the end of the flexible limb.

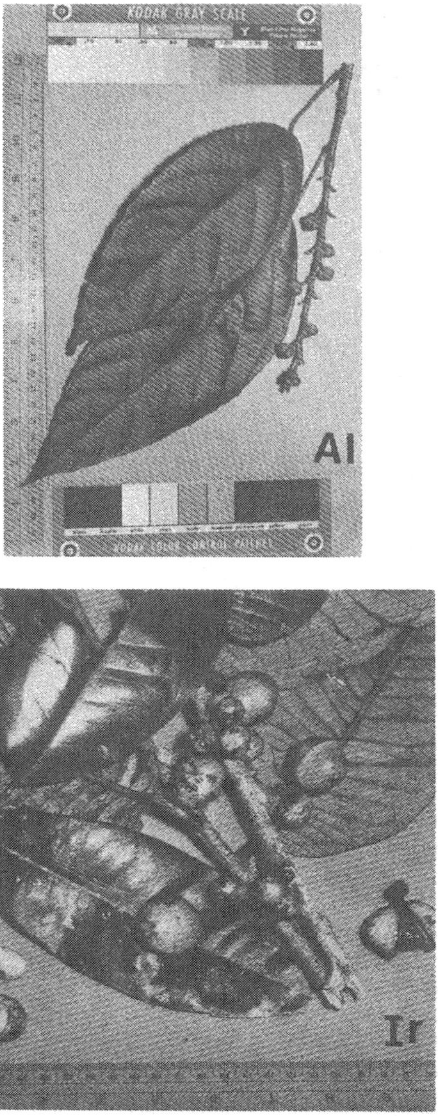

Fig. 66. Native fruits utilized as food sources: selected specimens photographed and measured spectrophotometrically in the laboratory. Al: *Alchornea* leaves and berries with grey scale and color separation guide to insure proper exposure and reproduction. Each of the short stems had a fruit on it before the plant was fed upon. The fruit is yellow at the stem and red at the

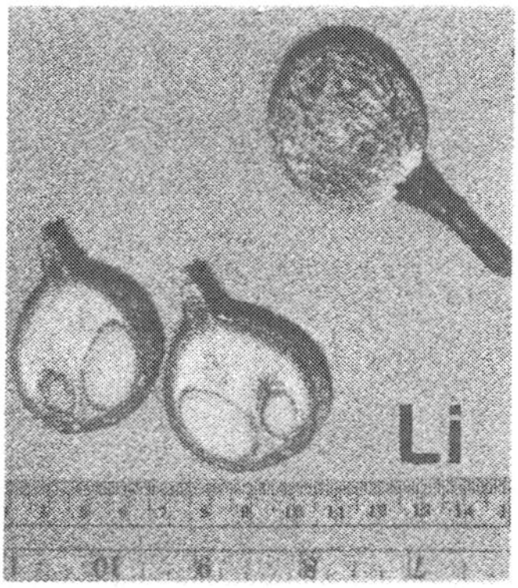

apex, so that an undisturbed cluster of fruit has alternating areas of yellow and red. Ir: *Iryanthera* fruits on branch broken and bent double. At lower right is a dehiscent fruit exposing a red aril. At lower left is an opened fruit husk below a seed with a light, unripe aril on half the seed, and the other half of the seed scraped bare. Li: green liana fruit (probably a species of *Salacia*) with yellow interior cut in half to show soft seeds eaten by the monkeys. Psa: *Psychotria axillaris* with green, unripe berries in leaf axillae. Groups of unripe, green, and ripe, purple berries are placed on a dark top side of a leaf and a light underside of a leaf to the right. To: *Tovomita*, a dehiscent fruit with fruit wall curved back to open four red cells and release the orange seeds shown in the upper left. Intact fruit in right center. For appearance of *Tovomita* specimen bitten open by monkeys while feeding, see Kinzey (1977b, Fig. 6).

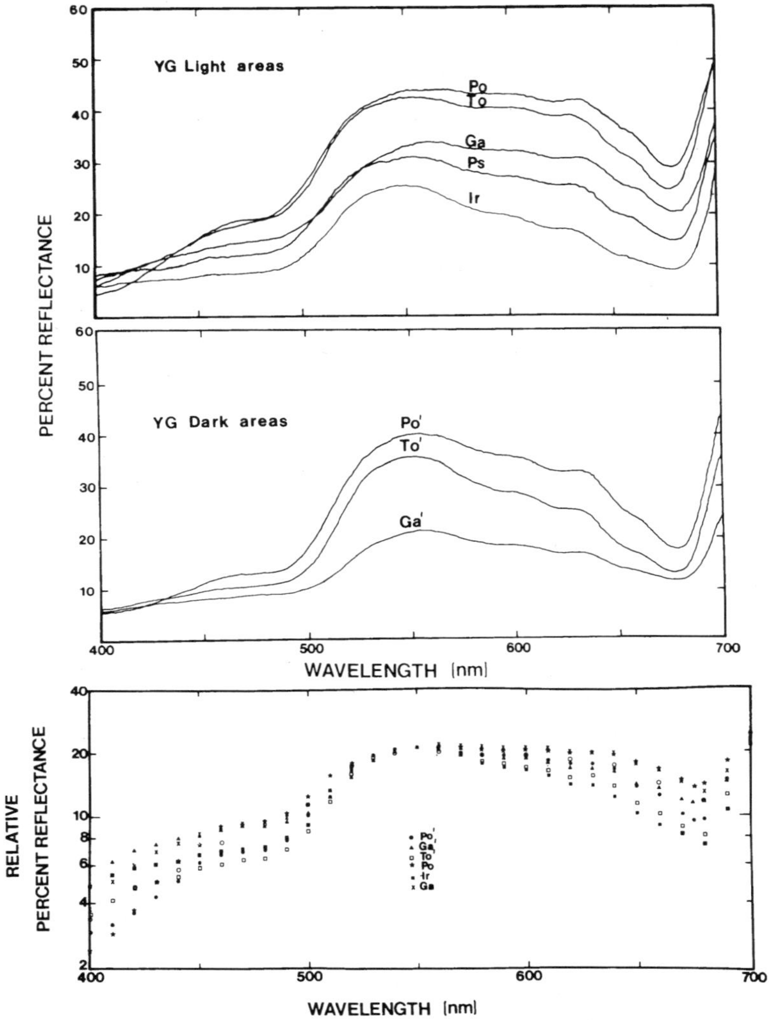

Fig. 67. Yellowish-green fruits. Top panel--light samples and light subareas: *Po*, *Pourouma*; *To*, *Tovomita*; *Ga*, *Gavarretia*; *Ps*, *Psychotria axillaris*; *Ir*, *Iryanthera*. Middle panel--dark areas of three of the same fruits. Bottom panel--relative reflectance of light and dark areas plotted on a logarithmic scale and equated at 550 nm.

An example of the effects of countershading on the reflectance spectrum is shown in Figure 68 for a sample of *Gavarretia*. Here a light region and a dark area of the fruit are compared with the top surface of two leaves. The dark region is close in reflectance to the leaf topside, whereas the light area is much more reflective. It is probably more similar to the leaf underside, which unfortunately was not measured for this sample.

A clear example of correspondence between fruit surface and leaf underside is illustrated in the middle panel for *Iryanthera*. The leaf underside differs from the topside in having an additional component of reflectance that is nearly constant across the spectrum. Here there can be little doubt that the color properties of the fruit are well matched to those of the leaves.

One feature of the reflectance of the dark area of the *Gavarretia* specimen that does not conform to the leaf spectrum is its relative flatness. This is probably due to the fuzzy, hairy surface of the *Gavarretia* fruit that gives it a yellowish cast.

In the case of *Duroia*, which has a smooth green surface penetrated by sparsely distributed hairs, the effect of removing the hairs can be demonstrated by gently rubbing the fruit surface (bottom panel). The smooth fruit has a dark green appearance more similar to the leaf top than the leaf underside. The hairs add reflectance at longer wavelengths that makes the fruit appear more yellowish and makes it more similar to the leaf underside at long wavelengths, while the middle and short wavelengths are relatively unaffected. The significance of this kind of surface texture is unclear at present, but it may represent a compromise between inconspicuousness when viewed from above or from below. *Duroia* is a relatively short tree, branching in the first story of the canopy, and is probably approached frequently from above by the arboreal monkeys.

The dramatic changes in the reflectance spectrum as fruits ripen are illustrated in Figure 69. In the top panel, the berries of *Psychotria axillaris* can be seen to have reflectance properties very similar to leaf undersides before they ripen. This is not as cryptic a coloration as it would be if the berries matched the leaf topsides, since *P. axillaris* is a short shrub less than two meters high, and is usually seen from above by the foraging monkeys. Nevertheless, it is still very different from the spectra

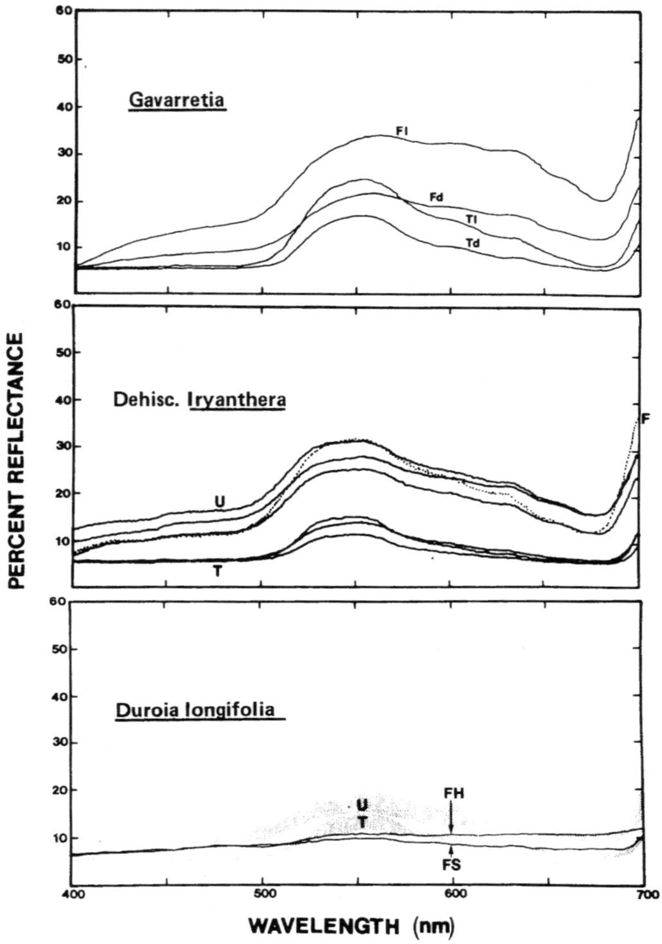

Fig. 68. Top panel--Light (Fl) and dark (Fd) areas of a *Gavarretia* fruit compared with top side of a light (Tl) and dark (Td) leaf. Middle panel--Dehiscent *Iryanthera* fruit exterior (F) compared with underside (U) and topside (T) of three leaves chosen to illustrate range of leaf lightness and darkness. Bottom panel--Fruit and leaves of *Duroia longifolia*. Shaded areas show range of leaf undersides (U) and top sides (T). A normal hairy surface of a fruit (FH) and a smooth fruit with the hairs rubbed off (FS) are compared.

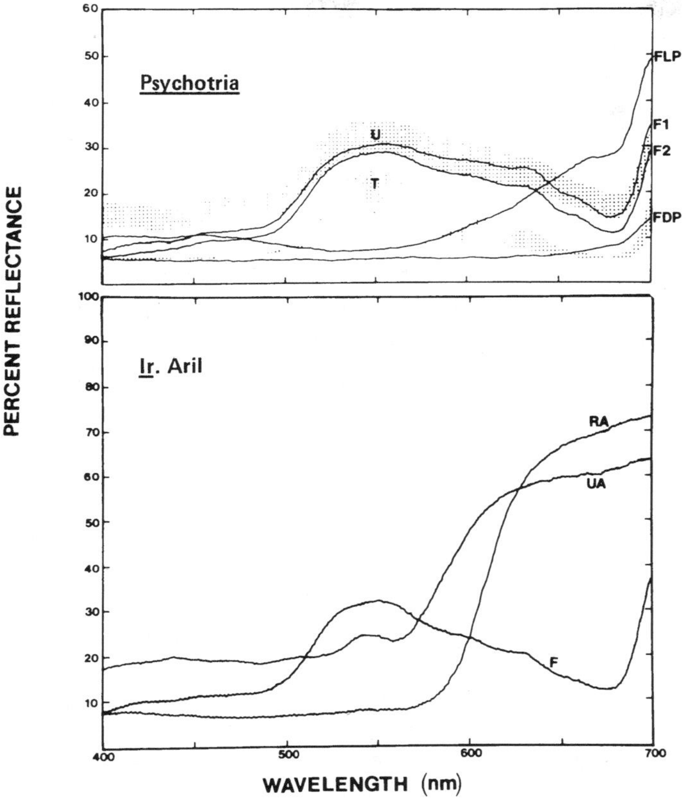

Fig. 69. Top panel--Leaves of *Psychotria axillaris* compared with fruit at different stages of ripeness. The ranges of leaf undersides (U) and topsides (T) are the shaded areas. Reflectance spectra for two green fruits (F1, F2), a fruit turning light purple (FLP), and a fully ripe, dark purple fruit (FDP) are shown. (The FLP curve is the highest solid line at 400 nm.) Bottom panel--Ripe (RA) and unripe (UA) red aril of dehiscent *Iryanthera* with exterior of fruit (F).

of berries that turn purple as they ripen. In fact, the ripening berries have a spectrum that is neatly complementary to the leaves.

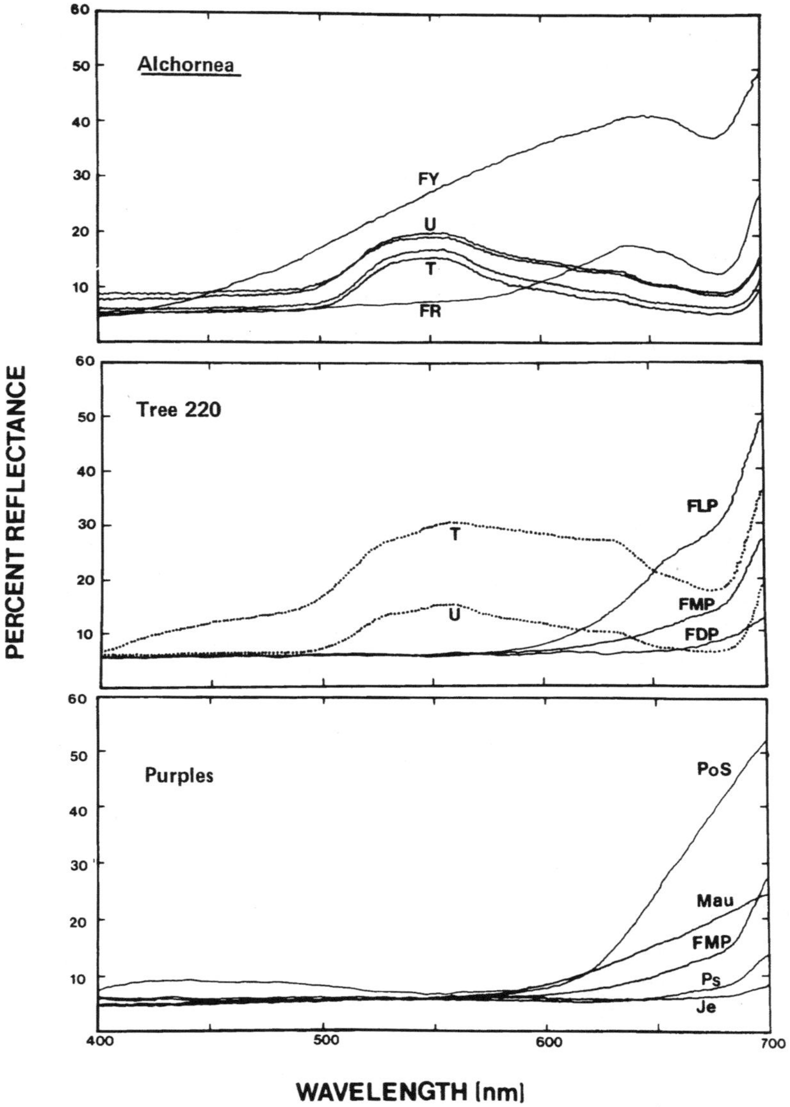

Fig. 70. Top panel--Light and dark leaf undersides (U) and topsides (T) of *Alchornea* with yellow stem region (FY) and red apex region of fruit (FR). Middle panel--Leaf topside (T) and underside (U) with three fruits illustrating the range of darkness from light (FLP),

Similar alterations can be seen in the ripening sequence of the aril of a dehiscent *Iryanthera* species in the bottom panel. The external fruit wall, which matches the leaf underside so exactly, contrasts with the red aril by having the main peak of reflected energy in a completely different part of the spectrum.

This same complementarity is apparent in two other noncryptic fruits as shown in the top two panels of Figure 70. *Alchornea*, one of the most conspicuously patterned fruits, has a completely different reflectance pattern from the leaf for both its yellow and red portions. The complementarity between fruit and leaf remains true even when there is considerable variation in degree of pigmentation of the fruit, as shown for an unidentified purple fruit. Note that the lightest fruit in this group has a quite reddish cast, whereas the other two fruits are dominantly purple in appearance and all three are very different from the leaves.

Reflectance Spectra Grouped by Color

The distinctive characteristics of the reflectance spectra encouraged me to compare plant specimens of similar colors to determine whether their reflectance spectra could be categorized in some parsimonious way. It is already clear from the measurements presented in Figures 67 and 68 that green fruits and leaves from a wide variety of plants have a common pattern of reflectance. In Figures 70 (bottom panel), 71, and 72, reflectance spectra are superimposed to demonstrate that common patterns also exist for five other natural color categories--purple, red, yellow, orange, and brown. I was unable to obtain any blue specimens for measurement because they appear to be relatively rare, at least in this environment.

---

to medium (FMP), to dark (FDP) purple. Unidentified species. Bottom panel--Samples of a purple *Pourouma* seed (PoS) and purple fruit exteriors, as follows: *Mau*, *Mauritia*, the aquaje palm fruit eaten by humans and by birds but not by *C. torquatus*; FMP, unidentified medium purple fruit from middle panel; Ps, *Psychotria axillaris* dark purple fruit; Je, palm fruit of *Jessenia polycarpa*.

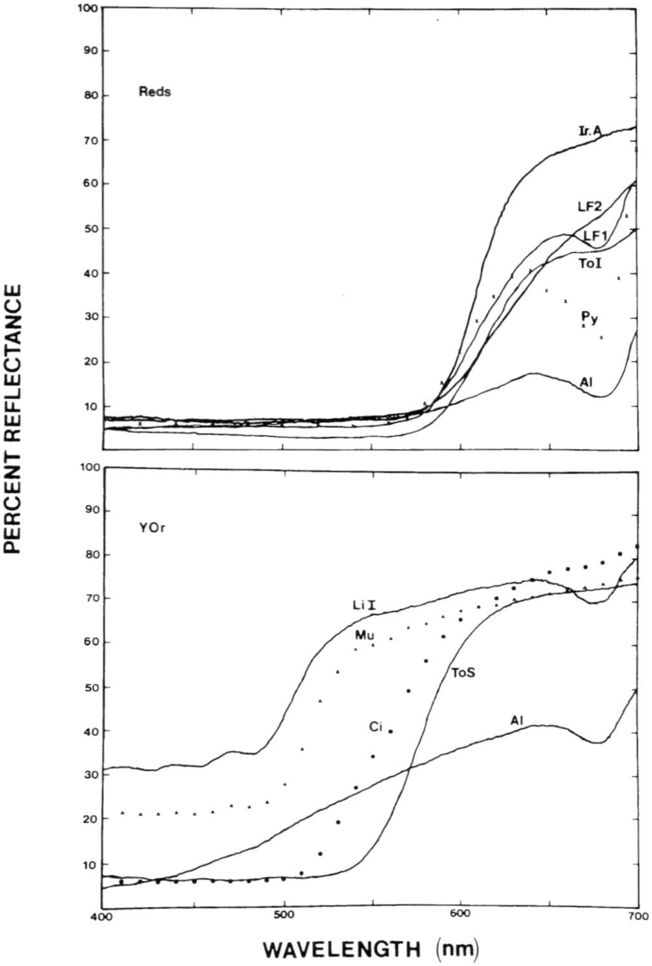

Fig. 71. Upper panel--Samples of red fruits and fruit parts: Ir.A, ripe *Iryanthera* aril; LF1 and LF2, exterior surfaces of two samples of unidentified liana fruit not eaten by *C. torquatus*; ToI, interior of dehiscent *Tovomita* fruit; Py, exterior of temperate-zone apple *Pyrus malus* eaten by humans; Al, apical end of *Alchornea* fruit exterior. Lower panel--Yellow and orange fruits and fruit parts: Yellow, LiI, interior of liana fruit (probably a *Salacia* species) eaten by *C.*

The spectra of purple plant specimens show a relatively low reflectance throughout most of the visible spectrum until they get to around 620 nm where the curves begin to rise in a characteristic manner. As a first approximation, one can consider many of the plant specimens to be cut-off filters. Purple specimens cut off at the longest wavelengths; as the cut-off point moves to shorter and shorter wavelengths, the perceived color becomes red, then orange, and then yellow (Fig. 71). In this respect, the plant pigments are similar to pigments used commercially for paints (Wyszecki and Stiles 1967, Snodderly 1978). One interesting consequence is that the color and luminance of a sample are closely linked: as the color of an object moves toward the middle of the spectrum, its luminance increases. (For a definition of luminance, which is an approximation to brightness, see Riggs 1965, or Chapter 7). Several examples of temperate-zone fruits eaten by humans--an apple, a banana, and an orange--are included to show that they also conform to the same general pattern.

Two of the specimens, one in the red and the other in the purple group, are native fruits that *C. torquatus* does not eat. The red liana fruits were collected only one meter from a *Duroia* tree where the monkeys had fed and the aquaje palm (*Mauritia*) was only 4¼ meters from a favorite *Jessenia* palm tree. The close proximity of accepted and rejected fruits suggests that the selection of food is deliberate and does not result merely from failure of the monkeys to encounter fruits that are not eaten.

It is also important to emphasize that food selection is *not* just a simple color preference. For example, the berries of *Psychotria klugii* are a bright orange and are clustered at the top of the plant where they are visually conspicuous (Fig. 64). This species is plentiful throughout the monkeys' home range, yet they never eat it. Preliminary results indicate that the berries are rich in toxic alkaloids and they may be avoided for that reason (W. Kinzey, M. Hladik, personal communication). However, the presence of toxic alkaloids has little correspondence with the

torquatus; Al, *Alchornea* fruit, yellow region near stem; Mu, banana, *Musa*, eaten by humans; ToS, *Tovomita* seed; Ci, orange, *Citrus*, eaten by humans. The dip in some spectra at 680 nm is probably due to small residual amounts of chlorophyll in those specimens.

color, since an equally bright orange tree fruit (Fig. 65) in the same locale is eaten avidly by the monkeys. I assume that the monkeys have learned to use cues other than color to identify the edible fruit.

Some aspects of food selection remain puzzling. Perhaps the most difficult to understand is the omission of the aquaje palm fruit (*Mauritia*) from the diet. Since this fruit is collected and eaten without difficulty by local humans, it probably is safe for the monkeys, too. Furthermore, its reflectance characteristics are so similar to those of other *C. torquatus* food sources that it is very unlikely that the monkeys are making some subtle color discrimination missed by human observers. In this case, other, still unknown factors must play a dominant role.

Importance of Fruit Size

The size of the fruit influences both the probability of seed dispersal and the fruit's spectral appearance. Other things being equal, large objects appear more saturated in color than small ones (Evans 1974) and hence will be more conspicuous. Plants achieve increased color saturation

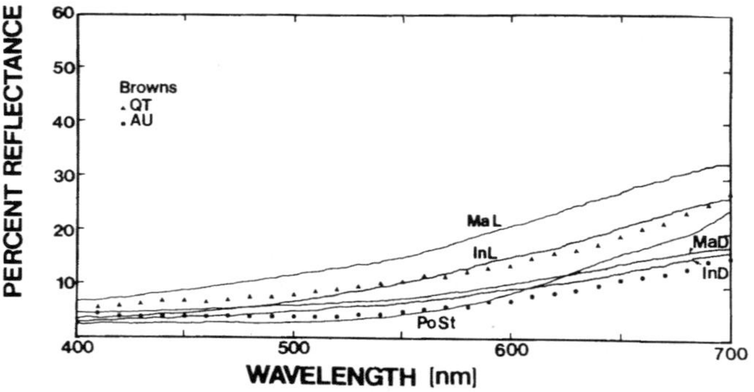

Fig. 72. Natural browns--vegetation samples: light (MaL) and dark (MaD) specimens of *Maripa* fruit exteriors; light (InL) and dark (InD) *Inga* pods; stems of *Pourouma* fruit (PoSt); dry topside of temperate zone oak leaf *Quercus* (QT); damp temperate zone maple leaf underside, *Acer* (AU).

by producing large fruit or by grouping small fruits in large clusters. The production of large fruit, especially if the seed is correspondingly large, probably indicates that the plant is adapted to seed dispersal by relatively large animals that can easily swallow the seed. In this regard it is interesting to point out that the small monkey (less than 1 kg body weight) that we studied feeds on relatively small fruits (Tables 8 and 9). In contrast, large primates such as chimpanzees (*Pan troglodytes*) are known to eat fruits several times as large as those eaten by *Callicebus* (Hladik 1973, A. Hladik and C. M. Hladik, personal communication).

PLANT ADAPTATIONS AND PRIMATE FORAGING BEHAVIOR

The feeding behavior of primates is very diverse (Gaulin and Konner 1977) and one can find many examples of both seed dispersal and seed destruction. It has been shown that seeds will germinate after passing through the digestive tracts of neotropical primates (Hladik and Hladik 1969, Glander 1975) but whether more seeds are destroyed or are dispersed is difficult to determine. Plants have several defense mechanisms to prevent seeds from being destroyed. Toxic chemicals (Janzen 1971), mechanical barriers, and visually cryptic appearance are some of the deterrents that affect primates.

The extent to which a plant must protect itself may depend on its local habitat. Janzen (1974) has argued that plants in blackwater, poor-soil areas such as our study site are richer in toxic chemicals than those growing in better soil types because it is more costly for them to lose vegetation to predators. Gartlan and McKey (in press) have described extensive chemical and mechanical defenses of plants in a primate habitat in Africa that has sandy soil poor in nutrients. It is, therefore, conceivable that plants in the kind of habitat we have studied would also have more extensive visual defenses and thus differ from the situation in many other primate habitats.

However, the available evidence suggests that primates specialize in their feeding patterns and some are more destructive than others regardless of the habitat. For example, the *Cebus capucinus* of Barro Colorado island (not a poor-soil area) eat approximately half their fruit while it is still green (Oppenheimer 1968), whereas the *Ateles* of Colombia eat only ripe fruit (Klein and Klein 1975). Some primates in dry climates will eat plant foods either when green or when dry (e.g., African vervets, *Cercopithecus aethiops*, Struhsaker 1967). These observations must be interpreted cautiously, since seeds of green fruits can often germinate (A. Hladik, personal communication), and quantitative comparisons of the survival of seeds dispersed by primates in their complex tropical environments would be difficult to conduct.

RELATIONSHIP OF FORAGING BEHAVIOR TO COLOR VISION

Environmental Selection

The idea that color vision should have coevolved with colored fruits was suggested by Polyak (1957, pp. 973-974) and was commonly accepted long before that by botanists and zoologists interested in plant-animal interactions (van der Pijl 1969). In view of this, it is surprising that no prior studies have attempted to measure the optical characteristics of fruits in order to specify their stimulus properties for animal visual systems.

Investigations of plant pigments have been restricted primarily to extracts prepared from species of economic importance (Chichester 1972, Goodwin 1976). This has the disadvantage of failing to include the optical effects of such features as surface texture or structure of the fruit's wall. However, the chemical studies do indicate that plant colors are frequently derived from mixtures of a few classes of compounds--the chlorophylls, carotenoids, anthocyanins, and so on. This may account for the finding that visual judgments by humans of the colors of natural objects occupy only a small part of the theoretically possible range of color perceptions (Hendley and Hecht 1949).

The reflectance spectra convey the same overall impression: a limited number of patterns can describe their main characteristics. The crucial question to which we must return is how this might explain the difference in color vision between the New World and the Old World primates. In my opinion, the critical factor is likely to be the color of the background against which the colored fruits contrast. The neotropical primates live in arboreal evergreen habitats that have the green background color of the forest. Most of their color discriminations are either among subtle shades of green or between contrasting colors and green. There are no demanding discriminations between similar colors in the long-wavelength part of the spectrum such as yellow vs. orange, or orange vs. red. Consequently, an animal with poor color discrimination at the long wavelengths could presumably still survive.

In the Old World tropics, however, many primates live in regions with lengthy dry seasons where the vegetation turns brown, and this, together with the soil, provides the background against which visual discriminations must be made (e.g., Kummer 1971, Altmann and Altmann 1970). The brown vegetation and most soils reflect light most strongly in the red end of the spectrum (Fig. 72, and Nickerson et al. 1945) and this means that yellow, orange, and desaturated red objects will be more similar to the background and more difficult to detect. Consequently, an animal in a dry environment with poor color discrimination at the long wavelengths might be handicapped at finding, say, dry yellow seeds amid brown vegetation. If food is a limiting variable, then natural selection would tend to eliminate such color-deficient animals from populations of Old World primates.

Mechanistic Considerations

One can consider the probable mechanisms responsible for the color vision differences between New and Old World primates on at least three different levels: genetic, physiological, and environmental (considered above). Concerning genetic differences, there is general agreement (Simons 1972, Orlosky and Swindler 1975) that the ancestral lines of New and Old World primates diverged very early and probably evolved independently from prosimian-like predecessors. Thus the genetic determinants of color vision may not be the same in both groups. The phylogenetic separation is important because of recent findings that the red-deficiency (protanomaly) in New World monkeys occurs in all males of some groups, but not the females (Jacobs 1977; see also Lepore et al. 1975). Not all studies on squirrel monkeys have reached this conclusion (e.g., DeValois and Morgan 1974, Jacobs 1972), which suggests that the situation may differ even from one population of *Saimiri* to another. Nonetheless, the presence of such a pattern in any group is incompatible with the same mode of inheritance as human color deficiencies (Jacobs 1977), which are also sex-linked, but do not affect all males or only males.

DeValois and Jacobs (1968) have suggested that one underlying physiological mechanism for the red-deficient color vision of squirrel monkeys is an anomalous visual pigment in cone receptors that preferentially absorb light of longest wavelengths. However, there may also be differences in the properties of the central visual pathways. For example, squirrel monkeys have fewer of the spectrally opponent neurons that are thought to carry color information in their lateral geniculate nucleus than do macaque monkeys (DeValois and Jacobs 1968). Squirrel monkeys also differ from macaques in the geometrical arrangements assumed by nerve fiber inputs from the two eyes in the visual cortex (Allman 1977). These results imply that there may be a whole cluster of genetically determined differences between the visual systems of New and Old World primates; whether these traits are linked or not remains to be determined. In any event, we can view the genetic and physiological traits related to color as responses to the kinds of environmental selection pressures that are the focus of this chapter.

Theoretical Issues

The gap between laboratory studies of color vision and the study of vision in the natural environment is very wide. Laboratory studies usually employ very narrow-band stimuli, whose luminance can be tightly controlled, whereas natural objects reflect light over a broad band of wavelengths and the illumination conditions vary over large ranges (Henderson 1970, Hailman 1977, Burtt, in press). Any complete description of natural objects as visual stimuli would have to utilize the product of the spectral energy distribution of the ambient light and the reflectance spectrum of the object to specify the light actually being received by the eye of an observer (see Chapter 7, Burtt, in press). To some extent, the dilemma is less acute as long as we think of the problem as a contrast discrimination, because both the object (fruit) and the background (foliage) receive the same illumination and will be affected similarly by changes in illumination conditions. This is particularly true when both the reflecting surfaces and the illumination have broad wavelength distributions like those which occur in natural environments.

One way to view natural stimuli is as a mixture of many narrow bands of wavelengths. This makes it plausible, at least, to compare the laboratory studies and field observations. The CIE color diagram shows that mixtures of wavelengths longer than about 520 nm are nearly equivalent in appearance to single wavelengths with a hue that matches the mixture (e.g., see discussion in Evans 1974). This implies that the laboratory wavelength discrimination data derived with narrow-band stimuli probably will predict performance on broad-band stimuli of the same color appearance at the red end of the spectrum. Experimental confirmation of this inference would be welcome.

Modern theories of color vision are based on red/green and blue/yellow opponent processes whose balance determines the color seen (see Chapter 5, also Jameson 1972). These processes are also differentially affected by changes in luminance, with the yellow/blue system favored by higher luminances. If we assume that the opponent systems have evolved in part to detect colored natural objects, then the observation that natural yellow pigments are likely to impart a higher luminance to objects than natural red pigments is an intriguing correspondence with the properties of the perceptual mechanisms (as well as physiological ones, e.g., DeValois et al. 1977), and it deserves further exploration. Other features of the reflectance spectra, such as the notch near 680 nm that is sufficient to change the appearance of a surface from yellow to green, and the predominantly long wavelength reflectance of purple objects, would also be interesting to compare with predictions derived from opponent process theory.

Refining the Approach

Future work might achieve greater predictive power by taking into account nutritional balance of the diet (Hladik 1975). This would help to identify which foods and which visual discriminations were critical for survival. Of course, this requires a coordinated effort, because no single investigator has the expertise or the time to conduct all the necessary studies. It would be most helpful if study areas could be established in primate habitats to encourage diverse approaches focused on a particular environment that could draw upon the insights of many different disciplines.

The Need for Habitat Conservation

In this chapter I have argued that understanding the primate visual system is critically dependent on an adequate description of the selection pressures exerted by the environment. To extend this work, I would like to study other primates, especially squirrel monkeys and terrestrial Old World monkeys, in their natural habitats. Then it would be possible to directly relate the laboratory data to the field observations. This will become increasingly difficult as primate habitats disappear at an accelerating rate. Natural areas in the neotropics where primates have been studied as recently as 1967 to 1970 have been altered so drastically that wild primates no longer can live there (Thorington and Heltne 1976). Unless vigorous actions are taken to preserve primate habitats, we may lose the opportunity to understand a key factor in the evolution of our primate brethren--their environment.

ACKNOWLEDGMENTS

I thank Warren Kinzey and his colleagues for sharing their resources with me, for obtaining samples for optical measurements, and for providing species identifications, with the help of Dr. Al Gentry and the Missouri Botanical Garden. Field assistance from Rogerio Castro, Sorin Davis, Mary Pearl, and Barb Sleeper is gratefully acknowledged. Financial support from the National Institutes of Health (Grant EY 01520), the American Heart Association (Grant 74-760), Earthwatch of Belmont, Massachusetts (a teacher fellowship), and the Massachusetts Lions Eye Research Fund made the study possible. The field station Estacion Biologica Callicebus was established under project AMRO-0719 on the conservation of Peruvian primates, sponsored by the Pan American Health Organization (PAHO) in cooperation with the Peruvian Ministry of Health. The station is administered by Rogerio Castro of the Instituto Veterinario de Investigaciones Tropicales y de Altura and by W. R. Kingston. I am grateful to Annette and Marcel Hladik for their hospitality and discussions of unpublished observations; to Francois Delori for assistance with the optical measurements; and to Sandra Spinks and Rita Raskin for expert help in preparing the illustrations.

REFERENCES

Allman, J. 1977. Evolution of the visual system in the early primates. In *Progress in Physiological Psychology*, Vol. 7, J. Sprague and A. Epstein (eds.). New York: Academic Press.

Altmann, S. A., and Altmann, J. 1970. *Baboon Ecology: African Field Research*. Chicago: Univ. Chicago Press.

Baldwin, J. D., and Baldwin, J. I. 1972. The ecology and behavior of squirrel monkeys (*Saimiri oerstedi*) in a natural forest in western Panama. *Folia Primatol.* 18: 161-184.

Burtt, E. H., Jr. The coloration of wood warblers (Parulidae). *Nuttall Ornithol. Monogr.* (In press.)

Chichester, C. O. (ed.). 1972. *The Chemistry of Plant Pigments*. New York: Academic Press.

Cott, H. B. 1957. *Adaptive Coloration in Animals*. London: Methuen. (Orig. pub. 1940.)

DeValois, R. L., and Jacobs, G. H. 1968. Primate color vision. *Science* 162:533-540.

DeValois, R. L., and Jacobs, G. H. 1971. Vision. In *Behavior of Non-human Primates*, Vol. 3, A. M. Schrier and F. Stollnitz (eds.). New York: Academic Press.

DeValois, R. L.; Morgan, H. C.; Polson, M. C.; Mead, W. R.; and Hull, E. M. 1974. Psychophysical studies of monkey vision. I. Macaque luminosity and color vision tests. *Vision Res.* 14:53-67.

DeValois, R. L., and Morgan, H. C. 1974. Psychophysical studies of monkey vision. II. Squirrel monkey wavelength and saturation discrimination. *Vision Res.* 14:69-73.

DeValois, R. L.; Snodderly, D. M.; Yund, E. W.; and Hepler, N. K. 1977. Responses of macaque lateral geniculate cells to luminance and color figures. *Sensory Processes* 1: 244-259.

Edmunds, M. 1974. *Defence in Animals*. New York: Longmans.

Esau, K. 1965. *Plant Anatomy*, 2nd ed. New York: Wiley.

Evans, R. M. 1974. *The Perception of Color*. New York: Wiley.

Gartlan, J. S., and McKey, D. B. Soils, forest structure, and feeding strategies of primates in a Cameroon coastal forest. In *Recent Advances in Primatology*: *Behavior*, D. J. Chivers and J. Herbert (eds.). London: Academic Press. (In press.)

Gaulin, S. J. C., and Konner, M. 1977. On the natural diet of primates, including humans. In *Nutrition and the Brain*, R. J. Wurtman and J. J. Wurtman (eds.). New York: Raven Press.

Gilbert, L. E., and Raven, P. H. (eds.). 1975. *Coevolution of Animals and Plants*. Austin: Univ. Tex. Press.

Glander, K. E. 1975. Habitat description and resource utilization: a preliminary report on mantled howling monkey ecology. In *Socioecology and Psychology of Primates*, R. H. Tuttle (ed.). The Hague: Mouton.

Goodwin, T. W. (ed.). 1976. *Chemistry and Biochemistry of Plant Pigments*, 2nd ed., Vols. 1 and 2. New York: Academic Press.

Hailman, J. P. 1977. *Optical Signals: Animal Communication and Light*. Bloomington and London: Ind. Univ. Press.

Halle, N. 1974. Attractivité visuelle des fruits pour les animaux. *J. Psychol. Normale Pathol.* 4:389-405.

Harrington, H. D., and Durrell, L. W. 1957. *How to Identify Plants*. Chicago: Swallow Press.

Henderson, S. T. 1970. *Daylight and its Spectrum*. New York: American Elsevier.

Hendley, C. D., and Hecht, S. 1949. The colors of natural objects and terrains, and their relation to visual color deficiency. *J. Opt. Soc. Amer.* 39:870-873.

Hilz, R., and Cavonius, C. R. 1970. Wavelength discrimination measured with square-wave gratings. *J. Opt. Soc. Amer.* 60:273-277.

Hladik, A., and Hladik, C. M. 1969. Rapports trophiques entre vegetation et primates dans la forêt de Barro Colorado (Panama). *Terre Vie* 1:25-117.

Hladik, C. M. 1973. Alimentation et activité d'un groupe de chimpanzés réintroduits en forêt gabonaise. *Terre Vie* 27:343-413.

Hladik, C. M. 1975. Ecology, diet, and social patterning in Old and New World primates. In *Socioecology and Psychology of Primates*, R. H. Tuttle (ed.). The Hague: Mouton.

Hunter, R. S. 1937. Methods of determining gloss. *J. Res. Nat. Bur. Std.* 18:19-38.

Jacobs, G. H. 1972. Increment-threshold spectral sensitivity in the squirrel monkey. *J. Comp. Physiol. Psychol.* 79: 425-431.

Jacobs, G. H. 1977. Visual sensitivity: significant within-species variations in a nonhuman primate. *Science* 197: 499-500.

Jameson, D. 1972. Theoretical issues of color vision. In *Visual Psychophysics: Handbook of Sensory Physiology*, Vol. VII/4, D. Jameson and L. M. Hurvich (eds.). New York: Springer-Verlag.

Janzen, D. H. 1971. Seed predation by animals. *Ann. Rev. Ecol. Systematics* 2:465-492.

Janzen, D. H. 1974. Tropical blackwater rivers, animals, and mast fruiting by the Dipterocarpaceae. *Biotropica* 6:69-103.

Janzen, D. H. 1975. *Ecology of Plants in the Tropics*. London: Edward Arnold.

Judd, D. B. 1967. Terms, definitions, and symbols in reflectometry. *J. Opt. Soc. Amer.* 57:445-452.

Kinzey, W. G. 1977a. Positional behavior and ecology in *Callicebus torquatus*. *Yearbook of Physical Anthropology* 20:468-480.

Kinzey, W. G. 1977b. Diet and feeding behaviour of *Callicebus torquatus*. In *Primate Feeding Behavior*, T. Clutton-Brock (ed.). New York: Academic Press.

Kinzey, W. G. Feeding behaviour and molar features in two species of titi monkey. In *Recent Advances in Primatology: Behaviour*, D. J. Chivers and J. Herbert (eds.). London: Academic Press. (In press.)

Kinzey, W. G.; Rosenberger, A. L.; Heisler, P. S.; Prowse, D. L.; and Trilling, J. S. 1977. A preliminary field investigation of the yellow-handed titi monkey, *Callicebus torquatus*, in northern Peru. *Primates* 18:159-181.

Klein, L. L., and Klein, D. J. 1975. Social and ecological contrasts between four taxa of neotropical primates. In *Socioecology and Psychology of Primates*, R. H. Tuttle (ed.). The Hague: Mouton.

Kummer, H. 1971. *Primate Societies. Group Techniques of Ecological Adaptation.* Chicago: Aldine.

Lavin, E. P. 1971. *Specular Reflection.* Monographs on Applied Optics No. 2. New York: American Elsevier.

Lepore, F.; Lassonde, M.; Ptito, M.; and Cardu, B. 1975. Spectral sensitivity in a female *Cebus griseus*. *Percept. Mot. Skills* 40:783-788.

Napier, J. R., and Napier, P. H. 1967. *A Handbook of Living Primates.* New York: Academic Press.

Nickerson, D.; Kelly, K. L.; and Stultz, K. F. 1945. Color of soils. *J. Opt. Soc. Amer.* 35:297-300.

Oppenheimer, J. R. 1968. Behavior and ecology of the white-faced monkey, *Cebus capucinus*, on Barro Colorado Island, Canal Zone. Ph.D. thesis, Univ. Ill., Urbana.

Oppenheimer, J. R., and Lang, G. E. 1969. Cebus monkeys: effect on branching of Gustava trees. *Science* 165:187-188.

Orlosky, F. J., and Swindler, D. R. 1975. Origins of New World monkeys. *J. Human Evol.* 4:77-83.

Polyak, S. 1957. *The Vertebrate Visual System.* Chicago: Univ. Chicago Press.

Ptito, M.; Cardu, B.; and Lepore, F. 1973. Spectral sensitivity in primates: a comparative study. *Percept. Mot. Skills* 36:1239-1247.

Riggs, L. A. 1965. Light as a stimulus for vision. In *Vision and Visual Perception*, C. H. Graham (ed.). New York: Wiley.

Simons, E. L. 1972. *Primate Evolution.* New York: Macmillan.

Smythe, N. 1970. Relationships between fruiting seasons and seed dispersal methods in a neotropical forest. *Amer. Naturalist* 104:25-35.

Snodderly, D. M. 1974. Outline of a primate visual system. In *Perspectives in Primate Biology*, A. B. Chiarelli (ed.). New York: Plenum Press.

Snodderly, D. M. Eggshell removal by the laughing gull, *Larus atricilla*: normative data and visual preference behaviour. *Animal Behav.* 26:487-506.

Snow, D. W. 1971. Evolutionary aspects of fruit-eating by birds. *Ibis* 113:194-202.

Struhsaker, T. T. 1975. *The Red Colobus Monkey*. Chicago: Univ. Chicago Press.

Struhsaker, T. T. 1967. Ecology of vervet monkeys (*Cercopithecus aethiops*) in the Masai-Amboseli game reserve, Kenya. *Ecology* 48:891-904.

Thorington, R. W. 1967. Feeding and activity of *Cebus* and *Saimiri* in a Colombian forest. In *Progress in Primatology*, D. Starck (ed.). Stuttgart: Fischer.

Thorington, R. W. 1968. Observations of squirrel monkeys in a Colombian forest. In *The Squirrel Monkey*, L. A. Rosenblum and R. W. Cooper (eds.). New York: Academic Press.

Thorington, R. W., and Heltne, P. G. (eds.). 1976. *Neotropical Primates. Field Studies and Conservation.* Washington, D.C.: National Academy of Sciences.

van der Horst, G. J. C.; de Weert, C. M. M.; and Bouman, M. A. 1967. Transfer of spatial chromaticity--contrast at threshold in the human eye. *J. Opt. Soc. Amer.* 57: 1260-1266.

van der Pijl, L. 1969. *Principles of Dispersal in Higher Plants*. New York: Springer-Verlag.

Wright, W. D. 1969. *The Measurement of Colour*, 4th ed. New York: Van Nostrand.

Wyszecki, G., and Stiles, W. S. 1967. *Color Science*. New York: Wiley.

Comments on Coevolution: Discussion

C. Richard Tracy

Max Snodderly's hypothesis of "coevolution" between monkeys and trees is interesting. It is worth noting that (a) the monkeys prey on the fruit without direct damage to adult trees, and (b) the trees doubtlessly have a generation time that far exceeds that of the monkeys. Many animals (e.g., condors, whales, and humans) and plants (e.g., elms, maples, and ashes) have life history strategies that place a premium on adult survivorship, sometimes at the expense of infant survivorship (see Mertz 1971). Any adaptations of the trees that manifest themselves in terms of fruits colored for camouflage or for attraction would present an interesting problem for the population biologist or evolutionary ecologist who might ask why the trees adopted this kind of strategy rather than the one employed by maple trees.

Snodderly: Monkeys can certainly affect trees directly, as shown by the impact of *Cebus* feeding activity on tree branching patterns (Oppenheimer and Lang 1969). I suspect the monkeys have been superimposed upon pre-existing adaptive relationships. Squirrels and birds as well as other kinds of animals feed on fruits that have developed defense mechanisms. Spiny fruits, for example, sometimes contain wind-dispersed seeds or soft seeds that are eaten by monkeys. It would be interesting to know if there is a spiny fruit that lacked spines before there were monkeys. Gentry (personal communication) stated that most generic evolution of trees (correlating with fruit dispersal types) has taken place since the Eocene and hence may have been subject to the influence of primates.

Tracy: People who work with spiny objects are toying with the alternative hypothesis that spines help prevent overheating of fruits that are in full view of the sun.

REFERENCES

Mertz, D. B. 1971. Mathematical ecology of the California condor. *Condor* 73:437-453.

Oppenheimer, J. R., and Lang, G. E. 1969. Cebus monkeys: effect on branching of Gustava trees. *Science* 165:187-188.

Are Selection Pressures Different?: Discussion

W.J. Hamilton III

One of the features of Max's discussion that fascinates me is his suggestion that the selection pressures for color discrimination might be different for Old and New World primates. I have studied the food habits of baboons (*Papio ursinus*, an Old World primate). Much of their food is unripe, green fruit. For example, a troop of baboons visits the same persimmon tree (*Diospyros mespiliformis*) day after day. To a human observer all the green persimmons look the same, yet on each visit the baboons select and eat only a few of the incompletely ripened fruits. These observations suggest that Old World primates, just like their New World brethren, may make subtle distinctions among green colors. The selection pressures on color vision in Old and New World primates may be more similar than Max suggests.

Snodderly: When I began work on the problem, I thought of it in terms of the color of the fruit, but vision works by contrast. That is why I cast the problem in terms of visual contrast and that is why I presented reflectance spectra of the fruit and the background against which the monkey sees the fruit.

There are two additional points that need to be made relative to Bill's comment. First, at the present time there is no reason to believe that human color discrimination is surpassed by any other animal. This is not to say that humans can rival all the optical sensing specializations of animals. After all, insects use ultraviolet, snakes use infrared, and humans cannot use either type of radiation. However, within the visible spectrum, one must go a long way to beat human color vision. To my knowledge there is no literature indicating that a deviation from what we consider normal human-type color vision can offer any advantage. If the squirrel monkey could have better discrimination in the green by giving up something in the red, we could think of it as a positive adaptation. However, the bulk of our present data indicates that there is little need for New World primates to discriminate among similar reds. Selection for red discrimination is lax; hence New World primates have poorly developed sensitivity in the red portion of the spectrum.

Now, if one asks what one would have to look for in the environment of Old World monkeys having normal human-type color vision, it would be the following: there should be situations that would force them to make subtle discriminations at the red end of the spectrum. These situations would provide sufficient selection pressure to force them to retain normal human-type color vision. The proposal I have made is that a dry environment necessitates subtle red discriminations because it is brown and browns are desaturated reds (see Fig. 72 above). Consequently, if baboons are picking green against brown, the discrimination is not difficult. However, if they are picking orange against brown, the discrimination can get subtle, or if they are choosing among shades of brown, then they may, in fact, be making subtle red discriminations.

Hamilton: Another alternative is suggested by your line of thought. Macaques, baboons, and man are omnivorous and range widely in search of prey, whereas New World primates reside in forests exclusively. Old World primates range through diverse habitats, which may broaden the selection pressure to make discriminations against diverse backgrounds and to discriminate signals provided by insects and other animal prey that are part of the diet of Old World primates, in addition to selecting greens from green backgrounds.

Audience Questions:
Discussion

Question: Old World primates possess excellent wavelength discrimination; yet, despite everything mentioned, the wavelength discrimination of New World primates appears to be equally excellent. Is that a correct assessment of the data?

Snodderly: Your assessment is not entirely correct. Figure 62 (above) shows a very important difference in the spectral sensitivity of New and Old World primates (*Saimiri* vs. *Macaca*). However, these few data allow only a preliminary comparison. Data on other species are needed to determine the magnitude and extent of the difference.

A point that I might have emphasized and that has been frequently overlooked is the extent to which primates destroy the plants on which they feed. It may be that primates have some special adaptations as destructive feeders (e.g., opposable thumb) that set them apart from other species.

Hamilton: Primates are an important destructive force. Over 90% of the seeds of some *Acacia erioloba* trees are eaten before they ripen.

Question: What differences in ability to discriminate wavelengths would you expect among leaf-eating and insect-eating primates in the New World?

Snodderly: One thing you must realize is how very, very tedious it is to study color vision of monkeys. The data that I have summarized represent years of work, and the answer to your question will require a lot more work. Furthermore, we need to coordinate laboratory and field studies so that both physiological and behavioral data will be available for certain key species. To date, the leaf-eating monkeys have not been studied. Nobody knows the first thing about their visual systems.

Question: *Saimiri oerstedi* is one of the New World monkeys that feeds in the lower deciduous forest which, unlike the canopy, would be green throughout the year. How would this affect your hypothesis?

Snodderly: Well, that would be extremely interesting to study, and I would like to do it. *Saimiri oerstedi* is known to feed on fruits as well as insects (Thorington 1967, 1968, Baldwin and Baldwin 1972), so the kind of analysis I have presented here could be easily extended. *Saimiri* is a sufficiently widespread genus that it probably inhabits different habitats and one would like to know whether the color-vision deficiencies are associated with particular habitats. If you could establish a correlation between habitat and color-vision deficiencies within one species or genus, you would have a powerful starting point. So I think *Saimiri* is a key primate for further study.

Baylis: I was delighted to see in Dr. Snodderly's slide that he photographed it against a neutral gray card and a Kodak color scale. Can I please ask anyone who photographs animal or plant coloration not to do so against a black or white background.

REFERENCES

Baldwin, J. D., and Baldwin, J. I. 1972. The ecology and behavior of squirrel monkeys (*Saimiri oerstedi*) in a natural forest in western Panama. *Folia Primatol.* 18: 161-184.

Thorington, R. W. 1967. Feeding and activity of *Cebus* and *Saimiri* in a Colombian forest. In *Progress in Primatology*, D. Starck (ed.). Stuttgart: Fischer.

Thorington, R. W. 1968. Observations of squirrel monkeys in a Colombian forest. In *The Squirrel Monkey*, L. A. Rosenblum and R. W. Cooper (eds.). New York: Academic Press.

Part 4

Coloration for Communication

Chapter 7

Environmental Light and Conspicuous Colors

Jack P. Hailman

Strategy for Investigating Conspicuous Coloration
- Functions of Biochromes and Schemochromes
- Principles of Conspicuousness
- Physical and Perceptual Variables
  - Radiometry
  - Photometry and Colorimetry
- Environmental Factors of Conspicuousness
  - Light Availability
  - Background
  - Transmission

Available Light
- Methods and Habitats
- Southeastern Pine Subclimax and Ecotone
  - Forest vs. Ambient Irradiance
  - Variables Affecting Irradiance
- Tropical Rain Forest
  - Forest Irradiance
  - Height Within the Forest
- Ponderosa Pine and Altitude
  - Altitude and Ambient vs. Forest Irradiance
  - Times-of-Day and Forest Irradiance
- Conclusions Concerning Available Light
- Implications for Animal Coloration

Optical Background
- Habitats and Methods
- Radiance Spectra in Southeastern Habitats
  - Sky, Water, Sand, and Dune Vegetation
  - Marshes, Bushes, and Oldfield
  - Woodland Leaves, Trunks, and Litter

Conclusions Concerning Background
Achromatic Backgrounds
Blue Backgrounds
Orange Background
Brown-Green Complex
Implications for Animal Coloration
General Discussion
Ecological Problems
Conceptual Problems
Future Prospects

No one has explained the coloration of the tiger swallowtail, queen parrotfish, painted bunting, and other beautifully colorful animals. Even when biologists agree that colors have been selected for conspicuousness--such as aposematic coloration of a noxious prey to ward off its predators or display coloration used in social communication with conspecifics--why a particular color or pattern has evolved remains largely unexplained. My present task is to identify ways in which the environment helps determine conspicuousness of colors.

My original talk in the symposium was drawn largely from Chapter 7 in *Optical Signals* (Hailman 1977), where I emphasized the paucity of relevant data concerning environmental light in different habitats. Happily, a travel grant allowed me to begin filling the void of data immediately after conclusion of the Animal Behavior Society meetings at which the symposium was held. These data were analyzed so that this volume might contain the first statements of the kind of information needed to make sense of conspicuous colors of animals. Therefore, this chapter opens theoretically by outlining the strategy for investigation and closes empirically by reporting initial progress toward the stated goals.

STRATEGY FOR INVESTIGATING CONSPICUOUS COLORATION

A strategy for solving problems of animal coloration was laid out in *Optical Signals* (hereafter *O.S.*) and is summarized here, the details being available in *O.S.* (Hailman 1977). First, one needs to consider the range of possible functions of animal coloration, since it seems probable that most coloration is some kind of resultant compromise among many, often conflicting, selection pressures (see the questions and answers at the end of Chapter 3). Second, one needs to identify the general principles that render coloration visually conspicuous. Lastly, one can outline how differences in environmental light favor selection of different colorations for conspicuousness under different ecological conditions.

Functions of Biochromes and Schemochromes

The perceived color of a nonbioluminescent animal depends upon either reflecting pigments (biochromes) or microstructures (schemochromes); see Chapter 4 of *O.S.* Some biochromes, melanin in particular, often confer benefits that are unrelated to the appearance of the animal. In other cases the "ideal" coloration may not have evolved within an animal group due to biochemical inabilities to synthesize a relevant biochrome. Birds, for example, must obtain carotenoids from their food, so when placed on carotenoid-deficient diets, they change color, as when captive flamingoes turn white. For these reasons, it is useful to study the physical and chemical basis of the coloration, an area of research in which a great deal more comparative work needs to be done.

Benefits derived from biochromes and schemochromes may be divided into three major categories: those unrelated to the appearance of the possessor, those that decrease the conspicuousness of the animal, and those that increase its conspicuousness. Some of the advantages unrelated to appearance are covered by Chapters 2 through 4 in this volume, and a summary list of advantages is provided in *O.S.* (Table 4-V, p. 114). These include various forms of protection that are unrelated to absorption of electromagnetic radiation: resistance to abrasive wear of the integument (Chapter 3 of this volume), water-proofing, anhydrous excretion, and chemical defenses against predators. A larger group of functions depends upon the interaction of the animal with radiation, although not necessarily radiation in the visible spectrum. For example, melanin may be used to absorb harmful ultraviolet radiation (Chapter 3) or to absorb visible and infrared radiation for thermal balance (Chapter 2). An important subset of this radiation-related group of functions concerns photoreception of the possessing animal. External coloration may reduce specular reflectance about the eyes, provide sighting lines, promote dermal light-sensitivity (Chapter 4) or shield internal photoreceptors from light (Chapter 4). Eyes themselves contain various biochromes and schemochromes, but since most of these have only minor effects on the general appearance of the animal, they are largely irrelevant to the present discussion; the important exception is iris color in some vertebrates, especially fishes, where it may change color.

The second of the three major functional categories of benefits derived from biochromes and schemochromes relates to decreasing the possessor's visual conspicuousness. This subject includes traditional concerns of concealment and mimicry (Chapter 8), which is covered by Chapter 6 in *O.S.* under the rubric of deception. There are at least four general strategies of such visual deception: (1) suppression of shadow-contrasts (including countershading); (2) suppression of outline-contrasts (including disruptive coloration, transparency, and coloration that matches the background); (3) specific imitation (including imitation of plants and mimicry of other animals); and (4) creation of various optical ambiguities (including symmetry-deception, deceptive polymorphism, and motion-deception).

Finally, the category with which this chapter is concerned is the use of coloration to increase the visual conspicuousness of an animal, usually for intraspecific social communication, but also for interspecific communication, as in aposematic (or warning) coloration of noxious prey animals. In attempting to analyze why an animal's signals are colored as they are, it is always necessary to consider simultaneously the other benefits of biochromes and schemochromes, for it seems likely that most coloration results as a compromise among conflicting selection pressures. Melanin in particular confers many potential advantages upon an animal, so whenever black coloration is under scrutiny, a host of alternative explanations should be kept in mind.

Principles of Conspicuousness

It is by no means always obvious when coloration has been selected for conspicuousness, and in *O.S.* I repeatedly assumed that coloration appearing conspicuous to me has been selected for conspicuousness to other animals. This seems a necessary starting point for analysis of conspicuous coloration until detailed ethological studies demonstrate that particular colors and patterns are or are not used as optical signals. Therefore, the analytical strategy is to derive from these presumably conspicuous colors and patterns some general principles of conspicuousness, so that one may analyze how these principles are differently manifest in different ecological environments.

Some principles of conspicuousness have been summarized in Table 7-I (p. 208) of *O.S.*, and fall into five major categories: (1) movement; (2) enhancement of shadow-contrast (reverse counter-shading); (3) enhancement of shape (including uniform coloration of complex shapes, outlining borders of flat surfaces, and geometric regularity of shape); (4) surface contrast (brightness, hue, and saturation); and (5) miscellaneous principles (optimal image-size, spatial repetition of signals, and so on). However, these general principles do not operate in the abstract; they depend at least upon the visual capacities of the observer and upon the optical environment in which they are seen.

It is virtually necessary to predicate all present analysis on an assumption that we know to be a lie--namely, that the visual capacities of other animals are similar to our own. Chapter 5 of *O.S.* concerns the capacities of the receiver of optical signals as understood from studies of sensory physiology and psychophysics, and presents ample evidence that animals differ in visual capacities. Some animals see well over a greater dynamic range of intensities than others (even some species of owls see better in low light than other owls). Some animals are sensitive well into the near-ultraviolet spectrum (e.g., apparently most invertebrates). Other differences occur in color analysis, pattern-recognition mechanisms, flicker-fusion curves, peak spatial-contrast frequencies, and so on.

The present concern is mainly with color *per se*, and, although there is a large literature documenting widespread possession of color vision in animals, there is little literature documenting quantitative similarities or differences among color vision systems of animals. We know that all vertebrate eyes exhibit certain basic structural similarities, that cone-shaped photoreceptors are the primary mediators of color vision, that photopic spectral sensitivities of many vertebrates are similar (although by no means identical), and that three (or four) cone pigments are commonly found. We do *not* know whether spectral discrimination functions and color-matching functions are similar among vertebrates.

These two latter sets of data are the critical ones in judging color-perception of animals, and as far as I can determine our sum of reliable comparative information is as follows. Spectral-discrimination curves--a plot of discriminability thresholds throughout the spectrum--are known only from a few primate species and the domestic pigeon. The curves are very similar in these species (see Figure 5-10, p. 133 in *O.S.*). Color-matching functions, sufficiently complete to construct a tentative chromaticity diagram, appear to be known only from man and the domestic honey bee (*Apis mellifera*). The diagrams differ appreciably (compare Figures 5-11 on p. 136 and 5-12 on p. 137 of *O.S.*) because the insect has good sensitivity in the ultraviolet spectrum. We are constrained therefore to make the outrageous assumption that color vision may be reasonably similar among vertebrates and certainly dissimilar from insects. What remains in this chapter is perforce restricted to considerations of coloration as a vertebrate predator or social companion may perceive it.

Physical and Perceptual Variables

In this chapter I shall argue from a combination of physical data and human color-perception calculations, so that a brief explanation of the two is in order.

Radiometry

The physics of light is covered in detail in Chapter 3 of *O.S.* (see also Chapter 1 of this volume), and only two crucial concepts need be pointed out here: spectral irradiance and radiance. Spectral irradiance is the light falling upon a surface, expressed as spectral increments throughout the visible spectrum. The "amount" of light may be measured according to energy or (less commonly) quanta, and its spectral position by wavelength or (less commonly) frequency. Energy per unit time is radiant power, the basic unit of which is the Watt, so irradiance spectra are usually plots of $W \cdot m^{-2} \cdot nm^{-1}$ vs. nm (i.e., spectral increments of power falling on a surface area as a function of wavelength). Irradiance could just as well be expressed as $quanta \cdot s^{-1} \cdot m^{-2} \cdot THz^{-1}$ vs. THz (i.e., photon flux increments incident on a surface area as a function of frequency), or as power-frequency or quantal-wavelength functions.

Spectral radiance is the light emitted from a surface area, and hence has the same units as spectral irradiance, although the two quantities differ importantly in meaning. Spectral irradiance has been measured in some environmentally relevant ecological situations, but spectral radiance measurements are rare. Burtt (in press) made the first attempt to fill this gap by calculating theoretical radiance from irradiance measured in a forest and the reflection spectra of leaves and museum specimens of birds measured in a laboratory with a reflection spectrophotometer. In the empirical part below, I present what appear to be the first data of direct field measurements of spectral radiance in different ecological situations.

Photometry and Colorimetry

The physical measurements document the basic data but cannot by themselves tell us how different two colored surfaces appear to an observer. This latter question can be approached through analysis by photometry and colorimetry (Chapter 5 of *O.S.* and Chapter 1 of this volume). There are three psychological variables by which we assess the coloration of a surface: brightness, hue, and saturation. The Commission Internationale de l'Eclairage (C.I.E.) has established standard analytical techniques that express these subjective variables by measurable luminance (or illuminance), dominant wavelength (or frequency), and excitation purity, respectively.

Luminance measures approximately the human brightness sensation by weighting radiance according to a standard luminosity curve that approximates the spectral sensitivity of the human eye. Luminance values express the approximate brightness of a stimulus to an animal's eye only if the spectral sensitivity of that eye is similar to the standard luminosity curve of the C.I.E. For some species the similarity is reasonable--e.g., the pigeon (*Columba livia*) and bullfrog (*Rana catesbeiana*)--whereas for others it is not (e.g., stump-tailed macaque, *Macaca arctoides*); see Figure 5-7, p. 128 of *O.S.* Because they see into the ultraviolet, most insects should probably be considered to have quite different curves of spectral sensitivity.

Dominant wavelength and excitation purity are calculated from the C.I.E. chromaticity diagram, which arbitrarily uses an equal-energy spectrum as the reference white color. The diagram is based on the amazing fact that any stimulus can be matched (approximately) by a superposition of some monochromatic stimulus plus white, with their relative radiances properly adjusted. The monochromatic stimulus used is called the dominant wavelength, and the amount of equal-energy white needed for a mixture that visually matches is measured by the excitation purity. Excitation purity has values from zero (pure white) to unity (pure monochromatic radiation). Both dominant wavelength and excitation purity may be calculated from the radiance spectrum of a stimulus. These two variables express subjective hue and saturation to eyes that have color-analyzing systems resembling that of the human eye, but we know so little about color-matching phenomena in animals that it is difficult to say how great the similarities actually may be. Colorimetric analysis, in any case, probably provides a better appreciation of the stimulus as seen by many vertebrate species than would simple physical measurements.

Luminance, dominant wavelength, and excitation purity characterize a stimulus but do not measure conspicuousness as expressed by the visual contrast between surfaces. Contrast in luminance and excitation purity is straightforward: the greater the difference in values of these variables, the more visually contrasting are the stimuli (although the scaling may be nonlinear). Contrast in hue, however, is not sensibly measured by mere differences in dominant wavelength. Short-wavelength stimuli (which we see as violet) and long-wavelength stimuli (red) have the greatest difference in dominant wavelength values, but they may not contrast as much with one another as each does with some middle-wavelength stimulus such as a green or yellow hue. I proposed in *O.S.* that contrast in hue might best be measured by complementary dominant wavelengths.

The complementary dominant wavelength is that monochromatic stimulus which when combined in correct proportion with the dominant wavelength yields the same visual sensation as equal-energy white. Like dominant wavelength, the complementary may be calculated from the radiance spectrum. Dominant wavelengths in the center of the visible spectrum have no spectral complements; instead, their complements are some form of the unique sensation we call purple. Physically, purple is a mixture of extreme wavelengths (violet or blue plus red).

Although various schemes have been devised for creating a three-dimensional color space, none is totally satisfactory (see Burtt, in press; also Figure 7-11, p. 242 in *O.S.*). Part of the difficulty comes in scaling the variables of luminance, dominant wavelength, and excitation purity so as to reflect properly their discriminability to the eye, and another part of the difficulty comes in scaling the three variables relative to one another. In this contribution I shall just consider each kind of contrast separately, rather than attempting to reduce contrast to a single variable in three-dimensional space.

Environmental Factors of Conspicuousness

My thesis is that three principal factors determine conspicuousness of animal coloration in any given light environment: the irradiance available for reflection by the animal, the background against which the animal is seen, and the attenuation of light between the animal and the observer. These factors are discussed extensively in Chapter 7 of *O.S.* and are summarized here.

Light Availability

Because most coloration is created by reflecting sunlight, the question of light availability concerns primarily factors that dictate the spectrum of light received ultimately from the sun. The chief exception is in animals that display at night by starlight or moonlight, where the illuminance is so low that color vision is generally believed to be impossible, so that white coloration is selected for as providing the greatest brightness contrast. (I also omit consideration of bioluminescence.) If one considers first a surface in the open on the earth's surface, three principal variables determine the spectral irradiance: the sun's angle above the horizon, the altitude above sea level, and the weather conditions of the atmosphere.

Ignore for the moment the problem of clouds and other weather variables, so that an animal in the open is illuminated by direct sunlight, skylight (which is sunlight scattered from the atmosphere), and such sunlight and skylight as are reflected from the substrate and surrounding objects. The irradiance spectrum changes with the sun's angle due to the amount of atmosphere through which the light must travel before striking the animal, the shortest path being when the sun is directly overhead. The sun's angle is determined by the time of day (low near sunrise and sunset), the latitude (low at higher latitudes), and the season (lower in winter than in summer): see Figure 7-6, p. 211 in *O.S.* The effect of a low sun angle is to eliminate short wavelengths (the "blue" end of the spectrum) because of Rayleigh scattering (Figure 7-7, p. 212 in *O.S.*). A surface facing the low sun is irradiated primarily by long wavelengths (yellow, orange, and red), whereas that facing opposite the sun receives much less radiation, and that with a short-wavelength emphasis due to back-scattering from the open sky. Therefore, animals that display early or late in the day, in the winter, or at high latitudes cannot create bright blue signals: available light favors display coloration of white, yellow, orange, or red (other things being equal).

Altitude has a different effect on the irradiance spectrum because increasing altitude, as on mountains, eliminates the lower part of the atmospheric light path selectively. Increasing elevation leads to higher overall spectral irradiance and slightly higher irradiance at short wavelengths, so that blue, violet, and purple signals become particularly feasible (see Figure 7-8, p. 215 in *O.S.*).

Weather has complex effects on irradiance, and this subject was not treated in *Optical Signals*. Obviously, cloud cover decreases the total irradiance, and the ambient light may become dim indeed when rain clouds obscure the sun. Not all animals experience the same weather conditions when displaying because the weather differs geographically, seasonally, and even by time of day in statistically predictive patterns. These variables need closer attention relative to animal coloration than they have so far received.

Finally, vegetation and water both absorb appreciable amounts of the ambient light striking the earth, and objects in the environment may reflect light upon an animal. Whereas open areas such as fields, prairies, deserts, and the surfaces of bodies of water provide an environment with high illuminances and spectrally complete light, vegetated and aquatic environments will have low illuminances and spectrally dominant light. In open areas we expect to find signal coloration that includes dark colors such as blue and structural coloration such as iridescence and dichromatism. In the forest, however, branches absorb and reflect light, and leaves absorb, reflect, and transmit light. The light level may drop by two log units (Burtt, in press) and its spectral composition may change markedly to a middle-spectrum emphasis (see Figure 3-13, p. 79 in *O.S.*).

Burtt (in press) showed that the mid-spectrum emphasis is stronger in hardwood forests of various types than it is in coniferous forests of various types, presumably due to transmission of green light through the broad leaves of the former. The low irradiance, diffuse nature of the light, and its greenish emphasis should select for white or yellow coloration to maximize conspicuousness due to brightness contrast in deep forests.

Pure water selectively absorbs long wavelengths and scatters light so that irradiance becomes diffusely blue with depth in an aquatic habitat (Figure 3-15, p. 83 in *O.S.*). However, suspended and dissolved materials may markedly change the spectrum of ambient light underwater, and at least some kinds of turbid water have long-wavelength emphasis. As expected, some species of turbid-water fishes have red or orange display coloration.

Background

The second of the three variables that dictate the conspicuousness of coloration is the background against which the coloration is seen. Commonly, general body coloration of animals provides the background for display coloration, as in the black body against which the male redwing blackbird's bright red epaulets are displayed. In other cases the environment is the relevant background, as with the all-red male cardinal. In these latter cases we need to know the spectral radiance of the relevant background, but no one has measured these radiances directly and in many cases we do not even know what the specific backgrounds are. (For example, many studies have been made of courtship displays by male birds, but almost none document from where the female watches, so that the relevant background remains unspecified: is it leaves, tree trunks and branches, the leaf litter on the ground, the open sky, or what?)

In *Optical Signals* I made the first speculative attempt to classify backgrounds for display and predict colorations that might be maximally conspicuous against them. This beginning distinguished homogeneously bright backgrounds, a bivalent homogeneous background, and a class of regularly patterned backgrounds. Homogeneously bright backgrounds include clear sky, open sand beaches, salt flats, and water *depths*. Against such backgrounds one expects signal coloration to be dark. The water's *surface* has two extremes of appearance: in the direction of the sun, specular reflection provides white radiance (full visible spectrum), whereas in the opposite direction reflection off the surface is primarily that of scattered skylight of bluish emphasis. Waterbirds and other animals that display habitually on the surface must contrast against both backgrounds, which predicts dark coloration with light patches such as orange, yellow, or desaturated green. Finally, some habitats, such as cattail marshes, prairies, and eelgrass beds, have a patterned structure of principally vertical elements. We can speculate here that uniform coloration or horizontal striping would be conspicuous patterns. What is needed in vegetated habitats is radiance measurements of the brown, yellow, and green vegetation to predict the coloration that would be most conspicuous.

Transmission

The last of the three variables of environmental light is the transmission characteristics of the medium between displayer and observer. Although we ordinarily think of the medium as being perfectly transparent, this is rarely true in aquatic habitats and often untrue in terrestrial habitats. Transmission noise may be decomposed into translucency and opacity, the former due to suspended particulates such as water vapor in air and turbidity in water, and the latter due to large objects such as plants, rocks, and coral. Turbidity, as mentioned above under consideration of available light, tends to filter out short wavelengths, and thus promotes yellow, orange, and red signal coloration for conspicuousness. The effects of fog, mist, and other suspensions in air are complex and require closer scrutiny in relation to optical signals of animals. Opaque objects in the environment may select for the size, shape, or placement of patches of signal coloration, but have no known effects on color *per se*.

In sum, our knowledge of how available irradiance, background radiance, and transmission of the medium affect coloration is in a primitive state, largely due to the lack of relevant physical data in different ecological situations. Even where predictions have been made, little more than a preliminary test of their reasonableness is presently available. However, a strategy for analysis has been mapped and there is at least some hope of better understanding within the capabilities of present technology. The empirical sections that follow present some preliminary attempts at further understanding.

AVAILABLE LIGHT

The light available to an animal for reflection as a signal is measured by irradiance spectroradiometry. Although the ecological literature contains irradiance studies in various habitats, the measurements are often restricted to total irradiance rather than the spectral distribution of available light, which is the critical aspect for studies of animal coloration. Even when the spectral distribution is reported, it is not analyzed colorimetrically, and hence Burtt's (in press) study of irradiance spectra in relation to the coloration of wood warblers was virtually the pioneering effort in this area. Here I report some old but recently analyzed measurements from a tropical forest in Panama, recent measurements from southeastern forests in the United States, and some data from forests in the Rocky Mountains. These are not offered as final characterizations of light available in these habitats, but rather as part of an initial survey to see how much difference occurs in different environmental loci and what the causes of the differences may be.

Methods and Habitats

Eastern North America may be divided into three major terrestrial biomes (Odum 1971): the coniferous forests of Canada, the deciduous forests of most of the eastern United States, and the subtropical forests of the tip of southern Florida. Between each is a broad transition zone (ecotone) containing a mixture of forest types. Burtt's (in press) measurements were made in habitats within the ecotone between the coniferous and deciduous forests in northern Minnesota, and represent the first strong data for these two biomes. The eastern deciduous biome includes a distinct southeastern area where the coastal plain soils apparently prevent the forest succession proceeding to hardwood climax. In this "edaphic subclimax" area, southern pines of various species represent the ultimate forest, and in the piedmont regions above the coastal plain there is a transition zone (ecotone) of mixed pines and scrubby oaks. It was this southeastern region of forests with associated coastal habitats such as marshes that I surveyed in June 1977.

I recorded the irradiance spectra in forests and when possible in an adjacent clearing so that the optical filtration by the forest could be characterized. For nearly the entire field period the weather was rainy or highly changeable, making it difficult to achieve records under stationary conditions; reasonably complete weather data were taken with each spectrum (cloud over, winds, temperature, and humidity). Irradiance measurements were made with an ISCO model SR battery-powered spectroradiometer, calibrated in the Engineering Instrumentation Laboratory of the University of Wisconsin in the fall of 1976. Field data were reduced by computer program in FORTRAN-V, listing being available upon request to the author. I am grateful for support from an N.S.F. BioMedical Sciences Grant from U.W. to carry out the field work, and to my wife, Liz, for aid in the computing and the field work.

During the summer of 1976 I was able to make some preliminary measurements in the Rocky Mountains of Colorado on a research trip funded for studies of phototaxis by the National Science Foundation. In 1973 I made similar measurements on a research trip to Barro Colorado Island in the Panama Canal Zone, supported by N.S.F. and a grant from the National Geographic Society to my co-worker, Dr. Robert G. Jaeger. I am grateful to him and to Linda Jaeger for help in the field. The same instrument was used in these older studies, but the data were not previously analyzed and reported because the calibration on the instrument was old and required checking.

All measurements were taken on or near the ground with the spectroradiometer vertical, except where specifically noted. In forested areas, the instrument was always in the shade, except where specifically noted otherwise. Although these irradiance data by no means survey all relevant habitats, even in America--and do not characterize any given habitat under all conditions of lighting--they do provide some interesting and unpredicted results that point the way for further studies.

Southeastern Pine Subclimax and Ecotone

The attempt of this recent survey was to make measurements near the summer solstice, when birds, butterflies, and other colorful animals display and are active.

Forest vs. Ambient Irradiance

Figure 73 summarizes four sets of direct, vertical irradiance spectra taken in forests and adjacent clearings: loblolly pine (*Pinus taeda*) stands in two different states, a mixed coastal hardwood thicket, and an area where both mixed hardwoods and tall pine woods were adjacent to a small clearing. Where the woodlands are relatively thick,

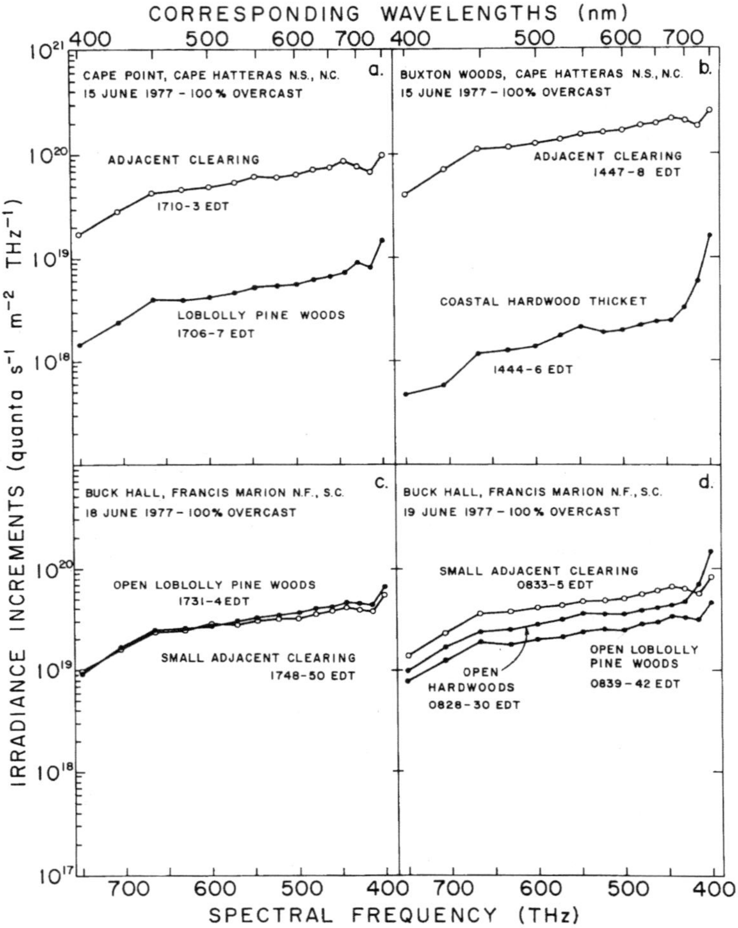

Fig. 73. Irradiance spectra from various southeastern coastal woodlands compared with reference spectra of ambient irradiance in adjacent clearings. The spectra are plotted on a scale of equal frequencies (in Tera Hertz) with corresponding wavelengths (in nanometers) given above. Quantal irradiance increments (in quanta per second, per square meter of surface area, per THz of spectral increment) are plotted logarithmically in order to compare spectra in the same graph that differ by several log units in absolute

the pine decreases available light by about one log unit (Fig. 73a) and the hardwoods by about two (Fig. 73b), but where the woods are more open, the decrease is much smaller in woodlands of both types (Figs. 73c and 73d). Furthermore, in the South Carolina locality (Figs. 73c and 73d), the adjacent clearing was small, so irradiance measurements there may not closely approximate the light falling upon the tops of the woodlands. Another problem relates to the sun's angle above the horizon, for at low angles early or late in the day, light may penetrate obliquely into the forest much more readily than at noon when it falls more vertically upon the trees. Finally, changing weather conditions--even when irradiance seems stable to the observer's eye--can create apparent paradoxes. Note that in Figure 73c the open pine woods are actually slightly brighter than the small adjacent clearing and that in Figure 73 the open hardwoods appear to transmit more light at low frequencies (far red) than is seemingly available for transmission. Despite the fact that woodland and reference data were taken only minutes apart, small shifts in cloud cover caused small shifts in irradiance.

Scrutiny of the spectral curves of Figure 73 reveals conformity to Burtt's (in press) discovery that the light quality is little changed by coniferous woods (e.g., Fig. 73a), but takes on a mid-spectrum peak in hardwoods (Fig. 73b). However, when filtering by open woodlands is minimal, this difference in spectral emphasis is not apparent (Fig. 73d). (These differences are more evident when energy rather than quanta is plotted, and when the scaling is arithmetic rather than logarithmic.)

---

value. (Furthermore, over middle intensities, the response of the eye is approximately proportional to the logarithm of the light level.) Times given are Eastern Daylight Times (EDT). The data come from two localities in Cape Hatteras National Seashore (N.S.), North Carolina (N.C.), and one locality in Francis Marion National Forest (N.F.), South Carolina (S.C.), all within the pine edaphic subclimax portion of the eastern deciduous biome. For discussion of features of the data, see text; for photometric and colorimetric analysis of these data, see Table 10.

The visual characteristics of the available light are best appreciated by photometric and colorimetric analysis, as shown in Table 10. The lines of the table correspond to the spectra graphed in Figure 73. The comparisons of illuminances show that differences are very nearly the same as the differences in irradiance levels mentioned above. This correspondence is due to similarities in the spectral distribution of light. The excitation purities are all low, meaning that the light is whitish (about 85-95% whitish). All the dominant frequencies save one are in the part of the spectrum we see as (greenish) blue, the exception being the coastal hardwood thicket, which is in the "green" region (522 to 611 THz) due to its mid-spectrum emphasis mentioned above. One does not "see" irradiance, of course, but if a perfectly reflecting white card were placed in the irradiated area and viewed next to a self-luminous surface emitting equal energy throughout the spectrum, the card would have a light greenish-blue tinge to it compared with the self-luminous white surface.

Variables Affecting Irradiance

Forests, as noted above, are not homogeneous. As Burtt (in press) found in his study of warbler coloration, the forest environment has patches of shade and sunlight, with all sorts of intermediates between these extremes. Therefore, I made a special test to see if patches of sunlight within the forest showed the same irradiance spectrum as that obtained in a nearby clearing, and compared these with the spectrum of a shaded area in the forest, as shown in Figure 74a. Because the National Forests in northern Florida are planted in loblolly (*Pinus taeda*), slash (*P. elliottii*), and hybrids between the two pines, I could not identify the species with certainty. The sky was partly cloudy, but all three spectra were taken during a period in which the sky near the sun was totally cloudless. As Figure 74a shows, the Florida woods filter out about one log unit of ambient light (also found in North Carolina: Figure 73a). A patch of sunlight within the forest, however, has virtually the same irradiance as in an adjacent clearing. Unfortunately, I was not able to make similar measurements in a hardwood forest.

Table 11 helps to make the comparisons inherent in the spectra of Figure 74. The illuminance values follow the irradiance levels and the light has a greenish-blue emphasis, but becomes distinctly more saturated in the shaded pine woods (excitation purity large: 0.23).

TABLE 10

Photometric and Colorimetric Analysis of the Irradiance Spectra of Figure 73

Spectrum	Illuminance (lux)[a]	Dominant Frequency (THz)[b]	Excitation Purity
73a--Cape Point			
adjacent clearing	1.5×10^4	620	0.12
loblolly pine woods	1.3×10^3	622	0.13
73b--Buxton Woods			
adjacent clearing	3.8×10^4	622	0.12
coastal hardwood thicket	4.7×10^2	608	0.08
73c--Buck Hall			
open loblolly pine woods	8.2×10^3	622	0.12
small adjacent clearing	7.6×10^3	623	0.16
73d--Buck Hall			
small adjacent clearing	1.2×10^4	622	0.14
open hardwoods	8.5×10^3	617	0.12
open loblolly pine woods	5.8×10^3	624	0.15

[a]To find foot-candles, divide these values by 10.8.

[b]To find the equivalent dominant wavelength in nm, divide these values into 3×10^5.

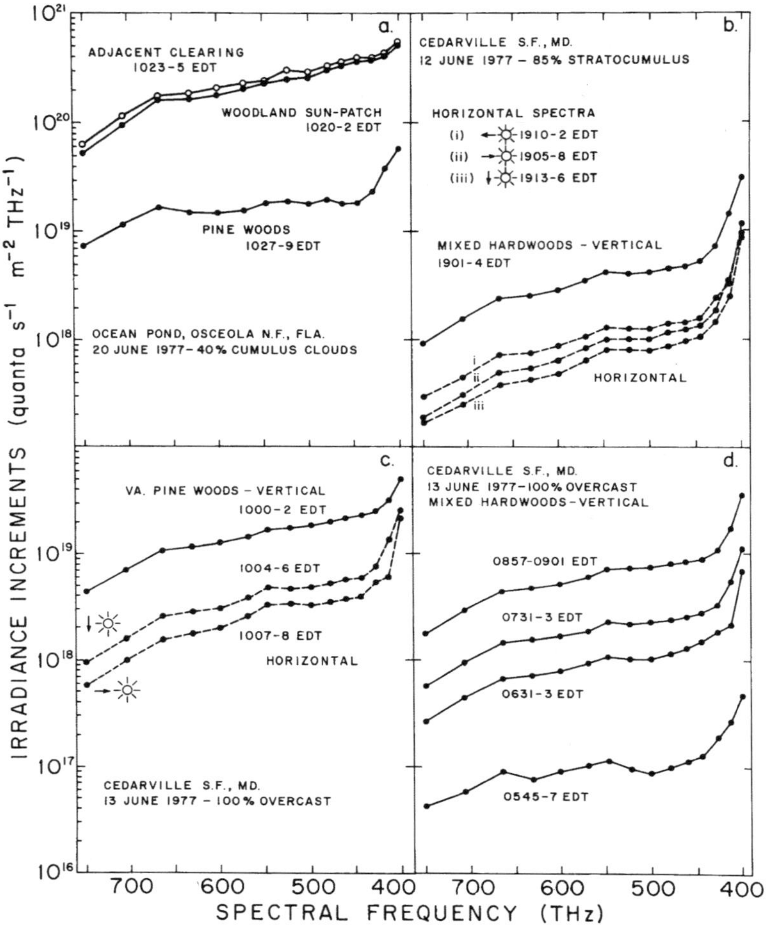

Fig. 74. Some effects of variables affecting local spectral irradiance in southeastern woodlands. For explanation of scaling, units, and abbreviations, see Figure 73; further abbreviations used here are: FLA., Florida; S.F., State Forest; VA., Virginia; and MD., Maryland. Note that the lower graphs here have been scaled down by one log unit relative to the upper graphs and those in Figure 73. For further analysis, see Table 11; and for interpretation of features, see text.

TABLE 11

Photometric and Colorimetric Analysis of the Irradiance Spectra of Figure 74

Spectrum	Illuminance (lux)	Dominant Frequency (THz)	Excitation Purity
74a--Ocean Pond (pine subclimax)			
adjacent clearing	6.6×10^4	621	0.08
woodland sun-patch	6.0×10^4	620	0.07
pine woods shade	4.5×10^3	628	0.23
74b--Cedarville mixed hardwoods (ecotone)			
vertical	9.8×10^2	609	0.07
away from sun's azimuth	3.0×10^2	604	0.06
toward azimuth	2.4×10^2	599	0.04
at right angles to azimuth	1.8×10^2	563	0.04
74c--Cedarville Virginia pine			
vertical	4.1×10^3	617	0.09
at right angles to azimuth	1.1×10^3	600	0.04
toward azimuth	7.3×10^2	563	0.04
74d--Cedarville mixed hardwoods			
0857 EDT	1.7×10^3	613	0.08
0731	5.2×10^2	617	0.11
0631	2.5×10^2	615	0.11
0545	2.5×10^1	620	0.23

In an area of mixed hardwoods within the ecotone, where no clearing was available for comparative spectra, I measured the forest irradiance not only vertically, but also in three directions horizontally: toward, away from, and at right angles to the sun's azimuth. These measurements help to characterize the spectrum illuminating the lower portions of an animal near ground level (Fig. 74b). The sun was obscured by nearly stationary stratoculumus clouds. The vertical spectrum is similar to that of a coastal hardwood thicket (Fig. 73b), but spectrally shifted to the "green" (609 THz) because it was taken later in the day (Table 11). The horizontal spectra taken about 1 m from the ground are lower in level by more than a half log unit. Curiously, the irradiance taken with the spectroradiometer pointed away from the azimuth of the obscured sun is highest, with that taken toward the sun slightly lower and that taken at right angles lower yet. At least part of this effect is due to reflection back from plants in the direction away from the sun.

Similar measurements in the same area were made in a stand consisting largely of Virginia pine (*Pinus virginiana*) the next day, during frustratingly variable weather. The sun was obscured by 100% overcast clouds while three spectra were taken, but the clouds broke during the fourth spectrum and the weather remained changeable so that no other measurements could be taken that day. Figure 74c shows the vertical and two horizontal spectra. The spectral irradiance in Virginia pine is similar to that in loblolly woods (e.g., Fig. 73), and the horizontal irradiances are about a half log unit below the vertical irradiance, as in the hardwoods (Fig. 72b). In this case, however, the irradiance (and illuminance: Table 11) looking at right angles to the azimuth is greater than that toward the approximate azimuth. (The sun was obscured by clouds, and from the woods I could not tell the exact azimuth.) The possible reasons for this difference include both the changing weather mentioned above and slightly denser vegetation in the direction of the sun than at right angles to it. Again, the horizontal irradiances are shifted to lower frequencies, in the "green."

Finally, within the hardwood forest of Figure 74b measurements, I determined the vertical irradiance at four other times of day, as shown in Figure 74d. The spectral irradiance (and illuminance: Table 11) increases with the rising sun, of course, but interestingly the spectrum appears to flatten as well, and the forest light becomes whiter as the sun rises in the sky (decreasing values of excitation purity).

Tropical Rain Forest

The Smithsonian Tropical Research Institute (S.T.R.I.) maintains a series of trails through the forest on Barro Colorado Island (B.C.I.) in the Panama Canal Zone, the trails being named and marked with numbered posts every 100 m. Bennett (1963) defined three forest types on B.C.I.: one-stratum forest of variable height showing recent disturbance; high two-strata forest, with foliage layers at 25-40 and 75-100 feet; and low two-strata forest, the lower layer of which is lower and more variable than the high forest. I surveyed vertical and horizontal irradiance spectra in each type of forest and also preliminarily investigated other variables.

Forest Irradiance

The only clearing on B.C.I. sufficiently large to provide a reference for forest spectra (such as the references in Fig. 73) is the clearing containing the buildings of the S.T.R.I. research station. Therefore, it was not possible to record reference spectra for the forest measurements, but I did take one vertical spectrum in the clearing from the roof of the main building (dining hall/dormitory), immediately adjacent to the weathervane. Even at this height, the tall tropical trees extend well above the horizon. The spectrum recorded was reported in Figure 3-10b (p. 75) of *O.S.* to compare it with a simulated spectrum from the program by McCullough and Porter (1971). I have now recalculated that spectrum using the more recent instrument calibration, and include it here in Figure 75a. This spectrum serves as a partial reference for the forest spectra shown in the remainder of Figure 75.

The lower portion of Figure 75A shows the same data replotted on axes that allow comparison with the simulated output of the program by McCullough and Porter (1971). The replotting on wavelength vs. energy basis demonstrates how different the same data appear when plotted in different ways. The simulation provides a good fit to the recorded data, both in terms of absolute levels and in the shape of the spectral distribution of the irradiance. The correspondence is better than that reported in Figure 3-10b of *O.S.*, where the data were analyzed with the older instrument calibration values. The top part of Figure 75a serves as a general reference for the remaining curves in Figure 75.

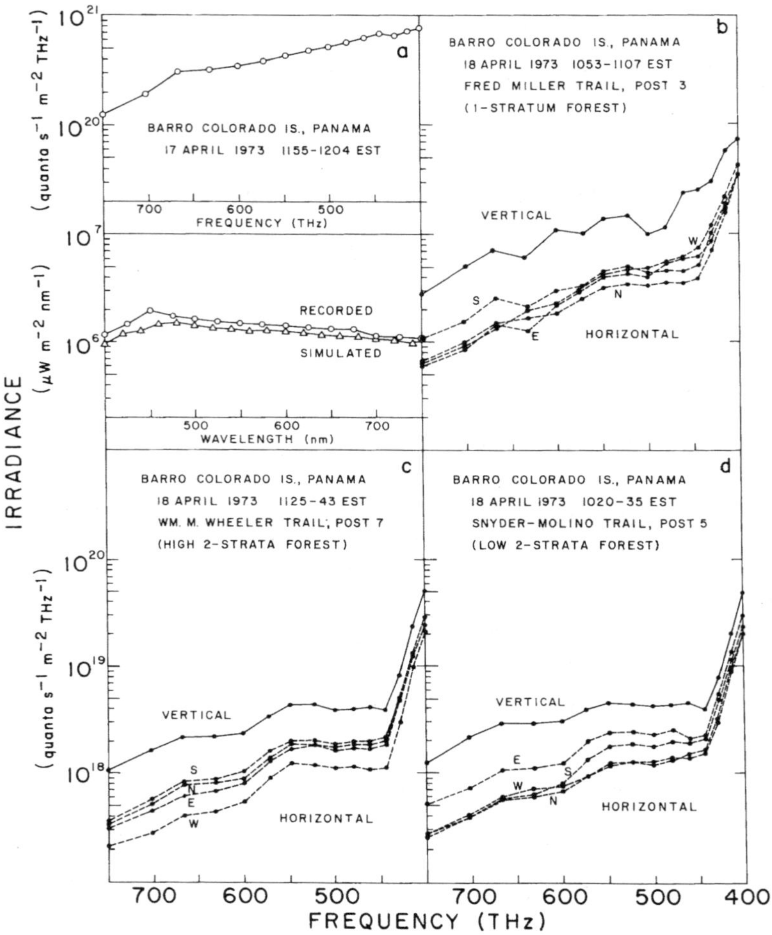

Fig. 75. Irradiance spectra from the tropical forest biome. The upper spectrum in part a is scaled for comparison with the spectra in parts b through d. The lower spectra in part a are plotted on energy/wavelength scales, comparing the same recorded data (upper curve) with the spectrum simulated by the program of McCullough and Porter (1971). See also Table 12. New abbreviations appearing in this figure are: IS., island; N, North; E, east; S, south; and W, west.

TABLE 12

Photometric and Colorimetric Analysis of the Irradiance Spectra of Figure 75

Spectrum	Illuminance (lux)	Dominant Frequency (THz)	Excitation Purity
75a--Open ambient			
vertical	1.1×10^5	623	0.09
75b--1-stratum forest			
vertical	3.0×10^3	597	0.06
horizontal-south	1.0×10^3	597	0.04
horizontal-west	9.9×10^2	523	0.25
horizontal-east	9.1×10^2	525	0.24
horizontal-north	7.3×10^2	543	0.06
75c--High 2-strata forest			
vertical	9.5×10^2	601	0.06
horizontal-south	4.4×10^2	544	0.10
horizontal-north	4.0×10^2	541	0.09
horizontal-east	3.7×10^2	535	0.14
horizontal-west	2.6×10^2	534	0.20
75d--Low 2-strata forest			
vertical	1.0×10^3	617	0.13
horizontal-east	5.2×10^2	553	0.07
horizontal-south	3.9×10^2	528	0.25
horizontal-north	2.8×10^2	539	0.06
horizontal-west	2.7×10^2	555	0.03

The tropical forest strongly attenuates the ambient light, lowering it by about two log units. Forest irradiance is strongest in the one-stratum forest (Fig. 75b) and weakest in the low, two-strata forest (Fig. 75d). Horizontal spectra in all cases are a half to a full log unit less than the vertical irradiance, but there are no strong or consistent differences correlating with direction of the horizontal spectra. As in the case of spectra in temperate broadleaved forests (e.g., Fig. 73 above), the spectra of Figure 75 show a mid-spectrum hump, in some cases quite pronounced. As can be seen in Table 12, the excitation purities are mostly small, although a few are in the range from 0.20 to 0.25. These exceptions also have the lowest dominant frequencies, around 525 THz, in the part of the spectrum we see as yellowish-green. Indeed, all the dominant frequencies lie within the "green" part of the spectrum, making the light in these tropical forests more greenish than in the temperate forests discussed above.

The illuminance measurements of Table 12 are tolerably similar to those made directly by Allee (1926) more than a half-century ago. He found illuminances of about 197 lux at the forest floor and 8.7×10^4 lux above the canopy.

Height Within the Forest

S.T.R.I. erected a platform 50 feet (15.2 m) above the ground between posts 3 and 4 on the Snyder-Molina Trail,

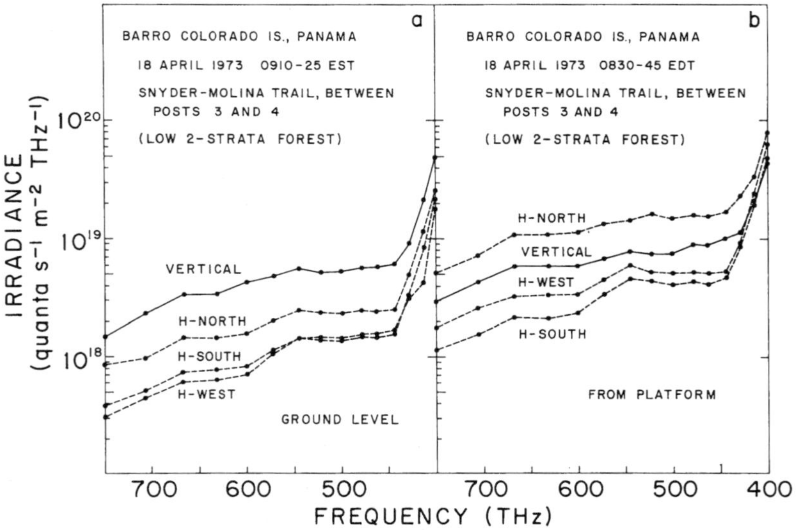

Fig. 76. Irradiance as affected by height within the tropical forest. Measurements shown in part b were taken from a platform about 15 m above the ground. See also Table 13.

TABLE 13

Photometric and Colorimetric Analysis of the Irradiance Spectra of Figure 76

Spectrum	Illuminance (lux)	Dominant Frequency (THz)	Excitation Purity
76a--Ground level			
vertical	1.3×10^3	611	0.11
horizontal-north	5.5×10^2	611	0.09
horizontal-south	3.2×10^2	598	0.03
horizontal-west	3.1×10^2	541	0.08
76b--Platform (15 m)			
vertical	1.8×10^3	622	0.18
horizontal-north	3.6×10^3	620	0.14
horizontal-west	1.2×10^3	613	0.12
horizontal-south	9.7×10^2	589	0.04

offering an opportunity to determine the effects of height on irradiance spectra within the forest. I recorded a vertical spectrum and three horizontal spectra from the platform and from the ground beneath, as shown in Figure 76. The platform was on the west side of the tree to which it was attached so that no east-facing spectrum could be recorded. The vertical spectra were compared in Figure 3-13 (p. 79) of *O.S.*, plotted on an arithmetic energy/wavelength basis, but that analysis was based on the former instrument calibration. The reanalysis using the new calibration is only slightly different (higher irradiance toward short wavelengths or high frequencies), and is here plotted on log-quantal/frequency axes, along with the six previously unpublished horizontal spectra. Table 13 provides photometric and colorimetric analyses of the spectra, and it is evident from both figure and table that light levels are higher aloft than they are at ground level. Peculiarly, the northward horizontal spectrum aloft shows higher irradiance and illuminance than the vertical spectrum. My reference photographs from the platform suggest an explanation: the vegetation is thin at this height, and the spectroradiometer was looking at a large amount of open sky horizontally, as well as reflectance off leaves. The vertical photograph also shows some open sky, but other contributions are primarily light transmitted through rather than reflected from leaves.

All the spectra have relatively low excitation purities, and hence are not strongly colored. At both heights the vertical and north-facing spectra have dominant frequencies in the "greenish-blue," but the south- and west-facing spectra are shifted noticeably toward the "green," although their excitation purities are lower so that the light quality is actually whiter. In every case, the illuminance is higher aloft than in the corresponding spectrum at ground level.

Ponderosa Pine and Altitude

Ecological structure in the Rocky Mountains and other heights in western North America depends strongly upon altitude. Most ecologists follow some system similar to the original life-zone concept of Merriam, which distinguishes Upper Sonoran, Transition, Canadian, Hudsonian, and Arctic-alpine zones as one climbs in altitude. My preliminary measurements come from the tundra of the Arctic-alpine zone in Rocky Mountain National Park, Colorado, and from ponderosa pine (*Pinus ponderosa*) forests in the Canadian zone on both sides of the Colorado Rockies. I looked at the effect of altitude upon open, ambient irradiance and the filtration by the pine forest, and specifically at time-of-day effects in the forest in a second study.

Altitude and Ambient vs. Forest Irradiance

I took vertical spectra at two times of day in an open area next to the foothills in Boulder, Colorado (1760 m) and compared these with a spectrum taken on the highest through-road in the United States: Trail Ridge Road in Rocky Mountain National Park (3720 m). Figure 77a

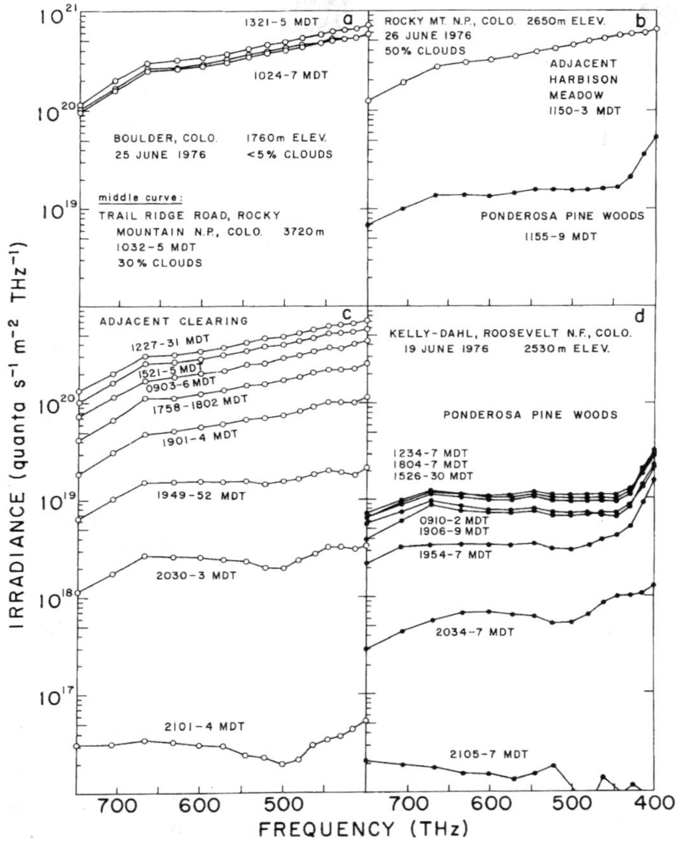

Fig. 77. Irradiance in ponderosa pine forests and clearings in the Rocky Mountains. Part a shows ambient spectra at different elevations, and part b shows the filtering effect of the forest. Parts c and d compare ambient irradiance in a clearing with irradiance in an adjacent forest through various times of day. See also Table 14. New abbreviations used in this figure: N.P., National Park; COLO., Colorado; MDT, Mountain Daylight Time; and ELEV., elevation above sea level (in meters).

shows that within this range, altitude has little effect on the ambient spectrum. I made a similar measurement in Harbison Meadow (2650 m) on the western slopes of the Rockies, and as shown in Figure 77b, this spectrum is similar to the others. In an adjacent ponderosa pine forest the irradiance is diminished by nearly one and a half log units, and flattened spectrally compared with the ambient reference. As shown in Table 14, the forest has little effect on the dominant frequency, but it does increase the excitation purity noticeably: the light quality shifts from nearly white to having a greenish-blue tinge.

Times-of-Day and Forest Irradiance

As mentioned above in conjunction with the tropical forest, McCullough and Porter (1971) provided a computer program that simulates the ambient irradiance on earth. The simulation provides for light at any day of the year and at any time of the day, at any geographic locality and altitude. If one could predict the effects of forest filtration on light, then an extension of the McCullough-Porter simulation would make possible modeling of forest light. My study of open ambient light and irradiance in an adjacent ponderosa pine forest in Colorado provides some background data for beginning such modeling.

The data were taken to test a simple approach to forest filtration. Suppose the forest were a filter that could be placed in the beam of a spectrophotometer, where the fate of incident light (I_0) is governed by:

$$I_0 = rI_0 + aI_0 + tI_0 \qquad (7.1)$$

where r, a, and t are the coefficients of reflection, absorption, and transmission, respectively (see pp. 62ff in *O.S.*). If forest filtration is the combined effects of reflection and absorption of ambient irradiance ($f = r + a$), it follows that the filtered forest light (fI_0) is $I_0 - tI_0$, so that:

$$f = (I_0 - tI_0)/I_0 \qquad (7.2)$$

If f were a constant, then one could model forest spectra (tI_S) by using the McCullough-Porter program to calculate the simulated incident light (I_S) from which the forest spectrum could be calculated by:

$$tI_S = I_S - fI_S \qquad (7.3)$$

TABLE 14

Photometric and Colorimetric Analysis of the Irradiance Spectra in Figure 77

Spectrum	Illuminance (lux)	Dominant Frequency (THz)	Excitation Purity
77a--Ambient spectra			
Boulder, 1321 MDT	1.1×10^5	623	0.10
Trail Ridge Road, 1032 MDT	9.2×10^4	623	0.10
Boulder, 1024 MDT	8.8×10^4	623	0.11
77b--Harbison Meadow			
meadow clearing	1.0×10^5	622	0.10
ponderosa pine woods	3.9×10^3	625	0.23
77c--Ambient spectra			
1227 MDT	1.1×10^5	624	0.11
1521	8.9×10^4	624	0.11
0903	6.3×10^4	622	0.10
1758	3.8×10^4	620	0.09
1901	1.7×10^4	620	0.11
1949	3.9×10^3	626	0.26
2030	5.9×10^2	627	0.34
2101	6.7	630	0.45
77d--Ponderosa pine woods			
1234 MDT	2.7×10^3	629	0.34
1804	2.7×10^3	628	0.31
1526	2.5×10^3	629	0.34
0910	1.9×10^3	629	0.37
1906	1.8×10^3	628	0.33
1954	1.1×10^3	626	0.30
2034	1.6×10^2	624	0.30
2105	3.8	629	0.41

To test the constancy of *f*, measurements were made at eight times of day, as shown in Figures 77c and 77d (see also Table 14).

It is clear that this simple approach to modeling light in a forest will not do for the ponderosa pine forest measured. While the ambient irradiance changes continually throughout the day according to the sun's angle in the sky (Fig. 77c), irradiance reaches an asymptote in the forest and remains remarkably constant through the middle of the day. In terms of eq. 7.2, this result means that *f* cannot be a constant.

Another extraordinary phenomenon is revealed by the analysis in Table 14. Although the dominant frequency remains fairly constant through the day, and is similar in the clearing and the woods, the excitation purity of the clearing irradiance is not so constant. In the ambient spectra, the light becomes more saturated as the illuminance decreases, varying from about 0.09 to about 0.45. However, within the forest the excitation purity of illumination is remarkably constant, having values of about 0.3 to 0.35.

Put simply, the ponderosa pine forest is unexpectedly resistant to changes in ambient irradiance. What factors cause this phenomenon, completely unpredicted by theory? I believe the answer is as follows. In midday, when the sun is high in the sky, light falls vertically on the forest and hence must traverse the maximum amount of vegetation, so it is strongly filtered. This filtering flattens the ambient spectrum (compare Figs. 77c and 77d). As the sun's angle decreases later in the day, more light penetrates the forest, which tends to be structured in horizontally protruding tree limbs. Filtration is therefore diminished, but so is the sun's irradiance, and the two factors tend to balance, keeping vertical forest irradiance constant. As filtration decreases, the forest no longer has such a pronounced effect on the spectral distribution of light, so one would expect light quality to change, even if total irradiance and illuminance were constant. However, the ambient vertical spectrum itself changes because a greater portion of the vertical irradiance comes from scattered skylight rather than direct sunlight. This can be seen in Figure 77c, where the ambient spectrum flattens as a function of decreasing irradiance. So again changes in the ambient light cancel changes in forest filtration, and the forest light remains relatively constant in excitation purity. Also note that purity is higher in this forest than in *any* of those mentioned above (cf. Tables 10 through 14). Whereas one must abandon the facile attempt to model forest irradiance as if the forest were a simple filter (eqs. 7.1 through 7.3), the empirical data have revealed a totally unpredicted constancy of available light in the forest.

Conclusions Concerning Available Light

On the basis of these admittedly preliminary data, what conclusions may be drawn about the ecological effects of light available for reflection or optical signals? The objective is clearly to discover generalities or shortcuts that eliminate the need to measure light empirically at every locus relevant to an animal's movement through its habitat, but the data suggest that we are presently far from being able to model environmental light accurately. The principal roadblock is the large number of interacting variables that affect irradiance. Nevertheless, the results suggest some generalities that may be useful first guides for further field work.

First: The simulation of McCullough and Porter (1971) appears to work well in predicting the vertical ambient spectrum in an open area under cloudless skies. Clouds are not, of course, constant filters, but with further study it may prove possible to extend the simulation to take into account cloudy conditions. For example, one might be able to measure the ambient illuminance with a simple photometer, and from it and the program simulate the spectral distribution of light--without having to make complicated spectroradiometric measurements in the field. If this were to prove possible, a large body of ambient lighting conditions would be taken care of, leaving vegetated areas and underwater environments as the remaining problems. In this chapter, I exclude consideration of the latter because of the added complexities (see *O.S.* for a discussion).

Second: Altitude above sea level seems to have little effect on visible light at the earth's surface.

Third: Areas within the forest that are illuminated by sunlight appear to have the same irradiance characteristics as ambient irradiance. This case is thus accounted for by the first point above.

Fourth: In shaded areas of the forest the light is always more saturated (less white), lower in total irradiance (and illuminance), and shifted toward lower dominant frequencies (greener) than the ambient light falling upon the top of the forest. This generality holds true for all kinds of forests measured, regardless of type of trees, weather conditions, geographic location, and other variables. The *quantitative* effects, however, vary widely.

Fifth: As one climbs in height within the forest, the light quality becomes more similar to ambient, and as one considers increasingly horizontal irradiance, the effects of the forest are exaggerated. That is, horizontal irradiances have higher excitation purity, lower dominant frequencies, and lower illuminances than vertical spectra made from the same locus in the environment. This conclusion also seems qualitatively independent of other variables.

Sixth: The quantitative effects of forest filtration of light appear too complicated to be modeled without considerably more information. Some factors quantitatively affecting forest light appear to be as follows. (a) Broad-leaved forests affect light more strongly than do needle-leaved forests, presumably because the broad leaves transmit highly saturated green light whereas needles affect light primarily by reflection. (b) The physical structure of the forest appears to have complex effects on available light. Because of the horizontal layering of the forest, sunlight penetrates best at low sun angles; when the irradiance levels are lowest, the spectrum is flattened and absorption by the forest is least. (c) The total amount of vegetation in the light path (density of forest) is also quantitatively important in determining forest light. This fact is revealed both by changes with height above the ground within the forest, and also by the comparison between denser tropical and less dense temperate forests.

Perhaps the most surprising result that emerged from this initial survey was the fact that the ponderosa pine forest in Colorado was so resistant to changes in the ambient light. The forest light remains remarkably constant in illuminance, dominant frequency, and excitation purity. We can only hope that such serendipitous results will continue to emerge in order to simplify the task of understanding and predicting environmental light.

Implications for Animal Coloration

Do the conclusions concerning available light reached above suggest any predictive effects on conspicuousness of animal coloration? I believe that the answer is a definite "yes," but this answer must be tempered by considering all the other factors of light (i.e., background and transmission through the medium) and vision (e.g., spectral sensitivities of observing animals) that affect conspicuousness.

The major difference between open ambient irradiance and forest irradiance is the absolute level. Animals that display in direct sunlight can afford (from strictly visual considerations) to utilize coloration that reflects little light. Without considering the complex subject of reflection spectra of animals, one may note that blue colors usually have a comparatively narrow reflection spectrum, which also peaks at frequencies to which the eye is not very sensitive--saturated blue is an inherently dark color. One expects, then, that dark blue animals will be restricted to open areas of sunlight, whereas their forest relatives must utilize coloration that reflects broader spectral bands nearer the peak sensitivity of the eye (e.g., yellow). A relevant comparison was suggested during our southeastern field work: the all-blue male indigo bunting (*Passerina cyanea*) always sings from a high perch in direct sunlight, whereas the congeneric painted bunting (*P. ciris*) seems to slink about thickets and other vegetated areas. This latter bird has a dark purple head, but also a bright yellowish-green back and a brilliant red breast and rump. A similar difference occurs with the eastern orioles (*Icterus*). The male northern oriole (*I. galbula*) sings and displays its bright yellowish-orange plumage within the canopy layer of tall deciduous forests, whereas the congeneric orchard oriole (*I. spurius*) is much more likely to be found at the forest edge, in orchards, or in other places where its dark reddish-brown coloration is illuminated by direct sunlight.

Burtt (personal communication) points out that the surprising constancy of light in the ponderosa pine forest suggests another possible principle worth noting. Animals confined to habitats where the ambient illumination is fairly constant may evolutionarily adapt their signal coloration to these specific conditions, whereas animals that communicate in a variety of habitats or in habitats where the available light shifts importantly through the day (e.g., direct sunlight) may have to adopt other strategies. These strategies might include using a variety of colors, each most conspicuous under a certain condition, or making various compromises in coloration.

The strength of analyses at this stage would appear to lie primarily in predicting differences in coloration between closely related species, and it would seem worthwhile pursuing this subject on the basis of present information about available light. However, the available light, by itself, cannot dictate animal conspicuousness because that is dependent upon contrast with the background against which the displaying animal is viewed. I therefore turn to analyses of surface radiances in the environment.

OPTICAL BACKGROUND

There are virtually no studies of the coloration of surfaces against which displaying animals are viewed. Burtt (in press) pioneered attempts to define background coloration by measuring the spectral reflectance of leaves in a laboratory spectrophotometer, and then calculating a measure of leaf radiance in a particular forest where the irradiance was measured spectroradiometrically. This approach entails several sources of error, but even if it did not, the approach would be inadequate because one cannot place a tree trunk, mixed branches and leaves, the surface of a pond, the beach, or the sky into a spectrophotometer for reflectance measurements. In this section I report what I believe to be the first direct spectral radiance measurements made in ecologically relevant situations.

Habitats and Methods

All the data come from habitats in the southeastern pine edaphic subclimax (and ecotone) area within the eastern deciduous biome, and all measurements were made in June 1977. Measurement of spectral radiance is somewhat more involved than irradiance measurement, so additional discussion of instrumentation is necessary.

Spectral radiance measurements were taken with a modular system manufactured by Gamma Scientific, consisting of a telescope with four apertures, a Bausch and Lomb high efficiency monochromator mounted in a Gamma housing containing an electrically operated shutter, an S-11 type photomultiplier-cum-housing, and a model 2900 autoranging photometer. Wavelengths were selected by hand-dialing at 25-nm increments from 400 to 725 nm and read out on the monochromator, and light values were read out on the nixie-tube digital display of the photometer. The instrument system was standardized in the field at night using a standard source with highly regulated power supply; the source was relamped and recalibrated against standards traceable to the National Bureau of Standards by Gamma in April 1977. The luminance of the source's screen is only about 100 foot-Lamberts (within the unfiltered range of this photomultiplier tube), so for much higher daytime readings, particularly in direct sun, an Optics Technology neutral density filter of 3.0 density was used; the filter was calibrated spectrally by the manufacturer and checked in a Beckman DK recording spectrophotometer in the laboratory. The entire field system was driven from a 12-V automobile battery and Tripp Lite 1000-W inverter to provide square-wave AC. For reasons that are not clear, the photometer's dark-current suppression was often not adequate to stabilize the voltage on the PM-tube when little other current was drawn from the 1000-W inverter. Therefore, a smaller inverter was often used to drive the photometer, the inverter connected either to the auto battery or to a smaller 12-V motorcycle-type battery.

Spectral irradiance measurements could be taken using the Gamma system and a cosine-diffuser head, but this would have required time-consuming reconfiguration of the apparatus in the field and unfeasible restandardization of the photomultiplier prior to each measurement. As will be explained below, it was important to make radiance and irradiance measurements in quick succession in the same locality. Therefore, comparative irradiance spectra were taken with the ISCO spectroradiometer described previously.

Field radiance data were reduced by computer program in FORTRAN-V run on the UNIVAC 1110 system of the Madison Academic Computing Center; copies are available upon request. The program corrects raw data for telescope aperture, calibration, and neutral-density filtration to provide spectral radiance curves in both power and quantum-flux units as functions of both wavelength and frequency. The curves are also integrated with appropriate weighting factors to deliver total luminance values from the spectral curves, and for each curve the x and y coordinates for the C.I.E. chromaticity diagram, the excitation purity, dominant wavelength, and complementary dominant wavelength are calculated.

Because of the nature of the instrumentation, the spectral radiance measurements cannot be considered as accurate as the irradiance measurements. The electronics of the instrument used for the former have less long-term stability, errors of movement are introduced by the telescopic optics, there may be diffraction effects when small apertures are used on the telescope, optical alignment of assembled modules may affect repeatability of measurements, and there are additional sources of error introduced with the neutral density filter utilized in many of the measurements. The instrument was calibrated in the laboratory on the standard source mentioned, and then standardized to it frequently in the field; yet my empirical measurements of the radiance and luminance of this source do not exactly duplicate the reference calibration of the standard source as provided by Gamma Scientific. Because the instrument corrections were calibrated to the standard source, the radiance increments (in $\mu W \cdot m^{-2} \cdot nm^{-1} \cdot sr^{-1}$) replicate Gamma Scientific's values, with rounding errors in the fourth significant digit. Luminance and chromaticity values derived through spectral integration do not match exactly, presumably because Gamma's Riemann sums are at 10-nm increments and mine are at 25-nm increments. Sample values are: luminance, 1.056×10^3 apostilbs (Gamma) vs. 1.023×10^3 apostilbs (my analysis); dimensionless $\times$ tristimulus coordinate, 0.446 vs. 0.447; and y coordinate, 0.410 vs. 0.410.

Radiance Spectra in Southeastern Habitats

I measured twenty-two different backgrounds, two of them twice, against which animals might be seen in various habitats in the southeastern pine subclimax and ecotone areas. I also report eight new irradiance spectra taken as references for some of these radiance measurements (some irradiance spectra reported above also serve as references). I have organized the data along an imaginary transect beginning at the ocean's edge and moving inland. Brown (1959) provides a detailed vegetational study of Cape Hatteras National Seashore, where many of these measurements were made.

Sky, Water, Sand, and Dune Vegetation

The first set of measurements, seven radiance spectra shown in Figure 78, are of backgrounds that one sees while standing in the open, on or behind the open ocean beach. Before pointing out features of the results, a few words of

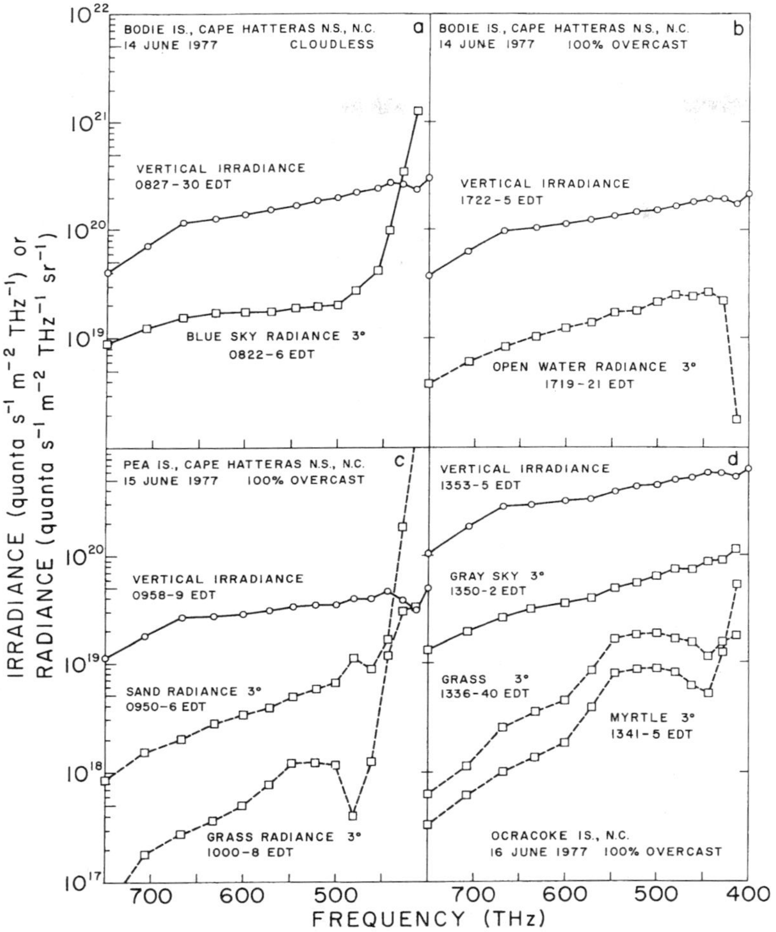

Fig. 78. Radiance spectra of backgrounds seen from the ocean beach, with vertical irradiance spectra for reference. The irradiance increments are in the same units as previous spectra (quanta$\cdot s^{-1}\cdot m^{-2}\cdot THz^{-1}$) and the radiance increments are in (quanta$\cdot s^{-1}\cdot m^{-2}\cdot THz^{-1}$) *per steradian*, the unit solid angle. Note that the vertical axes in the lower graphs (c and d) are one log unit displaced in the figure relative to the upper graphs (a and b). The telescopic aperture used is indicated with each radiance curve. For photometric and colorimetric analyses, see Table 15.

TABLE 15

Photometric and Colorimetric Analysis of the Spectra Shown in Figure 78

Spectrum	Illuminance or Luminance[a]	Dominant Frequency (THz)	Excitation Purity	Complementary Frequency[b] (THz)
78a--Ocracoke Island				
vertical irradiance	4.3×10^4	620	0.08	--
blue sky radiance	1.6×10^4	658	0.14	525
78b--Bodie Island				
vertical irradiance	3.4×10^4	621	0.11	--
open water radiance	1.3×10^4	526	0.07	--
78c--Pea Island				
vertical irradiance	8.3×10^3	623	0.17	--
sand dune radiance	4.4×10^3	504	0.23	614
Amer. beachgrass radiance	8.0×10^2	525	0.37	660

78d--Ocracoke Island				
vertical irradiance	9.8×10^4	624	0.10	--
gray sky radiance	3.9×10^4	516	0.03	--
grass radiance	1.0×10^4	522	0.54	641
myrtlebush radiance	4.9×10^3	523	0.59	642

[a]Illuminance (in lux) for irradiance spectra; luminance (in apostilbs or "equivalent lux") for radiance spectra.

[b]Given only for radiance spectra and only when excitation purity > 0.10 (i.e., when the background surface has a noticeable hue).

explanation are necessary to make the correct conceptual comparison between radiance and irradiance units in Figure 78 (and subsequent figures). Irradiance is simply the total radiant flux (e.g., quanta/s) falling upon a given surface area, but the radiance of a real surface emitting light, as by reflection, depends upon the viewing angle. Therefore, radiance in a particular direction of view is ordinarily expressed in units of radiant emitted flux per surface area--per solid angle. The figures plot radiance in terms of the unit solid angle (steradian), which is a radian of revolution. (For a detailed discussion of radiance, irradiance, and steradians, see Chapter 1 of this volume.) The purpose of the figures is merely to compare the spectral distribution of irradiance and radiance, so both are reported in their commonly used units. As explained below, however, it becomes instructive to make a closer comparison between illuminance and luminance values.

The radiance spectrum of blue sky shown in Figure 78a was purposely taken toward the northwest, about 45° above the horizon--the portion of the sky that looked bluest to me. The reference irradiance spectrum (like all those to follow) was the vertical spectrum, which thus accepted light from other parts of the sky. Because of this difference, the spectral characteristics and absolute light levels cannot be compared too closely for the sky measurements. (The comparison is closer for reflecting surfaces reported below.) Because vertical irradiance spectra can be modeled for clear sky conditions (see discussion in the irradiance section, above), these vertical spectra are used as the standard reference condition, and may help ultimately to model radiance and other irradiance spectra.

Table 15 shows the photometric and colorimetric analyses of the data in Figure 78, but again a few introductory remarks are necessary to insure correct interpretation of tabulated values.

The relations between illuminance and luminance are similar to those between irradiance and radiance, explained above, except that two kinds of expressions of luminance are commonly used. Suppose a 1-m^2, ideally diffusing surface is illuminated by one lumen, so that its illuminance is 1 lux. Then the total luminance of that ideal surface is 1 lumen/m^2, which is called the apostilb. This ideal surface must not only reflect all the light falling upon it (which real surfaces never do), but must also diffuse the light uniformly according to Lambert's cosine law, so that the surface appears equally bright from all angles of view (again, something that no real surface does). Assuming that the complex "surfaces" measured in this study approach uniformly diffusing matte surfaces in reflecting characteristics, the difference between the illuminance in lux and the luminance in apostilbs (as reported in Table 15 and subsequent tables) provides a rough idea of the average reflectance coefficient of the "surface."

The photometric analysis (Table 15) of the two curves in Figure 78a shows that the blue sky is darker than would be a perfectly diffusing, perfectly reflecting surface illuminated by light from that sky. This is not a real paradox because the irradiance spectroradiometer was receiving direct sunlight and skylight from a brighter part of the sky, as mentioned above. These empirical data are consistent with the theoretical analysis I made in *O.S.* (p. 229), where I indicated that homogeneously bright backgrounds "will *almost* always be brighter than any object seen against them" (emphasis added). I noted that "a bird seen against the open sky away from the sun . . . might be as bright or brighter than the sky if the bird be very highly reflecting." In this case, if a white bird were illuminated by the light represented by the irradiance spectrum in Figure 78a, it would need to reflect only about 40% of the light falling on it in order to be brighter to the eye than the background of blue sky.

The colorimetric analysis (Table 15) shows both curves of Figure 78a to have dominant frequencies in the "blue," but the small excitation purity value of the irradiance spectrum shows the available light to be principally white to the human eye. Interestingly, the dominant frequency complementary to the sky is in the yellowish-green part of our visible spectrum. However, this fact does not predict that animals should be yellow-green in order to contrast with the blue sky, because factors of luminance and excitation purity enter into the best contrast. These problems are discussed after presenting the empirical data.

We now turn our eyes from the sky to the open water just off Oregon Inlet at the south end of Bodie Island, looking about 90° from the obscured sun's azimuth (Fig. 78b; see also Table 15); the water is relatively calm. The graph shows the extraordinary absorption of far-red frequencies by the water, but reflectance through the rest of the spectrum is high, even considering the shallow angle at which measurements were made (telescope about 20° below the horizontal); also compare photometric calculations in Table 15. The water's surface appears nearly white (low excitation purity), as would a perfect diffuser reflecting the ambient irradiance.

Now consider the sand beach and the American beachgrass (*Ammophila breviligulata*) growing on it (Fig. 78c). The radiance spectra here were taken with the telescope nearly horizontal. As would be expected, the radiance (also luminance, Table 15) of the sand is higher than that of the dune vegetation, but the spectra also differ markedly in shape. The sand highly reflects low frequencies, increasing dramatically toward the infrared, with an unexplained dip at about 465 THz. The beachgrass, on the other hand, shows a peaked spectrum, the dip near 480 THz, presumably being due to absorption by chlorophyll. The excitation purities of these radiances are relatively high (Table 15), meaning they appear colored rather than white to the human eye. The dominant frequency of the sand is in the region of our spectrum we call orange, whereas that of the vegetation is yellowish-green. The former will appear tan under high illuminance and brown with lower light levels. Interestingly, the complementary to the sand color is in the greenish-blue part of our spectrum, whereas that of the grass color is firmly within the blue.

At another locality, we look again at the sky and grass, and this time include wax myrtle bushes (*Myrica*), which begin growing just inland from the sandy dunes. Figure 78d shows the gray sky to be brighter than the blue sky shown in Figure 78a, confirmed by the comparisons of luminances in Table 15. The vertical irradiances are similarly related in illuminances, and have nearly identical dominant frequency, compared with the blue of the blue sky, but its excitation purity is so low it is essentially white to the eye. The radiance of the grass (an unidentified species planted in the Park Service's campground area on Ocracoke, and hence probably not native) is similar to that of American beachgrass in Figure 78c, except that the "dip" of the spectrum is at slightly lower frequencies. Interestingly, the radiance spectrum from the myrtle bush is extremely similar to that of the adjacent grass (Fig. 78d), a fact reflected in their similarly yellowish-green dominant frequencies and similarly high excitation purities. The complementary colors to all three backgrounds are in the blue part of our visible spectrum.

Marshes, Bushes, and Oldfield

To continue the imaginary transect, we now walk inland past the dunes to brackish marshes, and on higher ground an oldfield successional area, with pine woods visible in the distance. Figure 79a shows the radiance of another gray sky and the cattail (*Typha*) marsh below it, along with a reference irradiance spectrum. Nearby, the marsh is made up of dried needlegrass (*Scirpus*) which appears largely tan, with myrtle bushes on higher ground around the marsh edge (Fig. 79b). The sky spectrum shows an unexplained dip near 430 THz that does not appear in the gray sky reported above (Fig. 78d); the data have been checked, and if this point is in error, the error was made in recording data from the photometer in the field, not in subsequent analysis. The radiance of the myrtle bush is nearly identical with that reported above (Fig. 78d) and the cattail spectrum is similar, but the dried needlegrass reflects quite differently.

Table 16 shows the appearance of these backgrounds to the eye, and confirms the comparisons of the spectra. The myrtle and cattail "surfaces" are highly saturated, the needlegrass decidedly less so, and the gray sky, as before (Table 15), is neutral. The cattail and myrtle have yellowish-green hues, but the dominant frequency of the needlegrass is within the "yellow" part of the spectrum, so that it appears tan. The complementary of the myrtle is in the blue as before (Table 15), but that of the cattail is shifted to the bluish-purple part of the spectrum (hence the designation "529c" or purple complementary of 529 THz). The complementary of the needlegrass is also in the blue part of the chromaticity diagram.

We now cross the shallow marshes to higher sandy land farther inland, where we first encounter a logged field where the tallest invading loblolly pines (*P. taeda*) have grown to 3-4 m and some deciduous saplings reach a height of 2-3 m. The telescope is pointed horizontally at the scrubby vegetation (Fig. 79c), where a yellow-breasted chat (*Icteria virens*) sings sporadically from the undergrowth under overcast but varying skies. The radiance spectrum appears to result from a mixture of green foliage and either branches or more neutral substrate showing through it, and the dominant frequency is just between yellow and green with high saturation (Table 16). The complementary to this background is, again, in the blue part of our spectrum.

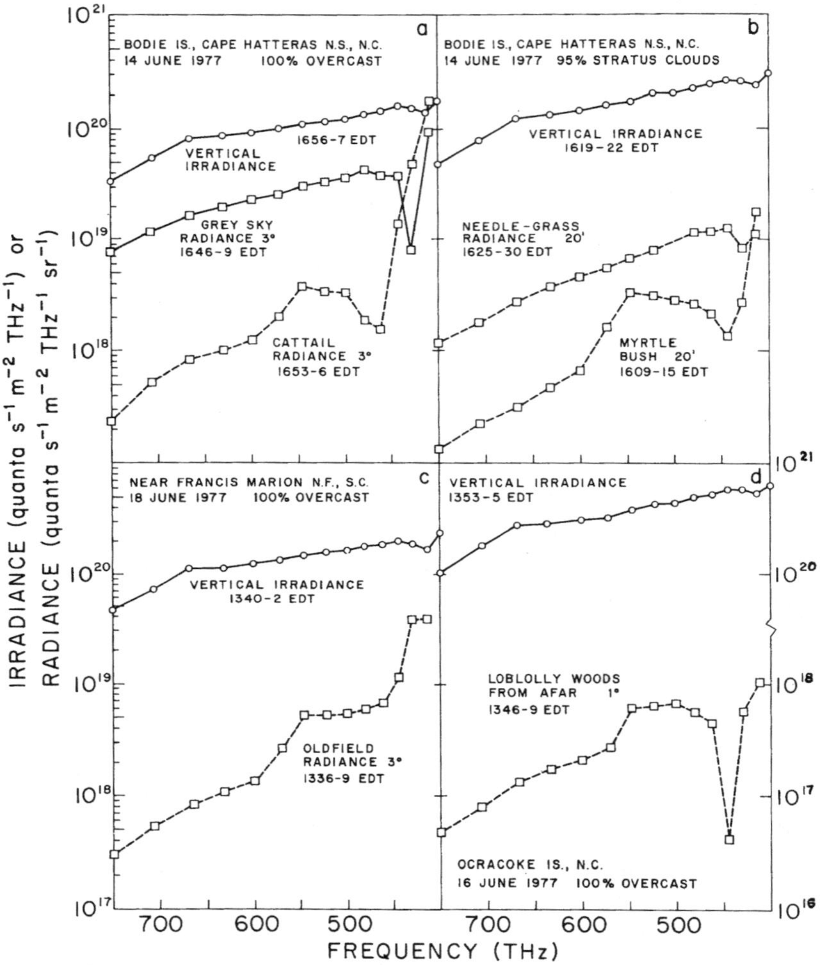

Fig. 79. Radiance spectra of backgrounds seen from just inland of the ocean beach, with vertical irradiance spectra. Units as in Figure 78; all graphs scaled the same, except lower curve in part d, where the scale (right vertical axis) has been raised one log unit to show the entire bottom curve and then broken to show the entire top curve in the same relative position as other curves in this figure. See Table 16 for photometric and colorimetric analyses.

TABLE 16

Photometric and Colorimetric Analysis of the Spectra Shown in Figure 79[a]

Spectrum	Illuminance or Luminance	Dominant Frequency (THz)	Excitation Purity	Complementary Frequency (THz)
79a--Bodie Island				
vertical irradiance	2.8×10^4	623	0.13	--
gray sky radiance	2.5×10^4	581	0.02	--
cattail radiance	2.3×10^3	529	0.34	529c
79b--Bodie Island				
vertical irradiance	4.6×10^4	620	0.09	--
brown needlegrass	5.6×10^3	519	0.19	628
myrtle bush	1.9×10^3	526	0.61	682
79c--Near Francis Marion N.S.				
vertical irradiance	3.7×10^4	623	0.13	--
oldfield radiance	3.3×10^3	521	0.53	634
79d--Ocracoke Island				
vertical irradiance	9.8×10^4	624	0.10	--
loblolly radiance	4.0×10^2	526	0.39	686

[a]See footnotes to Table 15.

We look beyond to the distant woods of loblolly pines, where the radiance spectrum from the canopy has the now-familiar vegetational "hump" between 450 and 550 THz (Fig. 79d). (The irradiance reference in this case is the same as in Fig. 78d, replotted here and retabulated in Table 16 for convenience of comparison.) The canopy spectrum is a saturated green to the eye, its complementary being a far blue, almost violet shade. The luminance is very low (note that the radiance spectrum in Fig. 79D has been raised by a log unit relative to other spectra).

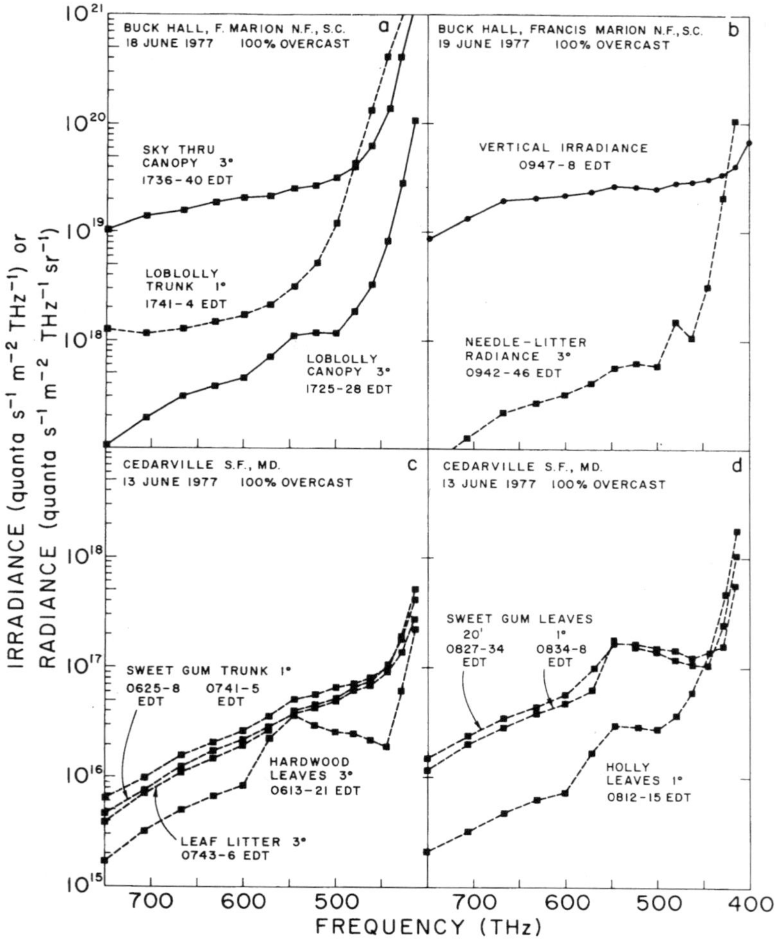

Fig. 80. Radiance spectra of backgrounds seen from within the woods. Units are as in

Woodland Leaves, Trunks, and Litter

We continue to walk inland, reaching the pinewoods and entering them to sample woodland backgrounds. The telescope is pointed about 30° above the horizontal to record spectra from the trunk of a loblolly pine, the canopy of branches and leaves, and the gray sky seen through breaks in the canopy (Fig. 80a). The sky here has a strong low-frequency emphasis, unlike the spectra shown in Figures 78d and 79a. The radiance from the trunk is unlike any reported above, actually dipping at high frequencies (around 700 THz) and then accelerating throughout the rest of the visible spectrum. The canopy as seen from within the pine woods is quite different from that seen without (cf. Fig. 79d), resembling more the background of an oldfield (cf. Fig. 79c) --probably because both are combinations of green vegegation and relatively neutral elements like gray sky, or brown branches in the case of the canopy. The irradiance references are those curves shown in Figure 73c.

These unusual radiance spectra are translated into photometric and colorimetric terms in Table 17, which includes data on reference spectra in Figure 73, used in the analysis of available light. The sky seen through the canopy actually has a purple tinge (dominant frequency 547c THz), but the excitation purity is sufficiently low that the appearance is chromatically neutral. The trunk of the loblolly pine is actually dark orange to the eye, with its complementary dominant frequency being in that part of the spectrum we see as bluish-green. The trunk's excitation purity is the highest encountered in this study. The canopy's dominant frequency is borderline between yellow and orange, probably due to the contribution of branches, which tend to resemble the main trunk, and the complementary is in the blue.

Figure 79; note that lower graphs (c and d) have been raised two log units relative to upper graphs (a and b). A reference irradiance spectrum is given only in part b because the other references are graphed above, as follows. For part a, the reference irradiance spectra are given in Figure 73c; for part c, in Figure 74d (curves at 0631 and 0731 E.D.T.); and for part d, in Figure 74d (curve at 0857 E.D.T.). The photometric and colorimetric analyses of these reference spectra are included in Table 17 to facilitate direct comparison.

TABLE 17

Photometric and Colorimetric Analysis of the Spectra Shown in Figure 80[a]

Spectrum	Illuminance or Luminance	Dominant Frequency (THz)	Excitation Purity	Complementary Frequency (THz)
80a--Buck Hall				
vertical irradiance, clearing (Fig. 73c)	1.2×10^4	622	0.14	--
sky radiance	2.2×10^4	547c	0.10	--
vertical irradiance, woods (Fig. 73c)	5.8×10^3	624	0.15	--
loblolly trunk radiance	8.4×10^3	481	0.79	609
canopy radiance	8.5×10^2	512	0.41	620
80b--Buck Hall				
vertical irradiance	6.4×10^3	621	0.17	--
needle litter radiance	4.7×10^2	510	0.31	617

80c--Cedarville				
vertical irradiance, 0631 EDT (Fig. 74d)	2.5×10^2	615	0.11	--
sweet gum trunk radiance, 0625 EDT	3.1×10	519	0.30	629
hardwood leaf radiance	2.1×10	531	0.50	531c
vertical irradiance, 0731 EDT (Fig. 74d)	5.2×10^2	617	0.11	--
sweet gum trunk radiance, 0741 EDT	3.9×10	520	0.31	633
broadleaved litter radiance	3.1×10	518	0.37	626
80d--Cedarville				
vertical irradiance, 0857 EDT (Fig. 74d)	1.7×10^3	614	0.08	--
sweet gum leaf radiance (20')	1.1×10^2	529	0.38	529c
sweet gum radiance (1)	9.6×10	527	0.42	527c
holly leaf radiance	2.0×10	518	0.54	628

[a] See footnotes to Table 15.

The telescope is now pointed about 30° below the horizontal to record the radiance of the litter of pine needles on the ground (Fig. 80b). The spectrum shows an unexplained wiggle at low frequencies like that of the sand beach (cf. Fig. 78c), which it resembles. The dominant frequency is in the orange, with its complementary in the blue.

In order to finish the imaginary transect from the ocean, we must now walk a long distance to reach the ecotone between the pine subclimax area and the major mixed-hardwoods climax area of the eastern deciduous biome. Figure 80c shows the radiance from the trunk of a sweet gum tree (*Liquidambar styraciflua*) taken twice during the morning, a spectrum of the leaf litter of mixed broad leaves and mixed leaves of the forest as seen looking horizontally through it about 1 m off the ground. Irradiance references were plotted in Figure 74d above, and are provided in Table 17 for ease of comparison. The sweet gum spectra differ from that of the loblolly trunk (cf. Fig. 80a): the sweet gum's dominant frequency is in the yellow (not orange), so that it appears tan rather than orange-brown, its excitation purity is less than half that of the loblolly, and its complementary is in the blue. The leaf litter, consisting of mixed broad leaves, differs from needle litter (cf. Fig. 80b) and, in fact, resembles the spectra of the sweet gum trunk. Like the needle litter radiance, however, its dominant frequency is in the yellow portion of the spectrum, with the complementary in the blue. Finally, the mixed hardwood leaves that form the background to horizontal view in the forest have a radiance spectra similar to other vegetation considered previously: grasses (cf. Figs. 78c and 78d), myrtle (cf. Figs. 78d and 79b), and cattails (cf. Fig. 79a). The broadleaved radiance has a dominant frequency in the green part of the spectrum, with a complementary in the purple, and a high excitation purity.

Are there differences among leaves from different species of plants? It is difficult to answer this question by comparing spectra made at different places on different days, so the final set of measurements compares sweet gum leaves with those of American holly (*Ilex opaca*), as shown in Figure 80d. The sweet gum spectra were made with two different apertures of the telescope in order to see what difference, if any, the size of the viewfield makes: it proves irrelevant in this case. There are, however, differences between sweet gum and holly spectra, which are reflected in the green dominant frequencies of the former and yellow of the later (Table 17), with consequent complementaries in the purple and blue respectively. Holly leaves have a tendency to curl up, and the viewfield of the telescope revealed that the radiance measured was primarily that of the underside of the leaves; the upper surfaces of holly leaves are much darker, and doubtless would provide a different spectrum. Actually, Burtt's (in press) direct measurements of reflectance spectra of leaves clearly show differences among species of broadleaved trees and among conifers as well.

Conclusions Concerning Background

On the basis of empirical measurements and their colorimetric analysis, terrestrial backgrounds may be placed into four primary categories: (1) achromatic, (2) blue, (3) orange, and (4) the brown-green complex. Although each background is different from every other one measured, those within a category share resemblances with one another that are sufficiently strong to allow this tentative classification. The scheme coincides roughly with intuition--after all, the human eye is a sophisticated colorimetric instrument--but further reveals important generalities about surfaces that would contrast optimally with the backgrounds.

Achromatic Backgrounds

The first category includes gray skies (Figs. 78d, 79a, and 80a) and reflection of gray sky from the water's surface (Fig. 78b). The spectra are characterized by a gradual but monotonic increase in radiance through the spectrum from high to low frequencies, although in the extreme red end there may be an unexplained dip in radiance, or a sudden increase, or both. All these backgrounds have small excitation purities (0.1 or less) and high luminances (greater than 10^4 apostilbs). The most contrasting surface against them is thus a dark one, with chromaticity playing little role.

Blue Backgrounds

The second category is represented only by the blue sky (Fig. 78a) in the empirical sample, but might include reflection of such sky off the water's surface (see Fig. 7-9, p. 233 of *O.S.*). The radiance spectrum is characterized by a flat curve from higher to lower frequencies, with a sudden acceleration at the "red" end of the spectrum. The luminance is high (10^4 apostilbs) and the excitation purity relatively low (0.14), so that again the most contrasting surface will probably be a dark one.

Orange Background

One spectrum is so different in colorimetric indices that it falls into its own category: the radiance from the trunk of a loblolly pine tree (Fig. 80a). It is the only spectrum where the radiance at the violet end at 750 THz is *not* the lowest point on the spectrum: the curve dips shallowly and then accelerates strongly as one moves toward lower frequencies. The excitation purity is extremely high (nearly 0.8), approached by no other spectrum in the sample, and the dominant frequency (481 THz) is the lowest in the sample (toward the red side within the orange). The complementary frequency is therefore in the green (near blue), the only background measured with such a complement.

Brown-Green Complex

The largest and most heterogenous category of backgrounds may be appreciated by Figure 81, which plots excitation purity as a function of dominant frequency. None of the other spectra mentioned above would plot within this diagram: blue sky is way off the diagram to the left, orange loblolly trunk off to the upper right, and the achromatic backgrounds would plot below the lower boundary of Figure 81. Although there are apparent groupings within Figure 81, I have treated this entire range of spectra within one major category because we do not know the effects that ambient irradiance (changes in sun angle, weather conditions, etc.) might have in shifting these points around. However, it does seem worthwhile to consider the groupings and their possible distinctions. The most ready distinction is by excitation purity, where there are three groupings: (a) low purity, below 0.25; (b) medium purity, between 0.3 and 0.45; and (c) high purity, above 0.5.

(a) *Low purity* backgrounds include the dried needlegrass marsh (Fig. 79b) and sand dunes (Fig. 78c). Their spectra resemble those of gray skies, and hence these

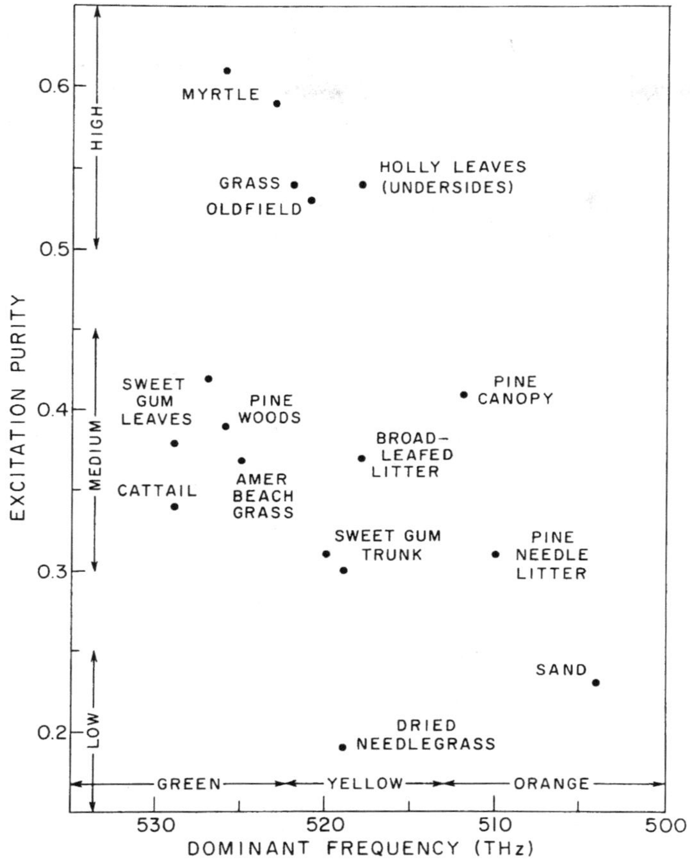

Fig. 81. A plot of the excitation purity/ dominant frequency indices of various background radiances in the "brown-green" category. The spectra are grouped readily into three classes of excitation purity, but show more of a continuum along the dimension of dominant frequency.

backgrounds appear only slightly chromatic: principally tan. Their complementary dominant frequencies are on the greenish side within the part of the spectrum we see as blue, but their luminances are relatively high (about 5 × 10^3 apostilbs), so dark objects probably contrast best against them.

(b) *Medium purity* backgrounds include a large range of dominant frequencies which divide roughly between brownish and greenish stimuli. Pine needle litter (Fig. 80b) is the most orange of the brown stimuli, with the loblolly canopy as seen from below (Fig. 80a) intermediate in hue but much more saturated, and sweet gum trunks (Fig. 80c) and litter of hardwoods (Fig. 80c) being the yellowish of the brown stimuli. These brownish spectra are characterized by monotonic (or nearly monotonic) increase in radiance from high to low frequencies, with strong acceleration at the low-frequency end; they thus resemble the low-purity spectra in general shape. All have relatively low luminances with complementaries in the blue, so that saturated (but bright) blue surfaces would contrast well.

The greenish stimuli of the medium purity backgrounds include pine woods as seen from afar (Fig. 79d), American beachgrass (Fig. 78c), sweet gum leaves (Fig. 80c), and cattails (Fig. 79a). These greenish spectra are characterized by a peak of radiance around 550 to 500 THz, the "hump" being due to chlorophyll absorption on both sides. The pine woods as seen from afar (Fig. 79d) is the most unusual of these spectra, but its low radiance at low frequencies has little effect on the eye, which is quite insensitive in this part of the spectrum. One might also notice that the spectrum of the loblolly canopy as seen from *within* the woods (Fig. 80a) shows a hint of this vegetational hump, but branches and perhaps gray sky showing through the foliage render the effect yellowish-brown rather than green. Again, the luminances are low enough that bright, but saturated, blues would contrast well, although the complementary of the cattails is pushed into the bluish part of the purple range. However, all these medium purity backgrounds are sufficiently bright that dark surfaces would also contrast well.

(c) *High purity* backgrounds are the most chromatic in appearance, consisting of the yellow undersides of holly leaves (Fig. 80d), and the green of myrtle bushes (Figs. 78d and 79b), grass (Fig. 78d), and vegetation in an oldfield (Fig. 79c). The spectra of these high purity backgrounds are not qualitatively different from the greenish backgrounds of medium purity, and only the colorimetric analysis brings out the evident differences in saturation. The yellow holly leaves have a complementary in the purple, but the complementaries of all the high purity greens are in the blue. The excitation purities of these backgrounds are sufficiently high--like that of the orange tree trunk--

that more desaturated, neutral stimuli begin to provide useful contrast. However, the luminances of these stimuli are also high, so a neutral contrasting color would have to be dark. It would appear more efficient to contrast by being a dark, saturated blue.

Implications for Animal Coloration

Perhaps the most counter-intuitive generalization that emerges from the data is that blue would be an excellent color to contrast with the predominant greens and brown of the background. This fact may help solve the puzzle I raised in *O.S.* (p. 229) concerning the blue dorsal coloration of trunk-creeping nuthatches (*Sitta*). It also reinforces the hypothesis offered in discussion of irradiance data that birds displaying in treetops should be deep blue like the indigo bunting: I argued above for the importance of high irradiance at high frequencies available for reflection, and argue here that a dark, highly saturated blue provides excellent contrast with the green vegetation.

The radiance spectra also serve to quantify a fairly obvious point, namely that brown animals will tend to match their backgrounds. One finds that almost all the small passerine birds that stay primarily on or near the ground are brown: emberizine sparrows, woodland thrushes (*Hylocichla* and *Catharus*), ground-dwelling warblers (*Seiurus*), and so on. These birds are concealed against leaf litter and dried vegetation, just as brown creepers (*Certhis familiaris*) are against tree trunks and small plovers (*Charadrius*) and sandpipers (*Calidris*) are against sand.

However, it is really display coloration--optical signals--that require explanation, for their characteristics are not intuitively obvious as are many characteristics of concealing coloration. It seems likely that the very dark body coloration of highly social icterids such as blackbirds of several genera (e.g., grackles and cowbirds) is the most contrasting coloration possible against the open sky, be it blue or gray, against which these birds see one another in flocks sometimes exceeding a million individuals. Crows and swifts are similarly aerial in habits, and tend to be very dark, although unitary explanations of dark coloration should be avoided, as emphasized at the outset. The fact remains that no background was found against which red, orange, or yellow would be the complementary color, yet these colors are commonly used for display among birds and other animals.

GENERAL DISCUSSION

Having articulated an approach to explaining conspicuous colors of animals relative to the optical environment in which they display, and then having presented new data surveying light available for reflection and backgrounds against which terrestrial animals are viewed, I will try finally to identify where we are along the road to understanding animal coloration and what remains to be done.

Ecological Problems

With the empirical demonstration that the complementary dominant frequencies of the commonest backgrounds in terrestrial environments are in that part of the spectrum we see as blue, the obvious question is: why are there not more blue animals? I will try to give perspective to the answer by concentrating on birds (a colorful group that I know best) and by breaking the question down into component parts.

As pointed out in the final subsection on backgrounds, there *are* a number of blue, violet, or purple birds. Most of these species share the dual characteristics of displaying in bright sunlight--where there is sufficient irradiance at high frequencies to make their chromatic component noticeable to the eye--and being seen against a background where high-frequency emphasis provides contrast in hue. In addition to the indigo bunting, mentioned above, these characteristics apply to many male hummingbirds, which have blue or purple caps or throats for display; to the eastern kingbird (*T. tyrannus*), which is blue dorsally; to the barn swallow (*Hirundo rustica*), whose blue dorsum is evident against the green foliage over which it flies catching insects; to the male purple martin (*Progne subis*); to male bluebirds (*Sialia*); male phainopepla (*Phainopepla nitens*), evident when perched in sunlight amidst desert scrub; the male blue grosbeak (*Guiraca caerulea*), which often sings from exposed perches like the indigo bunting; and the nearly black male lark bunting (*Calamospiza melanocorys*) of the prairies. The question does not, then, concern the paucity of blue birds, but really is three residual questions: (a) Why are not all birds that display in the open blue?

(b) Why are there blue birds that do not display in the open? (c) How can we account for other display colors commonly used by male birds, such as yellow, orange, and red?

To answer the first question, consider the brown thrasher (*Toxostoma longirostre*), which commonly sings from the highest part of a tree, not unlike the indigo bunting. Unlike the bunting, the thrasher spends considerable time foraging on the ground and often nests near the ground; its brown color and countershaded pattern suggest that it is under stronger selection pressures for concealment than the bunting, which might by itself account for the thrasher's coloration. One could also speculate that the thrasher depends more on its elaborate acoustical communication than its optical signals. The point is that one must consider not only the interaction of available light and optical background to predict animal coloration, but also the entire set of selection pressures governing the behavior and ecology of the species.

The second question, concerning blue birds in other environmental situations, was partially answered above. There are woodland birds such as nuthatches that have blue coloration in a situation where environmental light is not strong, so that the chromatic component is less noticeable, and hence the advantage of contrast in hue is diminished. Such woodland species include the blue jay (*Cyanocitta cristata*), blue-gray gnatcatcher (*Polioptila caerulea*), northern parula warbler (*Parula americana*), cerulean warbler (*Dendroica cerulea*), and blue-gray tanager (*Thraupis virens*). As American bird-watchers know, all of these species are differently colored from the blue birds mentioned previously. The woodland birds are *light* blue: they have sacrificed saturation (which would render them largely black in the forest environment) for hue, and hence pose no real paradox.

There are, however, a few bluish species of American birds that are not explained well on the basis of present data. For example, the bluish-gray belted kingfisher (*Megaceryla alycyon*) is seen in the open, yet has a desaturated blue color, *contra* prediction. The Steller's jay (*Cyanocitta stelleri*), on the other hand, is a woodland species that is very dark: black on the head and saturated blue behind, against apparently opposite to expectation. Lighting conditions in the habitats of the Steller's jay should be explored. The male mountain bluebird (*Sialia currucoides*), like the kingfisher, is seen in the open and

and is highly desaturated, a fact for which I offered a special hypothesis in *O.S.* (pp. 243-244). And the black-throated blue warbler (*Dendroica caerulescens*) is more highly saturated than expected for a woodland species. Therefore, the approach adopted has predicted correctly some avian colors, but exceptions remain to demonstrate the lack of a completely predictive theory.

Last, the important question arises as to why *any* species of bird uses yellow, orange, or red for display colors. There is, of course, ample low-frequency irradiance for reflection, so that available light favors such colors, but these are the complementaries of blue or bluish-green hues (see Fig. 7-3, p. 203 of *O.S.*), which I did not find as optical backgrounds in the present survey. There are a number of potential classes of explanation for these low-frequency colors. Among them are the following: (a) Perhaps there *are* bluish backgrounds in the environment but for one reason or another they were not included in the empirical survey. There are, for example, loci where I could not or did not take the radiance spectroradiometer (e.g., I was not able to secure permission to take it up in firetowers to measure radiances as seen from a height). (b) Similarly, perhaps under different weather conditions or other factors of lighting, some of the backgrounds I measured are actually more bluish. (c) Perceptual effects may play an unappreciated role. My colleague, Dr. Jeffrey R. Baylis, points out that under high light conditions shadowed areas sometimes appear dark purple--an effect that apparently shows up even in color photography. I have not yet been able to find a physical explanation for this phenomenon, but it may lie in spatial induction of color. At any rate, it is possible that animals perceive violet or purple backgrounds when in fact physical instruments fail to record them.

The solution to the low-frequency display colors may actually lie in quantitative interaction among the three perceptual variables of brightness, saturation, and hue, coupled with restrictions on the evolution of reflective surfaces. (d) For example, surfaces that appear blue to our eyes usually have a band of reflection peaking at high frequencies; to be saturated, these blue colors must be of narrow bandwidth and hence intrinsically dark. Red, orange, and yellow surfaces, on the other hand, are created by cut-off spectra that reflect highly at all frequencies lower than a particular value: they are intrinsically bright while maintaining high saturation. It may be that better contrast is achieved in the dark forest by maximizing saturation and brightness through some sacrifice in hue separation. This kind of explanation points up the need both for data on reflectance spectra of animal surfaces and also for a better conceptual color space in which trade-offs among the perceptual variables could be assessed quantitatively. This latter problem is discussed in the next section. (e) Finally, it could be that the entire approach suggested in this chapter is inadequate: my basic theory requires revision or even replacement.

Conceptual Problems

To begin, it is useful to recall from the outset that the entire use of colorimetric analysis is based on the unproven assumption that the color vision of animals discussed is similar to that of man. For this reason I have avoided discussing the coloration of butterflies, for example, because insects see well into the ultraviolet frequencies and have different colorimetric properties. Burtt and I, in an unpublished study, photographed a number of bird species with ultraviolet and visible light to see if any evident differences occurred that could be significant *if* birds had ultraviolet visual sensitivity, but we found nothing. It is possible, however, that quantitative differences in color-analyzing systems among vertebrate species could sufficiently change colorimetric analyses and render measurements more predictive of animal coloration.

A large roadblock still occurs in constructing a quantitative theory of contrast among surfaces. When Burtt and I constructed our first attempt (Burtt, in press; see also *O.S.*, pp. 242-243), we knew it to be inadequate. It consisted of a "colorimetric cube" of orthogonal axes of dominant frequency, excitation purity, and relative luminance. Each radiance spectrum plots as a single point in three-dimensional space, and the distance between two points is defined as the surface contrast. Such a system, if it could be perfected, would allow more accurate prediction of animal coloration because one could plot a series of backgrounds, and then search within the color space for areas that are farthest from the backgrounds.

The problems with the "colorimetric cube" are, however, considerable. There is the obvious problem of how to scale the three axes relative to one another, which was treated arbitrarily by equating their absolute distances. Then there is the problem of how to scale each axis internally. We scaled excitation purity arithmetically, relative luminance logarithmically (because over middle values the eye responds approximately linearly with log luminance), and dominant frequency nonlinearly (according to discrimination thresholds of the pigeon, *Columba livia*). For a first approach this color space worked predictively for warbler coloration (Burtt, in press), but further consideration suggests two new problems, as follows.

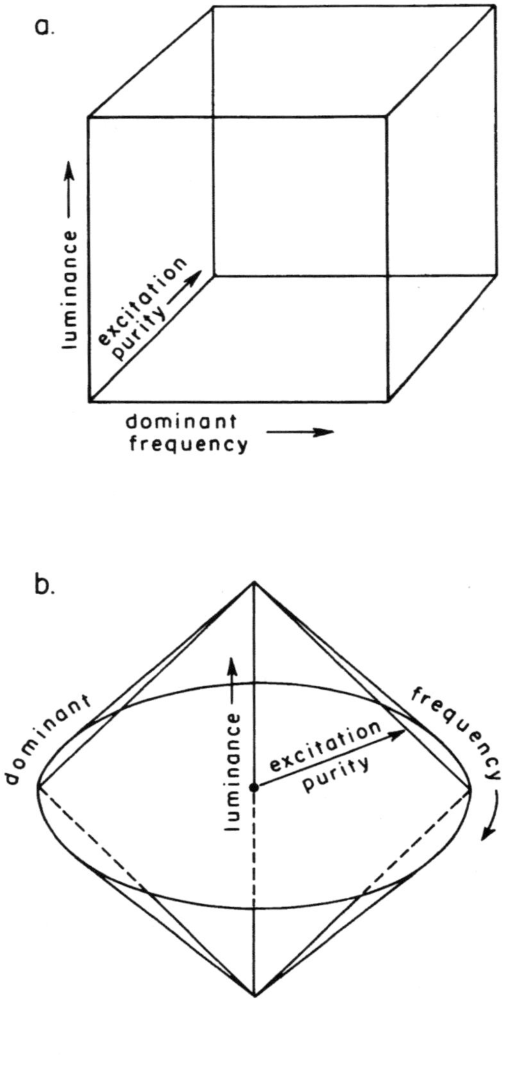

The range of relative luminance in the "colorimetric cube" was bounded by real stimuli that could be created in the available irradiance. That is, we took reflectance values for the most perfectly reflecting white surface commonly available and the most perfectly absorbing black surface. The spectral products of these surfaces and the ambient irradiance were used to define the end-points of the relative luminance scale: the brightest and darkest surfaces that could occur in the environment. My new data on sky radiance, however, suggest that the luminous sky may, under certain conditions, be brighter than any possible reflecting surface in the environment. For deep woodland warbler species, this exception may not be of any ecological relevance, but it does require attention for development of a general theory.

The other problem is more serious, namely, how to treat contrast in hue. Because dominant frequency was plotted on one of the orthogonal axes of the "colorimetric cube," purple stimuli were omitted and distance in hue was expressed as a function of dominant frequency *per se*, rather than perceptual distance.

Although I am not prepared to offer a quantitative color space that cures all the ills apparent in our first attempt, I can suggest an approach. Figure 82 presents the "colorimetric cube" (part a) and my suggested approach (b). The latter is conceptually similar to the Ostwald and Munsell color systems, based on color samples of real

---

Fig. 82. Two three-dimensional color spaces. (a) The "colorimetric cube" based on orthogonal axes from which purple stimuli are excluded. (b) A conception resembling the Ostwald and Munsell systems in which dominant frequency is a closed boundary including purple; complementaries plot opposite one another and excitation purities are represented by the horizontal distance from the vertical axis of luminance. In (a) white is the horizontal line across the top of the front face of the cube (maximum luminance, minimum purity) and black across the bottom line on the front face; in (b) white is the apex of the upper cone and black is the apex of the lower cone. Grays cover the entire front face of (a) whereas they plot on the vertical axis in (b).

surfaces for reference, and has the advantage of treating hue as a closed circle in which purple stimuli can be plotted. Complementary dominant frequencies are opposite one another on any circular cross section. The exact shape of this conceptual space, however, is a highly technical problem; ideally one wants all distances within the space to be equally discriminable, and it could be that in order to have that property the space would have to be distorted considerably from the double-cone shape drawn in the figure. The ultimate question, however, is really an empirical one: How "good" does such a concept have to be in order to predict animal coloration relative to the background?

Future Prospects

Finally, one must ask where we should go from here. It seems to me that there are seven fruitful directions in which further exploration promises to yield more complete understanding of conspicuous coloration relative to ecological situations. (a) Considerably more work on sensory physiology and perceptual psychophysics is necessary to put the entire analysis on firmer foundation. (b) Using available data, it should be possible to improve the existing theory of color space, perhaps along the lines suggested by Figure 82b. (c) The survey of environmental spectroradiometry needs to be expanded to other biomes and major habitats within them. (d) Following the expanded survey, which sketches the boundaries of the lighting conditions with which one is working, we need more detailed, parametric studies of environmental light: how does it change with time of day, time of year, weather conditions, height within the forest, direction of view, and so on. Ultimately, it would be useful to be able to model such conditions. (e) Finally, on this tack, we need a survey of reflectance spectra of animals to discover what their colors really are under different conditions of irradiance, an effort pioneered by Burtt (in press).

(f) Turning to more behavioral topics, we need far more accurate information on where and when animals display their conspicuous colors, and especially from where they are viewed by receivers so that the relevant optical backgrounds can be identified. (g) Last, we require the kinds of detailed ethological and ecological analyses that help to show all the competing selection pressures that dictate the final compromise we view as the animal's coloration.

As I stressed in *Optical Signals*, the most rewarding research at this stage may come from explaining the differences in coloration between closely related species, or populations within a species. I believe that the theory as so far applied helps explain the differences in color between indigo and painted buntings mentioned above and perhaps the differences between orchard and northern orioles, not to mention differences in flash-pattern color among wood warbler species (Burtt, in press). But why do the rufous-sided towhee (*Pipilo erythrophthalmus*) and brown towhee (*P. fuscus*) differ so strikingly in coloration, the male of the former being conspicuously colored and that of the latter concealingly colored? Why are the male rose-breasted grosbeak (*Pheucticus ludovicianus*) and black-headed grosbeak (*P. melanocephalus*) so different? (The two forms may even be conspecific.) How about the male western (*Piranga ludoviciana*) and scarlet (*P. olivaces*) tanagers? Male American (*Setophaga ruticilla*) and painted (*S. picta*) redstarts? These problems might be soluble now by proper field study and measurement. The dawn of understanding animal coloration may really be at hand.

ACKNOWLEDGMENTS

In addition to persons cited previously as having helped with specific parts of the empirical studies, I am grateful to Edward H. Burtt, Jr., Jeffrey R. Baylis, and Steve Witkin for having criticized the manuscript, and to my wife, Liz, for having read the final copy.

REFERENCES

Allee, W. C. 1926. Measurement of environmental factors in the tropical rain forest of Panama. *Ecology* 7:273-301.

Bennett, C. F., Jr. 1963. A phytophysiognomic reconnaissance of Barro Colorado Island, Canal Zone. *Smithsonian Misc. Collect.* 145 (no. 7):1-8.

Brown, C. A. 1959. *Vegetation of the Outer Banks of North Carolina*. Baton Rouge: Louisiana State Univ. Press.

Burtt, E. H., Jr. The coloration of wood warblers (Parulidae). *Nuttall Ornithol. Monogr.*: in press.

Hailman, J. P. 1977. *Optical Signals: Animal Communication and Light*. Bloomington and London: Ind. Univ. Press.

McCullough, E. C., and Porter, W. P. 1971. Computing clear day solar radiation spectra for the terrestrial ecological environment. *Ecology* 52:1008-1015.

Odum, E. P. 1971. *Fundamentals of Ecology*, 3rd ed. Philadelphia: Saunders.

Audience Questions:
Discussion

Hamilton: "Why is the male wood duck strikingly colorful?" Jack's question, raised many years ago (Hailman 1959) and reiterated today, prompts me to offer a few comments of my own. When I looked at coral-reef fishes in the Indian Ocean, I found I could make no sense of coloration within a particular community of fish unless I considered the diversity of coloration among all fish of the Indian Ocean and all species of fishes that interacted with fish living in the Indian Ocean. In other words, it was not possible to resolve questions of animal coloration from the inter- and intraspecific relationships of a single species within a single community.

Isn't it also possible that the phylogenetic history, the extinct species that determined past selective pressures on contemporary species are a partial answer to Jack's question? Could there at one time have been twenty species of strikingly colorful ducks that are now represented only by the wood duck (*Aix sponsa*) and mandarin duck (*Aix galerrculata*)?

Barlow: Coral-reef fishes pose a special problem because they play a dispersal game. They disperse sometimes for thousands of miles. So one species of coral-reef fishes may not occur in the same community of fish from one atoll, or island, to the next. On the other hand, a fish such as *Haplochromis burtoni* occurs in a fairly stable community and does not play a dispersal game. Hence I think the accepted rules would apply to *Haplochromis*.

Hamilton: I am less familiar with the behavior of coral-reef fishes than you, so my analysis may lack accuracy, but I still wonder about the phylogeny and I wonder about balanced polymorphism instead of a backward drift to the least common denominator under an absence of selection pressures. How much energy is required for an animal to maintain bright, complexly patterned coloration, if such coloration is no longer functional?

Hailman: Bill's question is a good one because the wood duck remains a troublesome case. In the original paper raising this question, Dilger and Johnsgard (1959) proposed just such an explanation of extinct, closely related species that the wood duck was selected to differ from. One has to admit the possibility, but I was unconvinced then--which is why I wrote the reply (Hailman 1959)--and I remain unconvinced. We know little about the energetic cost of maintaining coloration, but pigmentless cave animals and changes in pigmentation of the house sparrow (*Passer domesticus*) since its introduction into North America suggest that pigmentation is an evolutionarily labile trait. If the male wood duck had no need for bright colors, I think it would have lost those colors long ago.

Let me also introduce an outlook that I emphasized in *Optical Signals* (Hailman 1977). I believe that there has been far too much stress on "interspecific" explanations of animal coloration and behavior: mimicry, species distinctiveness, and so on. Closely related species often differ only slightly in acoustical or optical signals--slightly but consistently. We need a more comprehensive viewpoint, that includes traditional interspecific explanations, but concentrates now on new areas of exploration, such as how sensory capacities and the environment dictate the characteristics of signals.

Barlow: How can you decide when an animal or its color pattern is conspicuous?

Hailman: I have often assumed, in the absence of good ethological study, that color patterns appearing conspicuous to me are also conspicuous to social companions. This is why many of my examples came from male birds that are brightly colored compared with their brown, striped female counterparts. In some cases, my guesses may be wrong.

Barlow: Would you entertain the possibility that a particular signal in a given situation can be both conspicuous and cryptic?

Hailman: The same color pattern can be both conspicuous and concealing. In fact, in *Optical Signals* (pp. 236-244) I laid out five classes of hypothesis of how this might come about.

Barlow: Is conspicuousness a function of distance?

Hailman: Yes, definitely. One of my classes provides three specific hypotheses of how animals can appear concealing at a distance and conspicuous up close. These relate to mosaic backgrounds into which animals blend at a distance, mosaic color patterns of animals themselves that perceptually fuse to a cryptic blur when seen from afar, and the perception of spatial contrast frequencies.

Snodderly: I wish to address the issue of how we know when an optical signal is conspicuous or how we know when it is inconspicuous, particularly when the signal is viewed by observers of many different species. Is a particular animal conspicuous to its ecological competitors, its predators, or its prey? The different visual systems may determine conspicuousness and inconspicuousness differently. Except for measurements by Burtt (in press) and Hailman (1977 and above), there are few published measurements of the physical characteristics of optical signals or the illuminance of the habitats in which the signals are used. Researchers have relied on human color vision which, fortunately, is very good. However, there are visual systems capable of wavelength discriminations that are radically different from human discriminations (e.g., honeybee). How can we *a priori* judge what is conspicuous to an entire panoply of animals without (a) knowing the physical characteristics of the stimulus in its proper habitat and (b) the spectral sensitivity of each observer.

REFERENCES

Burtt, E. H., Jr. The coloration of wood warblers (Parulidae). *Nuttall Ornithol. Monogr.*: in press.

Dilger, W. C., and Johnsgard, P. A. 1959. Comments on "species recognition" with special reference to the wood duck and the mandarin duck. *Wilson Bull.* 71:46-53.

Hailman, J. P. 1959. Why is the male wood duck strikingly colorful? *Amer. Naturalist* 93:383-384.

Hailman, J. P. 1977. *Optical Signals: Animal Communication and Light*. Bloomington and London: Ind. Univ. Press.

Chapter 8

Optical Signals and Interspecific Communication

Jeffrey R. Baylis

The Context of Interspecific Optical Communication
- Unilateral Optical Communication
  - Correct Unilateral Communication
  - Incorrect Unilateral Communication
- Bilateral Optical Communication
  - Competitive Bilateral Communication
  - Cooperative Bilateral Communication

Evolutionary Origins
- Correct Unilateral Communication
  - Aposematic Coloration
  - Predictions of Apsomatic Color and Pattern
  - Startle Displays
- Incorrect Unilateral Communication
- Competitive Bilateral Communication
- Cooperative Bilateral Communication

Conclusion

Rather than attempt to review the immense literature on the use of optical signals for interspecific communication, I have chosen to explore several especially well documented examples of interspecific optical communication. From these few examples I attempt to deduce the selection pressures responsible for maintaining the communication system, and from knowledge of the selection pressures I predict some of the general properties we might expect interspecific optical signals to have.

By "interspecific communication" I mean all cases in which the probability distribution of the behavioral acts of a member of one species is altered as a result of an optical signal generated by a member of another species. I exclude acts of overt predation by visually oriented predators, and flight behavior by visually alarmed prey.

I have defined what I mean by interspecific communication; but what are "optical signals?" I consider only a restricted subset of the rather large set of optical signals (Hailman 1977), namely the set of signals that are "sign stimuli." These are optical stimuli, in the environment, to which the animal pays particular attention, and which have special significance to the animal when compared with the huge array of optical signals that constantly confront it. An example of a sign stimulus is the response of anuran amphibians to small, dark, moving spots. A hungry frog responds to such a stimulus by striking with its tongue and attempting to feed. The optical stimuli "small," "dark," "moving," have special significance to a frog, and that significance is "insect prey."

Within the subset of sign stimuli is the smaller set of "releasers." These are sign stimuli whose characteristics have been shaped to some extent by natural selection based upon the response the stimuli elicit in the receiver. That is, the forms of such signals are the result of coevolution between the sender and the receiver. "Social releasers" are signals that have evolved for intraspecific communication, where both communicants are members of the same species (see Chapter 9). I am concerned only with signals used in interspecific communication for purposes of this chapter, so social releasers are not discussed.

Throughout this chapter I deal only with situations in which I can assume that the color patterns or displays in question are releasers. The restriction is reasonable because my intention is to explore the significance of color patterns used in interspecific communication; hence I assume that the signal's form is the result of selection for an optical signal. My focus is the adaptive significance of animal coloration in relation to the behavior of individuals belonging to another species.

THE CONTEXT OF INTERSPECIFIC OPTICAL COMMUNICATION

Unilateral Optical Communication

There are two major situations involving interspecific communication. The first of these is the unilateral case, where an individual of one species influences the behavior of another, but the reverse is not true. This might really be called "trophic" or "ecological" communication, as it involves relationships that are primarily predator-prey. Please note that I am excluding overt predator-prey interactions; a predator that ingests a prey organism might be said to influence its future probability of various types of behavior rather drastically, but I do not consider it to be communication in any sense useful to the present discussion.

Correct Unilateral Communication

In any communications system, the signal sent can be either correct (it carries "true" information about the sender) or incorrect (it carries "misinformation" about the sender) (Wallace 1973, Hailman 1977). The category of unilateral communication of correct information contains the most spectacular and extensive examples of biological coloration. Unfortunately, most of the examples lie outside the scope of this chapter, as they involve plant/animal interactions. For example, most flower pollination by animals involves floral cues that fall into this category (van der Pijl and Dodson 1966, Baker 1963). Seed dispersal by animal ingestion of brightly colored fruits and berries is also a good case (McKey 1975; also, Chapter 6 of this volume).

This chapter is confined to animal/animal interactions, and here too we find dramatic examples. However, virtually all involve "aposematic" or warning coloration of various noxious organisms.

Most documented cases of aposematic coloration concern species employing allelochemical weapons. The chemical defenses may be systemic toxins that act when the prey is ingested; a bad-tasting or toxic fluid that is released by the prey animal when alarmed; or may involve the actual injection of venom, as in many insects, spiders, fishes, and molluscs.

Not all examples of aposematic coloration involve chemical defense. Some species that are pugnacious or even suicidally aggressive to other species may have aposematic coloration (Baylis 1974, Eaton 1976).

Incorrect Unilateral Communication

The second major category of unilateral communication involves deception ("misinformation"). A deceptive signal benefits the sender at the expense of the receiver. Most importantly, the selective advantage depends on the receiver's response, and such a system must, like birth control, face constant selection for its own failure. There are many suspected examples of optical signals involving deception (Hailman 1977). I list only a few.

Deflective markings, supposedly conspicuous markings that direct attack away from vital areas of the body, have been well studied in a series of classic experiments on animal coloration by Blest (1957). The so-called startle displays of many species of underwing moths may function in this way. Where the markings are large and ocellated, they may simply cause a predator to hesitate to strike immediately, and thus increase the probability of the prey's escape.

Deceptive coloration is almost certainly responsible for the flower-like leaves of many species of insectivorous plants; indeed some even produce limited quantities of nectar near the entrance to the traps (Lloyd 1942). Many orchid flowers mimic female insects, and are visited only by males of the species who then pollinate the flower, in some cases by "pseudocopulation" (van der Pijl and Dodson 1966). This may represent the ultimate in bestiality.

Batesian mimicry is the area of interspecific communication that has generated the largest literature and appears to be the best studied. This is the classic type of deceptive mimicry, where a relatively harmless or palatable species mimics a noxious, aposematic species. An example of such a mimicry complex is the monarch-viceroy butterfly model-mimic complex of North America. The toxic monarch (*Danius plexippus*) contains cardiac glycosides derived from the milkweed that it feeds upon as a larva, and has a conspicuous red, white, and black aposematic color pattern. The viceroy (*Limenitis archippus*) mimics this coloration in rather elaborate detail, although it is itself apparently not noxious (Brower 1958, 1960; Brower and Collins 1963; Brower et al. 1967, 1968).

Many harmless insects mimic stinging wasps and bees to a remarkable extent. Clyde Gorsuch of the Entomology Department of the University of Wisconsin recently showed me a species of clear-winged moth that resembles a yellow-jacket wasp almost exactly. Even the flight behavior of a wasp is copied. The species appears to be underscribed, which may testify to the degree of its protective resemblance. Mr. Gorsuch only recognized his specimens as moths because he was surprised to find wasps attracted to his moth sex pheromone baits.

Bilateral Optical Communication

The second major situation involving interspecific communication is the bilateral case, where both parties influence each other's behavior. This might be termed interspecific "social" communication. Bilateral or reciprocal interspecific communication can be thought of in two large categories: those cases in which the communication is the result of behavioral competition between the two species, and those cases in which the communication involves cooperative behavior benefitting individuals of both species.

Competitive Bilateral Communication

Cody (1969) suggested that many examples of character convergence in bird plumage in zones of sympatry are the result of interspecific territoriality, with two or more species converging on a similar plumage pattern to facilitate spacing. The argument is given strength by the observation that the convergence only applies to those signals used for territorial spacing; signals used in courtship remain species specific or actually diverge in the zone of sympatry. In areas of allopatry, the territorial signals diverge also. The former observation is necessary if the argument that the similarity in signals is simply a result of having to meet similar signal transmission problems in the environment (refer to Chapter 7) is to be countered.

Agonistic behavior often occurs across species lines. As with the intraspecific case, we can expect that such displays would tend to emphasize weapons. Any animals with a similar general gross morphology might be expected to share displays that correlate with "intent," and hence recognize such displays across species lines. An open-mouthed frontal display is a nearly universal threat among teleost fishes; felids and canids retract the ears and expose their teeth in an open-mouthed snarl. In both cases, the threat is used in agonistic encounters with other species as well as intraspecifically.

Cooperative Bilateral Communication

The most intriguing examples of interspecific communication are those involving bilateral communication that is cooperative. The individuals of the two species involved in such a system interact in a coordinated manner that results in a net benefit to individuals of both species.

Certainly one of the most readily observed examples of interspecific communication is the occurrence of mixed-species flocks of birds, herds of mammals, and schools of fishes. Evidence from a variety of sources suggests that the mixed-species groupings are not chance assemblies of short duration; many cases suggest that the assemblies are long term and are actively maintained by the individuals of the participating species. The existence of such mixed-species groups has been cited as evidence for the "selfish herd" hypothesis, as such aggregations cannot be explained by kin selection (Hamilton 1971). Familiar examples of this type of cooperative behavior are mixed-species feeding assemblies. These have been described for fishes and birds, and similar examples can probably be found for most phyletic groups (Barlow 1974, Moynihan 1968, Morse 1970). Here we would expect convergence on those signals that tend to coordinate the activity of individuals within the group, and signals that would serve to promote group cohesiveness (Moynihan 1968).

A similar case might be made for mixed-species communication involving mobbing behavior or alarm reactions.

Here we would expect convergence of species signals indicating alarm in response to potential predation or general disturbance. These signals may or may not involve convergence in form by the species involved; but recognition of the signal and an appropriate response is certainly possible. The now classic example of the hawk alarm call given by many passerine birds is well known, although it does not involve a visual signal (Marler 1959). Simple observation and recognition of another animal's panicked flight may be enough to serve as an example.

The most spectacular examples involving cooperative interspecific communication in the visual channel are the famous series of associations between aquatic organisms, termed "cleaning symbiosis." These associations frequently involve species from different phyla. Where one or both of the participants in the association are fishes, vision appears to be the most important signalling medium. The cleaning association generally takes the form of an individual "visiting" a site-attached individual of another species (the "cleaner") in order to have ectoparasites removed. The ectoparasites are eaten by the cleaner, and may represent a primary or a supplementary food source for the cleaner. Cleaners usually display a conspicuous color pattern, and have conspicuous "advertising" displays involving posture and motor patterns. Often the displays are restricted to the cleaning situation, and are not used at all in intraspecific social encounters. The reciprocal nature of the association is emphasized by the "solicitation" display postures and coloration assumed by the individual to be cleaned (Limbaugh 1961; Losey 1971, 1972; Sulak 1975; Brockmann and Hailman 1976; Wyman and Ward 1972).

EVOLUTIONARY ORIGINS

In the preceding section I have made no mention of how a given "message" is agreed upon by the sender and receiver. The reader may find himself thinking of associative learning, the evolution of sign stimuli, or even Darwin's "Principle of Associated Habits." I have purposely left the question of mechanism open, because I do not think the mechanism matters for the present arguments, as long as it involves what might be called the principle of association. The actual mechanism by which the receiver makes the association between sender and signal is not important. Whether the response to the signal is "learned or innate," the form of the signal is subject to selection pressure based on the receiver's response.

I have briefly presented some of the typical contexts in which interspecific visual communication can occur, and I gave a few examples. I now examine the origins of some of the systems discussed in the earlier section, with an eye toward defining the kinds of selection pressures that preserve the signals used for interspecific communication. I then predict some of the general properties I would expect such signals to have, given that I can identify the context in which communication takes place.

Correct Unilateral Communication

Aposematic Coloration

In the case of aposematic coloration, the actual selective mechanism producing the signal is unclear. The selection pressures maintaining the signal, once evolved, are much easier to understand. If an animal has evolved some mechanism for being distasteful, the advantage is greatest if potential predators recognize the individual as distasteful. The greatest advantage occurs when the predator's initial attack is avoided. This might best be accomplished by a dramatic and unambiguous signal that discourages an initial attack. It follows that the same properties of a dramatic and unambiguous color pattern would also apply to mimicry systems involving aposematic models.

The trouble with this argument is that it applies to selection at the level of the individual, and is adequate only to explain the preservation of conspicuous traits in the population, once the traits come to dominate. Explaining how the traits evolved in the first place is more difficult, as most of the cases of aposematic coloration involve forms of noxiousness that are effective only if the animal is substantially or fatally injured (i.e., systemic toxins), and a fatally injured animal cannot pass on its genes for aposematic coloration.

I would expect that an aposematic color pattern would be selected for on the basis of the optical receptors of the predator rather than the optical systems of conspecifics. Since the maximum advantage to prey animals occurs when the initial attack by a predator is circumvented, the "signal" should always be "on"; that is, the color pattern involved should be relatively fixed and invariant.

Because none of the above arguments assume any degree of genetic relatedness between individuals, convergence of color patterns of species noxious in similar ways and preyed upon by similar predators is to be expected. The selection advantage is to all individuals concerned, regardless of species. The risk to each individual prey of having to "train" a predator is reduced when the prey species has similar coloration. This is the argument underlying the concept of Müllerian mimicry: unfortunately, similarity alone is not enough to prove the theory. I would expect in general that the form of the conspicuous color pattern would be dictated by the predator's visual perception. Thus, the introduced European honey bee and many New World wasps have similar coloration; but it is unlikely that they are direct Müllerian mimics. Noxious animals facing predation from a common class of predators may have similar aposematic color patterns, even if no mimicry is involved.

Predictions of Aposematic Color and Pattern

I am now in a position to predict the sorts of properties we would expect of color patterns involved in interspecific communication that is unilateral and transmits correct information (e.g., aposematic coloration); such coloration should be conspicuous and unambiguous. Color and pattern should identify the sender as belonging to a specific set of signalers; hence correct identification is very important to both receiver and sender. This would result in stabilizing selection for the color pattern, selecting for very low variation in those characters used for discrimination by the receiver's optical system. Moreover, the aposematic visual signal should be fixed and always present; attacks by predators will be discouraged by conspicuousness regardless of whether or not the predator is detected by the prey.

I could not find a study that directly addressed itself to the above predictions. However, in a study on the aposematically colored soldier beetle (*Chauliognathus pennsylvanicus*), Mason (1976) found that in spite of strong sexual dimorphism in size and other characters, males and females had virtually identical means and low variation for the sizes of the prothoracic and elytral spots (chief elements of the contrast-rich color pattern). He attributed this to stabilizing selection acting through predation, presemably by birds.

This could prove to be a very easily tested hypothesis in other cases of interspecific communication. For example, the same kinds of predictions can be made for plant/animal communication in flower pollination. Flowers that are pollinated by many species should show more variation in color pattern than flowers that are pollinated by only one species. Similarly, flowers pollinated by birds should show visual characteristics more closely tuned to the vertebrate eye than to the visual properties of the insect eye. This observation has in fact been made by a number of authors who have commented upon the predominance of red in bird-pollinated flowers (van der Pijl and Dodson 1966, Raven 1972, Hailman 1977).

Aposematic insects will be an especially fruitful group to study. The action spectra of insect and vertebrate eyes are sufficiently separated that the insect can pack two signals into one channel; it is entirely possible for a butterfly to have two optical signals in the same area on its wings, one visible only to insect eyes, the other conspicuous (or inconspicuous!) to the vertebrate eye. This aspect of insect coloration allows unique opportunities to look at the signal components of an optical pattern from a functional viewpoint.

Startle Displays

"Startle displays," of the type given by underwing moths, are another case where I would predict that the signals should be dramatic and conspicuous. However, in this case the selective advantage is based on a *change* of appearance; thereby increasing the prey's chance of escape from a predator. Thus, the display must not be "always on," but should be hidden most of the time and only exposed under duress. The display should appear suddenly, in a manner that contrasts sharply with the normal appearance of the organism giving the display, and the environment in which the display is given. Blest (1957) has documented many cases of startle display that have these properties.

Incorrect Unilateral Communication

The most widely known example of unilateral interspecific communication involving misinformation is Batesian mimicry. Here a non-noxious species has evolved to resemble individuals of a noxious, aposematic species. The selection pressure involved is assumed to be the escape from predation by protective resemblance. Several lines of experimental evidence suggest that this interpretation is correct (Brower 1958, 1960; Brower and Collins 1963; Brower et al. 1967, 1968; Alcock 1971). The properties of the color pattern would, of course, be the same as those specified for aposematic organisms; the mimic's coloration should converge strongly on the model; should be conspicuous; always present; and selected for on the basis of the predator's optical system. As might be expected, where a mimic's range overlaps the range of several more locally distributed model species, the mimic is polymorphic (Clarke and Sheppard 1963).

The degree of match to the model may depend on the behavior of the chief predator in the system. Klopfer (1961) and Alcock (1971) both have demonstrated that bird species differ strongly in their ability to detect models and mimics, their ability to learn by observation, and their willingness to "experiment" with noxious prey after training. The dictum that the model needs to be more common than the mimic is probably not always true. Songbirds stung by large wasps refused to even approach hover flies that mimic wasps for months afterward, even though they ate the flies prior to exposure to the wasp (Moestler 1935, Tinbergen 1958).

Competitive Bilateral Communication

Many of the most interesting examples of interspecific communication involving animal coloration are cases of reciprocal or "social" interspecific communication. The interactions between individuals of different species often fully approach the complexity that we expect to see in intraspecific communication (Chapter 9); however, the signals used cannot be explained on the basis of shared evolutionary history. This implies the communication is of selective advantage to both participants.

An obvious example of interspecific social communication is agonistic behavior. Ritualized combat involving threat and appeasement can be explained on the basis of individual selection (Maynard Smith 1972, 1974), and therefore we should not be surprised to find that such encounters occur between individuals belonging to separate species. The important aspect is the communication of individual intent, which is typically done by using "threat postures." These displays usually exhibit and emphasize weapons, such as the conspicuous coloration outlining the knives on many species of surgeon fishes (Barlow 1974). Many vertebrates have conspicuous teeth or mouth linings that dramatize open-mouthed threat displays. All we need assume is that win or lose, involvement in an aggressive encounter costs the individual something. Hence both parties benefit when the conflict is settled by ritualized signals rather than overt attack. Since no relatedness is assumed, this model can be invoked to explain the selective advantage of interspecific recognition of threat signals.

Many cases of convergence in animal coloration might be explained as signals to promote and maintain interspecific territoriality. Cody (1969) and Moynihan (1968) argue that many pairs or groups of species show convergence in coloration where the species are sympatric, and divergence where the species are allopatric. Cody and Moynihan provide some well documented cases of this phenomenon in birds, and similar examples may occur in fishes (Myrberg and Thresher 1974, Barlow 1974). The bird examples are weakened by the very few actual observations of territorial interactions between the species concerned. An exception to this is the notoriously territorial mockingbird (*Mimus polyglottos*). Mueller (1971) has suggested that the mockingbird reacts territorially to a wide variety of birds having white wing flashes similar to its own. A general difficulty is that the observed convergence could also be the result of overcoming similar optical transmission problems in the same environment (Hailman 1977; also, Chapter 7 of this volume).

There are no clear theoretical objections to the evolution of interspecific territoriality. It can be accounted for by simple Darwinian selection, much as territorial behavior has been explained on an intraspecific basis (Brown 1975). No assumptions about kinship are needed to explain the evolution of territorial displays within species, and none are needed to explain their occurrence across species lines. The chief problem is how species that compete so directly can long remain in sympatry, a point that Cody (1969) briefly mentions. Luckily, I can dismiss that question as being primarily ecological, and beyond the scope of this chapter.

The prediction about the form of the signals used is that, as with territorial signals in general, they should have the optical properties associated with "advertisement" (Cott 1957). That is, they should be conspicuous in the normal visual environment (Chapter 7) and serve to identify the species as to general ecological guild or niche.

According to Cody, where such signals are reciprocal, territorial displays should show convergence across species lines in sympatry, with greater variation and possible divergence in allopatry.

Cooperative Bilateral Communication

The most complex examples of interspecific communication involve overtly cooperative behavior between two or more species. The simplest case is that of mixed-species aggregations. Multi-specific bird flocks (Moynihan 1968) and fish schools (Barlow 1974) are the best known examples of this phenomenon. Here I would expect to see the species involved share common signal patterns that promote coordination and orientation of the group. This would result in the convergence of such signals to one type. Convergence would also be promoted by the "selfish herd" selection for aggregation proposed by Hamilton (1971). Such signals used to promote group communication generally emphasize motion and orientation. I would expect to see markings placed on appendages, or the anterior and posterior portions of the body where these functions can best be realized.

There is some evidence that this form of signal convergence does occur in species that move in mixed groups. Moynihan (1968) cites some examples of birds from mixed flocks. Another example is the case of fish belonging to the genus *Tilapia*. The juveniles of this genus commonly form very large mixed-species shoals. The spot, located on the posterior base of the dorsal fin, is often referred to as a "tilapia mark," as it is nearly universal within the genus.

A sophisticated example of interspecific communication employing optical signals is the symbiotic cleaning association between individuals of different species living on tropical marine coral reefs. Here the communication system may involve several "host" species interacting with a single cleaner species. The signals involved are frequently subtle and the communication is definitely reciprocal (Losey 1971). The host has a typical pose and often a color pattern used to solicit cleaning. The cleaner generally has a conspicuous, species-typical color pattern and adopts unusual display or swimming postures to advertise the cleaning station.

In general, there is a large size disparity between the large host species and the diminutive cleaner. It would appear that the cleaner may face a real risk of being eaten by the host. Whether this actually happens or not is open to question. Certainly the color pattern of such cleaning species as *Labroides dimidiatus* could be considered contrast-rich enough to qualify as aposematic. It would be interesting to know if it is a palatable species to potential fish predators.

Because of the potential for predation, Trivers has invoked a "reciprocal altruism" model to explain the evolution of such symbiotic cleaning relationships (Trivers 1971). I do not feel that this approach is particularly heuristic; the association can be explained quite easily on the basis of classic Darwinian selection without the addition of hypothetical elements.

The communication of intent is clearly important to both participants in the interaction. The cleaner can signal intent by a species-typical color pattern, and immediate willingness to clean by a solicitation "dance." The host species must communicate its intent by a more transient and general means, as many species may be cleaned by one cleaner in a given area. The signals used by the host species are usually body postures. Tonic immobility appears to be an almost universal signal. Conspicuous changes in coloration may also code intent, but do not seem to be used to identify species and are not universal (Losey 1971, 1972; Sulak 1975; Wyman and Ward 1972).

The most important attribute of the system is the clear identification of the cleaner. As with aposematic coloration, stabilizing selection will produce a conspicuous "advertising" coloration in cleaners, and the coloration of such species should be species-typical with low variation. The signals should emphasize motion and be high in contrast.

If Trivers' model of reciprocal altruism is correct, then we would expect individual recognition to be important across species lines. This would predict variation in the basic coloration to allow for individual recognition. However, individual recognition could easily be coded for by site constancy; virtually all obligatory cleaners are territorial and site constant. Moreover, factors involved in intraspecific social interaction might also produce variation for individual identification. Hence, the Trivers model is not testable by looking at the visual signals involved.

CONCLUSION

In general, we can expect that the selective forces shaping the color patterns used in interspecific communication will be the same forces that shape the signals used in intraspecific communication. The primary differences between the two cases will be seen in instances where special relationships occur between species, as with aposematic coloration and cases of symbiosis such as cleaning, that involve mutualistic relationships. In interspecific interactions, the question of individual identification is rarely present. This removes the hypothetical source of selection producing variation to aid in individual recognition. A premium is placed on correct identification of the individual as belonging to a set of individuals (a species) with special properties. Thus we would expect to see very low variation within the species for color pattern, if the color pattern has been shaped primarily by selection based on interspecific communication. This is borne out by the few studies that have been made on such systems where variation has been looked at.

The advantage of investigating interspecific communications systems is that such systems are more easily broken into components where the "meaning" of the signal and its resultant form can be clearly linked. This is because the receiver's visual apparatus is often very different from the sender's. The aspects of the color pattern that pertain only to the signal system at hand can be separated from the color patterns used for intraspecific communication, or serving primarily physiological functions. Vertebrate/invertebrate aposematic systems would be particularly good systems for testing these predictions.

REFERENCES

Alcock, J. 1971. Interspecific differences in avian feeding behavior and the evolution of Batesian mimicry. *Behaviour* 40:1-9.

Baker, H. G. 1963. Evolutionary mechanisms in pollination biology. *Science* 139:877-883.

Barlow, G. W. 1974. Contrasts in social behavior between Central American cichlid fishes and coral-reef surgeon fishes. *Amer. Zoologist* 14:9-34.

Baylis, J. R. 1974. The behavior and ecology of *Herotilapia multispinosa* (Teleostei, Cichlidae). *Z. Tierpsychol.* 34: 115-146.

Blest, A. D. 1957. The function of eyespot patterns in the Lepidoptera. *Behaviour* 11:206-256.

Brockmann, H. J., and Hailman, J. P. 1976. Fish cleaning symbiosis: notes on juvenile angelfishes (*Pomacanthus*, Chaetodontidae) and comparisons with other species. *Z. Tierpsychol.* 42:129-138.

Brower, J. VZ. 1958. Experimental studies of mimicry in some North American butterflies I. *Evolution* 12:123-136.

Brower, J. VZ. 1960. Experimental studies of mimicry IV. *Amer. Naturalist* 44:271-282.

Brower, J. VA., and Collins, C. T. 1963. Experimental studies of mimicry 7. *Zoologica* 49:65-84.

Brower, L. P.; Brower, J. VZ.; and Corvino, J. M. 1967. Plant poisons in a terrestrial food chain. *Proc. Nat. Acad. Sci.* 57:894-898.

Brower, L. P.; Ryderson, W. N.; Coppinger, L. I.; and Glazier, S. C. 1968. Ecological chemistry and the palatability spectrum. *Science* 161:1349-1351.

Brown, J. L. 1975. *The Evolution of Behavior*. New York: Norton.

Clarke, C. A., and Sheppard, P. M. 1963. Interactions between major genes and polygenes in the determination of the mimetic patterns of *Papilio dardanus*. *Evolution* 17: 404-413.

Cody, M. L. 1969. Convergent characteristics in sympatric populations: a possible relation to interspecific competition and aggression. *Condor* 71:222-239.

Cott, H. B. 1957. *Adaptive Coloration in Animals*. London: Methuen.

Eaton, R. L. 1976. A possible case of mimicry in larger mammals. *Evolution* 30:853-856.

Hailman, J. P. 1977. *Optical Signals: Animal Communication and Light*. Bloomington: Ind. Univ. Press.

Hamilton, W. D. 1971. Geometry for the selfish herd. *J. Theor. Biol.* 31:295-311.

Klopfer, P. H. 1961. Observational learning in birds: the establishment of behavioural modes. *Behaviour* 17:71-80.

Limbaugh, C. 1961. Cleaning symbiosis. *Sci. Amer.* 205:42-49.

Lloyd, F. E. 1942. *The Carnivorous Plants*. New York: Ronald Press.

Losey, G. S. 1971. Communication between fishes in cleaning symbiosis. In *Aspects of the Biology of Symbiosis*. T. C. Cheng (ed.). Baltimore: University Park Press, pp. 145-176.

Losey, G. S. 1972. The ecological importance of cleaning symbiosis. *Copeia* 1972:820-833.

McKey, D. 1975. The ecology of coevolved seed dispersal systems. In *Coevolution of Animals and Plants*, L. E. Gilbert and P. H. Raven (eds.). Austin: Univ. of Tex. Press.

Marler, P. 1959. Developments in the study of animal communication. In *Darwin's Biological Work*, P. R. Bell (ed.). Cambridge: Cambridge Univ. Press, pp. 150-206.

Mason, L. G. 1976. Color variation and bisexual Muellerian mimicry in an aposematic insect. *Evolution* 30:841-846.

Maynard Smith, J. 1972. Game theory and the evolution of fighting. In *On Evolution*, by J. Maynard Smith. Edinburgh: Edinburgh Univ. Press.

Maynard Smith, J. 1974. The theory of games and the evolution of animal conflict. *J. Theor. Biol.* 47:209-221.

Moestler, G. 1935. Beobachtungen zur Frage der Wespenmimikry. *A. Morphol. Oekol. Tiere* 29:381-455.

Morse, D. H. 1970. Ecological aspects of some mixed species foraging flocks of birds. *Ecol. Monogr.* 40:119-168.

Moynihan, M. 1968. Social mimicry: character convergence versus character displacement. *Evolution* 22:315-331.

Mueller, H. C. 1971. Flashes of white in wings of other species elicit territorial behavior in mockingbirds. *Wilson Bull.* 83:442.

Myrberg, A. A., and Thresher, R. E. 1974. Interspecific aggression and its relevance to the concept of territoriality in reef fishes. *Amer. Zoologist* 14:81-96.

Raven, P. P. 1972. Why are bird-visited flowers predominantly red? *Evolution* 26:674.

Sulak, K. J. 1975. Cleaning behavior in the centrarchid fishes, *Lepomis macrochirus* and *Micropterus salmoides*. *Anim. Behav.* 23(2):331-334.

Tinbergen, N. 1958. *Curious Naturalists*. Garden City, New York: Doubleday.

Trivers, R. L. 1971. The evolution of reciprocal altruism. *Q. Rev. Biol.* 46:35-37.

Van der Pijl, L., and Dodson, C. H. 1966. *Orchid Flowers: Their Pollination and Evolution*. Coral Gables, Florida: Univ. of Miami Press.

Wallace, B. 1973. Misinformation, fitness and selection. *Amer. Naturalist* 107:1-7.

Wyman, R. L., and Ward, J. A. 1972. A cleaning symbiosis between the cichlid fishes *Etroplus maculatus* and *Etroplus suratensis*. I. Description and possible evolution. *Copeia* 1972:834-838.

Chapter 9

The Use of Color in Intraspecific Communication

William J. Rowland

Mechanisms by Which an Animal May Attain Coloration
Encoding Information with Color
The Use of Color in Intraspecific Communication
    Species Recognition
    Species and Sex Recognition
    Individual Recognition
    Motivational State
    Color Signals for Localization and/or Orientation
    Color Signals Physically Detached from Their Sender
The Behavioral Effects of Signals on the Receiver
Conclusions

The great diversity of colors and patterns that occurs in animals has interested man throughout history. In his *Historiae Animalium*, Aristotle describes the coloration of fishes, lizards, birds, etc., and notes the seasonal color changes of avian plumage and the more rapid color changes of chameleons and cuttlefish. The coloration of many animals is discussed by Pliny, who remarked that cuttlefish males were darker and more variegated than females, a point whose significance was demonstrated only in recent times (Tinbergen 1939).

By the middle of the nineteenth century, the role of color and patterns of color in animal communication was recognized. Darwin concluded that conspicuous coloration could function to warn other species of an animal's potential danger or unpalatability or to advertise the animal to a prospective mate. The last point was central to Darwin's theory of sexual selection. Darwin noted that among brightly colored species the sexually mature male amost always possesses the brightest coloration and that castrated males failed to attain the bright coloration of intact males during the breeding season.

Despite Darwin's extensive treatment of coloration in animals and its development through sexual selection, neither he nor his contemporaries fully appreciated its role in other contexts. Thus, the presence of conspicuous coloration or marking patterns in both sexes (e.g., the narrow white vertical lines on the hind flanks and angular white mark on the forehead of the koodoo, *Tragelaphus strepsiceros*) was assumed to be the result of sexual selection. Darwin also believed that sexual selection, operating primarily on males, resulted in features later transmitted to both sexes.

The beginning of the twentieth century marked a period of rapid growth in ethology. Individuals who had an interest and training in zoology began to carry out detailed, descriptive studies on a variety of species. Concerned with the adaptiveness of naturally occurring behavior, these individuals recognized that certain combinations of behavior, color, and morphological features occurred together. They concluded that such combinations evolved, in part, for the purpose of communication, and labelled these displays. Thus a fuller appreciation of the role of color and marking patterns in communication was achieved.

I intend to survey the use of color in intraspecific communication. However, before beginning I consider briefly the ways in which such signal coloration is achieved in animals and how such coloration is used to encode information in a signal.

MECHANISMS BY WHICH AN ANIMAL MAY ATTAIN COLORATION

In animals that possess integumentary pigments, true color or hue is imparted when these pigments absorb certain wavelengths of light and reflect or transmit others (see Chapter 1). Neutral shades are imparted when a pigment absorbs equally across the visible spectrum; the more light absorbed the darker the resulting gray coloration. When such pigments are sparse, they have minimal effect and the background color of the integument is expressed. When the pigment is dispersed and/or its production increased, the animal assumes a color determined by the pigment.

Color change may be due to a physiological mechanism whereby pigment is concentrated or dispersed by chromatophores or to a morphological mechanism whereby pigment is gained or lost by chromatophores. Most color change in animals involves both mechanisms simultaneously, although the physiological mechanism is generally thought to operate more rapidly and to be more easily reversible. Thus the chromatophores, through neural and endocrine control, provide the animal with a means of rapid color change encompassing changes in overall body color and patterns as well as subtle variations in hue and saturation.

Not all coloration results from conventional pigment cells; color also results from selective reflection of certain wavelengths through a redirection of energy rather than a loss by absorption (see Chapter 1). Colors that result from this process are known as structural colors and are found in the glistening bluish-green bodies (iridophores) of fish and the plumage of many birds. Rapid changes in such structural colors usually rely on masking and unmasking by other pigments or structures within the animal.

A less common mechanism by which an animal attains coloration is adornment. Elliot (1882) claimed that the great Indian hornbill (*Buceros bicornis*) obtains a bright yellow secretion from its preen gland and smears this oily substance on the conspicuously placed white feathers at the angle of its wings. The carotenoid pigment is soon oxidized on exposure to air, but the bird carries out this painting behavior continuously. Vevers (1964) describes similarly imparted pink coloration produced by the preen gland sections in various species of gull (*Larus*) and in the white pelican (*Pelecanus onocrotalus*). Crustaceans place bright pieces of extraneous material on their bodies, presumably another example of adornment for communication (Vevers 1964).

Finally, an animal's coloration may result from production of visible energy (see Chapter 1). In fireflies and certain marine animals, this bioluminescence is due to the highly efficient reaction of luciferin and luciferase. The emission spectra of the light produced is apparently a function of the luciferase involved, since the luciferin from different fireflies is identical even though the color of the luminescence differs. In fact, in the railroad worm (*Phrixothrix*) different bioluminescent organs on the same individual produce different colors, red and green, which appear to be attributable to differences in specific luciferases (Seliger and McElroy 1964). In certain deep-sea fishes, however, the bioluminescent organs are covered by a membrane that acts as a transmission filter, imparting a particular color to the emitted light (McCosker 1977).

ENCODING INFORMATION WITH COLOR

Color stimuli can be specified by three psychophysical variables--dominant wavelength, purity, and luminance--which are perceived by humans as hue, saturation, and brightness. Since these variables are not independent of each other, a change in one often affects the other two (see Chapters 5, 6, and 7). Although many ethological studies have not stringently controlled for this interaction, it would appear that each of these three variables might be used to encode information in visual signals.

Animals with color vision can discriminate different wavelengths, although different species have different spectral sensitivities (see Chapters 5, 6, and 7). Wavelength (hue) could therefore serve as a component for the construction of discrete signals. In addition, the perception of wavelength (hue) in nonaquatic habitats is less affected by distance than the perception of spatial patterns and is therefore of use to species with relatively poor visual acuity under adequate illumination levels. As expected, we find that hues are used in such functions as species recognition where discrete, long-distance signaling is of particular importance.

In some animals, color saturation can be continuously varied by increasing or decreasing the factors that impart hue. This implies that saturation could be used to code graded signals and indeed there is evidence to suggest that this occurs. In many animals, especially certain teleosts and lizards, color changes occur gradually and cyclically, reaching their maximum intensity at mating time. Such changes are often under hormonal control (see Chapter 4). For example, the gradual acquisition of red nuptial coloration in the threespine stickleback (*Gasterosteus aculeatus*) is due to an increase in the number of erythrophores that occur with increasing testosterone level (Reisman 1968), and the development of similar breeding coloration in certain cichlid fishes (e.g., *Hemichromis*) is probably due to the same process (Baerends and Baerends-van Roon 1950). Since the few studies of fish done so far indicate that females prefer more intensely colored males to ones less intensely colored (Noble and Curtis 1939, Haas 1976), one might assume that color saturation is a reasonable measure of an appropriate, sexually mature mate. Indeed, the idea of sexual selection is based on such assumptions. However, there is little evidence that animals respond to continuously graded signals with continuously graded behavior and further study is needed here.

Brightness, the sensation of light intensity, is very much a function of hue and saturation. The perception of brightness depends on the viewer's spectral sensitivity as well as on the background against which hue is viewed (see Chapter 6). For example, a hue to which an animal is very sensitive appears brighter than one of equal or higher luminance to which the animal is relatively insensitive, simply because the former provides greater retinal stimulation (see Chapter 5). However, perception of brightness may be confounded by psychological factors of which, in animals, we know little. For example, pink may have a much higher luminance than a fully saturated red of the same hue and yet the latter may appear brighter to the subject. Hues also appear brighter and more saturated when viewed against a background of complementary color than when viewed against a noncomplementary one. Likewise, a gray appears lighter ("brighter") when viewed against a black background and darker when viewed against a white one.

Although intensity would appear to be of little use for construction of a signal when it is a function of ambient light levels, when the signal depends on reflected or transmitted light, intensity variation could be used to encode information in bioluminescent signaling systems. For example, bioluminescent animals might alternate dimmer with brighter light pulses or modulate the intensity of a longer duration light pulse in order to achieve variation in signals.

Finally, information may be encoded by spatial and/or temporal patterning of light. The alternating color patterns that occur in many animals, as well as the spatial patterning of light organs that characterize certain species of *Lampyridae*, are good examples of the former mechanism, while the flash patterns that are characteristic of fireflies of the genera *Photinus* and *Photurus* provide an example of the latter.

Thus, by combining several of these mechanisms it should be possible to produce as many kinds of signals as a species is capable of interpreting. The mechanisms used depend on the visual abilities of the animal as well as the physical (see Chapters 2 and 3) and biological (see Chapter 7) constraints of the environment in which the animal occurs.

THE USE OF COLOR IN INTRASPECIFIC COMMUNICATION

I interpret color in its widest sense (see Chapter 5) to include the presence of hues or neutral shades (i.e., black, gray, and white) achieved by integumentary pigmentation, specific reflective, refractive, and light-transmitting properties of the body surface or bioluminescence. Intraspecific communication is interpreted as the process by which the behavior of one individual affects that of a conspecific, with the assumption that such a process ultimately increases the fitness of the former animal, i.e., the sender.

In considering display behavior in birds, Armstrong (1947) wrote that "colour, sound, form and function are integrated so intimately that to scrutinize one aspect of the performance, as we sometimes have to do, is apt to compromise our conclusion." I wish to extend this warning to include other groups of animals. It is especially applicable to color insofar as it interacts so intimately with structure and movement, each aspect affecting the conspicuousness of the other two. For example, in fiddler crabs of the genus *Uca*, the males possess a greatly enlarged and often conspicuously colored claw that is waved in a species-typical pattern during courtship and threat. An equally bizarre example of interaction of color pattern, structure, and movement occurs in the courtship display of the peacock, (*Pavo cristatus*) where the male fans out its gaudy, oversize upper tail coverts and shakes them in front of the female.

Another point, one so obvious that it is often overlooked, is that signals are often context specific. Failure to find an effect for a given stimulus or configuration of stimuli does not eliminate the possibility that the stimulus has meaning when presented at another time, distance, place, or in another context. For example, intensification of color in certain fishes has different meanings, depending on the context in which it occurs; in the presence of a sexually receptive member of the opposite sex it may be interpreted as a willingness to mate, while in the presence of a member of the same sex, it may serve as a threat. The configuration "red belly" elicits attack in the male three-spine stickleback (*G. aculeatus*); red alone is insufficient. Red on the dorsum of a stickleback dummy has little or no effect on the male's behavior, but when the venter is red, the dummy immediately elicits attack.

Finally, the use of color in communication may be overlooked because it occurs only under very specific, infrequent circumstances or because it is normally invisible to us. The apparent use of ultraviolet light for mate attraction in certain species of butterflies provides an example of the latter. In such butterflies, the wing scales are arranged to reflect ultraviolet light in a flickering pattern as the wings are flapped. Since these animals are capable of perceiving ultraviolet light, one assumes that this mechanism allows them to signal to each other without attracting the attention of vertebrate predators and other animals insensitive to ultraviolet light.

With these points in mind, I discuss some ways in which color is involved in intraspecific communication. To do this I wish to consider what it is that one animal needs to communicate to another member of its species. Color signals might help advertise the following:

1. the sender's species or subspecies
2. the sender's sex

3. the sender's individuality
4. the sender's internal state and/or status
5. the presence, localization, and/or orientation of certain body parts or objects such as nests, breeding sites, territories, enemies, etc.

The order in which I have listed the first four aspects corresponds in some degree to the order in which such information may be received and/or processed by the signal receiver. However, this ordering is only a very rough approximation since a signal often provides information relevant to several of the above categories simultaneously. Thus it is difficult, if not impossible, to construct any meaningful divisions that are mutually exclusive and yet reflect the way nature operates.

Species Recognition

In monomorphic species, coloration may be involved simply in species recognition. One of the most spectacular uses of color and pattern for this purpose occurs in fishes that inhabit tropical coral reefs. Field observations (Lorenz 1962) and field experiments (Fricke 1966, Brockmann 1973, Potts 1973) indicate that the characteristic "poster coloration" is an important cue for species recognition among these fishes. Furthermore, such coloration is not only limited to the body, but sometimes includes the eyes, which are made conspicuous through various techniques of ornamentation: dark pupil set against a contrasting, light-colored iris, conspicuously colored irises, and ancillary eye markings of contrasting colors (Thresher 1977). An effective species-recognition mechanism presumably insures that a species will direct aggressive behavior to conspecifics, since the latter represent the major source of ecological competition.

Species-specific coloration often promotes social contact among species. For example, it is known that the young of certain species of cichlid fishes are attracted to discs of the same color as their parents (Noble and Curtis 1939, Baerends and Baerends-van Roon 1950). In some species (e.g., *Hemichromis*) the preference for red is innate, or at least resistant to experiential factors, while in other species (e.g., *Cichlasoma*) color preferences can be altered by rearing the young with foster parents of a different color. This imprinting-like phenomenon has been reported to occur between different color morphs of the same species (Noakes and Barlow 1973, Fernö and Sjölander 1973, 1976) and between different species (Sjölander and Fernö 1973, Kop and Heuts 1973).

A dramatic effect of color used in conjunction with movement is seen in some cichlid fishes when they are calling their young. For example, in the jewel fish (*Hemichromis bimaculatus*) both parents possess brightly colored medial fins that are accentuated by a series of reflective blue-green flecks. When alarmed, the parents rapidly raise and lower their fins in alternation, causing the brightly colored pattern to be flashed on and off like a miniature neon sign (personal observation). Such behavior is believed to cause the young to aggregate and approach the parents or sink to the bottom where they may be less easily noticed by predators, but it may also be a distraction display calling the predator's attention to the parents and away from the young.

Many monomorphic birds possess conspicuous color or marking patterns that are probably utilized in species recognition. In the European robin (*Erithacus rubecula*) both sexes possess a reddish-brown breast, which Lack (1943) showed was an important cue for species recognition.

Immelmann (1959) presented models of zebra finches to live zebra finches (*Taeniopygia castanotis*) and found that the red beak of mature males and females was an important factor in species recognition. Smith (1967) demonstrated that the eye-head contrast of several sympatric species of gulls was a major factor in species recognition. Females were highly selective; they rejected conspecific males whose eye rings were painted to look like those of another species but accepted heterospecific males whose eye rings were painted to look like those of their own species. Once a female had formed a pairbond with a male, alteration of his eye ring had no measurable effect. However, males showed little concern for a female's eye-head contrast during pair formation but would not copulate with females bearing eye ring coloration of another species. Thus even such subtle visual cues as these can operate as effective reproductive isolating mechanisms.

The influence of early experience on an animal's response to color is probably best documented in birds. Hess (1973) presents considerable evidence for the role of color in imprinting in chicks, and Immelmann (1972) has shown how early experience can influence the preference for different color morphs in the zebra finch. Studying the white and gray morphs, Immelmann found that later sexual preference was for the color morph of birds with which the individual was reared. Recent investigations on the lesser snow goose (*Anser caerulescens*) have also shown that color preferences for a given morph (white or grayish blue) are influenced by an individual's early experience with its parents as well as with its siblings (Cooke, Mirsky, and Seiger 1972, Cooke and McNally 1975). These preferences are exhibited in the individual's approach tendencies, association preferences, and mate selection.

The ability of some birds to distinguish their own species' eggs from those of social parasites is yet another example of species recognition. It is believed that egg recognition depends in part on color and marking patterns (Wickler 1968, Baerends and Drent 1970) and the close matching of these characteristics by successful nest parasites, such as the European cuckoo (*Cuculus canorus*), tends to support this contention.

Color cues are also important for the parents' recognition of nestlings of their species. This is especially evident in the bright color patterns on the inside of the mouth of nestling estrildid finches (Eibl-Eibesfelt 1975). Such patterns act as releasers for parental feeding when the birds gape, and at the same time they aid in orienting the parents' response.

One of the most fully investigated cases of intraspecific communication involving color is that of the begging response of gulls and terns. Tinbergen and Perdeck (1950) investigated the stimuli involved in elicitation of the begging response of young herring gulls (*Larus argentatus*). Using cardboard dummies, they found that the red patch on the lower mandible of the parents was the most important feature for eliciting begging in the young. Red produced a stronger response than any other color but a patch that contrasted strongly with the mandible produced a greater response than one with less contrast. Therefore, a very strong response was obtained with a red patch on a yellow mandible, the naturally occurring color pattern of the parents' bills. However, in the sandwich tern (*Sterna sandvicensis*), where the parents' bills are black, young of this species respond more strongly to black than to red (Weidmann 1961).

Among mammals, the use of marking patterns occurs in the rump patches of male and female ungulates. Since these animals have little or no color vision and generally poor visual acuity, it is understandable that such rump patches consist of highly contrasting combinations of black, gray, and white. It has been suggested that rump patches have evolved through ritualization of anogenital presentation, supporting subordination behavior by remotivating an aggressor into a sexual mood (Guthrie 1971). Guthrie argues that the use of rump patches as a warning signal or as a signal for the young to follow developed secondarily to its appeasement function in ungulates. More recently, however, Alvarez, Braza, and Norzagaray (1976) have argued that the rump patch of the fallow deer (*Dama dama*) serves primarily as a warning signal that has evolved from tail-raising during defecation and from the autonomic response of piloerection. In any case, there is little doubt that the color pattern of rump patches serves in intraspecific communication.

Species and Sex Recognition

In dimorphic species, where characteristic color and marking patterns are exclusive to one sex, usually the male, sex and species recognition occur simultaneously. Both kinds of information are crucial to a mate-seeking female. The blackspotted stickleback (*Gasterosteus wheatlandi*) occurs sympatrically with the threespined stickleback (*G. aculeatus*) along the North Atlantic coast of North America. The breeding coloration of males of the former species is bright greenish-gold, that of the latter species grayish-blue and red. Although males court females of other species with equal vigor, females show a clear preference for males of their own species, apparently basing the choice initially on color cues (McInerney 1969, Rowland 1970). Furthermore, when a female *G. aculeatus* has the opportunity to choose between two conspecific males that differ in the degree of development of the red throat and belly, she tends to select the brighter one (Semler 1971; McPhail 1969, Wootton 1976). Additional, though indirect, support for the significance of red coloration to the female stickleback comes from a physiological study by Cronly-Dillon and Sharma (1968), who used the optomotor response as a behavioral measure. They found that female *G. aculeatus* are more sensitive to red light than males are during the breeding season, but that this difference disappears when the animals are out of reproductive condition. They suggested that this greater sensitivity to red may be due to selective sensitization within visual pathways or at synapses concerned with transmitting impulses from red-sensitive photoreceptors to the brain.

Haas (1976) investigated the preference of female killifish (*Notobranchius guentheri*) for males and found that females chose red-tailed congeners to congeners lacking this feature. Furthermore, when the choice was between two conspecific males that differed in the intensity of tail coloration, females chose the brighter male 61-67% more often. In an earlier experiment, Noble and Curtis (1939) likewise found that *Hemichromis* females preferred to mate with brighter red males than with duller ones. However, since in this experiment the color of the males was varied pharmacologically, it is possible that the males' behavior was also affected and that females were responding on the basis of male behavior rather than color.

In the common guppy (*Poecilia reticulata*), males have elaborately colored caudal fins that they flutter in front of females during courtship. In a recent laboratory study, Farr (1977) found that females show a sudden increase in copulation rates with novel males when the latter are introduced into a small group of males and females that are familiar with each other. Such effects were rare if the newly introduced male was of the same color as those already present. Farr suggests that the high degree of polymorphism in tail color of male guppies may be maintained by such selection on the part of the females. By habituating to common color patterns and responding to novel ones, females are selecting males of a new and different genotype, thereby lessening inbreeding and producing offspring of greater genetic variability. Such variability should be adaptive in an environment as variable as that in which the guppy occurs.

In view of the extensive work on *Anolis*, it is surprising that little experimental evidence exists to confirm the use of dewlap color in species recognition. On the contrary, some investigations on the most widely studied species, *Anolis carolinensis*, have indicated color to be unimportant. For example, Greenberg and Noble (1944) found that females responded equally well to males with normal, pink dewlaps or green painted dewlaps. Furthermore, Crews (1975) found that males whose dewlaps were colored blue by injection of india ink were just as successful in stimulating oogenesis in females as were control males. However, W. Sigmund, working in our laboratory, has recently found that when female *A. carolinensis* are given the choice of approaching a pink dewlap male or a green dewlap male, both two meters away and displaying against a green background, females preferred pink dewlaps. By varying the background color against which the females viewed displaying males, Sigmund found that contrast between dewlap and background was also important (see Chapters 6 and 7 for a further discussion of backgrounds and contrast). Thus the preference for red dewlaps over green dewlaps became insignificant when a red background was used instead of a green one (Table 18). These results indicate that the normal pink coloration of *A. carolinensis* dewlaps has evolved to enhance conspicuousness of threat and courtship displays against the green foliage in which this species often occurs.

Many avian displays involve the presentation of bright colors or marking patterns. For example, the courtship of some species of ducks incorporates courtship preening, a movement in which the male preens a specific part of its plumage that is conspicuously colored (Lorenz 1941), while in the blue-footed booby (*Sula nebouxii*), the male lifts its bright blue feet high in the air as it struts in front of a prospective mate (Welty 1975).

A more extreme case of male coloration is found in the peacock, *Pavo cristatus*. Here the males have attained gaudy coloration, especially of the upper tail coverts, which they display by fanning and rattling the plumes. When males gather at the display arena, they direct their displays mainly at the females, suggesting that such displays play a role in the female's choice of a mate (Bastock 1967).

Experimental studies have confirmed the role of male color and marking patterns in avian communication. Noble (1936) showed that the black "moustache" marking at the corner of the mouth of the male common flicker (*Colaptes auratus*) was used for sex recognition. A female that had a moustache painted on her was attacked by her mate but accepted when the marking was removed.

In a recent study of nuptial plumage in the male mallard, Klint (1973) found that the green color of the head was an important feature eliciting inciting display in females. Females preferred males in full nuptial plumage to those whose green head coloration was artificially removed; this preference was shown also by white mutant females raised in isolation. The author concluded that females recognize males on an innate basis that might be modified by sexual imprinting.

TABLE 18

Female Preference for Males in *Anolis Carolinensis*

Dewlap Effects	Background Effects
On Green Background	With Red Dewlap
Red dewlap vs. green dewlap	Red background vs. green background
(16) (4)	(7) (14)
$p < .01$	$.05 < p < .10$
On Red Background	With Green Dewlap
Red dewlap vs. green dewlap	Red background vs. green background
(10) (8)	(13) (6)
$.10 < p$	$.05 < p < .10$

There is some evidence that bright coloration or marking patterns may, in some species, play a major or exclusive role in intrasexual communication. Males with more pronounced secondary sexual traits may be better able to intimidate other males, maintain their territories and/or status and thereby have better access to reproductive females. For example, Jacobs (1955) found that male dragonflies (*Perithemis tenera*) whose characteristic amber wings were painted black were much less successful in securing mates than were control males whose wings were painted with clear lacquer. Although females reacted normally to blackened males, other males treated them as females or ignored them. Therefore, painted males were less successful in acquiring females because they were unable to intimidate intruding males and maintain territories.

Studies on several other invertebrates have utilized dummy presentations to investigate the role of coloration and marking patterns during agonistic encounters. Tinbergen (1939) found that the most important feature releasing aggressive behavior in the cuttlefish is the dark purple and white stripes of the body and ventral arms of displaying males. Plaster dummies possessing these features were displayed to and eventually attacked by males, but when these features were lacking, the dummy was courted. Dummy presentation studies also reveal a role for coloration in the agonistic behavior of salticid spiders (Crane 1949, Drees 1953) and hermit crabs (Hazlett 1969, 1972).

Ewing and Evans (1973) have described the patterns of coloration assumed by aggressive male killifish of the genus *Aphyosemion* during encounters with other males. Although their conclusion was not experimentally demonstrated, they believe that these color patterns serve a signal function among males in their fights to establish themselves in the social hierarchy. Different color patterns are observed in frightened or in courting males.

Noble and Bradley (1933) found that if the ventral surface of a female lizard (*Sceloporus undulatus*) is painted blue (the male's color) it will be attacked by males. On the other hand, males whose ventral surfaces are painted gray are courted. Similar experiments using the European lizard (*Lacerta viridis*), where the blue coloration is confined to the male's throat, lead to the same conclusions (Tinbergen 1951).

Experimental evidence for the releasing function of male coloration has been obtained with birds, too.

Cinat-Thomson (1926) studied the budgerigar (*Melopsittacus undulatus*), a species in which the cere of the male is colored bright blue and that of the female dull brown. Newcomer females whose ceres had been painted blue were attacked by males, while newcomer males with brown-painted ceres were courted by them.

The red epaulets of the male redwing blackbird (*Agelaius phoeniceus*) contrast sharply against the solid black plumage that covers the rest of the bird's body. In a recent field study, Smith (1972) found that males whose red epaulets were obliterated with black dye were less successful in holding territories and in reproducing than control males. Since blackened males were still able to attract females, Smith concluded that the red epaulets communicate threat between rival males but have little if any role in intersexual encounters.

Grant, Mackintosh, and Lerwill (1970) found that male golden hamsters (*Mesocricetus auratus*) whose black chest patches were enlarged by dyeing won more fights than normal males, and concluded that the black patch functioned as a threat stimulus. Recently, however, Johnston (1976) reported that males do not display their chest patches in agonistic encounters. Although Johnston confirmed that males with dyed chest patches had an advantage over other males in their initial encounter, he concluded that the dyed chest patch scared the opponent because of its novel effect and not because it acted as a threat stimulus.

The color and marking patterns on the face of many primates, especially in males, suggest that they may be used as threat signals (Guthrie 1970). Guthrie points out that since primates lack elaborate fighting tools such as antlers, horns, and claws, the face has become emphasized in threat display and embellished by encircling ruffs, hair caps, sideburns, and chin whiskers.

The use of color patterns in males of certain species of Old World monkeys is particularly striking. In several species of catarrhine monkeys, for example, the penis is bright red and is usually contrasted with blue cutaneous coloration of the scrotum. Moreover, the intensity of color, which is influenced by hemoglobin circulating in the cutaneous capillaries (Hill 1955), is a function of the animal's arousal state (Wickler 1967). In the mandrill (*Papio sphinx*), the red-and-blue pattern of the genitals is essentially duplicated on the face, but the facial color is even more conspicuous because of its exposure and the larger surface area involved. The fact that genital display is common among such monkeys suggests that the colors have developed to enhance its conspicuousness as a threat signal.

Sometimes the specific coloration pattern of a sexually dimorphic species is possessed by the female. Buchholz (1951, 1956) investigated the visual features of females of two species of dragonflies that elicited courtship in males. In *Calopteryx splendens* the female must have a yellow or greenish-blue body and wings that transmit 60-80% of the incident light. In *Platycnemis pennipes* the female must be colored greenish-brown or greenish-yellow and have a pattern of alternating dark and light green stripes on the abdomen. Young female *P. pennipes* not yet ready to mate are yellowish-brown overall and are not approached by courting males, apparently because they lack the coloration of mature females.

In the butterfly *Hypolimnas misippus* the female's orange-brown wing with its black tip and white edges is important in eliciting male courtship (Stride 1958). A large white patch on the hindwing, characteristic of conspecific males and of other species, inhibits male courtship. In the grayling butterfly (*Eumenis semele*), however, sexual pursuit by the male is not controlled by the pattern of the female's wings or by any specific color, but rather by its darkness (Tinbergen et al. 1942). By presenting a series of gray and colored paper dummies to males in the field, Tinbergen found that not only were darker colors more effective than lighter ones but that a black dummy was "supernormal," eliciting more sexual pursuit than a dummy constructed from the brown wings of a female. Most importantly, males as well as females of this species show a definite color preference (for yellow and blue) when feeding and therefore are not color blind.

A particularly interesting system of visual communication occurs in the *Lampyridae*. Here glow worms, neotenic females of the genera *Lampyris* and *Phausis*, lift up their abdomens when they become sexually receptive, thereby revealing a pattern of glowing bioluminescent organs to which males are attracted. Using illuminated stencil decoys, Schaller and Schwalb (1961) investigated the importance of light intensity, hue, and spatial pattern on reproductive males. They found that males were attracted to decoys bearing the spatial pattern and intensity range of their own species. In the more discriminating *Lampyris*, males were only attracted to yellow wavelengths (the color emitted by their females) even though such males could perceive blue, red, and green wavelengths. Similar parameters may be involved in communication within other bioluminescent insects, but in fireflies of the genera *Photinus* and *Photurus* the temporal patterning of flashes is of greater importance (Lloyd 1971).

Among birds, the phalaropes are unusual in that the female bears the more brightly colored plumage. In most birds the male acquires brighter plumage, which is dependent on the male hormone testosterone, but in the northern phalarope (*Lobipes lobatus*) testosterone occurs in greater concentration in the female's ovaries than in the male's testes (Hohn 1970). As expected, it is also the female phalarope that takes the active role in courtship and territorial defense and the dull-colored male that cares for the brood.

A bright red patch of skin on the hindquarters of certain baboons and other Old World monkeys usually signifies a female in estrus. This sex skin varies in conformation and color, from flesh to bright red, in phase with the menstrual cycle. Females in heat present their anogenital region to males as an invitation to mate and it is believed that the bright red coloration underlines and magnifies the effect of this signal (Wickler 1967). It is also interesting to note that enlargement of the *labia minora* is extremely pronounced in some human females, such as the Koisanids, when they are sexually receptive. This enlargement, sometimes known as "Hottentot's skirt," shows a marked change of color from normal pale pink to purplish red during sexual excitement (Fischer 1955). Wickler (1967) concludes that this acts as an intraspecific signal and he points out that in some peoples in which enlargement of the *labia minora* does not naturally occur, it is brought about by artificial manipulation, e.g., among the Batetela, the Basutos, and the Bantu.

Individual Recognition

Certain kinds of social organization require that an animal be able to individually recognize other members of its group. In the simplest instance, an animal might recognize only its mate or offspring, while in a social hierarchy an animal might recognize each individual of the group. Although the evidence is scant, there is reason to believe that coloration and marking patterns are used in individual recognition among animals.

For example, Noble and Curtis (1939) showed that male and female jewel fish (*H. bimaculatus*) recognized their mates solely on the basis of visual cues. Although subtle movements are apparently involved in such recognition, the authors suggest that the patterning of the bluish-green flecks, especially those that adorn the head region of these fish, also plays a role. When an animal had its head region painted with a mixture of petcock grease and chrome yellow so that the fleck pattern on the opercula was covered, the altered animal was attacked by its mate as though it were an intruder. However, if the rest of the flank was covered with the paint but the head left unaltered, the animal was generally accepted by its mate. Since fleck patterns in the vicinity of the head vary considerably between individual *Hemichromis*, it would appear likely that these patterns are involved in individual recognition, but further experiments are needed to confirm this.

Several studies have provided evidence of individual recognition by visual cues in birds, especially the ability of parent birds to recognize their young. Davies and Carrick (1962) suggested that the great variation of plumage patterns (from pale silvery gray to dark olive green) in crested tern chicks (*Sterna bergii*) are important for recognition by the parents. The authors found that the parents can recognize their chicks when the latter are two days old, at which time the chicks begin to wander and might mingle with other chicks. Buckley and Buckley (1972) present evidence for individual chick recognition as well as egg recognition by adult royal terns (*Sterna maxima*) based on coloration and marking patterns.

Experimental evidence for the role of coloration and marking patterns in individual recognition of chicks by parents was obtained by Miller and Emlen (1975). The authors visually altered one member in each brood of ring-billed gull chicks (*Larus delawarensis*) with a marking pen, reshaping and adding spots on head and back plumage, darkening the margin of each eyelid and extending the black of the bill about 5 mm posteriorly. More than 50% of the altered chicks were attacked by their parents, but such attacks subsided and eventually ceased altogether as the parents apparently adjusted to the altered visual pattern of their chicks. The authors also found that devocalized but visually unaltered chicks were accepted by the parents immediately, indicating that visual cues are more important than auditory cues for parental recognition of young in this species. In other cases, however, visual cues may play only a secondary role in individual recognition. Tschanz (1968) found guillemot chicks (*Uria aalge*) recognize their parents primarily by auditory cues but show conditioning to color and/or visual pattern of the cloth on which they feed. Tschanz therefore suggests that there may be a predisposition for newly hatched guillemot chicks to get to know their parents individually by visual cues.

In colonial nesting budgerigars (*Melopsittacus undulatus*), individuals recognize their mates and perhaps other individuals of their group. By conditioning subjects to respond to projected images from 35-mm color transparencies of conspecifics, Trillmich (1976) demonstrated that these birds can discriminate individuals of either sex in a two-choice situation. The most critical feature for recognition was the head region, since subjects could discriminate between individuals when this was the only part of the body visible to them. Experimental manipulation, however, gave no clear indication of the specific characteristics involved. Although this discrimination ability was demonstrated in a conditioning paradigm, one would assume that the same mechanism is utilized for individual recognition under natural conditions.

The ruff (*Philomachus pugnax*) differs from most other bird species because of its extreme individual diversity in male nuptial plumage. During courtship, two groups of males, satellite males and independent males, congregate at the communal display arena or lek (Hogan-Warburg 1966). Independent males defend territories and are mostly dark-colored, nonterritorial satellite males behave peacefully and are mostly white. In addition, independent males show wide variation in basic and secondary color(s) of ruff and head tuft, contrast between ruff and head tuft, and color of the wattles. According to Hogan-Warburg, such differences provide for individual recognition among independent males. The fact that females prefer to mate with certain males on the lek, usually those with the more brilliant plumage (Selous 1907, Hogan-Warburg 1966), suggests that they, too, are capable of individual recognition based on color cues.

The use of color for individual recognition among mammals is even less well studied than it is for birds, but there is some experimental evidence in support of its occurrence. For example, in a recent study of mutual recognition among ewes and lambs of four breeds of sheep (*Ovis aries*), Shillito and Alexander (1975) found that such recognition was based on coat coloration, which varies widely in these breeds. In a two-choice situation, mutual recognition of ewes and lambs occurred more readily when a test partner of the same breed was of dissimilar color or color pattern than the natural partner.

General observations also reveal color or color pattern differences among mammals that could be used for individual recognition. For example, the right whale (*Eubalaena australis*) possesses a series of light-colored callosities that contrast sharply with the dark skin of this animal. Payne (1976) has found that the number, size, shape, and placement of these callosities are unique to the individual whale, "making it possible for us--and presumably the whales too--to tell individuals apart by sight."

Motivational State

Often animals must communicate their motivational state to other members of their species and this requires a communication mechanism whose signals can be changed over time to reflect corresponding changes in motivational state. In the visual modality, such communication is often achieved by gestural or postural signals, which may be made more conspicuous by the incorporation of color. However, in some animals, color or color patterns can be changed rapidly and are, therefore, capable of dynamic signaling relatively independent of body movement. In fact, many animals are capable of signaling by color change if one includes those changes that occur over a long timescale, such as the seasonal plumage and pelage changes in birds and mammals. The most impressive color changes, however, are those that occur rapidly enough to be seen, the kind of change that is especially well devloped in some cephalopods and fishes.

In the investigation of the cuttlefish, *Sepia*, cited previously, Tinbergen (1939) found that reproductive males develop a dark purple and white striped pattern when they encounter a conspecific. Positioning themselves alongside their opponent, they display their mantle coloration and especially their broad fourth arm. If the opponent happens to be another male, it rapidly assumes a similar color pattern that leads to agonistic behavior between the opponents.

If the encountered individual fails to assume this pattern, it is courted as a female, regardless of sex.

Many fish exhibit rapid and complex color changes. Associations between color patterns and a tendency to perform certain behavior is well documented in many species of fishes, including the Cichlidae (Baerends and Baerends-van Roon 1950, Neil 1964, Myrberg 1965, Baldaccini 1973), Poecilidae (Baerends, Brouwer, and Waterbolk 1955), Centrarchidae (Howard 1974), Chaetodontidae (Hamilton and Peterman 1971), Nanidae (Barlow 1963), Anabantidae (Forselius 1957), and so on. It is generally assumed that these color changes are involved in intraspecific communication, but surprisingly few studies have actually demonstrated this.

One of the best cases in which experimental evidence has been obtained for the role of coloration patterns in communication of motivational state is the study by Leong (1969) on the cichlid fish *Haplochromis burtoni*. Using painted dummies, Leong was able to show that only two aspects of the color pattern affected the tendency to attack in territorial males: a black oblique eyebar and an orange color patch located just dorsal to the gills (Fig. 83). When the black eyebar was present on the dummy, it caused an increase in attack behavior while the orange color patch inhibited attack. When a dummy with both features was presented to a territorial male, it elicited a level of attack that was the algebraic sum of the two opposing effects.

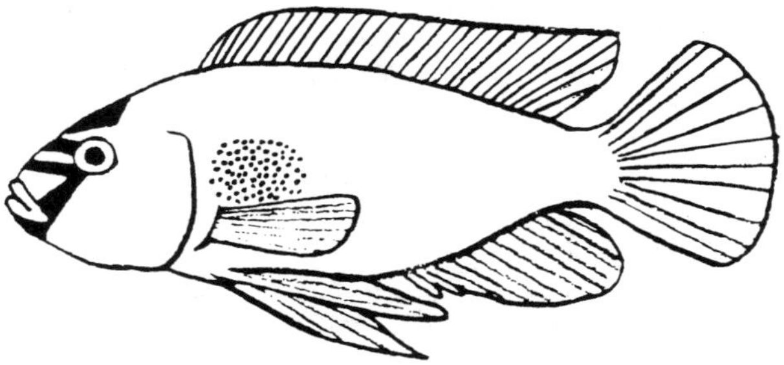

Fig. 83. *Haplochromis burtoni*, showing the dark eyebar pattern and orange color patch just posterior to the operculum.

Baldaccini (1973) has described the color patterns and associated behavior of the cichlid fish *Tilapia mariae*. Nine color patterns can be distinguished in this species, some of which represent combinations of the three major patterns. The major patterns consist of (1) a pattern of vertical bars, typical of nonterritorial fish moving about in schools; (2) a spotted pattern, typical of aggressive, territorial fish; (3) a dark pattern, indicating an animal tending to escape.

M. Slovin, working in our laboratory, has compared the effects of the barred and spotted patterns on territorial males of this species by presenting them with dummies (Fig. 84). The results of his experiments show that the spotted pattern elicits a greater amount of aggressive behavior than a barred pattern (Table 19).

Thus Slovin concluded that these color patterns communicate their possessor's internal state and status to other individuals, allowing the latter to act appropriately during a social encounter.

TABLE 19

Total Number of Responses of *Tilapia mariae* to Certain Stimuli

Behavioral Response	Dotted Dummy	Barred Dummy	$\underline{p}$[a]
Bite/butt	12,871	8691	0.001
Frontal display	207	31	0.001
Lateral display	1747	3226	0.001
Bite/butt to other objects	377	1155	0.004

[a]Wilcoxon distribution-free test.

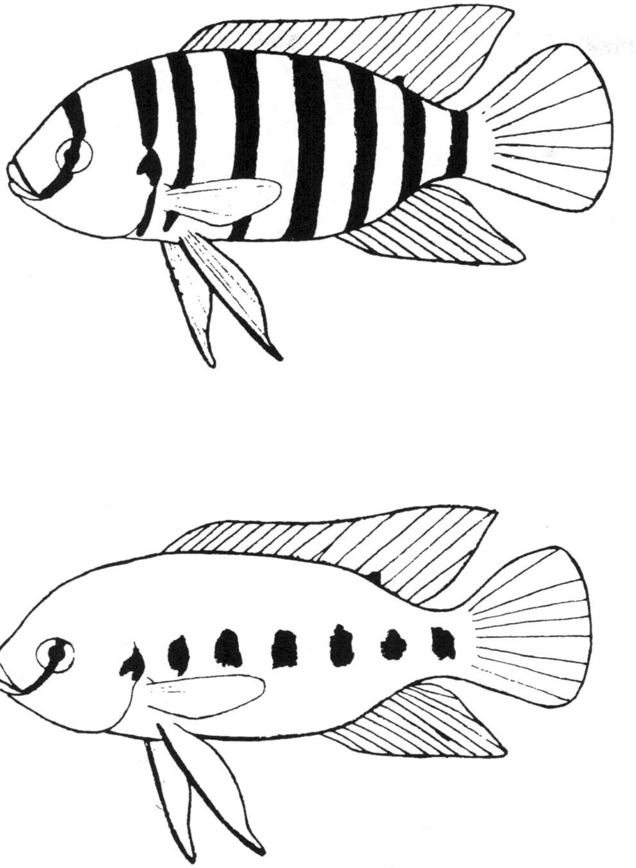

Fig. 84. Dummies used to test the effects of color pattern on *Tilapia mariae*; the nonaggressive pattern is shown above and the aggressive pattern, typical of territorial animals, is shown below.

Hadley (1969) found that in the longear sunfish (*Lepomis megalotis*) dominant fish have a greater amount of red in their irises than low-ranking fish. By presenting dummies to territorial males in their natural habitat, Keenleyside (1970) found that the dummies' effectiveness in eliciting aggression in this species was increased by (1) adding black pelvic fins, (2) adding rim coloring of the opercular patch to make it more conspicuous, and (3) making the iris red and the pupil black.

In the jewel fish (*H. bimaculatus*), there is often a rapid intensification in the red coloration, especially around the throat region, during a social encounter. Experiments have shown that red-colored dummies elicit higher levels of courtship or attack in males than dummies lacking such coloration (Seitz 1943, Rowland 1975) (Fig. 85). Likewise, Oehlert (1958) found that red light illumination makes *H. bimaculatus* appear brighter red and thereby intensifies fighting behavior in this species.

Picciolo (1964) carried out a detailed analysis of the visual stimuli involved in intraspecific communication in anabantid fishes of the genera *Colisa* and *Trichogaster*. Color patterns were found to be involved in sexual recognition for several species and the presence of male coloration

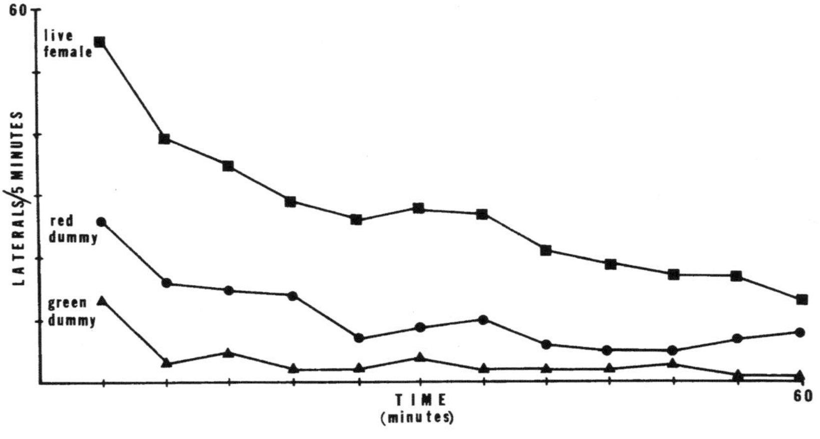

Fig. 85. Frequency of lateral displays/five minute intervals in male *Hemichromis bimaculatus* elicited by a live female, a red dummy, and a green dummy. The live female was allowed to move freely and therefore provided a more effective stimulus than either of the two stationary dummies.

elicited an aggressive response in conspecific males. In some species, e.g., *Colisa lalia*, a silvery dummy, similar in coloration to a female, elicited sexual behavior in the male.

The Asian fish (*Badis badis*) is known for its ability to alter color pattern. Barlow (1963) was able to identify eleven color patterns, each of which occur under characteristic situations in this species. Lighter color patterns reflect an increasingly greater fright tendency while darker color patterns are correlated with the advanced stages of aggressive behavior. Fights between males are accompanied by color change and indeed, incomplete fighting behavior consists mostly of changing colors.

Lizards are also capable of rapid color change, but the degree to which such color change is involved in intraspecific communication of internal state is unknown. Carpenter and Grubits (1960) studied dominance shifts in the tree lizard (*Urosaurus ornatus*) and found that dominant males were darker in color than other males. When a dominant male was removed from its enclosure, it became lighter in color in one to two hours. When returned to its enclosure again, it became darker if it became aggressive but remained lighter if forced to retreat and become subordinate. Whether such darkening enhances a dominant's ability to maintain its status was not tested.

Color Signals for Localization and/or Orientation

When signal coloration is highly localized on an animal, one might suspect its involvement in orientation as well as elicitation of the viewer's behavior. The bright red pelvic fins of the male fourspine stickleback (*Apeltes quadracus*) appear to function as targets on which the female fixates as she follows the courting male to the nest (Reisman 1963, Rowland 1974). In other stickleback species the pelvic fins are also colored more or less conspicuously and probably play a similar role.

Peden (1973) has elegantly demonstrated the functions of the black anal spot in fishes of the genus *Gambusia*. This spot, which is located at the genital opening of females, becomes most conspicuous when eggs are present in the ovaries and disappears when young are about to be born.

By constructing a dummy with a hollowed-out genital region filled with soft cooking fat and marked with a black spot of india ink, Peden was able to record the gonapodial impressions left by males attempting to copulate with the dummy. His data show that the black pigmentation of the female's anal spot both directs and elicits the male's copulatory thrusts.

In the schooling fish (*Pristella riddlei*) there is a conspicuous black mark on the dorsal fin that acts as a visual following and orientation signal (Keenleyside 1955). When a group of *Pristella* are deprived of this mark through amputation of part of the dorsal fin, they become much less attractive to an isolated conspecific. The existence of other conspicuous markings in strongly schooling fish, such as the silver line of the silverside (*Menidia*), might also function in this manner.

A remarkable use of color pattern involving mimicry has been reported to occur in certain species of mouth-brooding cichlid fishes (Wickler 1962). These fishes, especially the males, possess anal fins marked with a series of spots that are believed to mimic eggs. As soon as the female lays eggs, she picks them up in her mouth to incubate them. Mistaking the spots on the male's anal fin for her own eggs, the spawning female snaps at them but instead gulps in a mouthful of sperm from the male's genital papilla. Thus fertilization of the newly spawned eggs is virtually insured.

In the jewel fish (*H. bimaculatus*), darkly pigmented spots occur on the opercula, flank, and caudal peduncle. The flank patch is the largest of these and is capable of rapid changes of intensity, from black, associated with attack behavior, to white, associated with courtship behavior (Rowland and Rowlands 1978; Fig. 86). Although the spots on the opercula are thought to mimic eyes, making the animal appear larger when it raises its opercula during a frontal threat display (Baerends and Baerends-van Roon 1950), the function of the pigmented patches on the flank is uncertain. These may help direct an opponent's attack away from the eyes and other vulnerable areas, as suggested for the ocelli in the three-spotted gourami (*Trichogaster trichopterus*) (Picciolo 1964), but they may also play a role in communicating an animal's motivational state to others.

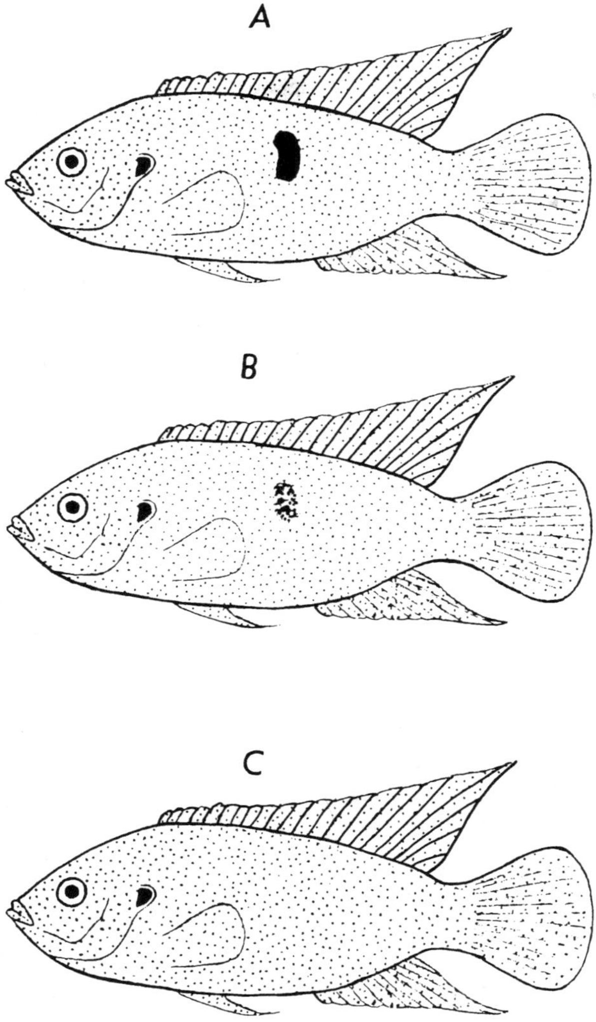

Fig. 86. Stages in the level of pigmentation of the flank patch of *Hemichromis bimaculatus*. The stages shown here represent typical conditions of such pigmentation, which varies along a continuum from A to C.

In birds, the bright colors and color patterns on the inside of the mouth of begging young serve as a target for the parents when they are feeding the young; such color patterns also are found on the young of socially parasitic bird species, where the patterns closely match those of the model (Nicolai 1965). Likewise, the color spots or patterns on the bills of gulls serve as a target for directing the begging response in chicks.

Color Signals Physically Detached from Their Sender

The orderly incorporation of color in the building of a structure occurs in fish and birds and such structures may serve in communication ("sematectonic communication"; Wilson 1975). Wunder (1930) noted that male threespine sticklebacks (*G. aculeatus*) tended to place brightly colored or contrasting nesting material around the entrance of their nests. Morris (1958) investigated this phenomenon in more detail by dissecting the nests of this species layer by layer and found that there was a shift in the male's choice of nesting material as the nest was being constructed. When provided with appropriate nesting material of various colors, males show an initial preference for green or yellow but switch to red during the final stages of nest building, when the nest entrance is being completed. Because red body coloration is significant for courtship in this species, the possibility arises that the use of red around the nest may also serve as an intraspecific signal. Referring to his observations on the nests of *Gasterosteus*, Morris states that the "unmistakable bright ring of color surrounded the entrance in such a way as to make it necessary to consider the possibility of a very special entrance-marking mechanism." His interpretation is that a sudden shift in preference for red nest-building material accomplishes this. Whether red material is available in the environment and whether the increase in conspicuousness of the nest entrance acts as a signal to which prospective mates orient is uncertain and deserves further study.

One of the most elaborate and widely known cases of color use in construction by animals occurs in the bowerbirds. These birds, of which there are eighteen species, are native to Australia and New Guinea. At least twelve species build a bower from twigs, grasses, ferns, beetle carcasses, stones, berries, etc. The bower serves as an arena for the male's courtship and may attract and/or arouse prospective mates. Gilliard (1969) found that in the genus *Amblyornis* there is an inverse relationship between the male's plumage and the complexity of its bower. For example, in *A. macgregoriae* the male has a long golden-orange crest and builds a simple bower; in *A. subalaris* the male has an intermediate crest and builds a somewhat more complex bower; in *A. inornatus* the male has no crest (it cannot be distinguished from the female!) but builds an elaborate bower decorated with berries, shells, and flowers. Thus transferral of signal function from plumage to an extrinsic structure provides the male with the ability to attract females to his mating arena but to remain inconspicuous to visual predators.

The complexity involved in the building of bowers is in some species quite remarkable. In the satin bowerbird (*Ptilonorhynchus violaceus*), the male decorates his bower with berries, flowers, parrot feathers, and other bright objects, showing a preference for dark blue and yellow-green colors (von Frisch 1974). Furthermore, using a piece of fibrous bark as a brush, the male sometimes paints the inside of its bower with the juice of blue berries which it crushes in its beak. Indeed, the great complexity and variation of color used in bower construction has even led to the suggestion that these birds possess an aesthetic sense (von Frisch 1974, Thorpe 1974).

Colored artifacts may also play a role in intraspecific communication. Bowerbirds have been observed holding brightly colored artifacts such as red berries, beetle carcasses, shells, flowers, and so forth, in their beaks during courtship, apparently as an offering for the female (Gilliard 1969). The use of grass, leaves, and other artifacts for intraspecific communication has also been reported for the great crested grebe (*Podiceps cristatus*) (Huxley 1914), the brown towhee (*Pipilo erythrophthalmus*), and the European starling (*Sturnus vulgaris*) (Hamilton 1973), and the mountain gorilla (*Gorilla gorilla beringei*) (Schaller 1963).

Finally, the significance of color adornment, use, and sign construction reaches its culmination in man. Owing to man's extraordinary ability to discriminate colors and color patterns and to think abstractly, color signals have attained an important role in communication, probably in early man (as suggested by the use of color in cave paintings), and certainly in extant, primitive societies as well as technologically advanced ones. The many ways in which we use color to decorate, advertise, and symbolize preclude its discussion in the present chapter, but a quick survey of one's surroundings will usually provide sufficient evidence of its importance. Although the signal value of specific colors or color patterns is for man an essentially culturally acquired trait, there is a possibility that it may in some cases have an innate basis (Battersby 1964). Further research along such lines would be most worthwhile.

THE BEHAVIORAL EFFECTS OF SIGNALS ON THE RECEIVER

From the foregoing examples, it is evident that an intraspecific signal may affect the receiver by release or stimulation, by inhibition or by orientation of the latter's behavior. Furthermore, a signal may simultaneously release and orient a response or at one time stimulate and another time inhibit a response. The red beak of the mature zebra finch, the blue throat of a male *Lacerta* lizard, and the amber wings of a dragonfly are all examples of releasing stimuli. However, such stimuli not only release responses but may provide relative long-term stimulation to maintain or enhance behavior. As pointed out by Hinde (1970), the distinction is often based on the way such stimuli are presented, releasing stimuli being presented suddenly and stimulating ones being continuously present. Therefore, while the nuptial coloration of a male may fail to elicit a receptive response in a female initially, his continued presence may act as a source of stimulation that brings her into a receptive state.

From a functional point of view a signal can be considered inhibitory if it prevents a response or decreases its probability. From a causal point of view the distinction may, in many cases, be only semantic, since some signals inhibit one response by stimulating another, incompatible one. Thus the striped pattern of a male cuttlefish inhibits another male's courtship by increasing aggression in the latter. In the case of rump patches of ungulates described earlier, the inhibition of aggression observed when an animal displays its rump to a would-be attacker may also occur indirectly. According to Guthrie (1971), the rump patch is effective as an appeasement signal because it "remotivates the aggressor into a sexual mood."

In other cases, it appears that a color signal can inhibit behavior directly. For example, in the cichlid fish (*Haplochromis burtoni*) discussed earlier, the color patch located above the pectoral fins inhibited biting but caused no apparent increase in other behaviors. Similarly inhibitory effects of coloration in cichlid fishes have been shown for *Tropheus moori* (Wickler 1967), *Tilapia mariae*(Slovin, personal communication), and most recently in gold morphs of *Cichlasoma citrinellum* (Barlow 1976).

Since vision is generally the most effective modality for stimulus localization, one would expect color and pattern to play a major role in the orientation of behavior. Several examples have been given that demonstrate the importance of such patterns in spatially guiding (or misguiding) an animal's response. For example, the dark anal spot of sexually receptive female gambusiin fishes or the red bill spot of parental gulls serve as targets toward which the response of a conspecific is directed. In other cases, such as certain schooling fishes or flocking birds, coloration and marking patterns may allow conspecifics to maintain a given orientation that is necessary for the cohesiveness and functioning of the group. Here the animal does not respond to the orientation signal as a target, but as a reference point.

CONCLUSIONS

A display, like any behavior or morphological trait, is the result of evolutionary compromise. The incorporation of coloration in display is also subject to selection that is unrelated to its role in intraspecific communication. We have had presented to us in this symposium evidence for the role of pigmentation in thermo- and hydroregulation (Chapter 2), resistance to feather wear and protection against ultraviolet radiation (Chapter 3), and interspecific communication (Chapter 8). Clearly, the coloration that we find associated with an intraspecific signal is not always the optimal pattern for communication with conspecifics; it might be possible to "design" a more effective "supernormal" stimulus by altering the color, form, etc., of the existing display in some way. But such changes could have negative effects on other parameters, thereby decreasing the animal's fitness. For example, studies by Semler (1971) and Moodie (1972) have shown that there exist on the Northwest Pacific coast of North America populations of threespine sticklebacks whose ventral region becomes black during the reproductive period. Females from such populations still show a preference for males with red venters, but the black coloration is maintained in the populations because black-bellied males are less prone to predation and therefore are more fit than the sexually attractive (and predator attractive!) red males.

We have also seen from the evidence presented in Hailman's chapter (Chapter 7) that there are some general conclusions one can draw concerning the design of visual signals in various habitats. Attempts to predict the characteristics of such signals should help us understand the pressures an organism faces in its natural environment and will, hopefully, lead us to the discovery of principles concerning the evolution of visual communication systems.

ACKNOWLEDGMENTS

I would like to thank D. French, P. Furspan, P. Percival, and M. Slovin for their helpful comments on the manuscript and C. Meyer for her assistance on some of the figures. I also thank W. Sigmund and M. Slovin for allowing me the use of their data. I would like to acknowledge support I received from Indiana University Faculty Grant-in-aid of Research 22-342-73. This chapter constitutes contribution 1074 from the Department of Biology of Indiana University (Bloomington).

REFERENCES

Alvarez, F.; Braza, F.; and Norzagaray, A. 1976. The use of the rump patch in the fallow deer (*D. dama*). *Behaviour* 56:298-308.

Armstrong, E. 1947. *Bird display and Behaviour*, 2nd ed. London: Lindsay Drummond.

Baerends, G. P., and Baerends-van Roon, J. M. 1950. An introduction to the study of the ethology of the cichlid fishes. *Behaviour Suppl.* 1.

Baerends, G. P.; Brouwer, R.; and Waterbolk, H. 1955. Ethological studies of *Lebistes reticulatus* (Peters). I. An analysis of the male courtship pattern. *Behaviour* 8:249-334.

Baerends, G. P., and Drent, R. 1970. The herring gull and its egg. *Behaviour Suppl.* 17.

Baldaccini, N. E. 1973. An ethological study of reproductive behaviour, including the colour patterns of the cichlid fish *Tilapia mariae* (Boulanger). *Monitore Zool. Ital.* (N.S.) 7:247-290.

Barlow, G. 1963. Ethology of the Asian teleost *Badis badis*. II. Motivation and signal value of the color patterns. *Anim Behav.* 11:97-105.

Barlow, G. 1976. Colour and levels of aggression in the midas cichlid. *Anim. Behav.* 24:814-817.

Bastock, M. 1967. *Courtship: A Zoological Study*. London: Heinemann.

Battersby, K. A. 1964. Applications of colour in everyday life. In *Colour and Life*, W. B. Broughton (ed.). Symposium Inst. Biol., No. 12. London, pp. 125-132.

Brockmann, H. J. 1973. The function of poster coloration in the beaugregory, *Eupomacentrus leucostictus* (Pomacentridae, Pisces). *Z. Tierpsychol.* 33:13-34.

Buchholtz, C. 1956. Eine Analyse des Paaruugsverhaltens *Caolpteryx* Leach unterbesonderer Berücksichtigung ethologischer Fragen. *Z. Tierpsychol.* 8:273-293.

Buchholtz, C. 1956. Eine analyse des Paaruugsverhaltens und der dabei werkenden Auslösen bei der Libellen *Platycnemis pennipes* und *Pl. dealbata*. *Z. Tierpsychol.* 13:13-25.

Buckley, P. A., and Buckley, F. G. 1972. Individual egg and chick recognition by adult royal terns (*Sterna maxima maxima*). *Anim. Behav.* 20:457-462.

Carpenter, C., and Grubits, G., III. 1960. Dominance shifts in the tree lizard (*Urosaurus ornatus*--Iguanidae). *Southwest Naturalist* 5:123-128.

Cinat-Tomson, H. 1926. Die geschlechtliche Zuchtwahl beim Wellensittich (*Melopsittacus undulatus* Shaw.) *Biol. Zentralbl.* 46:545-552.

Cooke, F., and McNally, C. 1975. Mate selection and colour preferences in lesser snow geese. *Behaviour* 52:151-170.

Cooke, F.; Mirsky, P.; and Seiger, M. 1972. Color preferences in the lesser snow goose and their possible role in mate selection. *Can. J. Zool.* 50:529-536.

Crane, J. 1949. Comparative biology of salticid spiders at Rancho Grande, Venezuela. Part IV. An analysis of display. *Zoologica* 34:159-214.

Crews, D. 1975. Effects of different components of male courtship behavior on environmentally induced ovarian recrudescence and mating preferences in the lizard, *Anolis carolinensis*. *Anim. Behav.* 23:349-356.

Cronly-Dillon, J., and Sharma, S. C. 1968. Effect of season and sex on the photopic spectral sensitivity of the three-spined stickleback. *J. Exp. Biol.* 49:679-687.

Davies, S., and Carrick, R. 1962. On the ability of crested terns, *Sterna bergii*, to recognize their own chicks. *Austral. J. Zool.* 10:171-177.

Drees, O. 1952. Untersuchungun über die angeboren Verhaltensweisen bei Springspinnen (*Salticidae*). *Z. Tierpsychol.* 9:169-207.

Eibl-Eibesfeldt, I. 1975. *Ethology: The Biology of Behavior.* New York: Holt, Rinehart.

Elliot D. G. 1882. A monograph on the Bucerotidae. London.

Ewing, A. W., and Evans, V. 1973. Studies on the behaviour of cyprinodont fish. 1. The agonistic and sexual behaviour of *Aphyosemion bivattatum* (Lonnberg 1895). *Behaviour* 46:264-278.

Farr, J. A. 1977. Male rarity or novelty, female choice behavior and sexual selection in the guppy, *Poecilia reticulata* Peters (Pisces: Poeciliidae). *Evolution* 31: 162-168.

Fernö, A., and Sjölander, S. 1973. Some imprinting experiments on sexual preferences for color variants in the platyfish (*Xiphophorus maculatus*). *Z. Tierpsychol.* 33: 417-423.

Fernö, A., and Sjölander, S. 1976. Influence of previous experience on the mate selection of two color morphs of the convict cichlid, *Cichlasoma nigrofasciatum* (Pisces: Cichlidae). *Behav. Processes* 1:3-14.

Fischer, E. 1955. Über die sogenannte Hottentotten-schürze nebst Bermerkungen über den descensus testiculorum. *Z. Morph. Anthro.* 47:58-66.

Forselius, S. 1957. Studies of anabantid fishes: I, II and III. *Zool. Bidrag. fran Uppsala* 32:97-598.

Fricke, H. 1966. Attrappenversuche met einigen plakatfarbigen Korallenfischen im Roten Meer. *Z. Tierpsychol.* 23: 4-7.

Gilliard, E. T. 1969. *Birds of Paradise and Bower Birds.* London: Weidenfeld and Nicholson.

Grant, E. C.; Mackintosh, J. H.; and Lerwill. C. J. 1970. The effect of a visual stimulus on the agonistic behavior of the golden hamster. *Z. Tierpsychol.* 27:73-77.

Greenberg, B., and Noble, G. K. 1944. Social behavior of the American chameleon (*Anolis carolinensis* Voight). *Physiol. Zool.* 17:392-439.

Guthrie, R. D. 1970. Evolution of human threat display organs. *Evolutionary Biol.* 4:257-302.

Guthrie, R. D. 1971. A new theory of mammalian rump patch evolution. *Behavior* 38:132-145.

Haas, R. 1976. Sexual selection in *Notobranchius guentheri* (Pisces: Cyprinodontidae). *Evolution* 30:614-622.

Hadley, W. F. 1969. Factors affecting aggressive behavior and social hierarchy in the longear sunfish *Lepomis megalotis* (Rafinesque). Ph.D. thesis, Okla. State Univ., Stillwater.

Hamilton, W. J. 1973. *Life's Color Code.* New York: McGraw-Hill.

Hamilton, W. J., and Peterman, R. M. 1971. Countershading in the colourful reef fish *Chaetodon lunula*: concealment, communication or both? *Anim. Behav.* 19:357-364.

Hazlett, B. 1969. Further investigations of the cheliped presentation in *Pagurus bernhardus* (Decapoda, Anomura). *Crustaceana* 17:31-34.

Hazlett, B. 1972. Stimulus characteristics of an agonistic display of the hermit crab (*Carcinus tibicen*). *Anim. Behav.* 20:101-107.

Hess, E. 1973. *Imprinting.* New York: Van Nostrand Reinhold.

Hill, W. C. 1955. A note on integumental colours with special reference to the genus *Mandrillus. Saugetierkd. Mitt.* 3:145-151.

Hinde, R. A. 1970. *Animal Behavior*, 2nd ed. New York: McGraw-Hill.

Hogan-Warburg, A. J. 1966. Social behavior of the ruff, *Philomachus pugnax* (L.). *Ardea* 54:109-229.

Höhn, E. O. 1970. Gonadal hormone concentration in northern phalaropes in relation to nuptial plumage. *Can. J. Zool.* 48:400-401.

Howard, J. W. 1974. Dominance and relation to coloration in green sunfish, *Lepomis cyanellus. Behav. Biol.* 12: 559-565.

Huxley, J. S. 1914. The courtship habits of the great crested grebe (*Podiceps cristatus*); with an addition to the theory of sexual selection. *Proc. Zool. Soc.* (Lond.): 491-562.

Immelman, K. 1959. Experimentelle Untersuchungen über die biologische Bedeutung artspezifischer Merkmale beim Zebrafinken (*Taeniopygia castanotis* Gould). *Zool. Jahrb. Abt. System.* 86:438-592.

Immelmann, K. 1972. The influence of early experience upon the development of social behavior in estrildine finches. *Proc. XV Int. Ornithol. Congress* (The Hague). 1970. pp. 291-313.

Jacobs, M. E. 1955. Studies on territorialism and sexual selection in dragonflies. *Ecology* 36:566-586.

Johnston, R. E. 1976. The role of dark chest patches and upright postures in the agonistic behavior of male hamsters, *Mesocricetus auratus. Behav. Biol.* 17:161-176.

Keenleyside, M. 1955. Some aspects of the schooling behavior of fish. *Behavior* 8:183-248.

Keenleyside, M. 1970. Aggressive behavior of male longear sunfish (*Lepomis megalotis*). *Z. Tierpsychol.* 28:227-240.

Klint, T. 1973. On the "sexual releaser" function of the male nuptial coloration of the mallard. *Zool. Rev.* 35 (1):11-21.

Kop, P., and Heuts, B. 1973. An experiment on sibling imprinting in the jewel fish, *Hemichromis bimaculatus* (Gill 1862, Cichlidae). *Rev. Comp. Animal* 7:63-76.

Lack, D. 1943. *The Life of the Robin.* London: Witherby.

Leong, C.-Y. 1969. The quantitative effect of releasers on the attack readiness of the fish *Haplochromis burtoni* (Pisces: Cichlidae). *Z. Vergl. Physiol.* 65:29-50.

Lloyd, J. E. 1971. Bioluminescent communication in insects. *Ann. Rev. Entomol.* 16:97-122.

Lorenz, K. 1941. Vergleichende Bewegungsstudien an Anatiden. *J. Ornithol.* 89:19-29.

Lorenz, K. 1962. The function of color in coral reef fishes. *Proc. Royal Inst. Gr. Br.* 39:282-296.

McCosker, J. E. 1977. Flashlight fishes. *Sci. Amer.* 236(3): 106-114.

McInerney, J. 1969. Reproductive behavior of the blackspotted stickleback, *Gasteristeus wheatlandi*. *J. Fish. Res. Bd. Canada* 26:2061-2075.

McPhail, J. D. 1969. Predation and the evolution of a stickleback (*Gasterosteus*). *J. Fish. Res. Bd. Canada* 26:3183-3208.

Miller, D., and Emlen, J. T., Jr. 1975. Individual chick recognition and family integrity in ring-billed gull. *Behaviour* 52:124-144.

Moodie, G. E. E. 1972. Predation, natural selection and adaptation in an unusual three-spined stickleback. *Heredity* 28:155-167.

Morris, D. 1958. The reproductive behavior of the ten-spined stickleback (*Pygosteus pungitius*). *Behaviour Suppl.* 6.

Myrberg, A. 1965. A descriptive analysis of the behavior of the African cichlid *Pelmatochromis guenteri* (Sauvage). *Anim. Behav.* 13:312-329.

Neil, E. H. 1964. An analysis of color changes and social behavior of *Tilapia mossambica*. *Univ. Cal. Publ. Zool.* (Berkeley) 75:1-58.

Nicolai, J. 1965. Der Brutparasitismus des Witwenvögel. *Naturwiss. Med.* 2:3-15.

Noakes, D., and Barlow, G. 1973. Cross-fostering and parent-offspring responses in *Cichlasoma labiatum* (Pisces: Cichlidae). *Z. Tierpsychol.* 33:147-152.

Noble, G. 1936. Courtship and sexual selection of the flicker (*Colaptes aurates luteus*). *Auk* 52:269-282.

Noble, G. K., and Bradley, H. T. 1933. The mating behavior of lizards: its bearing on the theory of sexual selection. *Ann. N.Y. Acad. Sci.* 35:25-100.

Noble, G. K., and Curtis, B. 1939. The social behavior of the jewel fish. *Hemichromis bimaculatis* Gill. *Bull. Amer. Mus. Nat. Hist.* 76:1-46.

Oehlert, B. 1958. Kampf und paarbildung bei einigen Cichliden. *Z. Tierpsychol.* 15:141-174.

Payne, R. 1976. At home with right whales. *Nat. Geog. Mag.* 149:322-339.

Peden, A. E. 1973. Variation in anal spot expression of Gambusiin females and its effect on male courtship. *Copeia* 1973:250-263.

Picciolo, A. R. 1964. Sexual and nest discrimination in anabantid fishes of the genera *Colisa* and *Trichogaster*. *Ecol. Monogr.* 34:52-77.

Potts, G. 1973. The ethology of *Labroides dimidiatus* on Aldabra. *Anim. Behav.* 21:250-291.

Reisman, H. 1963. Reproductive behavior of *Apeltes quadracus*, including some comparisons with other gasterosteid fishes. *Copeia* 1963:191-192.

Reisman, H. 1968. Effects of social stimuli on the secondary sex characteristics of male three-spined sticklebacks, *Gasterosteus aculeatus*. *Copeia* 1968:816-826.

Rowland, W. J. 1970. Behavior of three sympatric species of sticklebacks and its role in their reproductive isolation. Ph.D. thesis, State Univ. N.Y., Stony Brook.

Rowland, W. J. 1974. Reproductive behavior of the fourspine stickleback, *Apeltes quadracus*. *Copeia* 1974:183-194.

Rowland, W. J. 1975. The effects of dummy size and color on behavioral interactions in the jewel cichlid, *Hemichromis bimaculatis* Gill. *Behaviour* 52:109-125.

Rowland, W. J., and Rowlands, R. D. 1978. Flank patch pigmentation and behavior of the jewel fish, *Hemichromis bimaculatis*. *Behav. Biol.* (in press).

Schaller, G. 1963. *The Mountain Gorilla: Ecology and Behavior*. Chicago: Univ. Chicago Press.

Schaller, F., and Schwalb, H. 1961. Attrapenversuche mit Larven und Imagines einheimischer Leuchtkafer. *Zool. Anz. Suppl.* 24:154-166.

Seitz, A. 1943. Die Paarbildung bei einigen Cichliden. I. Die Paarbildung bei *Hemichromis bimaculatus* Gill. *Z. Tierpsychol.* 5:74-101.

Seliger, H. H., and McElroy, W. D. 1964. Enzyme structure and conformation in bioluminescence. *Proc. Nat. Acad. Sci.* 52:75-81.

Selous, E. 1907. Observations tending to throw light on the question of sexual selection in birds, including a day-to-day diary on the breeding habits of the ruff (*Machetes pugnax*). *Zoologist* 4:10.

Semler, D. E. 1971. Some aspects of adaptation in a polymorphism for breeding colors in the three-spined stickleback (*Gasterosteus aculeatus* L.). *J. Zool.* (Lond.) 165: 291-302.

Shillito, E., and Alexander, G. 1975. Mutual recognition amongst ewes and lambs in four breeds of sheep (*Ovis aries*). *Appl. Anim. Ethol.* 1:151-165.

Sjölander, S., and Fernö, A. 1973. Sexual imprinting on another species in a cichlid fish, *Haplochromis burtoni*. *Rev. Comp. Animal* 7:77-81.

Smith, D. G. 1972. The role of the epaulets in the red-winged blackbird (*Agelaius phoeniceus*) social system. *Behaviour* 41:251-268.

Smith, N. G. 1967. Visual isolation in gulls. *Sci. Amer.* 217(4):94-102.

Stride, G. O. 1958. Further studies on the courtship of African mimetic butterflies. *Anim. Behav.* 6:224-230.

Thorpe, W. H. 1974. *Animal Nature and Human Nature*. London: Methuen.

Thresher, R. 1977. Eye ornamentation of Caribbean reef fishes. *Z. Tierpsychol.* 43:152-158.

Tinbergen, N. 1939. Zur Fortpflanzungesethologie von *Sepia officinalis* L. *Arch. neerl. Zool.* 3:323-364.

Tinbergen, N. 1951. *The Study of Instinct*. Oxford: Clarendon Press.

Tinbergen, N.; Meeuse, B.; Boerema, L.; and Varossieau, W. 1942. Die Balz des Samtfalters, *Eumenis semele*(L.). *Z. Tierpsychol.* 5:182-226.

Tinbergen, N., and Perdeck, A. C. 1950. On the stimulus situation releasing the begging response in newly hatched herring gull chicks (*Larus a. argentatus*). *Behavior* 3: 1-38.

Trillmich, F. 1976. Learning experiments on individual recognition in budgerigars (*Melopsittacus undulatus*). *Z. Tierpsychol.* 41:372-395.

Tschanz, B. 1968. Trottellumenen: Die Entstehung der personlichen Beziehungen zwischen Jungvogel und Eltern. *Z. Tierpsychol.* Suppl. 4.

Vevers, H. G. 1964. Adornment by colour in man and other animals. In *Colour and Life*, W. B. Broughton (ed.). London: Symposium Inst. Bio. 12.

von Frisch, K. 1974. *Animal Architecture*. New York: Harcourt Brace.

Weidmann, U. 1961. The stimuli eliciting begging in gulls and terns. *Anim. Behav.* 9:115-116.

Welty, J. C. 1975. *The Life of Birds*, 2nd ed. Philadelphia: Saunders.

Wickler, W. 1962. Ei-Attrappen und Maulbruten bei afrikanischen Cichliden. *Z. Tierpsychol.* 19:129-164.

Wickler, W. 1967. Socio-sexual signals and their intraspecific imitation among primates. In *Primate Ethology*, D. Morris (ed.). Chicago: Aldine.

Wickler, W. 1968. *Mimicry in Plants and Animals*. New York, Toronto: McGraw-Hill.

Wilson, E. O. 1975. *Sociobiology: The New Synthesis*. Cambridge: Harvard Univ. Press.

Wootton, R. J. 1976. *The Biology of Sticklebacks*. London: Academic Press.

Wunder, W. 1930. Experimentell Untersuchungen am dreistachligen Stichlinge (*Gasterosteus aculeatus* L.) wahrend der Laichzeit. *Z. Morph. und Okol. Tiere* 16:453-498.

Visual Functions of Color: The Predictive Approach: Discussion

C. Richard Tracy

In the three chapters by Jack Hailman, Jeff Baylis, and Bill Rowland, we see an interesting blend of philosophical approaches to the topic of optical communication. Bill presented a comparative survey of intraspecific displays in which numerous known examples of color markings for display were simply lumped into groups often on the basis of function of the display. Jack, on the other hand (maverick that he is), attempted to predict the characteristics of display signals based on his own "principles of conspicuousness." In other words, he used something akin to the "evolutiono-engineering approach," which I described earlier (see discussion following Chapter 3), to deductively reason the directions of evolution by natural selection, and predict the actual displays of animals displaying in different environments. Clearly, this approach yields new insights into the selective mechanisms involved in the evolution of displays.

Jack's approach contains a hidden bias which becomes more apparent in light of Jeff's talk. Jeff reviewed the differences in inter- and intra-specific communication, and it became immediately apparent that an intraspecific display is an adaptation involving both the sender and receiver of the signal. Thus, in environments in which it is costly to send a signal, natural selection could simultaneously prevent the evolution of very conspicuous displays, and also select for individuals with the capacity to receive, and discern subtle displays. The latter are adaptations to reduce what Jack calls "detection noise" (noise that occurs when the receiver cannot distinguish signals from optical background). Therefore, Jack's "principles of conspicuousness" really emphasize the attributes of the sender, but tacitly assume a particular kind of receiver. For example, Jack said, "We know that movement is important in a signal, and now we need to know what attributes of movement are especially conspicuous." This statement has a built-in bias stemming from what is known about the receiver of the signals. The statement actually says, "Given what I know about a particular receiver (which may be a particular group of animals--such as birds), what signal would I send to it?"

An understanding of this bias actually allows us to gain even more information from the philosophical approach Jack has taken. The principles are apparently constructed with a bias from previous knowledge of the abilities of the receiving individuals (e.g., birds). If these "principles" (hypotheses) are tested on a group of animals (e.g., lizards or beetles), one could learn more about the similarities and differences between the evolutionary design of signal receivers. In other words, the approach taken by Jack has enormous potential for creative investigation of the mechanisms underlying patterns of adaptation in displays or signals.

Audience Questions:
Discussion

Question: You have cited examples of complex and intricate color patterns in a variety of animals, yet the experiments fail to address the function of specific patterns of color. Have you a comment?

Baylis: Several of the experiments I cited address the question of function at the behavioral level--*viz*., communication. However, it is always risky to address *the* function of such patterns because there may be several. For example, suppose that the sight of a particular color pattern of one animal causes predictable changes in the behavior of another and that these changes benefit the former animal. We might predict that there will be selection pressures to maintain and perhaps even to further develop this color pattern. We would then conclude communication of the sort that I describe in my chapter to be a function of the pattern in question, but this does not rule out the possibility that there is also a noncommunicative function, such as discussed in Chapters 2 and 3.

At a more proximal level we know little about the function of such patterns. Ethologists would like to know how these color patterns function physiologically to elicit, orient, or inhibit the behavior of an animal. The more recent findings of neuroethology, neurophysiology, and psychology are beginning to hint at answers.

Question: A bewildering variety of color patterns are available to animals. Is it possible to predict that a particular part of the body will be covered with a particular color or pattern? I mean egg spots are unlikely to appear on the head. Can you state predictive hypotheses?

Rowland: Yes, I believe that predictions are possible. If we can assume a specific communicative function for a given visual pattern, then there are certain predictions one could make concerning the location of these patterns. This is perhaps easiest to do when the pattern plays a role in orientation to some part of the signaler's body, nest, etc. The location of egg spots on the anal fins of some mouthbrooding cichlid fishes that you refer to is quite predictable--the pattern must be near the male's genital papilla and yet on some surface where it is visible from the side. Similarly, concentration of brightly colored material around the entrance of the nest of bowerbirds and sticklebacks is predictable. Many such patterns will be highly localized because they serve as landmarks or targets for the viewer when at close range.

If the color pattern serves as advertisement, for whatever reason, then it must be bold, representing improbable combinations of color, shape, and arrangement that would hardly ever occur accidently in nature (see Chapter 7 or Hailman 1977a). This would increase conspicuousness and decrease ambiguity. Since such patterns might also attract visual predators, we could expect these patterns to occur somewhere on the body where they are normally inconspicuous or hidden. Therefore, such locations would allow the animal to go unnoticed except during social encounters, when the pattern is displayed.

The normal postures and body parts used in various social encounters also influence the location of color patterns. Patterns often occur on the head region if the animals adopt a position where they are facing each other in an encounter. When animals take up other positions during social encounters, we often find that color patterns are concentrated on parts of the body that are most visible to the partner during these encounters. This is especially so when a color pattern is associated with a species-typical movement pattern, e.g., the chelae of certain crustaceans and the tail plumes of the peacock (see Chapter 9 above).

Baylis: Yes, such predictions can be made. For example, markings that are used to coordinate group movements should be placed on appendages used for locomotion, or on the posterior or anterior extremes of the body, where they provide orientational cues. Examples are the caudal spots present on many species of schooling fishes (Keenleyside 1955, Cott 1957). Markings used for intraspecific social interactions will be placed on the head in most vertebrates, as the interacting individuals usually face each other in such encounters. Examples here would be the use of opercular tabs or brightly colored branchiostegal membranes exposed during aggressive encounters in cichlid fishes (Baerends and Baerends-van Roon 1950), or the common occurrence of accessory plumage or structures such as wattles on the heads of birds. Many further examples can be found in Hailman (1977a, 1977b). However, to predict with accuracy we must know (1) the function of the signal, and (2) the context in which it appears.

REFERENCES

Baerends, G. P., and Baerends-van Roon, J. M. 1950. An introduction to the study of the ethology of cichlid fishes. *Behaviour Suppl*. 1:1-243.

Cott, H. B. 1957. *Adaptive Coloration in Animals*. London: Methuen.

Hailman, J. P. 1977a. *Optical Signals: Animal Communication and Light*. Bloomington and London: Ind. Univ. Press.

Hailman, J. P. 1977b. Communication by reflected light. In *How Animals Communicate*, T. A. Sebeok (ed.). Bloomington and London: Ind. Univ. Press.

Keenleyside, M. H. A. 1955. Some aspects of the schooling behaviour of fish. *Behaviour* 8:183-248.

Chapter 10

Conclusion

Edward H. Burtt, Jr.

The many, diverse hypotheses discussed in the preceding chapters lead to the inevitable conclusion that no single hypothesis can explain the coloration of living things. Nonetheless, we need not conclude that coloration is whimsical nor that the many hypotheses are chaotically unrelated.

One group of hypotheses relate pigment distribution to physiological (e.g., hydroregulation, vitamin D synthesis) requirements of plants or animals (Chapters 2 and 3). These hypotheses depend on chemical and physical properties of pigments. Color is a by-product and an animal's pattern of color is interpreted not as an optical signal, but as the visible evidence of a physiological need (e.g., a dark dorsum for protection from ultraviolet radiation).

Another, better studied group of hypotheses deal with color and patterns of color as optical signals (Chapters 8 and 9). Predictions from these hypotheses depend on the particular characteristics (e.g., spectral sensitivity) of the photoreceptors (Chapters 4, 5, and 6) and on environmental variables (e.g., spectral quality of ambient illumination, transmission properties of air or water) that affect the appearance of an optical signal (Chapter 7).

A third group of hypotheses, which has received very little attention, relate to color as it affects the animal's own vision. Polyak (1957) suggested that lines through the eyes act as sighting lines. The hypothesis was stated more precisely by Ficken and Wilmot (1968), who offered supportive data from a comparative study of North American songbirds. Data from a comparative study of wood warblers (Burtt, in press) also support the hypothesis, but these are the only tests of an interesting hypothesis that awaits critical evaluation. Ficken et al. (1971) suggested that lightly colored eyerings increase the light-gathering potential of the eye. However, such light cannot be resolved into an image and therefore can only cause the eye to adapt to a higher level of illuminance than is appropriate to the visual field. The hypothesis seems unlikely and is refuted by data from warblers (Burtt, in press). Dark patches or stripes around, about, or across the eye may reduce reflectance that interferes with the animal's own vision (Ficken et al. 1971). Wood warblers with pale upper mandibles forage in shade whereas those with dark upper mandibles often forage in direct sunlight (Burtt, in press), a result that suggests the importance of dark coloration on a highly reflective surface near the eye. However, no other data address the hypothesis that coloration near the eye reduces reflectance that interferes with vision. Color as it affects the animal's own vision is a poorly explored subject.

The hypotheses advanced in the preceding chapters and reviewed above are predictive and capable of rigorous testing. No longer need we resort to fanciful, *post hoc* explanations that are incapable of generating predictions. Formulation of predictive hypotheses often suggests important variables that were formerly unrecognized. Statement of the hypothesis encourages us to deduce and test predictions and ultimately to evaluate the hypothesis in the light of our new knowledge. Hence predictive hypotheses of coloration must lead to careful measurement of important variables and to discovery of new relationships.

Most importantly, we must assume that every patch of color on every animal exists for a reason. That is evolution's prediction. Perhaps coloration is the result of pleiotropisms, or pharmacological effects (see discussion following Chapter 4), or chance, but such explanations are nonproductive and should serve only as a last resort.

We are far from a comprehensive theory that predicts the coloration and pattern of color of animals. Such a theory requires the integration of many hypotheses that may or may not predict the same color or pattern of color under the same circumstances. To create new hypotheses, to critically test their predictions, and to integrate diverse hypotheses will be no easy task, but those who seek a comprehensive answer to the coloration of animals can anticipate many exciting discoveries.

REFERENCES

Burtt, E. H., Jr. 1977. The coloration of wood warblers (Parulidae). *Nuttall Ornithol. Monogr.*: in press.

Ficken, R. W., and Wilmot, L. B. 1968. Do facial eye-stripes function in avian vision? *Amer . Midland Naturalist* 79:522-523.

Ficken, R. W.; Matthiae, P. E.; and Horwich, R. 1971. Eye marks in vertebrates: aids to vision. *Science* 173:936-939.

Polyak, S. L. 1957. The vertebrate visual system. H. Kluver (ed.). Chicago: Univ. Chicago Press.

Index

Abramov, I., 186, 198, 200, 219
Acanthodactylus erythrurus, 140
Acris crepitans, 56
Acris gryllus, 56, 158
Adkisson, P. L., 135
Adler, K., 142, 155, 158, 159
Adrian, 215
Ageliuas phoeniceus, 395
aggregations, mixed-species, 365, 372
agonistic behavior,
  interspecific, 365, 370-72
  intraspecific, 394-96
Aix galerrculata, 355
Aix sponsa, 355
alarm signals and reactions
  interspecific, 365-66
  intraspecific, 388, 390
alchornea, as primate food, 254, 255, 265
Alciedinidae, 22
Alcock, J., 370
Aleksuik, M., 39
Alexander, G., 400
Allee, C., 314
Allen, L. H., Jr., 99
Allman, J., 272
Alpern, M., 200
Altmann, J., 271
Altmann, S. A., 271
Alvarez, F., 390
Ambler, M., 211
Amblyornis, 409
  inornatus, 409
  macgregoriae, 409
  subalaris, 409
Ambystoma tigrinum, 158, 159
Amiurus nebulosus, 153
Ammophila brevigulata, radiance
  spectrum of, 332
amphibians
  metachrosis in, 44-45
  photoreception
    and circadian rhythm, 142
    and color change, physiological, 152-53
    and orientation, 157-59
    and phototaxis and photokinesis, 155, 156-57
    and pineal system, 138-40, 142, 152-53, 159
  polymorphism, color, 45-46, 55-56
  thermoregulation
    behavioral, 40-42
    color, hydroregulation and, 44-56
    compared to that of lizards, 63-68
  see also names, subjects
Amphibolurus barbatus, 38

Amphibolurus fordi, 38, 43-44
Anabantidae, 401
Anas platyrhynchos, 24
Anderson, K. V., 159
Angolasaurus skoogi, 40
Anhinga anhinga, 86
Anolis, 95, 391
  carolinensis, 147-49, 152, 391-92
  marmoratus, 40
Anser caerulescens, 389
Antheraea pernyi, 135
Apeltes guadracus, 405
Aphyosemion, 394
Apis mellifera, 295
Aporosaura anchietae, 39
Ariëns-Kappers, J., 139
Aristotle, 381
Armstrong, E., 385
Assenmacher, I., 144, 145
Atsatt, S. R., 43
Auber, L., 22
Autrum, H., 225, 226
Averill, C. K., 80

Bachman, J., 79-80
backgrounds, optical and conspicuous color, see conspicuousness of color, and backgrounds, optical
Badis badis, 405
Baerends, G. P., 384, 387, 389, 401, 406, 426
Baerends-van Roon, J. M., 384, 387, 401, 406, 426
Bagnara, J. T., 152, 153
Baker, H. G., 362
Baldaccini, N. E., 401, 402
Baldwin, J. D., 285
Baldwin, J. I., 285
Barlow, G., 388, 401, 405, 411
Barlow, G. W., 365, 371, 372
Barlow, H. B., 215
Bartlett, P. N., 42-43
Barow, 355-57
basking, 38-40, 41, 44
Bastock, M., 392
Batesian mimicry, 363-64, 369-70
Battersby, K. A., 410
Baylé, J. D., 147, 162
Baylis, Jeffrey R., 285, 348, 359-77, 422-26 +
Becker, H. E., 157
begging response, 389, 408
Bennet, M. H., 159
Bennett, C. F., Jr., 311
Benoit, J., 144, 145, 163
Bunsen-Roscoe Reciprocity Law, 155
Benson, S. B., 120
Bentley, P. J., 41-42
Berends, W., 116
Bergmann, G., 140
Bernstein, J. J., 224
Beukers, R., 116
Bezold, W. von, 188
Binkley, S., 150
biochemical rhythms, photoreception, pineal system and, 149-51
biochromes, functions of, 292-93
biological clock, see circadian rhythms
bioluminescence, 25-26, 383
  and signaling systems, 385
    and sex recognition, 396-97
birds
  aggregations, mixed-species, 365, 372
  agonistic behavior, intrasexual, 394-95
  alarm reactions, 365-66
  begging response, 389, 408
  bower building, 408-09
  color preferences, and imprinting, 388-89
  conspicuousness of color relative to optical environment, 323, 345, 346-48

detection of models and mimics by, 370
feather abrasion resistance, 77-93, 111-12, 122
see also feathers
and flower pollination, 369
egg recognition, 389
individual recognition, 398-99
localization signals, 408
nest building, 408
nestling recognition, 389, 398
parent recognition, 399
photoreception
and biochemical rhythm, 150-51
and circadian rhythms, 142-44, 150-51
and color change, physiological, 152
and photoperiodism, 144-47
and phototaxis and photokinesis, 155-56
and pineal system, 140-47, 150-51
sexual activity
color preferences, 389
individual recognition, 399
sex recognition, 392, 397
and territoriality, 364-65
species recognition, 388-89
territorality, 364-65, 371
ultraviolet radiation and, 115
feathers and scales and, 96-106 +
leg color and, 97-106
mandible color and, 99-101, 103-06
vision, 226
see also names

blackbodies, 14-15, 16
Blattidae, 130
Blest, A. D., xiii, 363, 369
Blough, D. S., 222, 225
Blum, H. F., 93, 94, 115, 116
Bogert, C. M., 39, 57
Boll, F., 197
Bollum, F. J., 94
Boring, E. G., 191
Bowers, D. E., 80, 107
Boynton, R. M., 186, 187, 191, 195, 224
Bradford, D. F., 38, 41
Bradley, 191
Bradley, H. T., 394
Brain, C. K., 39
brain and vision
color vision, 189, 220-21
pineal system, see pineal system and photosensitivity
Brattstrom, B. H., 38, 39, 40, 41, 65
Braza, F., 390
Bridges, C. D., 198
Brockmann, H. J., 366
Brockmann, H. J., 387
Brouwer, R., 401
Brower, J. VA., 364, 370
Brower, L. P., 364, 370
Browman, L. G., 159
Brown, A. G., 40
Brown, J. L., 221, 371
Bruce, V. G., 132
Brush, A. H., 79, 98
Bruss, R. T., 159
Buceros bicornis, 382-83
Buchholtz, C., 396
Buckley, F. G., 398
Buckley, P. A., 398
budgerigars, 395, 399
Bufo boreus, 41
Bufo mauritanicus, 41
Burkhardt, D., 226
Burnham, R. W., 186, 188
Burtt, E. H., Jr., xiii, 75-

116, 121, 122, 272, 295-306+,323, 324, 341, 349-56+,427-31
butterflies
Batesian mimicry in, 364
ultraviolet light used in mate attraction by, 386
Byzov, A. L., 225

Calamospiza melanocorys, 346
Caldwell, M. M., 93
Calidris, 345
Calkins, J., 94, 115
Callicebus torquatus, field study of foods of
documentation, photographic, 243
food sources
appearance and reflectance spectra, 255-65
coevolution evidence, 246-55
fruit size, 268
major, characteristics of, 246-47
reflectance spectra grouped by color, 265-68
foraging behavior
and color vision, 269-73
and plant adaptations, 268-69
methods
group and locale, 241-42
plant specimens, 242-43
reflectance measurements, 243-46
Calopteryx splendens, 396
Campbell, F. W., 200
Cardinali, D. P., 160
Cardiosis, 69
carotenoids, 24, 98
in photopigments, circadian rhythm and, 132-33
Carpenter, C., 405
Carpodacus mexicanus, 96
Carrick, R., 398
Carrier, W. G., 116
Case, T. J., 38
Catharus, 345
Cavonius, C. R., 255
Cebus, 239, 280
capucinus, 269
Centrarchidae, 401
Cercopithecus aethiops, 269
Certhis familiaris, 345
Chaetodontidae, 401
Chan, R., 214
Chamnea fasciata, 80
Charadrius, 345
Chauliognathus pennsylvanicus, 368
Chelgren, P., 41
Chichester, C. O., 270
Chichlasoma, 387
citrinellum, 411
chlorolabe, 200, 202
chlorophylls, 24
chromophores, 198-200, 202, 382
Cichlidae, 401
Cinat-Thomson, H., 395
circadian rhythms, 129-30
of insects
extraretinal photoreception and, 130-34, 138
and photoperiodism, 135
photopigments and, 132-33
of vertebrates
biochemical, 149-51
and photopigments, 159-61
photoreception, pineal system, and, 138, 142-44, 149-51, 159-61
Claret, J., 135
Clarisia, as primate food, 254, 255
Clarke, C. A., 370
Claussen, D. L., 46
cleaning symbiosis, 366
Cloudsley-Thompson, J. L. 41
Cody, M. L., 364, 371, 372
coevolution of primates and their foods, 246-55

foraging behavior and color vision, 269-72
Cogger, H. G., 38, 39, 43-44
Colaptes auratus, 80, 392
Cole, L. C., 39, 42, 95
Coleonux variegatus, 95
Colisa, 404-05
lalia, 405
Collette, B., 95, 115
Collins, C. T., 364, 370
color(s)
blindness, 189, 195
of animals, 221
brightness, 383, 384-85
coevolution of colored fruit and color vision, 246-55, 269-72
conspicuous, see conspicuousness of color
definition of, 186-88
and emissivity, 16
fundamental or unitary, 190-92
hue, 383-84
interference and, 23-24
iridescence, 23-24, 382
measurement of
colorimetry, 296, 297
photometry, 18-21, 296-97
radiometry, 17-18, 295-96
monochromatic, 190
Munsell system of determination, 77-78
perceived, 6-7, 8, 73-74, 186-88, 190, 296-97
see also vision, color
saturation, 383, 384
scattering and, 22-24
spectrum, 7, 189-90
transmittance in water, 24
vision, see vision
see also coloration; light; pigments/pigmentation; specific subjects
coloration, 381, 429-30
aposematic or warning, 363, 367-69, 381
prediction of color and pattern, 368-69
change, physiological
and chromatophores, 382
and extraretinal phororeception, 151-53, 180-81
for localization and/or orientation, 405, 406
and motivational state, 400-05
ontogenetic, 44
and communication, see communication, interspecific; communication intraspecific
conspicuous, see conspicuousness of color
crypticity, 56, 57, 72-73
deceptive, 363-64
development through sexual selection, 381
mechanisms for attaining adornment, 382-83
bioluminescence, 25-26, 383
chromatophores and color change, 382
pigmentation, 24-25
reflection, 382
metachrosis
in amphibians, 44-45
in reptiles, 43-44, 57
patterning
evolutiono-engineering approach to, 111-13
and information encoding, 385
polymorphism in amphibians, 45-46, 55-56, 70-73
significance and implications of, 37, 185-86, 226-27
structural color, 382
and ultraviolet radiation protection, 96-106 +

see also ultraviolet radiation
see also color; specific species, subjects
"colorimetric cube," 349-52
colormetry, 296, 297
Columba livia, 155, 296, 356
Columbformes, 24
communication, interspecific, and optical signals
agnostic behavior, 365, 370-72
aggregations, mixed-species, 365, 372
alarm reactions, 365-66
aposematic or warning coloration, 363, 367-68
bilateral, 364
competitive, 364, 370-72
cooperative, 365-66, 372-73
cleaning symbiosis, 366, 372-73
deceptive color, 363
definitions, 361
deflective markings, 363
evolutionary origins, 366-67
and intraspecific communication, 374
mimicry
Batesian, 363-64
Müllerian, 368, 369-70
predictive approach to, 422-23
"reciprocal altruism" model, 373
releasers defined, 361
sign stimuli defined, 361
social releasers, 361
"startle" displays, 363, 369
territorial signals, 364-65, 371-72
unilateral, 362
correct, 362, 367-69
incorrect, 363-64, 369-70
communication, intraspecific, and color use in
artifacts, use of, 409-10
behavioral effect of signals on receiver, 410-11
bioluminescence and signaling, 385
and sex recognition, 396-97
context specificity, 386
definition of intraspecific communication, 385
individual recognition, 397-98
mate recognition, 398, 399
young, recognition of, 398-99
information encoding, 383-85
and brightness, 384-85
and hue, 383-84
by patterning, spatial and/or temporal, 385
and saturation, 384
interaction with structure and movement, 385-86
localization and/or orientation signals, 405-08
motivational state and color change, 400-05
purposes of, 386-87
predictive approach to, 422-23, 425-26
sex recognition, 390-92
and agnostic behavior, intrasexual, 394-96
mate recognition, 398, 399
and courtship and mating, 290-92, 296-97
of female maturity and readiness, 396-97
sexual activity and, 384
signals physically detached from their sender, 408-10

species recognition
and alarm behavior, 388
begging response, 389
egg recognition, 389
and color preferences, 388-89
in monomorphic species, 387-90
nestling recognition, 389, 398-99
and rump patches of ungulates, 389-90
and sex recognition, 390-97
social contact and "imprinting," 387-88
ultraviolet light, 386
Cone, R. A., 157
cone receptors, see eye, cones
conspicuousness of color, 291
and backgrounds, optical, 300
achromatic, 341
blue, 341-42
brown-green complex, 342-45
classification of backgrounds, 300-01
implications for animal coloration, 345-46
of marshes, bushes, and oldfield, 333-36
measurement of, and habitats, 324-26
orange, 342
of Southeastern habitats, 326-41
of sky, water, sand and dune vegetation, 326-32
of woodland leaves, trunks, and litter, 337-41
determination of conspicuousness, 356-57
investigation strategy, 291
and backgrounds, 300-01
and biochrome functions, 292-93
and environmental factors, 298-301
light availability, 298-300
and principles of conspicuousness, 293-95
and radiometry, 295
and schemochrome functions, 292-93
and transmission characteristics of medium, 301
and variables, physical and perceptual, 295-97
and light availability, 298-300, 321-22
and altitude, 316-18, 321
habitats studied, 302
height within forest and, 314-16, 22
implications for animal coloration, 323-24
measurement methods for irradiance, 302-03
in ponderosa pine forest, 316-21, 322, 323
simulation of vertical ambient spectrum, 311, 318, 321
in Southeastern pine subclimax and ecotone, 303-10
times-of-day and forest irradiance, 318-21
in tropical rain forest, 311-16
and phylogenetic history, 355-56
principles of, 293-94
problems remaining
conceptual, 349-52
ecological, 346-49
and prospects for future,

352-53
transmission characteristics of medium, 301
see also color; coloration
Cooke, F., 389
Cornsweet, T. N., 189, 191, 193, 197
Cott, H. B., xiii, 114, 241, 257, 371, 426
Coturnix Coturnix japonica, 147
Cowles, R. B., 39, 57
Crane, J., 394
Crews, D., 391
Cronley-Dillon, J. R., 222, 390
Crotaphytus collaris, 140
crypticity, color, 56, 57, 72-73
Cuculus canorus, 389
Cullen, E., xiii
Curtis, B., 384, 387, 391, 398
Cyanocitta cristata, 347
Cyanocitta stelleri, 347
cyanolabe, 202
Cyprinidae, 207-09

Dama dama, 390
Danius plexippus, 364
Dartnall, H. J., 185
Darwin, 366, 381
Davies, S., 398
Daw, N., 197, 209-17 +
deflective markings, 363
de la Motte, I., 154, 156
Dendroica caerulescens, 348
Dendroica cerulea, 347
desiccation, color and, 46-56, 71-72
De Valois, K. K., 209, 217, 219, 221
DeValois, R. L., 209, 215-26,+239, 255, 271-72, 273
De Witt, C. B., 38
diffraction, 14
Dilger, W. C., 356
Dipsosaurus dorsalis, 38, 95, 121
Dodson, C. H., 362, 363, 369
Dodt, E., 139, 140
Dowling, J. E., 202, 214
Drees, O., 394
Drent, R., 389
Drosophila, 131-33
melanogaster, 131, 132
pseudoobscura, 131, 132
Dumortier, B., 130
Dunn, J., 160
duplexity theory of vision, 193, 210
Duroia, as primate food, 247, 255, 261, 267
Durrell, L. W., 254
Dwight, J., Jr., 79, 82, 122

Eaton, R. L., 363
Edgren, R. A., 44, 45
Edmunds, M., 241, 257
Eibl-Eibesfeldt, I., 389
Eichler, V. B., 150
electromagnetic radiation
and blackbodies, 14-15, 16
emissivity, 15-16
geometrical optics, 8-14
mathematical description of, 7
measurement of
Inverse Square Law, 16
photometry, 18-21
radiometry, 17-18
quantum, 7
sources, 14-16
wave/particle characteristics of, 5-7
see also light; solar radiation; ultraviolet radiation
Elliott, D. G., 382-83
Emlen, J. T., Jr., 398
emissivity, 15-16
solar absorptivity, thermal emmissivity, and morphological adaptations, 28-32

Engbretson, G. A., 140
Engelmann, W., 131
Ephippiger, 130
Epinephelus striatus, 154
Eriksson, L. O., 142
Erithacus rubecula, 388
erythrolabe, 200, 202
Esau, K., 254
Escherichia coli, 94, 95, 114, 115
Eubalaena australis, 400
Eumeces gilberti, 95
Eumeces obsoletus, 44
Eumenis semele, 396
Evans, R. M., 268, 272
Evans, V., 394
Ewing, A. W., 394
eyes
  amacrine cells, 204, 220
    response potentials, 214
  bipolar cells, 204, 220
    response potentials, 214
  compound, 130-34, 162
  cones, 191, 193, 202-04, 220
    and color vision, 191, 210-11
    pigments, 198, 200-02
    response potentials, 207-10
  ganglion cells, 204, 220-21
    response potentials, 215-19
  horizontal cells, 204, 211, 220
    response potentials, 211-14
  lateral, 142 ff., 162-63
  Müller cells, 204
  parietal, 139-40, 149, 163-64
  retina, vertebrate, 190, 192
    electrical recording from, 205-20
    pigment absorption spectra and, 193-97
    structure of, 202-04
    see also eye, cones; eye, rods; specific subjects
  rods, 193, 202-04, 220
    and color vision, 210-11
    pigments, 193-95, 198, 220
    response potentials, 207-10
    rhodopsin absorption spectra, 193-95
  see also photoreception, extraretinal; photoreception, retinal; vision

Falco peregrinus, 80
Farmer, D. S., 147
Farr, J. A., 391
Farrell, M. P., 46, 50
Fasso, F., 84
feathers
  abrasion, 79-80
    by airborne particles, 84-93, 122
    distribution observed of resistant color, 87-93
    experiment with warbler feathers, 80-84
    melanin, and resistance to, 79, 80, 83, 84, 93, 112
    topography of resistant coloration, 84-87
  color determination for warbler study, 77-79
  ultraviolet radiation protection and, 96-106+
Ferguson, D. E., 157, 158
Ferno, A., 388
Feynmann, R. P., 26
Ficken, R. W., 429
Fischer, E., 397
fish
  agonistic behavior, in, 371
    sex recognition, 394
  alarm signaling, 388

bioluminescence in, 25-26, 383
cleaning symbiosis, 366, 372-73
color changes
for localization and/or orientation, 405, 406
and motivational state, 400-05
photoreception and, 154-55, 156-57
conspicuous color, 355-56
groupings, mixed-species, 365, 372
individual recognition by, 398
localization and/or orientation signals, 405-06
photoreception
color change, physiological, and, 152, 153
and phototaxis and photokinesis, 154-55, 156-57
and pineal system, 138-40, 142, 154-55
and sexual activity, 149
sexual activity
and color saturation, 184
mate recognition, 398
photoreception and, 149
sex recognition, 390-92, 394
social contact and "imprinting," 387-88
species recognition, 387, 390, 291
and ultraviolet radiation, 95
vision, 207, 226
receptor response potentials, 207-10, 215-19
see also names
Fitch, H. S., 44
flowers
"honey guides," 226
mimicry, 363
pollination, and plant/animal communication, 369
focal points, 12-13
Ford, K. W., 26
forests, irradiance in, and conspicuous color
ponderosa pine forest, 316-21, 322, 323
Southeastern pine subclimax and ecotone, 303-10
tropical rain forest, 311-16
see also conspicuousness of color
Forselius, S., 401
Fox, H. M., 24
Fricke, H., 387
frogs
metachrosis in, 44-45
photoreception
and orientation, 158-59
and pineal system, 139
polymorphism, color, in, 45-46, 55-56, 70-73
thermoregulation, 63-68
behavioral, 40-42
color, hydroregulation, and, 44-56
see also amphibians; names, specific subjects
fruits, as primate foods
coevolution evidence, 246-55
plant adaptations, and foraging behavior, 268-69
reflectance spectra
grouped by color, 265-68
and visual appearance, 255-65
size, importance of, 268
Fujimoto, K., 200
Fuortes, M. G., 209, 212
Furukawa, T., 207

Gallus, 146
Gambusia, 405-06
Gardiner, M. S., 22, 24, 26

Gartlan, J. S., 269
Gasterosteus aculeatus, 384, 386, 390-91, 408
Gasterosteus wheatlandi, 390
Gaston, S., 142
Gates, D. M., 28, 29, 42-43
Gaulin, S. J. C., 268
Gavarretia, as primate food, 254, 261
geometrical optics, 8
  diffraction, 14
  focusing, 12-13
  reflection, 9
  refraction, 9-11
Gern, William, 180
Gilbert, L. E., 241
Gilliard, E. T., 408
Gillis, J. E., 42, 56
Glander, K. E., 268
Goldsmith, T. H., 132, 133
Goodwin, T. W., 270
Gordon, J., 198, 200
Gorilla gorilla beringei, 409
Gorsuch, Clyde, 364
Gouras, P., 211, 212, 215
Graham, C. H., 193, 198, 204
Granit, R., 192, 207, 215
Grant, E. C., 395
Green, A. E. S., 99
Greenberg, B., 391
groupings, mixed-species, 365, 372
Gruber, Samuel H., 183, 236
Grubits, G., 405
Gryllidae, 130
Guiraca caerulea, 346
Guthrie, R. D., 390, 395, 410
Gwinner, E. G., 147

Haas, R., 384, 391
Hadley, M. E., 152, 153, 181
Hadley, W. F., 403
Hailman, Jack P., xiii, 106, 289-357, 361-71, 422-26+
Halberg, F., 159
Halle, N., 247
Hamaski, D. E., 139, 140, 225
Hamilton, W. D., 365, 372, 401, 409
Hamilton, William J., III, 40, 69, 112-22+,282-84, 355, 356
Hanaoka, T., 200
Hanawa, I., 207
Hanawalt, P. D., 95, 116
Haplochromis burtoni, 355-56, 401, 411
Harm, W., 94
Harrington, H. D., 254
Harrison, P. C., 147
Harth, M. S., 154
Hartline, H. K., 214, 226
Haynes, R. H., 116
Hazlett, B., 394
Heaton, M. B., 155
Hecht, S., 270
Heerd, E., 139, 140
Heinroth, K., 80
Heinroth, O., 80
Helmholtz, H. von, 191, 192, 205, 212
Heltne, P. G., 274
Hemichromis, 384, 387, 391
  bimaculatus, 388, 398, 404, 406
Henderson, S. T., 272
Hendley, C. D., 270
Hering, E., 192, 212
Hering (opponent-mechanism) theory of vision, 192, 211-12, 217
Herter, K., 226
Hess, E., 388
Hess, J. B., 45
Heuts, B., 388
Heward, C. B., 181
Hill, W. C., 395
Hilz, R., 255
Hinde, R. A., 410
Hirundo rustica, 346
Hladik, A., 268, 269

Hladik, C. M., 267, 268, 273
Hogan-Warburg, A. J., 399
Höhn, E. O., 397
Holmgren, F., 207
Homma, F., 147, 163
Honegger, H. W., 131
Hooper, E. T., 120
Hoppe, David M., 35-62, 70-74
Howard, J. W., 401
Huey, R. B., 40
Hunt, J. M., 159
Hunter, R. S., 244
Hurvich, L. M., 185, 191, 192
Hutchinson, V. H., 43
Huxley, J. S., 409
Hyalophora cecropia, 134
hydroregulation and thermoregulation
  behavioral, 41-42
  color and, 46-56, 71-72
  see also thermoregulation
Hyla labialis, 41
Hyla regilla, 55-56
Hyla versicolor, 45
Hylocichla, 345
Hypolimnas misippus, 396

Ichthyophis glutinosus, 155
icterids, 345
Icterus, 323
  galbula, 323
  spurius, 323
Iguana iguana, 139, 140
Ilex opaca
  radiance spectrum of, 340-41
Immelmann, K., 388-89
infrared radiation of biological tissue, 16
insects
  aposematic, 369
  bioluminescence in, 383
  color vision, 225-26
  mimicry, 363-64
  photoreception, extraretinal
    and clock entrainment, 130-34, 138, 164-65
    location of receptors, 133-38+,164-65
    and oclosion rhythm, 130-34
    and photoperiodism, 134-38, 164-65
    and photopigments, 132-33, 164
  sex recognition by, 394, 396
  thermoregulation, behavioral, of, 69
  and ultraviolet radiation, 121
    sensitivity to and "honey guides," 226
  see also names
interference, of light waves, 23, 24
Inverse-Square Law of radiation, 16-17
irridescence
  interference and, 23-24
  reflection and, 382
iridophores, 382
irradiance, spectral, and coloration, 295-96, 301-03
  environmental factors affecting, 298-300
  see also conspicuousness of color
Iryanthera, as primate food, 247, 255, 261
Ives, D., 131, 133

Jacobs, G. H., 215, 226, 239, 271-72
Jacobs, J. H., 197, 210, 211, 214, 226
Jacobs, M. E., 394
Jacobson, M., 139, 140
Jaeger, Robert S., 303
Jameson, D., 185, 191, 192, 273

Jameson, D. L., 56
Janzen, D. H., 242, 254, 269
Jessenia, as primate food, 255, 267
Johnsgard, P. A., 356
Johnson, C. R., 39-40
Johnston, R. E., 395
Jordan, H., 154
Justis, C. S., 158

Kaneko, A., 211, 212, 214
Kashkarov, D., 39
Keatts, H., 145
Keenleyside, M., 403-04, 406, 426
Kelly, D. E., 139
Kickleiter, E., 224
Kinzey, Warren G., 241, 242, 246, 267
Klauber, L. M., 95
Kleczkowski, A., 94
Klein, D. C., 160
Klein, D. J., 269
Klein, L. L., 269
Kleinholz, L. H., 152
Klint, T., 392
Klopfer, P. H., 370
Knight, J., 139, 141, 149
Konner, M., 268
Kop, P., 388
Kubitschek, H. E., 94
Kuffler, S. W., 215
Kühn, A., 222
Kühne, W., 197-98
Kummer, H., 271
Kurbatov, V., 39

Labroides dimidiatus, 373
Lacerta, 410
  sicula, 139-40
  viridis, 394
Lack, D., 388
Lagothrix, 239
Lampetra fluviatilis, 154
Lampetra planeri, 153-54
Lampyridae, 385, 396
Lampyris, 396-97
Landreth, H. F., 157
Lang, G. E., 280
Larimer, J. L., 43, 129
Larus, 383
  argentatus, 389
Lasiewski, R. C., xiii
Lauber, J. K., 147, 150
Laufer, M., 212
Lavin, E. P., 244
Lees, A. D., 137
Le Grand, Y., 186-87
Lent, C. M., 140
Leong, C. Y., 401
Lepomis megalotis, 403-04
Lepore, F., 271
Lerwill, C. J., 395
Licht, P., 40, 41
Lickey, M. E., 129
Liebman, P. A., 202
light
  absorption, 8
    by pigmentation, 24-25
  bioluminescence, 25-26
  and color, 6-8, 21-24
    see also color; coloration
  colored, and color vision theories, 191-92
  colorimetry, 296, 297
  diffraction, 14
  environmental, and conspicuous colors
    backgrounds and, 300-01, 324-46
    implications for animal coloration, 323-24
    irradiance available for reflection, 298-300, 301-24
    transmission characteristics of medium between displayer and observer, 301
  see also conspicuousness of color
extraretinal response to
  see photoreception,

extraretinal; specific subjects
focusing, 12-13
geometrical optics, 8-14
interference, 23-24
irradiance, spectral, 295-96
environmental factors affecting, 298-300
metamers, 191-92
photometry, 18-21, 296-97
polarization, 23
radiance, spectral, 295
of backgrounds, and conspicuous color, 300-01, 324-41
radiometry, 17-18, 295-96
reflection, 9
and coloration, 382
refraction, 9-11
response to, see photoreception, extraretinal; photoreception, retinal; subjects
scattering, 22, 24
speed of, 7
sunlight, see solar radiation; subjects
transmittance in water, 24
water penetration and angle of incidence, 22
wave and particle properties of, 5-6
see also electromagnetic radiation; solar radiation; ultraviolet radiation
Lillywhite, H. B., 40-41, 42
Limbaugh, C., 366
Limenitis archippus, 364
Limulus, 226
Linksz, A., 192
Liolaemus multiformis, 29, 30, 31, 38
Lipsett, L. P. 225
Liquidambar styraciflua
radiance spectrum of, 340-41
lizards
color change and motivational state, 405
emissivity, 29-31
metachrosis in, 43-44, 57
pineal system and photosensitivity, 139-40
and circadian rhythm, 142, 144
and photoperiodism, 147-49
sex recognition, 391-92
and agnostic behavior, intrasexual, 394
species recognition, 391
thermoregulation, 38-40
color and, 42-44, 57
compared to that of frogs, 63-68
and ultraviolet radiation, 94-95, 115
vision, 226
see also reptiles; names; subjects
Lloyd, F. E., 363
Lloyd, J. E., 397
Lobipes lobatus, 397
Loher, W., 130
Lomonsov, M. V., 190
Loop, M. S., 224
Lorenz, K., 387, 392
Lorenz, K. Z., xiii
Lorenzen, C., 118
Losey, G. S., 366, 372, 373
Loucks, O. L., 112
Lowe, C. H., 57
luciferin and luciferase, 383
luminance, 296
and illuminance, 330-31
luminosity, 19-21

Macaca, 239-40, 284
arctoides, 296
McCleary, R., 224
McCosker, J. E., 383
McCullough, E.C. 311, 318, 321
McDiarmid, R. W., 56

McElroy, W. D., 383
McFarland, W. N., 227
McGuire, R. A., 160
Machado, C. R. S., 150, 159
McInerney, J., 390
McKey, D., 362
McKey, D. B., 269
Mackintosh, J. H., 395
McLaren, A. D., 94
MacMahon, J. A., 46, 50
McMillan, J.P. 145
McNally, C., 389
MacNichol, E.F., Jr., 200, 202, 209, 212
McPhail, J. D. 390
Maki, T., 84
mammals
  individual recognition by, 399-400
  photoreception in, 162-63
    and biochemical rhythm, 149-50
    photopigments and, 159-61
    pineal system and, 140-42, 144, 149-50
  rump patches and intraspecific communication, 389-90
  and ultraviolet radiation, 94
  vision, 226
Maripa, as primate food, 247
Marks, W. B., 202
Marler. P., 366
Mariott, F.H., 189-200, 205, 210
Mason, L. G., 368
Matthews, T. C., 45, 70-71
Mauritia, 267, 268
Maxwell, J. C. 191
Maynard Smith, J., 370
Megaceryla alycyon, 347
Megoura, 137-38
  viciae, 137
melanin, 25
  and abrasion resistance of feathers, 79, 80, 83, 84, 93, 112
  and ultraviolet radiation protection, 95, 98, 105, 114-15, 121-22
melatonin, 144, 149-50, 152-53, 180-81
Melopsittacus undulatus, 395
Menaker, M., 142, 145
Menidia, 406
Mertz, D. B., 280
Mesocricetus auratus, 395
microspectrophotometry, 200-02
Milan, E., 212
Miller, D., 398
Miller, K., 48
mimicry
  Batesian, 363-64
  Müllerian, 368, 369-70
Mimus polyglottos, 371
Minis, D. H., 132, 135
Mirsky, P., 389
Moermond, Timothy C., 106
Moestler, G., 370
Moodie, G. E. E., 411
Moore, R. Y., 150
Morgan, B., 81
Morgan, H. C., 239, 271
Morita, Y., 140
Morris, D., 408
Morse, 121
Morse, D. H., 365
Mosauer, W., 39
Motokawa, 211
Moynihan, M., 365, 371, 372
Mueller, H. C., 371
Müller, 191
Müllerian mimicry, 368, 369-70
Muntz, W. R., 222
Munz, F. W., 227
Murphy, T. M., 94
Myrberg, A. A., 371, 401
Myrica
  radiance spectrum of, 332
Myxine glutinosa, 154

Nachtwey, D. S., 93, 94, 115
Naka, K-I., 195, 214

Nanidae, 401
Napier, J. R., 239
Napier, P. H., 239
Neil, E. H., 401
Nevo, E., 56
Newth, D. R., 154-55
Newton, I., 189-190
Nickerson, D., 257, 271
Nicolai, J., 408
Nishiitsutsuji-Uwo, J., 130
Noakes, D., 388
Noble, G., 392
Noble, G. K., 384, 387, 391, 394, 398
Norris, K. S., 29, 38, 39, 42, 44, 57, 95
Northmore, D. P., 207, 222, 225
Norzagaray, A., 390
Notobranchius guentheri, 391

Obreshkove, V., 155
O'Bryan, P. M., 209
oclosion rhythm and extra-retinal photoreception, 130-34
Odum, E. P., 302
Oehlert, B., 404
Ohmart, R. D., xiii
Oishi, T., 147
Oliver, J., 147, 163
Onamophorus, 121
Onymacius, 120, 121
Oppenheimer, J. R., 269, 280
opponent-mechanism (Hering) theory of vision, 192, 211, 212, 217
orientation
  color signals for, 405, 406
  extraretinal photoreception and, 138, 157-59
  polarized light and, 23, 159
Orlosky, F. J., 271
Orlov, D. Y., 225
O'Steen, W. K., 159
Ott, L., 145
Ovis aries, 400
Oxyuranus scutellatus, 39

Packard, G. C., 48
Page, T. L., 129
Palmer, G., 190
Pan, 239
  trogbdutes, 268
Papio, 239
  sphinx, 395-96
  ursinus, 282
Parker, G. H., 44, 151-55+
Parkhurst, D. F., 112
Parula americana, 347
Parulidae
  abrasion of feathers
    color relationship experiment, 80-84
    distribution observed of resistant colors, 87-93
    melanin, and resistance to, 79, 80, 83, 84, 93
    topography of resistant coloration, 84-87
  coloration, 77-79
  ultraviolet radiation and, 115
    and feathers and scales, 96-106
    and leg color, 97-106
    mandible color and, 99-101, 103-06
Parus caeruleus, 22
Passer domesticus, 80, 142, 145, 356
Passerina ciris, 323
Passerina cyanea, 323
Pavo cristatus, 24, 386, 392
Payne, R., 400
Pearlman, A. L., 189
Pearse, A. S., 155
Pearson, O. P., 29, 32, 38, 61

Pectinophora gossypiella, 132, 135, 137
Peden, A. E., 405-06
Pedler, C., 204
Pelecanus onocrotalus, 383
Pennycuick, C. J., 86
Pequegnat, S., 56
Perdeck, A. C., 389
Perithemis tenera, 394
Peterman, R. M., 401
Pettus, David, 45, 57, 70
Phainopepla nitens, 346
Phausis, 396
Pheucticus ludovicianus, 353
Pheucticus melanocephalus, 353
Philomachus pugnax, 399
Photinus, 385, 397
photochromatic interval, 193
photometry, 18-21, 296-97
photoperiodism, 129-30
  of insects, 134
    action spectra of, 137-38
    circadian rhythms and, 135
    and extraretinal receptors, 135-38, 164-65
    "hourglass" or interval timer hypothesis, 135
  of vertebrates and photoreception, 138, 144-49
photoreception, extraretinal, 129-30, 165, 179
  dermal light sensitivity, 129
  evolution of, 162
  of insects
    and clock entrainment, 130-34, 164-65
    location of receptors, 133-38+,164-65
    and oclosion rhythm, 130-34
    and photoperiodism, 134-38, 164-65
  of vertebrates
    and biochemistry, 149-51
    and circadian rhythms, 142-44, 149-51, 160-61
    coexistence of different kinds of, 164
    and color change, physiological, 151-53, 180-81
    and orientation, 158-59
    and photoperiodism, 138, 144-49
    and photopigments, 159-61
    and phototaxis and photokinesis, 154-57
    and pineal system, 138-44, 149-55, 159-61, 163-64, 165, 179-82
    site of, 163
photoreception, retinal, 162-63
  and biochemical rhythms, 149-51
  and color changes, physiological, 152-53
  and orientation, 158-59
  and photoperiodism, 144-49
  and phototaxis and photokinesis, 154-56
phototaxis and photokinesis, and extraretinal photoreception, 154-57
photurus, 385, 397
Phoxinus, 155
  laevis, 153
Phrixothrix, 383
Phrynocephalus mystaceus, 39
phycocyanin, 24
phycoerthrin, 24
phytochromes, 24-25
Picciolo, A. R., 404, 406
Pieris brassicae, 135
pigments/pigmentation
  and abrasion resistance of feathers, 77-93, 111-12, 120-22
  absorption spectra of,

24-25
and coloration, 24-25, 382
and ultraviolet radiation protection, 95, 98, 105, 114-15, 121-22
visual (photopigments), 198
absorption spectra of, 193-97, 198-200
and color vision, 197-202
and insect extraretinal photoreception, 132-33, 164
and photoreception in mammals, 160-61
retinal, 193-202, 220
see also color; coloration; pigment names
pineal system and photosensitivity, 138-39, 163-64, 179-82
of amphibians, 142, 138-40, 142, 152-53, 159
biochemistry and, 141, 144, 149-51, 160
of birds, 140-47, 150-51
and circadian rhythms, 142-44, 149-51, 159-61
and color change, physiological, 151-53, 180-81
in lower vertebrates, 139-40, 141, 142-44
of mammals, 140-42, 144, 149-50, 159-61
and orientation, 159
and photoperiodism, 144-49
and phototaxis and photokinesis, 154-55
of reptiles, 138-40, 142, 144, 147-49
Pinus ellioltii, 306
Pinus ponderosa
forest, light availability in, 316-21, 322, 323
Pinus taeda
forest, light availability in, 303-06
radiance spectrum of, 337
Pinus virgiana
forest, light availability in, 310
Piper, 207
Pipilo erythrophthalmus, 353, 409
Pipilo fuscus, 353
Piranga ludoviciana, 353
Piranga olivaces, 353
Pithecellobium, as primate food, 247-54
Pittendrigh, C. S., 130, 132, 135
plants, see vegetation; names
Platycnemis pennipes, 396
Pliny, 381
Podiceps eristatus, 409
Poecilia reticulata, 391
Poecilidae, 401
polarization of light, 22-23
Polioptila caerulea, 347
Polyak, S. L., 269, 429
Porter, K. R., 45
Porter, Warren P., 29, 63, 94-96, 106, 112, 114, 115, 121, 311, 318, 321
Potts, G., 387
primates
foods of, 241-74
differences in, and vision, 284-85
see also Callicebus torquatus, field study of foods of
habitat conservation need, 273-74
sex recognition by, 395-96, 397
vision
coevolution of colored fruits and, 269-72
and foods, see primates, foods of

of Old World and New World species compared, 239-41, 270-71, 282-84
response potentials, 215, 217, 226
Pristella riddlei, 406
Probstein, R. F., 84
Progne subis, 346
Pseudacris triseriata, 45-55, 70-74
Psychotria klugii, 267
Psychotria oxillaris, as primate food, 247, 261-62
Pterophyllum scalare, 139
Ptilonorhynchus violaceus, 409
Ptito, M., 239
Pyburn, W. F., 61

Quay, W. B., 139, 141, 149

radiance, spectral, 295
of backgrounds, and conspicuous color, 300-01
measurement methods and habitats, 324-26
in Southeastern habitats, 326-41
see also conspicuousness of color
radiometry, 17-18, 195-96
Ralph, C. L., 150, 180
Ramphocelus, 98
Rana catesbciana, 40, 158-59
Rana clamitans, 45, 155
Rana esculenta, 140
Rana pipiens, 63, 64-65
Rana temporaria, 139, 140
Rasquin, P., 149
Ratliff, F., 226
rats
photoreception
and biochemical rhythms, 150
photopigments and, 159-61
Raven, P. H., 241
Raven, P. P., 369
Ray, C., 46
"reciprocal altruism" model, 373
reflection, of light, 9
and coloration, 382
refraction, 9-11
Reinecke, W. G., 84
Reisman, H., 384, 405
Reiter, R. J., 160
Relkin, R., 139
reptiles
emissivity, 29-31
metachrosis in, 43-44, 57
pineal system, and photosensitivity, 138-40
and circadian rhythm, 142, 144
and photoperiodism, 147-49
thermoregulation, 63-68
behavioral, 38-40
color and, 42-44, 57
and ultraviolet radiation, 94-95, 115
vision, 209, 212-13, 226
see also names
Resnick, L. E., 56
Resnick, M. A., 93, 94
retina, see eye
rhodopsin, 198, 200
absorption spectra of, and vision, 193-95, 198
and photoreception, 160-61
Richmond, G. M., 73
Richter, C. P., 159
Riddiford, L. M., 134
Riggs, L. A., 267
Ripps, H., 198
Roberts, S. K., 130
Rodieck, R. W., 185, 190, 197, 202, 209, 215
Römer, 191
Roscoe, J. T., 97, 101
Rosen, R., 112
Rosenbloom, L., 149

Rosner, J. M., 151
Ross, D. M., 154-55
Rowland, William J., 379-422, 425
Rowlands, R. D., 406
Ruiter, L. de, xiii, 114
Rupert, C. S., 94
Rushton, W. A., 189-200+, 210-14+

Saccharmoyces cerevisiae, 94
Saimiri, 239, 271, 284
  oerstedi, 285
Sakakibara, Y., 147, 163
Salmo irideus, 139
Samia cynthia, 134
Saunders, D. S., 134, 135, 137, 138
Sauromalus obesus, 38
scattering, of light, 22
sceloporus, 38
  olivaceus, 142
  undulatus, 63, 64-65, 394
Schaller, F., 396
Schaller, G., 409
Scharrer, E., 175
schemochromes, functions of, 292-93
Scherer, E., 139, 140
Schlieper, C., 222
Schlosberg, H., 159
Schmel, G. A., 84
Schneiderman, N., 224
Schultze, M., 193
Schwalb, H., 396
Schwalm, P. A., 56, 73, 74
scotopic vision, see vision
Scyliorhinus caniculus, 139
Sechzer, J. A., 221
Seiger, M., 389
Seitz, A., 404
Seiurus, 345
"selfish herd" hypothesis, 365, 372
Seliger, H. H., 383
Selous, E., 399
Semler, D. E., 390, 411
Sepia, 400-01
Setlow, R. B., 94, 116
Setophaga picta, 353
Setophaga ruticilla, 353
sexual activity
  color preferences and, 389, 391, 392
  color saturation and, 384
  courtship displays and interaction of color, structure, and movement, 385-86
  localization and/or orientation signals, 405-06
  mate recognition, 398, 399-400
  photoperiodism and photoreception, 144-49
  selection, sexual, and color development, 381
  sex recognition, 390-92, 296-97
  and territorial signals, 364-65
Sharma, S. C., 222, 390
Sheppard, J. J., Jr., 185
Sheppard, P. M., 370
Shettle, E. P., 99
Shillito, E., 400
Shipley, T., 193
Shugar, D., 94
Sialia, 346
  currucoides, 347-48
Siefried, H., 79
Sigmund, W., 391-92
Silver, P. H., 222
Simon, E. J., 212
Simons, E. L., 271
Sitta, 345
Sjölander, S., 388
Slovin, M., 402, 411
Smith, D. G., 395
Smith, D. H., 84
Smith, K. C., 94
Smith, N. G., 388
Smythe, N., 254

Snell's Law, 10, 11, 24
Snodderly, D. Max, 237-85, 357
Snow, D. W., 247
Snyder, S. H., 159
Sokolove, P. G., 130
solar radiation
  absorption atmospheric, 21-22
  absorptivity of, thermal radiation, and temperature, 28-32
  scattering, atmospheric, 22
  spectral distribution, 21-22
  see also electromagnetic radiation; light; ultraviolet radiation
Spencer, A. W., 45, 52
Starrett, P. H., 56
"startle" displays, 363, 369
Stebbins, W. C., 222, 225
Stell, W. K., 202, 204, 211
Stephan, F. K., 150
Sterna bergii, 398
Sterna maxima, 398
Sterna sandvicensis, 389
Stetson, M. H., 150
Steven, D. M., 129, 154, 156
Stiles, W. S., 186, 205, 267
Storer, J. H., 86, 93
Storer, R. W., xiii
Streck, P., 139, 140
Streptopelia resoria, 155
Stride, G. O., 396
Struhsaker, T. T., 254, 269
Sturnus vulgaris, 409
Sula nebouxii, 392
Sulak, K. J., 366, 373
sunlight, see light; solar radiation
Sustare, B. Dennis, 3-29
Sutter, S. L., 84
Svaetichin, G., 207, 211
Swindler, D. R., 271

Taeniopygia castanotis, 388-89
Tamsitt, J. R., 41
Tansley, K., 186
Taricha rivularis, 40
Taylor, D. H., 157, 158, 159
temperature
  radiant emmittance and, 14-16
  regulation
    in amphibians, 40-42 44-56, 63-68
    behavioral, 38-42, 69
    color and, 37, 40, 42-57,
    hydroregulation, color and, 44-56, 71-72
      in insects, 69
      in reptiles, 38-40, 42-44, 57
  solar absorptivity, thermal emissivity and, 28-32
territorality, interspecific, 364-65, 371-72
Test, F. H., 80
thermoregulation, 38-40
Thomas, I., 225, 226
Thorington, R. W., 274, 285
Thorpe, W. H., 409
Thraupis virens, 347
Thresher, R., 387
Tilapia, 372
  mariae, 402, 411
Tinbergen, N., xiii, 185, 186, 370, 381, 389, 394, 396, 400
Tomita, T., 207, 209
Tordoff, W., 45, 55, 72
Tovomita, as primate food, 247
Toxostoma longirostre, 347
Tracy, C. Richard, 28-32, 52, 58, 63-68, 111-13, 117, 179-82, 280, 281
Tragelaphus strepsiceros, 381
trees, see vegetation; names
Trichogaster, 404-05

trichopterus, 406
Trillmich, F., 399
Trivers, R. L., 373
Trochilidae, 24
Tropheus moori, 411
Truman, J. W., 130, 134, 138
Tschanz, B., 399
Tucker, 93
Turek, F. W., 144, 147
turtles
  vision, 209, 212-13, 226
Tyrannus tyrannus, 346

Uca, 386
ultraviolet radiation
  birds and, 115
    and feathers and scales, 96-106
    leg color and, 97-106 +
    mandible color and, 99-101, 103-06
  butterfly use in mate attraction, 386
  damage from, 93-95, 114-18
    molecular basis for, 94
  insect sensitivity to and "honey guide" patterns, 226
  protection from, 94
    by feathers and scales, 96-106 +
    and melanin shield location, 121
    by tissue pigmentation, 95, 114-15, 120-22
  source and intensity, 99
Underwood, Herbert, 127-178, 181-82
Urasaki, H., 149
Urosaurus ornatus, 405
Uta stansburiana, 94-95, 96

Valdivieso, D., 41
van der Horst, G. J. C., 255
van der Pijl, L., 247, 254, 269, 362, 363, 369
van Ween, T., 142
vegetation
  as background, optical, and conspicuous color
    dunes, Southeastern, 332
    marshes, bushes, and old-field, 333-36
    woodland leaves and trunks, 337-41
  deceptive coloration, 363
  as food for primates, see Callicebus torquatus, field study of foods of; fruits, as primate food
  and light availability, 299
    in ponderosa pine forest, 216-21, 322, 323
    in Southeastern pine subclimax and ecotone, 303-10
    in tropical rain forest, 311-16
vertebrates, see names, subjects
Vevers, G., 24
Vevers, H. G., 383
Viaud, G., 226
vision
  assessment of, 221
    testing techniques, 222-25
  and central nervous system, 220-21
  and color, definition of, 186-88
  dichromacy, 195-97
  duplexity, 193, 210
  foods of primates and, 241-74, 282-84
    see also Callicebus torquatus, field study of foods of; primates
  Hering (opponent mechanism) theory of, 192, 211, 217
  and information encoding, with color, 383, 385
    and brightness, 384-85

and hue, 383-84
patterning, spatial and/ or temporal, 385
and saturation, 384
laboratory and field studies of, gap between, 272-73
and luminosity, 19-21
mechanisms, functional, 202-25
monochromacy, 195
photochromatic interval, 193
photopic, 19-21
phylogeny of color vision, 225-27
pigments and, 197-202, 220
absorption spectra, 193-97
scotopic (achromatic), 20-21, 210-211, 220
and luminosity, 20-21
rhodopsin absorption spectra and, 193-95
theories, 189-97
see also specific subjects
trichromacy, 190-92, 197, 200-02, 220
Young-Helmholtz, theory of, 190-92, 202, 205, 209, 211
see also eye
Vitt, L. J., 38
Voitkevich, A. A., 79
von Frisch, K., 152, 153, 226, 409
von, see also principal patronymic

Waldman, G. D., 84
Wallace, A. R., 227
Wallace, B., 362
Walls, G. L., 221, 222, 226-27
Ward, J. A., 366, 373
Wasserman, G. S., 190
water
dynamics of, and thermoregulation, 44-56, 71-72
and light
availability and coloration, 300
penetration by, 22
transmittance of, 24
Waterbolk, H., 401
Watkins-Pitchford, W., 95
Webster, 40
Weidman, U., 389
Welty, J. C., 392
Werblin, F., 214
Westphal, K., 81
Wetmore, A., 98
Wetterberg, L., 150, 159
Whatson-Whitmyre, M., 150
Wickler, W., 389, 395, 397, 406, 411
Wien's Displacement Law, 15
Williams, C. M., 135
Wilmot, L. B., 429
Wilson, E., 408
Witkin, E. M., 93, 95
Witkovsky, P. I., 211
Wolken, J. J., 24, 26
Wolstenholme, G. E. W., 139, 141, 149
wood-warblers, see Parulidae
Wootton, R. J., 390
Wright, W. D., 185, 243-44
Wunder, W., 408
Wurtman, R. J., 139, 141
Wykes, U., 152, 153
Wyman, R. L., 366, 373
Wyszecki, G., 186, 267

Xenopus, 152

Yager, D., 207, 222, 225
Yokoyama, K., 147
Young, J. Z., 153, 154
Young, T., 190, 191, 192, 212
Young-Helmholtz theory of vision, 191-92, 202, 205, 209, 211, 212

Zenaidura macroura, 96
Zimmerman, N. H., 142
Zimmerman, W. F., 131, 132, 153
Zonotrichia atricapilla, 147
Zonotrichia leucophrys, 147
Zucker, I., 150
Zweig, M., 159